W9-CTD-393

FAMILY THERAPY WITH ETHNIC MINORITIES

SECOND EDITION

SAGE SOURCEBOOKS FOR THE HUMAN SERVICES SERIES

Series Editors: Armand Lauffer and Charles Garvin

Recent Volumes in This Series

Health Promotion at the Community Level, 2nd Edition, edited by **Neil Bracht**

Qualitative Methods in Social Work Research: Challenges and Rewards by **Deborah K. Padgett**

Legal Issues in Social Work, Counseling, and Mental Health: Guidelines for Clinical Practice in Psychotherapy by **Robert G. Madden**

Group Work With Children and Adolescents: Prevention and Intervention in School and Community Systems by **Steven R. Rose**

Social Work Practice With African American Men: The Invisible Presence by **Janice M. Rasheed** & **Mikal N. Rasheed**

Designing and Managing Programs: An Effectiveness-Based Approach, 2nd Edition, by **Peter M. Kettner, Robert M. Moroney**, & **Lawrence L. Martin**

Promoting Successful Adoptions: Practice With Troubled Families by **Susan Livingston Smith** & **Jeanne A. Howard**

Strategic Alliances Among Health and Human Services Organizations: From Affiliations to Consolidations by **Darlyne Bailey** & **Kelly McNally Koney**

Effectively Managing Human Service Organizations, 2nd Edition, by **Ralph Brody**

Stopping Child Maltreatment Before It Starts: Emerging Horizons in Early Home Visitation Services by **Neil B. Guterman**

Organizational Change in the Human Services by **Rebecca Ann Proehl**

Family Diversity: Continuity and Change in the Contemporary Family by **Pauline Irit Erera**

FAMILY THERAPY WITH ETHNIC MINORITIES

SECOND EDITION

Man Keung Ho
University of Oklahoma

Janice Matthews Rasheed
Loyola University Chicago

Mikal N. Rasheed
Northeastern Illinois University

Sage Sourcebooks for
the Human Services

SAGE Publications
International Educational and Professional Publisher
Thousand Oaks ▪ London ▪ New Delhi

Por La Memoria

Por la memoria de mi hermano Ronald Philpot de Matthews
¡Trabaja duro y aprenderás rápido!
Descansa en Paz

Dedication
This book is dedicated to the late Dr. Man Keung Ho

For information:

Sage Publications, Inc.
2455 Teller Road
Thousand Oaks, California 91320
E-mail: order@sagepub.com

Sage Publications Ltd.
6 Bonhill Street
London EC2A 4PU
United Kingdom

Sage Publications India Pvt. Ltd.
B-42, Panchsheel Enclave
Post Box 4109
New Delhi 110 017 India

Printed in the United States of America

Library of Congress Cataloging-in-Publication Data

Family therapy with ethnic minorities / Man Keung Ho, Janice Matthews Rasheed, and Mikal N. Rasheed.—2nd ed.
      p. cm.—(Sage sourcebooks for the human services series ; v. 5)
Previous ed. cataloged under: Ho, Man Keung.
Includes bibliographical references and index.
ISBN 0-7619-2391-8 (cloth)
   1. Family psychotherapy-United States. 2. Minorities-Mental health services-United States.
I. Ho, Man Keung. II. Rasheed, Janice M. (Janice Matthews) III. Rasheed, Mikal N. (Mikal Nazir)
IV. Series.
RC451.5.A2H62 2004
616.89´156—dc22

                                                                        2003015929
Printed on acid-free paper

03   04   05   06   07   08   09   10   9   8   7   6   5   4   3   2   1

Acquiring Editor:	Arthur T. Pomponio
Editorial Assistant:	Veronica K. Novak
Production Editor:	Claudia A. Hoffman
Copy Editor:	Catherine M. Chilton
Typesetter:	C&M Digitals (P) Ltd.
Indexer:	Molly Hall
Cover Designer:	Michelle Lee Kenny

Contents

Acknowledgments

First, we give all honor and praise to God, who is the head and center of our lives.

We thank all the people at Sage Publications for entrusting this important project to us. A special thanks to Dr. Armand Lauffer and Dr. Charles D. Garvin (both of whom are Professors Emeritus at the University of Michigan, Ann Arbor). We also wish to thank our colleagues who so generously consented to review the prepublication drafts of this text (Daniel B. Lee, Jude Gonzales, Philip Brown, Maria Vidal de Haymes, and Maria Yellow Horse Brave Heart). We thank all of our colleagues, students, and administrators at both of our wonderful universities (Loyola University Chicago School of Social Work and Northeastern Illinois University Department of Social Work) who have contributed in various ways to the publication of this book. Finally, we give a very special thank you to the widow of Dr. Man Keung Ho (Jeannie Ho), who gave us permission to revise her late husband's work.

Preface

It has been 17 years since Dr. Man Keung Ho first published his groundbreaking and critically acclaimed text, *Family Therapy With Ethnic Minorities* (1987). His work represented an important contribution to the literature of family therapy theory and practice with families of color. A great deal has happened in these fields and in the lives of ethnic minority families since the initial publication of the book. In view of these pivotal developments, it is time to revise this important work. Unfortunately, Dr. Ho is now deceased, but the forward-thinking editors at Sage Publications recognized that much of what Dr. Ho originally wrote continues to be relevant and important scholarship. This led the people at Sage Publications to approach us with the prospect of revising Dr. Ho's original text with a view to updating the various demographics, incorporating information about the changes that have occurred in the lives of ethnic minority families, and noting the implications of these changes for practice with these families. Additionally, the revised text needed to reflect and integrate the movement that has been made in the scholarship of the mainstream field of family therapy itself.

It was not without a great deal of contemplation, reflection, and prayer that we agreed to take on this daunting task. Because we, like many other family therapists and academicians, hold Dr. Ho's work in the highest esteem, revising his critically acclaimed text is an honor that we feel represents one of our most important scholastic challenges to date. Throughout the revision, it was our intent to preserve the academic integrity of Dr. Ho's original work as well as updating its content to reflect important changes in the family therapy field and changes in the social, political, and economic reality of the daily lives of American ethnic minority families. In the end, we hope to have honored the memory and legacy of Dr. Man Keung Ho with our humble revisions. It is not our intent to alter the direction of Dr. Ho's original work. Rather, we hope that if he were alive today, he would give us his approval of the additions that we placed in his original piece.

Audience

This book is appropriate for all those who are involved in clinical practice with American racial and ethnic minority families.[1,2,3] To this end, this book is appropriate for family therapists, as well as for pastoral counselors, social workers, psychologists, and psychiatrists engaged in the practice of family therapy with ethnic minority families. Social service and human service practitioners who are involved with ethnic and racial minority families may also find this book helpful, especially the concise, updated demographics that assist in the identification and understanding of salient practice issues for these families from an ecosystemic practice perspective. Scholars and educators will find this text to be a valuable resource that can enhance the racial minority content of courses in family therapy and practice and courses about racial minorities. Specification of family therapy knowledge should facilitate the learning process of both undergraduate and graduate students. Practicing family therapists will find that the book also presents practical information that they can readily use in their work with ethnic minority families.

Overview of the Book

The proliferation of articles, book chapters, and texts on the subjects of family theory and therapy with ethnic minorities from 1983 to 2003 is a testament to the societal and, hence, professional importance of this field of study. Additionally, family-centered approaches to the resolution and treatment of emotional disturbances, including couple and marital stress and the difficulties of children, have taken a place of centrality in the various helping professions—even outside of the field of family therapy. From 1973 to 2003, a majority of these publications acknowledged the error of approaching the family problems of ethnic minority families using the white middle class American family as a conceptual frame of reference; as well, these publications warn family therapists to be wary of ego-dystonic, Eurocentric, class- and culture-bound family therapy models and techniques. However, many of us must surely ask ourselves often, "How much cultural tailoring am I really doing in my everyday clinical practice with ethnic minority families?"

Theories about the experiences of ethnic minority families have, for the most part, failed to capture the complexity and diversity of the experiences of these families. As a result, therapists and practitioners are frequently given a distorted, homogenized caricature of ethnic family life that has (in the not-so-distant past) tended to pathologize functional and culturally indigenous adaptive family behavior within these populations; at the very least, this picture has reified unfortunate negative cultural stereotypes. Even with some of the impressive advances made in the modification of family therapy models, many of these models still fail to conceptualize a practice approach within the *larger* contexts of these families. As well, there have been important conceptual advances (e.g., the use of a Nativecentric, Latinocentric, or Africentric perspective versus a Eurocentric perspective in practice with First Nations families, Latino families, or African American families) that may help family therapists to incorporate culturally based perspectives in theories of the development of family life and family process and hence facilitate practice. Failure to incorporate such culturally based perspectives has operated to unwittingly conceal important cultural strengths that often lie dormant or underused as therapists search for culturally indigenous approaches to (family) problem resolution.

Many of the prevailing family theories have also failed to acknowledge the uniqueness of individual, couple, and family developmental experiences within ethnic minority families (especially in light of the unique sociohistorical and politicoeconomic forces brought to bear on these families). These same theories and frameworks have not begun to explore the variety of these experiences or capture the variability of how *each* ethnic family (and each family member) *experiences similar circumstances*. This book uses existing and emerging theoretical and conceptual frameworks that can provide a more accurate basis from which family therapists can draw their "cultural maps," develop more realistic assessments, and hence provide more culturally competent, culturally sensitive, oppression-sensitive, and, potentially, more culturally effective approaches to family practice with ethnic minority families.

In this volume, we ground our thinking in *ecosystemic* theory and aim to provide practice strategies that use a *critical constructionist* perspective for an integrating and unifying conceptual and theoretical framework.[4] We contend that these theoretical and conceptual frameworks and perspectives can be used to better understand the family life and family processes of ethnic minority families and hence provide for a much more culturally balanced and culturally appropriate approach to family therapy. Furthermore, the ecosystemic framework and the critical constructionist perspective provide a broader, more complex, and more realistic context for assessment and therapy with ethnic minority families. Thus the family therapist is in a better position to form a multilayered analysis of the historical, socioeconomic, and cultural factors affecting the lives of these families (with an emphasis on how each individual family member uniquely experiences these events) and develop a more accurate cultural road map to follow in family therapy activities.

Four ethnic minority family groups are represented in this book. They are (a) Asian and Pacific Islander Americans, (b) First Nations peoples, (c) Latinos, and (d) African Americans. The book provides theory specification, integration, and systematization for ethnic minority families. Six important features frame the organization of this book.

1. We introduce a culturally relevant theoretical framework from which appropriate assessment and therapeutic guidelines in work with different ethnic minority families are derived (chapter 1).

2. This book provides family therapists and students with an up-to-date resource for the historical, political, social, and economic problems that each ethnic minority family group faces and the unique strengths and contributions of each ethnic minority family group.

3. This book gives family therapists and students a clear picture of the distinctive cultural values of each ethnic group and describes the changing family structure and interactive patterns.

4. This book provides a theory-based "how to"; that is, it gives specific guidelines for and suggestions about culturally relevant family therapy models, strategies, skills, and techniques.

5. These chapters also cover work with the single-parent family and the reconstituted family; additionally, the practice of couple therapy and divorce therapy is discussed.

6. In chapters 2, 3, 4, and 5, we discuss therapy with each ethnic group and (for the most part) follow the same standard outline. (This helps to prevent content unevenness.) Adherence to a single outline also facilitates comparison and integration of common core knowledge and differences in ethnic minority family therapy, which are covered in chapter 6 to help prevent content duplication and replication.

Each ethnic specific family therapy chapter is, however, written to stand alone on its own, without reliance on other ethnic-specific chapters. Cultural, theoretical, and conceptual content is provided in each of the four ethnic-specific family therapy chapters so the reader is not required to refer to or have to rely upon content presented in the other ethnic-specific chapters. With this format, the authors attempt to accommodate readers who may elect to review chapters only on specific ethnic groups at different times. Hence, some repetition (in theory) is unavoidable; however, chapter 6 is included specifically to minimize duplication and repetition of important material. Our hope is that the organization of this book will provide students and practitioners not only with a comprehensive, up-to-date examination of family therapy with ethnic minorities but with an analytical and functional format that lends itself to the scientific ordering of information and the promising challenge of providing quality in practice theory with ethnic minorities.

Because this book focuses on an ecological family systemic framework that uses critical constructionist practice approaches, psychodynamic and psychoanalytic theories have received only scant attention. Such unevenness should not be construed as implying that the intrapsychic world of ethnic minorities is unimportant or irrelevant. Given that this is a book for family therapy, the interpersonal resolution of inner conflict is examined because it forms the basis of most couple and family dysfunction. None of the family therapy models or approaches for ethnic minorities was adequately tested according to prevailing paradigms of social science and practice research. However, all the models and approaches relate closely to existing family therapy theories. Furthermore, all interventive approaches and principles suggested herein represent supplements to existing family therapy theories, not alternatives.

It is generally recognized that there is not only considerable interethnic group diversity but marked and significant intraethnic group heterogeneity. In an attempt to delineate and systematize knowledge about ethnic minority family structures and practice principles, the possibility of stereotyping, obviously, continues to be great—even with this second edition. As in Dr. Ho's initial work, we tried to avoid this danger and continued with the tradition set down by Dr. Ho to consult a panel of distinguished ethnic minority practitioners and educators. Yet, again, we undoubtedly have not been totally successful. If we have presented incorrect or stereotypical information, we apologize and invite readers' corrections.

1

Theoretical Framework for
Therapy With Ethnic Minority Families

At the dawn of the 21st century, the United States is witnessing an increase in the number of ethnic minorities (First Nations Peoples, Asian Americans and Pacific Islanders, Latinos, and African Americans). As these groups begin to represent a larger percentage of the population, there will be a corresponding increase in the demand for mental health services to these populations (Aponte & Wohl, 2000; Cheung & Snowden, 1990). Family-centered approaches to problem solving and the treatment of mental health issues, including couple stress, parent-child problems, and children's difficulties, have gained wider acceptance in the mental health profession. Green (1998) states: "The discrepancy between the proportion of people of color in the general population and in the profession of family therapy means that racial minority families are usually seen by White majority family therapists and that the caseloads of White family therapists will increasingly be composed of families of color" (p. 94). The challenges for the family therapy field are the needs to reformulate existing theoretical models of clinical intervention and to develop new ones that are attuned to the cultural uniqueness of these populations. These models are necessary to enable family therapy practitioners to provide culturally competent services to these populations (Sue & Sue, 1999).

The acceptance of the family-centered approach to problem solving has generated many treatment theories and models. The philosophical orientations and techniques employed by some of the theoretical approaches may diametrically oppose the indigenous cultural values and family structures of ethnic minority families (Mizio & Delaney, 1981; Sue & Sue, 1999). Further, the client's orientation to the process of help seeking and the "fit" between traditional paradigms and those used by providers may be critical to successful clinical process and treatment outcomes (Green, 1999; Tseng & McDermott, 1975). Given the historic and current underutilization of mental health services and the high drop-out rate by ethnic minority clients (Barrera, 1978; Fujii, 1976; Jackson, 1973; Jones, 1977; Sue & Sue, 1999), a wide gap clearly exists between the unmet needs of ethnic minority clients and families and the therapists' ability to provide for their needs successfully. It is also clear that family therapy with ethnic minorities requires organized culturally sensitive theoretical frameworks. From such frameworks, existing family therapy principles and techniques and innovative emic-based (culture-specific) therapy principles and techniques can be developed.

This chapter and discussion focuses on two conceptual frameworks that emanate from and consider the ethnic minority experience of racism and oppression, culture, biculturalism, ethnicity status, language, social class, and cultural narrative. The social work "person in environment" focus of the ecosystem theoretical framework and the "social justice and oppression–sensitive" focus of the critical constructionist framework are introduced as a unifying conceptual framework for practice with ethnic minority families.

These two perspectives, frameworks, or metatheories possess the ability to inform decisions about the use of specific explanatory theories, practice models, and interventions. Yet these frameworks do not prescribe any specific personality theories, explanatory theories, or family therapy practice models. Within the assumptive framework of each of these metatheories is an ideological commitment to an empowerment and strengths perspective. These frameworks further provide a broad conceptual foundation for selecting relevant practice models and allow for greater flexibility in developing strategies for assessment and intervention.

At this time, there is no single integrated family therapy practice model upon which family therapists can rely (Franklin & Jordan, 1999; Nichols & Schwartz, 2001; Sue & Sue, 1999). This problem is accentuated when therapists deal with ethnic minority families, even though there have been efforts to apply various practice models to ethnic minority families (Ariel, 1999; Boyd-Franklin, 1989; Brown & Shalett, 1997; DiNicola, 1997; Falicov, 1998; Hong & Ham 2001; McGoldrick, 1998; McGoldrick, Giordano, & Pearce, 1996). Notably, in the vast amount of family therapy literature, many concepts that address the same family phenomenon or processes are identified by different names within various practice models.

We take the stance that there are important common themes among theories and therapies, particularly those used in family therapy with ethnic minorities. Two criteria are used in this book to ensure an organized, common systematic format for analyzing, discussing, and presenting family therapy theories: (a) The theories used are rooted in and derived from the field of family therapy, and (b) our own practice experience, acquired through direct work with ethnic minority families, is used. A discussion of each of these important criteria follows.

This book applies theories that have developed within the field of family therapy. In spite of the contemporary influence of postmodern thought in family therapy, a large portion of the theory of family therapy today continues to derive its underlying conceptual framework from systems theory and developmental tasks. These family therapies differ in their points of emphasis within systems theory itself. One family therapy and theory group has emphasized the communicative-interactive system within families (Haley, 1976; Satir, 1967).

Yet another therapy group emphasizes a (family-environment transactions and intergenerational dynamic order) structural-functional framework represented by Minuchin (1974), Aponte (1994), and Kerr and Bowen (1988).

Newer formulations of family therapy that have been influenced by postmodern constructivist and feminist thought have provided a critique of system-based approaches (Nichols & Schwartz, 2001). The nature of the critique is that the systems approach represents a mechanist view of the family as an entity to be manipulated and changed by the "expert" therapist. Such an approach ignores the impact of the therapist's presence on the family system, the dynamics of gender and power, and the larger historical and cultural context in which the family is embedded (Nichols & Schwartz, 2001). We also contend that the families are the experts in their own lives, not the family therapist.

As a corrective measure to systems theories, postmodern constructionist and narrative-based approaches do provide significant insight into understanding families by giving attention to how family members construct their intrafamilial experiences through language and through individual and family narratives (de Shazer, 1988; Walter & Peller, 1992; White & Epston, 1990). The narrative emphasis on "meaning" is further supplemented by a focus on ways in which broader sociopolitical influences affect family and individual narratives. Although postmodern critiques may address some of the major limitations of family systems theories, these critiques do not necessitate a rejection of systems-based theories. The focus of the communicative-interactive and structural-functional practice models, within the context of ecological and critical constructionist metatheories, can provide a framework for understanding the actual structure of the family and the narrative meaning and interpretation of that structure by family members as affected by ethnic, cultural, historical, economic, and sociopolitical factors.

The second criterion this book uses, as mentioned earlier, is the emic approach. Emic-based models of mental health construe mental health in terms of divergent attitudes, values, and behaviors that arise out of specific cultures (Ridley, 1995). Thus an emic-based approach to family therapy offers considerable promise for enhancing the understanding of ethnic families, enlarging interventive repertoires, and developing "communicative competence" by understanding and grasping the narrative meanings that family members attach to their experiences within their family systems (Green, 1999). The emic approach is relevant to the immediate social and physical nurturing environment of the "dual perspective" advanced by Norton (1978) and the "cultural identity continuum" presented by Logan (1990) and colleagues (Logan, Freeman, & McRoy, 1987). According to Norton, every ethnic minority individual is embedded simultaneously in at least two systems: that of his or her immediate social and physical nurturing environment and that of the larger major society. The nurturing environment defines the various elements of each particular culture and determines an individual's needs and sense of identity. Logan's (1990; Logan et al., 1987) cultural identity continuum concept addresses the identity struggle that an ethnic minority individual has as he or she struggles with maintaining a connection with the culture of origin while striving for assimilation or acculturation within the dominant society. Thus ethnic minority families often struggle with negotiating their embeddedness in multiple environments, as reflected in the "dual perspective" and "cultural continuum" formulations. Using an emic approach with ethnic minority families enables a family therapist to generate practice principles that are relevant to understanding the experiences of these families.

In an attempt to systematize and integrate therapy practice models with ethnic minority families, each chapter pertaining to therapy with specific ethnic family groups (chapters 2, 3, 4, and 5) will first identify relevant principles of family behavior and then identify relevant principles of practice. A major assumption is made here that theories of family behavior that are at a high level of abstraction are appropriate for ethnic minority families, but the manner in which they may be translated into principles of therapy is ethnicity specific. The general and specific application of these practice models for therapy with each ethnic family group is contained in each chapter under "Part 2: Culturally Relevant Techniques and Skills in Different Phases of Therapy." The word *technique* here refers to the specific means or procedures through which a particular aim mutually agreed upon by the client or family and the therapist is implemented and accomplished. The word *skill* refers to the unique fusion of aptitudes and knowledge or capabilities essential to performing a professional task or activity (Barlett, 1958). Unique aptitudes that are part of skill may include a therapist's warmth, sensitivity (to the therapist's own ethnic background and the client's ethnic background and reality, and adaptation of skills in response to the client's ethnic reality), flexibility, and positive regard and respect for the client or family. Therapists' capabilities that are part of skill include therapeutic procedures responsible for accomplishing a task. To demonstrate the close relationship between theoretical perspectives and actual practice, case illustrations are presented in Part 3 and specific interventive modalities are explored in Part 4 of each chapter.

The Conceptual Framework for Therapy With Ethnic Minority Families

The development and selection of culturally sensitive theoretical frameworks for therapy with ethnic minorities must take into consideration seven major factors that distinguish minorities from mainstream middle-class white American families. These factors include the following:

- Ethnic minority experiences with racism and oppression
- The impact of external systems on minority cultures

- Biculturalism
- Ethnic differences in minority status
- Ethnicity and language
- Ethnicity and social class
- Ethnicity as a narrative identity

The following discussion aims to define these concepts and factors as they relate to the theoretical framework for therapy with ethnic minority families.

Ethnic Minority Experiences With Racism and Oppression

In spite of the growth of ethnic minorities, the pervasive presence of racism, poverty, and oppression shapes their life experiences. African Americans continue to live with the legacy of slavery, while First Nations Peoples live with the historical experience of genocide. For many ethnic minorities, racism and oppression are the causes of generational poverty and a diminished self-esteem that produces community violence, attempts to escape by using drugs and alcohol, and disproportional involvement with the criminal justice system (Thomas, 2000). Current demographic data indicate that ethnic minorities have made considerable gain in the areas of family income, education, and other indicators of social, economic, and political status (Karger & Stoez, 2002), but almost any set of data that is examined continues to show the subordinate position of ethnic minorities within the social order. In reviewing the continued disparity in wages, incomes, poverty levels, education, home ownership, job promotion rates, and middle-management and top-management positions, we find that the data reflect that ethnic minorities continue to bear a disproportionate share of social problems (Axinn & Levin, 1997; Jansson, 2001).

For example, the unemployment rate for African Americans is still more than twice that of whites. Although unemployment among African American men fell in 1997 to 8.6%, the lowest in 23 years, it was still twice the jobless rate for white men (Karger & Stoesz, 2002). In 1979, 28% of Latino children were below the poverty line. By 1990, that number had risen to 38%, which is twice the rate for white children. By 1995, Latinos had replaced African Americans as the most impoverished group in the United States (Karger & Stoesz, 2002). In 1990, more than 16% of First Nations males living on reservations were unemployed, compared to 14.5% of whites. Sixty-five percent of First Nations peoples on reservations were high-school graduates, compared to 75% of the total U.S. population. Asian and Pacific Islander Americans have the same unemployment rates as non-Hispanic whites, and as a group had the highest median family income in the United States in 1995, but these indicators conceal the reality of the many low-wage immigrants who work in "sweatshops" in urban Chinatowns. Furthermore, Southeast Asians are at a higher risk of poverty than whites. Finally,

Asians and Pacific Islander Americans are underrepresented in higher salaried public and private career positions (Karger & Stoesz, 2002).

The disparity in the social status of ethnic minorities clearly documents the realities of racism, poverty, and oppression as potent factors that continue to have a negative effect on the lives of ethnic minority individuals and families. These factors also affect minorities' help-seeking behaviors, which include underutilization of family therapists, who generally are white, monolinguistic, middle class, and ethnocentric in their family problem assessments and interventions (Acosta, Yamamoto, & Evans, 1982).

The Impact of External Systems on Minority Cultures

In addition to coping with racism, oppression, poverty, and societal constraints, ethnic minority families must also adjust to tensions created by conflicts with the value systems of white society. In contrast with middle-class white American cultural values, which emphasize man's *control of nature and the environment,* many ethnic minority groups emphasize man's *harmony with the environment.* The mainstream societal ideal is future oriented, requiring the worship of youth and sacrifices for a "better" tomorrow. In contrast, some ethnic groups reminisce about the past and take pleasure in the present. In the relational dimension, while the middle-class American cultural ideal is *individual autonomy,* the ethnic minority cultural value is a preference for *collectivity.* Because the *doing* orientation is basic to the middle-class white American lifestyle, *competitiveness* and upward mobility characterizes this mode of activity. The Asian and Pacific Islander American cultural ideal is self-discipline, many African Americans exhibit resiliency in the midst of suffering, and both First Nations peoples and Latinos may prefer a *being-in-becoming* mode of activity. Finally, the sociological structure of the mainstream society addresses itself basically to the nuclear family, which contrasts to the extended family common to many minority groups. Constraints are imposed on minority family members, who are required to adjust. Due to differences in value systems, discriminatory conditions, and societal constraints, ethnic minority members can be expected to experience significant family and individual problems and difficulties. Chestang (1976) labels minorities' shared experiences with the mainstream dominant systems as social injustice, societal inconsistency, and personal impotence. Social injustice is exemplified by the overrepresentation of minorities in prison. Societal inconsistency refers to the individual's personal rejection and personal impotence, which results when adequate supports are not available.

Biculturalism

Threats to survival and self-esteem require adaptation from ethnic minorities that causes "a split in the acculturative process resulting in the development in the duality of culture" (Dreyfuss & Lawrence, 1979, p. 78). Biculturalism demands the bilateral bringing together of items, values, and behaviors. It signifies participation in two cultural systems and often requires two sets of behavior. This characterization of dual response has both conscious and unconscious aspects. It can be internalized as a central aspect of the personality but does not mean dual personality; rather, it involves two distinct ways of coping with tasks, expectations, and behaviors (Chestang, 1976). For example, a Latino (male) may behave according to a hierarchical and vertical structure at home with his family and friends, as his culture demands; but he can behave competitively in the workplace, as the white American culture requires. In assessing an ethnic minority client's biculturalism, it is essential to consider age, sex, educational, economic, social, political, familial, and linguistic factors. Familiarity with the cultural values of each group should serve as a baseline for the assessment. Hence family therapy theory must consider the level of acculturation within the ethnic and mainstream culture, the degree to which the client is able to choose between two cultures or worlds, and the level of participation in each world that is desirable and obtainable by each client or family.

Ethnic Differences in Minority Status

Several factors affect the status and adjustment of ethnic minorities in this country. The status of each ethnic group or subgroup experience, in turn, affects social adjustment and family living in a white-dominant society. Historical and governmental relationships serve as important indicators in understanding the experiences of a particular ethnic group. The history of slavery of African Americans and their struggle to maintain African cultural roots in a society that challenges and oppresses them make African Americans feel precarious at best and demoralized at worse. Racism and colonialism have made First Nations peoples "immigrants" in their own homeland. In contrast to any other ethnic minority group in the United States, a person is not indigenous, or an authentic Native, unless he or she fits into categories defined by the federal government, including blood degree and tribal status. To be eligible for federal Native programs, a person must be able to prove that he or she has at least one-quarter indigenous "blood" as recognized by the federal government.

Immigration status also plays a vital role in the living experiences of many ethnic minority individuals. Some Southeast Asians and refugees realize that they may never be able to return to their homeland. They often experience *emotional cutoff* and wonder if and when there will be any reunion with relatives. Such geographical disconnection and intergenerational family emotional cutoff have adverse implications for family structure and functioning. Conversely, minority groups such as Puerto Ricans can consider their stay on the mainland transitory and know that they can easily visit their families again. Whether the ethnic minority individual is a legal resident or an undocumented resident is also significant. Incredible abuses toward undocumented residents are well known. Many live in fear of being reported.

Understanding and discerning the minority status of a particular ethnic subgroup is important in accurately assessing the need of the group's members for family therapy. For example, if society considered the Vietnamese merely as an immigrant group, then discrimination against them might be temporary if they followed the customary path of acculturation and assimilation into mainstream or dominant society. However, skin color is an important factor in determining the experiences of an ethnic minority person or family regardless of patterns of acculturation and assimilation. Because color is one of the most pervasive reasons for discrimination, some ethnic minority individuals may attempt to "pass" as white. Puerto Ricans (or any ethnic minority person) from a mixed heritage can easily be traumatized by societal pressure to define themselves as "African American" or "white," and this is complicated further when other family members are labeled differently.

Ethnicity and Language

The transactional definition of *ethnicity* "as an element of behavioral and cognitive participation in the decisions and symbolic construct which supply meaning to communication" (Bennett, 1975, p. 4) requires that family therapists be knowledgeable of the implications and ramifications of ethnic connections, especially the language used by an ethnic individual or family. Ethnicity is experienced and persists through language. A common language provides a psychic bond, a uniqueness that signifies membership in a particular ethnic group. It is comforting to speak one's own language, particularly when under stress. Bilingual family services should be made available to ethnic minorities, given that communication is crucial to effective service delivery. Although many ethnic minority clients are bilingual—and that bilingualism is a strong indicator of biculturalism—problems of miscommunication may still occur. Many ethnic minority clients do not have parallel vocabularies or may not know various meaning of words. An ethnic minority client may appear to have a flat affect when, in reality, the problem is linguistic. The use of interpreters may be limiting, for much of the state of the art in family therapy is gaining information from the way family members interact, exchange, and interpret communicative interaction. The use of children to interpret, particularly minors, can reverse the vertical hierarchical structure of some families (Asian and Latino) and therefore is inappropriate. Family therapy with ethnic minorities requires close examination of the language used by each ethnic family and family member and (ethnic) group. There can be many variations of a language, from ethnic group to ethnic group—intergenerational and even regional differences that may impede communication.

Ethnicity and Social Class

Social class refers to "differences based on wealth, income, occupation, status, community power, group identification, level of material consumption and family background" (Duberman, 1975, p 34). However useful the definition of social class may be for categorizing people for some purposes, by itself it may not be adequate for a full appreciation of ethnic differences as they relate to family therapy. Individuals may act in accordance with their perceived class interest in some situations and in accordance with their cultural preferences or minority identity in others. Gordon (1969) uses the term *ethclass* to describe the point at which social class and ethnic group membership intersect. This formulation helps in examining the meaning of membership in an ethnic minority group and in various social classes. A limited number of ethnic minority members may have more income and be in the upper or middle classes, work in more highly valued and rewarding occupations, and have more prestige than others. This in turn affects the extent of their well-being, including health, help-seeking patterns, real and perceived power to achieve desired goals, self-respect, and the degree of dignity conferred by others. For those who are in the lower social class, the ethnic reality may translate into continual and persistent discrimination in jobs, housing, education, and into the reception received in the workplace and in healthcare and welfare institutions.

Members of ethnic minorities who have achieved material goals continue to be frequently reminded of the oppression that plagues their kindred and of their identification with the specific ethnic group. Although economically and materially successful, some ethnic minority members still experience difficulty in being accepted by white, middle-class society. At the same time, they may feel alienated from their own ethnic group (Combs, 1978). There is evidence that ethclass among the ethnic minority is positively correlated to a member's English efficiency, educational level, and acculturation rate (DeAnda, 1984). However, ethnic minority members' higher social class status does not imply that ethnicity play a less important role in their life. As Mass (1976) indicates, the influence exerted by the value patterns that were acquired throughout childhood is often considerable even among those whose behavior is highly westernized. Other studies (Native American Research Group, 1979; McAdoo, 1978; Staples, 1976) have also indicated that "successful" or "acculturated" ethnic minority families show a strong interest in and need for keeping alive the folkways, arts and crafts, language, and values associated with their heritage. The ethnic minority family's retention of its traditional heritage and persistent adherence to its own ethnicity should have important implications in the conceptualization of a practice theory that addresses its needs and problems.

Ethnicity as Narrative Identity

Emerging conceptualizations of ethnicity and culture draw upon *narrative* and constructionist formulations. From a narrative perspective, ethnic identities are not static descriptions of attributes of a group of people who view themselves as being bonded together by a common history, traditions, language, and geographic origin. Rather, ethnic identities are fluid, socially and historically constructed within the context of "evolving products of material and social circumstances and the actions of groups themselves, wrestling with, interpreting and responding to those circumstances, building or transforming (ethnic) identities in the process" (Cornell, 2000, p. 42). Ethnic identities are embedded in those *collective narratives* that ethnic groups recount as their distinctive "connectedness." These *cultural narratives* are further reflective of their ongoing interpretations of those distinctive elements in an ever-changing and shifting economic, social, political, and cultural context. As Cornell (2000) points out, *ethnic narratives* contain the linking together of selected past, anticipated, or imagined events and experiences in a causal, sequential, and associational manner. Contained within these narratives are claims about the degree to which these selected and constituent events define the group as subjects. Laird (1998), in viewing ethnicity as a narrative construct, suggests that in addition to ethnicity being a constantly evolving set of meanings embedded within the context of a *narrativized past,* it is a political construct. The rendering of one's personal or *collective ethnic narrative* is shaped by the constraints of the broader sociopolitical context in which the narrative is told. *Ethnic identity narratives* and their production are affected by power relationships in terms of who gets to narrate what and whose version of an identity gains currency in a particular sociopolitical context (Cornell, 2000). For example, as African Americans speak of their identity, the history of slavery is incorporated into the narrative rendering of the African American experience. Yet embedded within the narration of African American history are historical and cultural spaces in which the voices of African Americans were rendered silent due to the constraints of racism and oppression. In these silent spaces, the *narration of oppression and resiliency* under racism, discrimination, and oppression was not allowed to be heard. The only *legitimate* narratives about the African American experience were rendered by the perpetrators of racism and oppression, thus shaping in multifarious ways the identity of African Americans.

For many ethnic minority families, *disempowering sociopolitical metanarratives* constrain the family's ability to construct more empowering and potentiating solutions to family problems. As ethnic minority families present themselves for family therapy, a culturally attuned therapist must take a stance that allows for the narrative rendering of the *ethnic themes* in a family's history. These narrative renderings, representing the family's emic interpretation of the interrelationship of family and ethnic themes, permits the therapist to enter into the family's narrative world to uncover, with the family, the interplay of ethnic, family, and broader *sociocultural metanarratives.* A family therapist cannot understand the significance of a family's problem or narrative without recognition of the material, power-laden, and affectively charged elements of the prevailing sociocultural metanarratives and their influence on the family member's lived experiences. A therapist assuming a *narrative stance* (Laird, 1998) in working with families can create a space where more empowering narratives can be coauthored.

The Ecosystem Framework

The ecosystem perspective is selected as one of the frameworks because of its "person-in-environment" focus, which takes into consideration the unique background experiences and contributions of each ethnic population. An ecosystems framework provides a lens in which the family and family members can be understood within the context of transactions with a variety of biological, psychological, cultural, and historical environments. By adopting an ecosystem perspective, a family therapist can focus on adaptive (and maladaptive) transactions between persons and between the person and various environments, that is, the interface between them.

In an ecological framework, people are understood in terms of their location within their environment or habitat. As the concept of environment is described with an ecosystems framework, it becomes much broader than one's habitat. The environment includes not only one's physical or geographical location or habitat but the sociopolitical, cultural, and economic context that surrounds one's lived space. It is the broader context of culture, economics, and politics that determines if one's habitat is supportive of the mental, physical, and social functioning of the individual and family.

The sustaining and nurturing resources within one's habitat are further determined by one's niche—that is, one's social position, class location, ethnic and racial identity, and economic status within the overall social structure. A good or *enabling* niche is one that avails the occupant of the rights of equal opportunity to educational and economic resources (Kilpatrick & Holland, 2003; Taylor, 1997). There are, however, individuals and families with devalued personal or cultural characteristics, such as color, ethnicity, gender, sexual orientation, age, poverty, or other types of bias and oppression, who are entrapped in niches that are incongruent with fulfilling their human needs and ensuring their well-being (Kilpatrick & Holland, 2003; Taylor, 1997).

Within an enabling niche are supports that can affirm one's sense of personal power, competence, and self-esteem. Furthermore, an enabling niche can represent a position from which one can express and affirm one's social power. An *entrapping* niche, however, contains elements that rob one of that self-affirming power. An entrapping niche further blocks one from those resources needed to acquire that power. Thus persons in an entrapping niche are people with a vulnerable status—a status of powerlessness. The concept of oppression denotes relationships that are unequivocally negative and that create a differential power imbalance. These relationships impair human growth and on a systemic level are destructive to both the physical and the social environment (Germain & Gitterman, 1996). Power withheld and abused by dominant groups becomes oppressive power. This form of power shapes and gives meaning to the experiences of those held captive within entrapping niches. The experiences of powerlessness and oppression become the primary themes in their transactions with the environment. This experience becomes one of the major themes in the captive's *life narrative.*

When using the ecosystem framework to assess the family structure and function of an ethnic client or family, a therapist should give special consideration to the family's particular cultural values and the *multiple niches* they occupy. Falicov (1983, 1998) presents a multidimensional view of culture that is imminently congruent with the ecosystem perspective:

> Culture is that set of shared world views, meanings and adaptive behaviors derived from simultaneous membership and participation in a variety of contexts, such as language; rural, urban or suburban setting; race, ethnicity, and socioeconomic status; age, gender, religion, nationality; employment and occupation, political ideology, and stages of acculturation. (Falicov, 1983, pp. xiv-xv)

Such a definition also suggests that there are *multiple ecological contexts* and perspectives where a therapist must look to discover the family's culture and its ecological niche (Falicov, 1998).

When using the ecosystem framework, there are several practice principles that are particularly relevant in therapy with ethnic minorities, characterized as a group or groups of "politically underprivileged" individuals who interact through maintaining their own sense of cultural distinctiveness (Bennett, 1975). These principles are grounded in an understanding of power dynamics and how powerlessness is reinforced through oppressive habitats and niches (Fong & Furuto, 2002). Four of the practice principles are discussed below.

First, individual or family problems are not conceived of as pathology; instead, problems or difficulties are understood as a lack or deficit in the environment (as in the case of migration or immigration) or a result of interrupted growth and development (role conflict and resource deficits in the environment). A therapist's change effort can thus focus on the interface between systems or subsystems. The goal will be the enhancement of the relationship between those systems.

Second, intervention efforts are directed to multivariable systems, and a single effect can be produced by a variety of means. The principle of *equifinality*, which means that a number of different interventions may, owing to the complexity of systems, produce similar effects or outcomes, encourages flexibility and creativity in seeking alternative routes to change. A therapist may try to relate interventive strategies to existing theories that are Western middle-class American oriented, but innovative strategies of change based on the client's cultural background and *ecological niche* are also encouraged.

Third, intervention strategies make use of natural systems and life experiences and take place within the life space of the client. The family itself is a natural helping system and an instrument of change. Emphasis on the client's life space and family as a natural helping system places the therapist in a role of *cultural broker* instead of intruder, manipulator, or cultural expert.

Finally, the ecological principle *reverberation throughout the system*, meaning that change in one part of the system has an impact on all other parts of the system, allows a therapist the flexibility to function within a practice constriction without involving all family members in the change process. Thus working with one family member who is more "acculturated" or motivated than other family members may well bring about significant change in the total family. When family interactions made rigid by traditional role structure and the family as a whole are not amenable to family therapy, the one-to-one therapeutic modality may be the only workable resolution for an ethnic minority family. In defending this therapeutic modality, Bowen (1978) writes, "A theoretical system that 'thinks' in terms of family and works toward improving the family system is family psychotherapy" (p. 157).

An ecosystem framework can guide the family therapist in conceptualizing and defining the *unit of attention*, defined as the universe or data that provide the raw material for the assessment process. The ecosystem framework begins with an analysis of the structure of the field by using common operational properties of systems as criteria to identify family systems, subsystems, and environmental systems. By tracing the communications within and between the family systems and other systems, the ecosystem framework can help clarify the structure, sources, pathways, repository sites, and integrative functions of messages. The holistic nonexclusive nature of the ecosystem framework minimizes the danger of excessive selectivity by the therapist in the collection and analysis of data.

When using the ecosystem framework to assess the family structure and function of an ethnic client or family, a therapist should give special attention to that family's particular values. In the study of ethnicity, culture can also be defined as those things that are relevant to communication across some kind of social boundary. Such a definition also suggests where a therapist must look to discover cultural differences. This assumes that some factors that characterize the family background and experience of each individual are, at least at the moment of presenting family concerns to a therapist, more important than other external factors. According to Kluckhohn (1951), cultural orientations are distinguished from concrete values by their levels of generality. A value orientation organizes and influences behavior in regard to time, nature, environment, and interhuman transactions. Such individual differences are particularly critical during the assessment phase of therapy. The ecosystemic framework is particularly helpful to a therapist in organizing and assessing data during the assessment phase of therapy. This framework will facilitate the development of emic (cultural-specific) practice principles and intervention techniques.

Critical Constructionist Perspective

Family practice theories describing family interventions have the possibility of being apolitical and relativistic in that they can ignore the broader sociopolitical context in which family therapy work practice is conducted. According to Fish (1993), in many family therapy models, politics and power are understood at the level of the helping relationship. The level of the clients' or the family therapist's position within the larger social order is not considered. The critical constructionist perspective as the second part of the conceptual framework used in this book provides a corrective to the potential apolitical nature of theories of family therapy (Heiner, 2002; Witkins, 1995).

The critical constructionist perspective represents a synthesis of social constructionism, critical social science, and conflict theory. Within a social constructionist perspective, ideas, beliefs, customs, subjective experiences, values and myths (and all those things that make up our psychological reality) are socially constructed within the context of human interactions and expressed through the medium of language (Ariel, 1999; Freeman & Combs, 1996). Language is the means of organizing and structuring life experiences. It is the narrative that individuals construct about their lives that provides them with a sense of personal identity. Narratives further reveal the significance of an individual's lived experience within the context of his or her social worlds (Gergen, 1991; Polkinghorne, 1988). Within a social constructionist framework, family therapists shift from a focus on action to a focus on meanings, for human actions and relationships are seen as efforts to create meaning out of personal experiences. These efforts at meaning construction are reflected in narratives or stories that give organization and structure to a person or family (Kilpatrick & Holland, 2003). Thus family problems are located within communication systems or language. Facilitating, in a collaborative manner, a change in the family's language from a problem-oriented discourse to a solution-focused discourse creates a space for increased individual or family competency. This perspective involves creating a therapeutic space for the emergence of alternative and more empowering interpretations, as problems are grounded in interpretations of intrafamily communication. Reality is thus a matter of interpretation rather than a description of an objective or external given. This feature (of the social constructionist perspective) has caused some theorists some discomfort in that viewing problems only as "interpretations" may ignore differentials in power in terms of what interpretation is socially valued and hence validated.

From the perspective of critical constructionism, this concern is addressed. Heiner (2002), in his synthesis of conflict theory and social constructionism, presents one variant of a critical constructionist perspective. For Heiner, critical constructionism articulates how the meanings of social problems are socially constructed and gives primary attention to the role of the elite in problem construction. Heiner (2002) states: "Critical constructionists do not argue that social problems that are successfully constructed are inconsequential and harmless. Instead they argue that our view of the problems that exist in society has been distorted by the power relations involved in the construction of social problems" (p. 11). Witkins (1995) views the critical constructionist perspective as a useful organizing framework for family social work. The critical constructionist approach is a heuristic (problem-solving) framework out of which the important activity of family practice may develop a distinctive approach. The critical constructionist perspective is not only an attempt to interpret social reality but a framework for recognizing the inherently political nature of social explanations of human conditions and family life.

A critical constructionist perspective draws many of its theoretical assumptions from critical social sciences and conflict theory. Healy (2000), drawing upon the works of Fay (1987), defines the following four basic characteristics of critical social sciences and conflict theory:

- Critical social theories and conflict theories seek to explain the social order in terms of an organizing principle or dominant ideologies that structure society as a totality. This organizing principle fundamentally orders social relationships at an institutional and personal level. For example, Marxists would describe this organizing principle as capitalism, radical feminists would identify it as patriarchy, and multiculturalists would describe it as racism. This form of totality is not permanently fixed but represents a particular dialectical historical and social process. Through analysis of these processes, critical social scientists seek to provide insight for social transformation.

- Critical social theories and conflict theories give primary attention to power relationships within the social order, with an understanding that there are clear power dimensions within the dialectical struggle between groups. The position and power of the oppressor and oppressed are structurally determined within the framework of the dominant social ideology. Yet even as these power dynamics exist, humans are social actors with the power to maintain or change the system of power relationships.

• As human beings are social actors, critical science theories and conflict theories promote rational, self-conscious thought as the basis for critical analysis of the social system, liberation, and transformation of the social system. This analysis and movement for action is grounded in acts of reflective activity or "critical consciousness." In this state of consciousness, individuals are able to identity the ways in which the social structure shapes their experience. This awareness becomes the basis for challenging and rejecting those dominant ideologies that constrain individuals from making more authentic choices for their lives.

• Critical social scientists then aim to empower their audience to transform the social order to one that meets their genuine needs.

Drawing from these assumptions, four major themes can be found in varying degrees in all of the critically oriented practice models (Fine, 1992; Healy, 2000; Lee, 1987; Leonard, 1994; Longres, 2000). These themes are (a) a commitment to standing alongside oppressed and impoverished populations; (b) the importance of dialogic relations between the therapist and family members; (c) the role of social, economic, and political systems in shaping family and individual experiences and social relationships, including interactions within the social context; and (d) a commitment to the study of change and the provocation of change. In summary, a critical constructionist perspective can be seen as oriented toward the transformation of processes and structures that perpetuate domination and exploitation. A critical constructionist perspective attunes the family therapy practitioner to the broader social, political, and economic issues that shape the experiences of the family members. As a framework to understand the meaning of the client's narrative and his or her ecological niche, a critical constructionist perspective keeps the practitioner focused and cognizant of the political dimensions of the personal, as well as cognizant of the personal dimensions of the political.

This perspective gives recognition that families exist as a dialectical social process that fundamentally represents conflicting interest between social groups. Yet most important in this dialectical struggle is the premise that the "conflicting interests of the opposed classes are fundamentally irreconcilable and that the power of the elite is maintained at the expense of the powerless" (Healy, 2000, p. 19). Although the dialectical tensions are generally described in terms of conflicting class interest, a critical constructionist perspective can highlight conflicting cultural interest and the structural dominance of a social, political, and cultural order that can marginalize another culture—thereby creating the dynamics of the oppressor and oppressed.

One of the important contributions of the critical constructionist perspective is that it can contextualize the meaning of both the family therapist's and the family member's *lived experience* in therapy by locating that experience with a specific ecological, historical, economic, and political context. To say that "the personal is political" underscores one of the basic assumptions of critical social theory. Any understanding of an individual or family system or family narrative must include an inquiry into the family's social, political, economic, and cultural position within the social order. The therapist must view her or his narrative (and the family's narrative) with a critical eye to uncover the extent to which the unique reality of both the therapist's and the family member's lived experience is shaped by the dominant social and political ideology.

The critical constructionist–oriented practitioner views liberation from oppressive ideologies and structure as an indispensable condition of the quest for human potential and authenticity (Stevens, 1989). Liberation is attained by first developing a state of "critical consciousness," which means achieving an awareness of how the social, political, and economic ideologies constrain our *sense of agency* and identity (Freire, 1973). Informed by this new awareness, the therapist and the families can take action against those oppressive structures and articulate in their own "voice" a narrative of self that represents their unique lived experience.

Communicative-Interactive Theories and Practice Models

The communicative-interactive practice models developed and advanced by Haley (1976) and Satir (1986) are based on George Herbert Mead's (1934) symbolic interactionism, which places a major emphasis upon the communicative and interactive process taking place between individual family members and sub-systems within the family. Contemporary family theorists may view these practice models as being eclipsed by constructionist and narrative theories, but there is great compatibility with communicative-interactive models and social construction theory in that both practice models give attention to the human need to make meaning out of every experience (Cheung, 1997; Satir, 1988) and the importance of language in creating that meaning. One of the assumptions of the communicative-interactive model is that family culture is sustained and maintained through communication and language and, more important, through subjective and everyday interpretations of behavior. One of the key elements of communication within families is not just the act of communicating but the interpretation of communicative events by others and the interpersonal meanings derived from that interpretation, followed by the subsequent response to that interpretation.

The contributions of the interactional framework center primarily upon changes within the family unit that are a result of interactions between members.

From this framework, an analysis can be made in which individual family members act and react to the actions of others and the interpersonal meanings attached to these actions. Interactive processes that are of particular importance to therapy with ethnic minority families include communication, conflict, role relations, and decision making. Because the communicative-interactive framework is concerned primarily with change rather than with stability, the concepts of family *equilibrium* and the family's transaction with the outside world are less important. The framework can also easily shift from one that concentrates upon interactive processes between system members to one that emphasizes intervention methods that focus primarily upon individual actions or behaviors.

Structural-Functional Theories and Practice Models

Strongly committed to the systems outlook, the structuralist position emphasizes the active, organized wholeness of the family unit. Like the communication theorist, the structuralist is interested in the components of the system, how balance or *homeostasis* is achieved, how the family *feedback mechanism* operates, how dysfunctional communication patterns may develop, and other system factors. There are also important differences between the two theories. Rather than observing the communicative interaction—the interpersonal meanings in a family transaction, and what messages members send back and forth—the structuralist adopts a more holistic view, observing the activities and functions of the family as a clue to how the family is organized or structured. The focus here is on using the content of a transaction in the service of understanding how the family organizes itself. Structualists in general are more concerned with how family members communicate than what they communicate and the interpretation of that communication. The study of power games, communication patterns, meaning systems, or rule processes is only marginally relevant and is monotheoretical because, in the structuralist view, these concepts fail to explain the complexities of human interactions.

The structural-functional framework primarily developed and advanced by Bowen (1976) and Minuchin (1974) was based on the anthropological and sociological work of Talcott Parsons (1951), Robert Merton (1957), and George Homans (1964). The relevance of this approach in therapy with ethnic minority families lies with its emphasis on the family as a *boundary-maintaining* social system in constant transaction with the environment or other systems. The internal family system is composed of individual members who define both the family as a whole and the various subsystems within the whole, that is, the marital, parent-child, and sibling units. In transacting with the environment, individual members are viewed primarily as reactors who are subject to influences and impingement from the greater social system. The healthy functioning of an ethnic minority family system can be measured by its adaptive boundary-maintenance ability following stressful situations caused by pressures from transactions with other environmental systems or with society as a whole (Kerr & Bowen, 1988; Minuchin, 1974). Hence, therapy as guided by this conceptualization suggests two levels of intervention: (a) strengthening the boundary-maintaining ability of the family for adaptive purposes that serve stability or equilibrium needs and (b) intervention at the broader societal level to reduce the impact on families of destructive influences that emanate from the environment (Aponte & DiCesare, 2000; Minuchin, 1974).

Some of the concerns regarding the limitations of the structural-functional–based practice models were addressed earlier, but it is important to reiterate that the use of a single model (as opposed to an integrative approach that employs several models) may provide limited explanatory power in understanding ethnic minority families and limited value in facilitating change in families. Yet when cast within an ecosystem and critical constructionist framework, these models have the potential to address the multiple realities of ethnic minorities.

Summary and Conclusion

The ecosystem framework and the critical constructionist framework are presented and explored here as organizing conceptual perspectives that can guide our understanding of the unique historical and cultural realities of ethnic minority families; we may thus more effectively guide family therapy activities. Within the assumptive framework of each of these frameworks is an ideological commitment to a strengths orientation. Thus decisions are made regarding the use of explanatory theories, practice models, and techniques. These frameworks draw deliberate attention to the indications of strength and resilience. Additionally, these frameworks suggest strategies for *challenging debilitating and depotentiating narratives* that may exist as a result of experiences with oppression, discrimination, and racism (Rasheed & Rasheed, 1999).

The ecosystems framework provides a conceptual lens with which to examine the transactions between ethnic minority families and their biopsychosocial environment, wherein the critical constructionist framework allows the practitioner to explore the unique individual and familial impact of societal factors on the construction of ethnic family members' identities through their language and personal narratives. Using a critical practice perspective, we can attend to how ethnic minority families construct their narrative identities and acknowledge the diversity in which these ethnocultural individual or familial identities are expressed. This perspective offers the family therapist the opportunity to recognize *multiple ethnocultural voices* as they resound within the "chorus" of a heterogeneous ethnic community.

Although these frameworks represent different lenses, they both revolve and converge around the integrating themes of strength, resilience, and empowerment. Namely, the ecosystems perspective sets the stage by addressing how the multiple environments in which ethnic minority families interact and transact can be supportive of or debilitating to the ethnic individual's and/or family's well-being. The ecosystems orientation also emphasizes how the life cycle allows one to focus on the impact of race, culture, ethnicity, and class factors on the ethnic minority family's ability to fulfill life roles and developmental tasks across the life span. The critical constructionist perspective gives attention to an articulation of a culturally sensitive narrative that supports an ethnic and communally based identity, value, and worldview. Finally, the critical constructionist perspective instructs us how to challenge those *dominant narratives* that rob ethnic minority individuals and families of their psychological, social, and spiritual vitality. These metatheories or perspectives that we strategically blend for family practice with ethnic minority families will enable family therapists to hear and give voice to the voiceless. Each ethnocultural voice is liberated to speak its own ethnocultural reality and is not constrained to keep to the metanarrative of the entire ethnocultural family or (community) group.

Having discussed the conceptual frameworks, the ecosystemic theoretical framework, and the critical constructionist perspective, as well as the application of communication and structural family therapy theories, we now direct our attention to the application of these theoretical frameworks and models to understand and provide effective therapy for each of the selected ethnic minority groups featured in this volume.

2

Family Therapy With Asian and Pacific Islander Americans

PART 1: PRETHERAPY PHASE CONSIDERATIONS: A CRITICAL PERSPECTIVE

D
ue, in part, to the economic and educational achievements of Asian and Pacific Islander Americans, this diverse ethnocultural group has come to be considered the "model minority." Asian and Pacific Islander Americans are held up as an example of what can be accomplished in America by ethnic minorities, "if one really works hard." As a "model minority," the Asian or Pacific Islander individual is portrayed as hard working, industrious, and (most important) compliant, as he or she strives to fully assimilate into mainstream American culture (Cooper, 1995; Ishii-Kuntz, 2000). The seemingly prevalent notion of a model minority ignores the many ways in which Asian and Pacific Islander Americans have been discriminated against and stigmatized throughout United States history. Two of the most shameful eras of racism, discrimination, and stigmatization in this country's history are the internment of Japanese Americans in detention camps during World War II and the hate crimes committed against Southeast Asian refugees in the 1970s and 1980s, during and immediately following the Vietnam War era.

Economic discrimination is a harsh reality confronting Asian and Pacific Islander Americans. Southeast Asians currently are at a higher risk of poverty than white Americans. There are many recent Asian and Pacific Islander immigrants working in low-wage sweatshops in urban Chinatowns. Asians are underrepresented in higher salaried public and private career positions (despite impressive academic achievements). While many Asian and Pacific Islander Americans have become successful small business owners, for some this role is forced upon them as a last-resort employment endeavor, given the consequences of racism and discrimination (Karger & Stoesz, 2002). The economic, occupational, and political realities of Asian and Pacific Islander life clearly do not support the notion of the happy, successful, and well-integrated model minority. It is ironic and unfortunate that the resentment toward Asian and Pacific Islander Americans' success, work ethic, and emphasis on education plays a role in the racism and discrimination displayed against Asian and Pacific Islander Americans.

In discussing family therapy with Asian and Pacific Islander families, it is important to consider the complexity of Asian and Pacific Islander Americans' experiences in the United States and the impact of these experiences in shaping Asian and Pacific Islander American family life. Asian and Pacific Islander American families, like other ethnic minority families, encounter multiple conflicts and tensions as they attempt to maintain cultural integrity and achieve a level of assimilation and acculturation into the mainstream culture. This struggle is compounded by myriad social, political, and economic forces, as cited earlier. The following section discusses multiple factors that should be considered by family therapists who engage Asian and Pacific Islander families in therapy. These pretherapy considerations will enable the family therapist to better understand Asian American families within their ecological (social, economic, historical, and political) context.

Demographics

The term *Asian and Pacific Islander* generally includes Chinese, Japanese, Korean, Filipino, Samoan, Guamanian, Hawaiian, and other Pacific Islanders. Recent immigrants and refugees from Vietnam, Thailand, Cambodia, Laos, and Indonesia; persons from India, Pakistan, and Ceylon; and children of mixed marriages in which one parent is Asian American are also included. Although the term *Asian and Pacific Islander* refers to a cluster of rather fixed ethnic identity markers based on country of origin, it also reflects a self-constructed ethnic narrative. The narrative basis of ethnic identity is clearly evident in the United States 2000 Census. The United States 2000 Census (U.S. Census Bureau, 2001a) allowed individuals to self-identify with various race mixings. In this census, the number of U.S. residents who reported as Asian alone or in combination with one or more other races made up 4.2% (11.9 million) of the U.S. population. This number represents an increase from 10.03 million in 1997 (U.S. Census Bureau, 1998). The leading Asian group is Chinese (2.7 million), followed by Filipino (2.4 million) and Asian Indians (1.9 million). What is further significant is that the term *Asian and Pacific Islander* is not used as a personal self-descriptor by those above identified as Asian or Pacific Islander. These individuals are more likely to define themselves in relation to their country of origin or ethnic category (e.g., Korean, Hmong, Bengalese, Pakistani).

For Westerners, the differences among the Asian and Pacific Islander groups may seem minimal, but vast differences do exist. The 2000 United State Census gave recognition to these vast differences by considering Asians, Native Hawaiians, and other Pacific Islanders as separate race categories (Lum, 2002). The subgroupings are as follows:

Asian Americans	Chinese, Japanese, Filipino, Korean
Southeast Asians	Cambodian, Hmong, Vietnamese, Laotian, Thai, Malaysian, Singaporean
Asian Indians	Bengalese, Bharat, Dravidian, East Indian, Goanese
Other Asians	Bangladeshi, Burmese, Indonesian, Pakistani, Sri Lankan

In addition to obvious language differences, the historical, social, and economic differences among these nations should not be overlooked. Within the context of living in the United States, there are within-group distinctions among individuals based on immigrant, refugee, and transnational status (Ishii-Kuntz, 2000; Lott, 1998; Lum, 2002).

Although they are vastly different with respect to ethnic, historical, and social factors, Asian and Pacific Islander groups do share some common features of family structure and function (Sue & Morishima, 1982). Application of family therapy concepts presented in this chapter should be preceded by a careful evaluation of the particular Asian and Pacific Islander family or client, including geographical origin, birthplace of family members, number of generations born or resident in the United States, and the family's social class or position in both its country of origin and in the United States. The family theory concepts and family therapy skills and techniques discussed in this book are potentially applicable to most Asian and Pacific Islander American families, especially those who are recent immigrants and older immigrants with strong traditional ties. This population is quite significant in that approximately 60% of the immigrants are foreign born (U.S. Census Bureau, 1998). These concepts may be least applicable to later generation Asian and Pacific Islander Americans such as Sansei (third-generation) Japanese Americans, who are usually thoroughly assimilated into American culture.

Cultural Values in Relation to Family Structure

Traditional Asian and Pacific Islander values governing family life have been heavily influenced by Confucian philosophy and ethics, which strongly emphasize specific roles and proper relationships among people in these roles. The influence of Taoism and Buddhism may be reflected in actual religious practices, values, and belief systems (Hong, 1993, Hong & Friedman, 1998, Hong & Ham, 2001). According to the Confucian system, the quest for spiritual fulfillment is to achieve harmony in this world and in this life through observing the five basic relationships of society: those between a ruler and his subjects, father and son, husband and wife, elder and younger siblings, and friends (Keyes, 1977). These five relationships demand loyalty and respect. Within the family, *filial piety,* or the respectful love shown to parents by children, is of paramount importance. It is the cornerstone of morality and is expressed in a variety of forms. *Oyakoko,* a Japanese version of filial piety, requires a child's sensitivity, obligation, and unquestionable loyalty to lineage and parents.

Highly developed feelings of obligation (*giri* in Japanese) govern much of the traditional life of members within a family. But although contractual obligations such as those between parent and child and teacher and pupil exist and are important, the unspoken obligatory reciprocity that rises out of human relationships, such as is seen in kindness and helpfulness, has a greater impact on the personal life of the individual. Parents are considered by their children as their greatest obligation because parents are the ones who brought them into the world and cared for them when they were helpless. Hence, regardless of what parents may do, the child is still obligated to give respect and obedience. The concept of *filial piety* further prescribes that children should repay their parents' love and care by providing and caring for them in their old age. It is not uncommon for aging parents to live with a married child, preferably a married son, as prescribed by the patriarchal structure of the traditional Asian family. For immigrant couples who have left their parents behind in their country of origin, inability to care for them may create constant guilt feelings, especially when there are no other siblings to assume this responsibility (Hong & Ham, 2001).

Closely related to the notion of obligation are the concepts of shame (*tiu lien* in Chinese) and shaming, which are used traditionally to help reinforce familial expectations and proper behavior within and outside of the family. Should a family member behave improperly, he or she may not only cause him- or herself to "lose face" but may also cause the family, community, or society to withdraw confidence and support. In Asian and Pacific Islander societal structures, where interdependence is so important, the actual or threatened withdrawal of support may shake a person's basic trust and cause him or her considerable anxiety over the thought of facing life alone. Hence the fear of losing face can be a powerful motivating force for conforming to family expectations.

As in Confucianism, the legacy of Buddhism is also strong in Asian and Pacific Islander folkways. Qualities essential to harmonious living involving compassion, respect for life, moderation in behavior, self-discipline, patience, modesty, friendliness, and selflessness are highly valued in Buddhist canons. The value *enryo* in a Japanese family requires that an individual maintain modesty in his or her behavior, be humble in expectations, and show appropriate hesitation and unwillingness to intrude on another's time, energy, or resources. *Gaman* for a Japanese means to evince stoicism and patience, be uncomplaining in the face of adversity, and display tolerance for life's painful moments. To maintain a harmonious family life, the Japanese family capitalizes on *kenshin,* which demands submission and devotion to group interest and purposes. The importance of these cultural values has a direct bearing upon the relationship subsystems, structure, and interactive patterns of Asian and Pacific Islander American families.

Key to a Buddhist perspective is the understanding of the phenomenon of suffering within human existence. Original Buddhist doctrine is summarized in the Four Noble Truths:

1. All life is suffering.

2. Suffering is caused by desire and attachment to the world.

3. Suffering can be extinguished and attachment to all things (including the self) can be overcome by eliminating desire.

4. To eliminate desire, one must live a virtuous life by following the eightfold path: right views, right thought, right speech, right conduct, right livelihood, right effort, right mindfulness, and right meditation.

Morelli (2001) and Lum (2002) speak to the Cambodian cultural construction of trauma and suffering as uniquely different from the Western perspective in that suffering builds family and extended family relationships and connects them to the cultural value of suffering. As Morelli (2001) states, "in the Khmer culture, the concept of pain extends beyond pain as the indication of illness. It is part of a larger process of suffering, which contributes to their kinship and familial solidarity, reciprocity, and ethnic identity maintenance" (pp. 202-203). This concept of suffering is crucial for Cambodian families as they strive to maintain family solidarity in the midst of their horrendous experiences during the Vietnam and post-Vietnam war era.

Extended Family Ties

The individual in traditional Asian and Pacific Islander culture is protected securely in a wide network of kinship. The Asian and Pacific Islander family system, with an emphasis on extended family, is the core of the Asian and Pacific Islander American life. The family member is clearly reminded that other social relationships or friendships should be secondary to the needs of the family and other kin relationships. Extended family ties are maintained by sharing a common domicile or by frequent visits. The fact that once an Asian and Pacific Islander family settles they are not likely to move also helps to keep extended family ties intact. Among Filipinos, kinship relationships extend beyond the set relations generally suggested by the concept of an extended family shared by other Asian and Pacific Islander groups. Filipino families tend toward bilateral equality in family relationships by incorporating relatives of both parents into the extended family. The *compadrazgo,* a Filipino system in which trusted friends and allies can be recruited to serve as godparents to children, further demonstrates the wide scope and viability of the family network. Extended family ties help maintain a good reputation for the partrilineage in the community and play important roles in the affairs of family life and the socialization of children (Chin, 1982; Ponce, 1977).

Immigration can seriously affect the support network provided by the extended family. Those individuals who have immigrated as single individuals may experience being cut off from emotional and social support provided by their network of relatives who still may reside in the immigrant's country of origin (Hong, 1989; Hong & Ham, 1992, 2001; Lee, 1997; Shon & Ja, 1982). For example, couples experiencing marital conflict are unable to turn to their families for consultation and support. Additionally, getting support for life and family development issues, such as marriage, childbirth, or other life events that may have culturally prescribed processes, may be absent. Such social isolation may create various forms of individual, family, and marital discord (Hong & Ham, 2001). The erosion of the extended family thus can be attributed to factors of migration, uprooting, and *mixed acculturation patterns* within Asian Pacific families.

Mate Selection and Husband-Wife Relationships

While the tradition of *omimai* (arranged marriage) is gradually disappearing among Asian and Pacific Islander families, the choice of mate is still heavily influenced by families on both sides. Within the traditional Asian and Pacific Islander framework, marriage serves to perpetuate the continuation of the husband's family line. Through marriage, the wife is considered to have left her family of origin and to have become absorbed into the family of her husband. The marriage ceremony symbolizes the death of the wife's relationship with her natal family (Sung, 1967). Arising from a patriarchal system adopted from Confucianism, this tradition places the wife in a low status in the family structure. A wife's position, in addition to being lower than that of her husband and her husband's parents, is also lower that that of her oldest son. Furthermore, a woman within the traditional Confucian framework is given three pathways to follow, of which all involve subservience to a man. In youth, she must follow and obey her father or uncle. In adult womanhood, she must follow her husband. In later years, she must follow her oldest son. In arguments between the wife and the parents-in-law, the husband is expected to ally himself with his parents (Yang, 1959). Because the most crucial factor of a marriage is the birth of male progeny, barrenness in a woman is deemed more than sufficient cause for divorce.

Today, among many Asian and Pacific Islander Americans, the status of a wife in her interaction with her husband and with the family is influenced by the following factors: Was the wife born in her native country or in the United States? Is she married to a foreign-born or native-born husband? What level of education does she have? Is there a scarcity of women of marriageable age? Generally, the higher a woman's education, the more acculturated she is and the higher her status in the family. Despite the wife's level of education and acculturation, she still has the tendency to assume the role of assistant director and helper to her husband rather than having a totally egalitarian relationship. Shifts toward more egalitarian roles, though achieved in some Asian and Pacific Islander couple relationships, may be stressful (Hong, 1989; Hong & Ham, 1992, 2001; Lee, 1997).

Parent-Child Relationships

The roles and expectations of a parent-child subsystem within an Asian or Pacific Islander American family are well-defined. The father is the head of the family. He makes the decisions, and his authority generally is unquestioned. In addition to being the breadwinner of the family, he is totally responsible for the welfare of the family as a whole. He makes and enforces the family roles and is the primary disciplinarian. Hence the father is frequently perceived as somewhat stern, distant, and less approachable than the mother. The mother, on the other hand, is recognized as the nurturing caretaker of both her husband and children. Her energy and creativity are channeled primarily into taking care of her children. In addition to providing the children with physical care and emotional nurturance, the mother intercedes occasionally with the father on the children's behalf. She forms a strong emotional bond with her children, especially her firstborn son, who later is expected to provide economic and social security for her upon her husband's death. Due to the strong emotional attachment the oldest son feels toward his mother, the wishes of the mother are frequently respectfully attended to by the son.

The primary role of the father is to provide and enforce the rules, the mother's role is to nurture and care for her children, and the child's responsibility at home is to obey and to be deferential to his or her parents. The Asian or Pacific Islander child is taught to behave only in ways that will not bring shame to his or her parents. The child is also reminded that the effect of his or her behavior on parents and clan must be the major consideration governing action (Ritter, Ritter, & Spector, 1965). Love and affection generally are not openly displayed in an Asian or Pacific Islander family. When the child is an infant, both parents usually show no hesitancy in pampering the child publicly. After these early years, the child quickly becomes incorporated into his or her role in the family structure and learns to live by the more rigid guidelines and expectations of the family and the society. Generally, Asian and Pacific Islander children grow up in the midst of adults, not only their parents, but also members of the extended family. Further, they are seldom left at home with babysitters or other adults (Hsu, 1972). Having been exposed to the companionship of adults, Asian and Pacific Islander children are also taught strict control of aggression.

One factor that is worthy of note is how an Asian or Pacific Islander child from a traditional family copes with the more egalitarian classrooms and school settings in the United States. Such settings may provide confusing experiences to both students and parents. As the Asian or Pacific Islander student, especially the teenager, searches for identity and acceptance within such a context, she or he may be viewed as "rebelling" against parental expectations or those in authority. These conflicting expectations may cause conflict between parents and children (Hong, 1996; Hong & Ham, 2001).

Sibling Relationships

Traditionally, Asian and Pacific Islander families favor a male child over a female child. Due to the patrilineal, patrilocal, and patriarchal principles guiding the Asian and Pacific Islander family, the birth of a boy is a particularly joyous event. Through the boy, the parent can be assured that the family name and the memory of the family's ancestors will continue to be worshiped in the afterworld. The birth of a daughter, on the other hand, is considered a liability to the family. She neither carries on the family name nor worships her natal ancestors (Fei, 1962).

The oldest son is the most desired and respected child in the sibling subsystem. Accordingly, he also carries more responsibilities than the rest of the siblings. He is expected to be a role model for his siblings, as well as to have authority over them. He is expected to provide continuous guidance to his younger siblings, not only when they are young but throughout their adult lives. He is to inherit the family authority and leadership upon the death of his father. Conflicts among siblings arise when the oldest son fails to fulfill his responsibilities, including other siblings' expectations of him. A daughter, despite greater freedom of choice in marriage and in seeking a career, is still seen primarily as the caretaker of a household.

Sibling rivalry and aggression are in general discouraged in Asian and Pacific Islander American families. Relationships among siblings are modeled after the Chinese concept of *jang,* in which older children are encouraged to set a good example for other siblings in gentleness, manners, and willingness to give up pleasure or comfort in favor of someone else. To show respect to the older sibling, the younger siblings use appropriate kin terms of address between brothers and sisters in different age groups. For example, one addresses siblings as, for example, Older Brother, Oldest Sister, Second Older Sister, Third Older Sister, or

Fourth Older Sister. Also implicit in this system of address are the explicit recip-rocal role expectations and interaction regulating "proper" sibling behavior.

The youngest daughter in the Asian or Pacific Islander American family usu-ally either comes to the United States at a young age or is American born. She may resent being left with responsibility for her parents as her older siblings leave home. Because she is likely to be the most acculturated, she may be the most vul-nerable to cultural value conflicts. The positions of oldest son and youngest daughter have been associated with the highest rates of psychopathology in Chinese culture, suggesting that the social roles that go with these positions may at times be highly stressful (Kleinman & Lin, 1981).

Intermarriages

With the custom of omimai (or arranged) marriages in decline, early and steady dating among young Asian and Pacific Islander Americans has become a common practice. Contracted marriage for economic and social gain and for con-venience may still exist, but marrying for love based on mutual interest and com-patibility has become a norm among young Asian and Pacific Islander adults. Third-generation Asian and Pacific Islander Americans become more assimilated, hence interracial and interethnic dating and intermarriages increase.

Up until 1948, California prohibited marriages between Asian and Pacific Islander Americans and Caucasian Americans. In 1959, more than ten years after the law was repealed, fewer than three out of every ten Japanese American mar-riages were interracial (Barnett, 1963). In 1972, Tinker completed a survey of the marriage records of Japanese Americans in Fresno, California, and found that 56% of them were interracial. Kikumura and Kitano (1973) also found that the vast majority of intermarriages involve Japanese women rather than men. The Office of Special Concerns of the Department of Health, Education and Welfare (1974) found high rates of intermarriage among other Asian and Pacific Islander groups as well. In their 1982 study, Kitano and Yeung indicate that the most strik-ing finding when compared to earlier studies is the increase in Chinese intermar-riage. The rise from under 10% in the 1950s to over 40% in the 1970s indicates the increasing acceptance of intermarriage with Chinese and other groups. We speculate that such acceptance is brought about by increased cultural contact and acculturation with other ethnic groups, as well as the decrease of racial prejudice and discrimination by other groups.

Current data based on the U.S. Census 2000 Supplemental Survey (Le, 2003) reveals that Asian Americans have the highest "outmarriage" rates; that is, they marry someone else outside their own ethnic group more often than other ethnic groups. The following table drawn from the 2000 Census shows the percentage of outmarriages among Asian Americans. The non-Asian category refers to whites,

African Americans, and Hispanics. Obviously, intermarriages can complicate the interaction and adjustment of couples and other family members involved. Generally, the greater the distance between spouses in cultural background, the more difficulty they will have in adjusting to marriage and family life.

Percentage of Six Asian Ethnic Groups Who Are Married to

Asian Indian American			Filipino American		
Husbands	88.4%	Asian Indian	Husbands	75.6%	Filipino
	4.6%	Other Asian		9.4%	Other Asian
	7%	Non Asian		15%	Non Asian
Wives	92.1%	Asian Indian	Wives	55.6%	Filipino
	4.0%	Other Asian		6.9%	Other Asian
	3.9%	Non-Asian		37.5%	Non-Asian
Chinese American			Japanese American		
Husbands	77.6%	Chinese	Husbands	66.7%	Japanese
	13.0%	Other Asian		16.5%	Other Asian
	9.4%	Non Asian		16.8%	Non Asian
Wives	72.9%	Chinese	Wives	52%	Japanese
	11.9%	Other Asian		12.6%	Other Asian
	15.2%	Non-Asian		35.4%	Non-Asian
Korean American			Vietnamese American		
Husbands	86.4%	Korean	Husbands	88.7%	Vietnamese
	9.2%	Other Asian		8.7%	Other Asian
	4.4%	Non Asian		2.6%	Non Asian
Wives	62.9%	Korean	Wives	82.9%	Vietnamese
	6.7%	Other Asian		8.5%	Other Asian
	30.4%	Non-Asian		8.6%	Non-Asian

SOURCE: U.S. Census Bureau, 2000b.

One of the significant outcomes of interracial marriages is the growing number of multiracial, biracial, and mixed-race Asian children. Based on the 2000 U.S. Census, multiracial Asians constitute 13.9% of all Asian Americans. As interracial marriages increase, multiracial Asians will also increase. In a social environment that increasingly tolerates interracial marriages, although it does not always completely accept them, the task of creating an ethnic identity is still a challenge for any multiracial person. This factor presents a special challenge to parents to ensure and support in their children an identity that incorporates both cultural diversity and personal uniqueness.

Another emerging phenomenon is the marked increase of cross racial or transracial adoptions of Asian children (particularly females) by white American couples. The social, emotional, and psychological implications and consequences of this trend are yet to be determined. Family therapy issues with transracially adopted Asian children, although beyond the scope of this volume, will no doubt be an important emerging concern for family therapists.

Divorce and Remarriage

Traditionally, Asian and Pacific Islander Americans consider divorce a great shame and tragedy, especially for females. In addition to barrenness, the husband has six other classical reasons for divorcing his wife, among which are filial impiety, jealousy, and talkativeness (Burkhardt, 1960). Asian and Pacific Islander Americans' disapproval of divorce is related to the fact that it elicits a serious social ostracism that few can afford, even at the risk of an unhappy household. Few traditional Asian or Pacific Islander American males would consider befriending a woman who previously had been engaged to or gone steady with another man, let alone a divorcee. Hence the divorce rate has been relatively low among Asian and Pacific Islander families as compared to other ethnic minority groups, although it has risen in recent years (Wilson, Kohn, & Lee, 2000). Based on data from the 1999 U.S. Census, Asian and Pacific Islanders were less likely than non-Hispanic whites to be widowed (4% compared with 10%) or divorced (5% compared to 10%). For the more traditional wives, discord and unhappiness are generally turned inward toward the self and are reflected in a high suicide rate rather than in divorce statistics. Sung (1967) notes:

> The suicide rate among the Chinese in San Francisco is four times greater than that for the city as a whole, and it is predominately women who decide to end it all. Suicide has been the traditional form of protest for Chinese women who find life unbearable with their matrimonial bonds. (p. 162)

The young generation of Asian and Pacific Islander Americans, especially those born in the United States, may not be as conservative as their foreign-born parents, for they are brought up in a culture where individual love and happiness are more important than what other people say about the family.

Impact of Immigration and Cultural Adjustments

The traditional Asian and Pacific Islander American family structure has provided stability, interpersonal intimacy, social support, and a relatively stress-free environment for its members (DeVos, 1978; Hsu, 1972). However, the process of immigration and cultural transition has been severely stressful to these families. The process of immigration necessitates a large number of life changes over a short period of time and is associated with lowered well-being and migration stress (Holmes & Masuda, 1974; Hong & Ham, 2001). This factor is especially critical because approximately 60% of Asian and Pacific Islander Americans are foreign born (U.S. Census Bureau, 1998).

As a consequence of this factor, coupled with the economic crisis and economic recession in Asia, many Asian and Pacific Islander families are experiencing new and troubling problems and issues. Many migrate only to face adjustment issues resulting in an increase in male depression and suicide, as well as an increase in incidents of family violence. The impact on children is quite evident as well. *Newsweek* (Ingrassia, King, Tizon, Scigliano, & Annin, 1994) reported on "America's New Wave of Runaways," addressing the cultural rift between Southeast Asian teens and their parents that is causing them to run away from home. The increase in outmarriages can cause or accentuate family value conflicts. Leaving key members, including parents, in the country of origin decreases the parental role in marital matchmaking, thus setting the stage for a weakened extended family. Advances in technology can also contribute to migration stress, cultural imbalance, and cultural lag, making it increasingly difficult for Asian seniors to play a role in the daily life of the family.

There are two interrelated levels of adaptive cultural transitions that every Asian and Pacific Islander American family in the process of immigration must face: (a) the physical or material, economic, educational, and language transitions and (b) the cognitive, affective, and psychological (individual members and family as a unit) transitions. The transformation from these two levels of cultural transitions can cause dysfunction in Asian and Pacific Islander American families.

Specifically, there are five major factors that contribute directly or indirectly to the cultural transitional difficulties that lead to the dysfunction of Asian and Pacific Islander families. These factors include (a) economic survival, (b) American racism, (c) loss of extended family and support systems, (d) vast cultural conflicts, and (e) cognitive reactive patterns to a new environment.

Asian and Pacific Islander Americans are known as survivors. Their need for economic security to provide the basic necessities of life such as shelter, food, and clothing, coupled with their desire to provide for their offspring, prompt the adult members of the family to begin employment immediately upon arrival in the United States. Those who lack professional skills and are deficient in the English language may find only working-class jobs with 6-day work weeks, 10- to 12-hour days, sub-minimum wages, and no or few benefits. If the parents' earnings are low, the family will only be able to afford to live in substandard housing. In the past, these new immigrants often have been subjected to discriminatory laws. Despite their accomplishments in the professional and technical fields, they are underrepresented in managerial and professional occupations and encounter bigotry, discrimination, unfair employment, and hate crimes (U.S. Commission on Civil Rights, 1992).

Many Asian and Pacific Islander Americans believe that they must perform better than white Americans to get ahead (Loo & Yu, 1980).

In the midst of oppression, the primary strength of a traditional Asian or Pacific Islander family structure is in providing an environment for mutual support and interdependence. The process of immigration drastically changes the scene. Relatives and close friends are often no longer available to provide material and emotional support to the nuclear family. The traditional hierarchical structure and rigidity of family roles make the expression and resolution of conflicts within the nuclear family very difficult, if not nearly impossible. The absence of interpersonal interaction outside of the nuclear family, in turn, forces greater demands and intense interaction within the nuclear family, leaving members with a high degree of vulnerability and unresolved conflicts.

Discrepancies in acculturation between husband and wife and between parents and children can have negative effects on the decision making and functioning of a family. Asian and Pacific Islander American youth are more receptive to Western culture and value orientation, for they wish to be accepted readily by the larger society, especially in a school setting. Individual family members' acceptance and incorporation into the Western orientation of individualism, independence, and assertiveness, especially in attitudes related to authority, sexuality, and freedom of individual choice, make the cultural values of traditional Asian and Pacific Islander families an extremely uncomfortable fit.

Inherent in immigration is a cognitive response that each family member goes through. Shon and Ja (1982) listed these responses as follows:

1. Cultural shock and disbelief at the disparity between what was expected and what actually exists
2. Disappointment at what exists
3. Grief at the separation from and loss of what was left behind
4. Anger and resentment
5. Depression because of the current family situation
6. Some form of acceptance of the situation
7. Mobilization of family resources and energy

There are many variations to this generalized scheme of responses, and each family member may experience these responses in a different order. These seven factors contributing to the cultural transitional difficulties have also drastically altered the structure and content (relationship) of current Asian and Pacific Islander American families. Two subsystem relationships (wife-husband, parent-child) are especially worthy of mention, for each has important implications for family therapy.

Wife-husband relationship. Because the wife has to work to help support the family financially, she can no longer devote equal time and energy to being a subservient wife to her husband and a nurturing mother to her children. If she still tries to adhere to the traditional roles and expectations of her as passive, accepting, and nurturing, she is bound to experience role conflict. Should her husband not accept the change and not accommodate her new role, conflict will occur. If her children experience adjustment problems, she may blame herself for not being able to stay home with them. She may displace her hostility onto her husband, who fails to live up to his role as the provider for the family. Because she is asked to assume more and more responsibilities, she expects more respect, power, and freedom in decision making pertaining to herself and the family. The fact that her in-laws and other extended family members are not around enables her gradually to shift from the traditional role of passive obedient spouse to more of an equal partner.

The demands on the husband to share his primary leadership role may lead to conflict and dysfunction within the family. He may interpret his wife's wish for an egalitarian relationship as a step to undermine his authority. His insecurity is further compounded by the fact that he fails to live up to the traditional role as the primary breadwinner for the family. His failure to assume his role as provider can bring shame and dishonor, not only to himself, but to the family lineage as a whole. To reassure himself and to compensate for his inadequacy, he may demand even greater respect from his wife.

Obviously, problems confronting the couple demand an immediate and constant renegotiation of roles and expectations. Negotiations are difficult and may be nearly impossible due to the traditional role rigidity and communication pattern and process that emphasize indirectness and prohibition of the expression of honest and true feelings. Further, if the couple's marriage is arranged, negotiation within a marital relationship will be a totally new concept that is practically impossible to acquire during a period of emotional duress.

Parent-child relationship. A child experiencing cultural transition also has increased demands placed upon him or her. Placed in a strange culture about which they have no choice, children may be overwhelmed by the numerous unexpected obstacles confronting them. At a time when children need and want comfort and security, they find themselves totally alone. Children may be ambivalent about their parents working long hours and may also feel upset by the fact that their grandparents, relatives, close friends, and recreational opportunities are no longer available. Children may be constantly reminded by parents that the parents have invested their future in their children. Children also are expected to do well in English-speaking schools even though they cannot speak English. When children become proficient in the English language, they also learn to accept and assimilate the cultural and value orientations that come with the English language. A child's assimilation into Western culture may then render him a total stranger in his or her own home. Children's newly learned assertiveness and freedom of choice and speech create more conflicts and physical and emotional distance between children and parents. Should a child disobey, the parent, especially the father, who is the disciplinarian in the family, will feel threatened and may demand more respect and deference from the child. Children's rapid acculturation, including greater proficiency in the English language, may cause role reversal in the family. Because of a child's proficiency in English, he or she may be appointed translator or spokesperson for the family in extrafamilial transactions and relationships. The status newly acquired by the child in such a situation may cause him or her to have less respect for the parents who remain traditional, rigid, and uneducated in English.

Family Help-Seeking Patterns and Behaviors

To successfully to help Asian and Pacific Islander American families, we need to understand their traditional cultural values in regard to dysfunctional behaviors. The cultural values presented here are highly applicable to first-generation immigrants, recent arrivals, and, to a lesser but still important extent, American-born ethnic minorities. As Mass (1976) indicates, the influences exerted by value patterns that are acquired throughout childhood are often considerable, even among those whose behavior is highly Westernized.

Very traditional Asian and Pacific Islander Americans do not typically consider psychiatric dynamics and psychological theories in attempts to account for behavioral difficulties (Green, 1999; Sue & Sue, 1999). Instead, social, moral, and organic explanations are used. When an individual behaves in a dysfunctional manner, external events such as physical illness, the death of a loved one, or the loss of a job are the cause of his or her problems. The individual is always the victim of unfortunate social circumstances over which the individual has no control, and therefore he or she is not to blame. *Shikata ga nai* (It can't be helped) in Japanese reflects such an attitude.

Moral explanation involves the transgressions of interpersonal duties and loyalties held sacred by a specific cultural group. Dysfunction is seen as a punishment or a direct result of immoral behavior. Hence the dysfunction or suffering of an Asian or Pacific Islander individual may be attributed to his or her violation of filial piety. Community elders or family members may be expected to exhort the individual to improve his or her dysfunctional behavior. Organic explanations for personal dysfunction are most common in Asian and Pacific Islander culture (Kleinman & Lin, 1981). The Chinese model of *Yin and Yang,* suggesting the balance between two basic life forces, has long been accepted as being the source of difficulty in physical and emotional functioning (when the two forces are out of balance or unequal, problems arise). Social, moral, and organic explanations to account for behavioral dysfunction not only maintain the individual's dignity but also help to safeguard the honorable family name.

Asian and Pacific Islander families may undergo several similar stages in their attempt to help family members, but different families may have different service needs and help-seeking patterns. Generally, there are three types of Asian and Pacific Islander American families in the United States, based on their level of acculturation and assimilation to American society.

(1) *Recently arrived immigrant or refugee families.* For a considerable period of time after their arrival in the United States, new immigrant families must direct most of their energy simply to adjusting to a completely new environment. Most experience the seven phases of cognitive reaction identified by Shon and Ja (1982), as listed previously in this chapter. Initial requests for services by this type of family tend to be predominantly requests for information and referral, advocacy, other concrete services, English-language instruction, legal aid, and child care (Kim, 1978; Lee, 1997; Ngo, Tran, Gibbons, & Oliver, 2001). Due to cultural differences and language barriers, these families seldom seek personal and psychological help.

(2) *Immigrant-American families.* Such families are characterized by foreign-born parents and their American-born children and the great degree of cultural conflict between the generations. Younger family members are usually more acculturated and Americanized—assertive, individualistic, and independent. Members of family subsystems (wife and husband, parents and child, siblings) may share different values and goals conflicting with those set previously by parents or grandparents. Some children may not know or speak their parent's native language, making communication and negotiation among family members nearly impossible. These families usually require help in resolving generational conflicts, communication problems, role clarification, and renegotiation. Bicultural and bilingual workers are required to help this group effectively.

(3) *Immigrant-descendent families.* Such families usually consist of second-, third-, or fourth-generation American-born parents and their children. They are acculturated to the Western value orientation and speak English at home. They usually reside outside the Asian and Pacific Islander American neighborhood and can seek help from traditional human service agencies or private practitioners with some degree of comfort and little stigma.

Applying Culturally Sensitive Family Theories, Models, and Approaches

Family Communication Theory

Family communication theory and practice offers enormous potential for family therapy with Asian and Pacific Islander American families. The following discussion focuses on family communication theories and therapy approaches and is organized into two parts. The first section describes principles of family communication behavior from the perspective of family communication theory. The second section describes practice principles derived from family communication therapy models.

Communication Principles of Family Behavior as They Relate to Understanding Asian and Pacific Islander American Families

Theory about communication has been an essential part of understanding families since the early days of some of the very first pioneers of family therapy (Duhl, 1989). Much of the following discussion about family communication theory and practice relies primarily on the work of Virginia Satir (1967, 1986; Satir, Stachowiak, & Taschman, 1975). Satir is acknowledged by family therapy historians as being the very first woman pioneer in family therapy (Duhl, 1989). The underlying value and theoretical assumptions of Satir's communication family therapy are not only an excellent philosophical and existential fit with the critical constructionist practice perspective, her techniques are extremely compatible with social construction theory. (A full discussion of the Satir model and its compatibility with social construction theory will be presented in chapter 6, "Family Therapy with Ethnic Minorities: Similarities and Differences.")

Satir conceptualizes the therapist as having many important tasks. These tasks take on a decidedly social constructionist flavor. Satir views her tasks as *observing* and *describing* what is going on inside the family system from a position outside of the system (a notion very central to the postmodernists), *facilitating* a better understanding of the meanings behind family communications, and *empowering* the family to discover new ways of coping by *opening up space for alternative stories or actions.* Satir has always believed in the growth potential of individuals, their ability to make their own choices, and has clearly displayed within her practice model how much she values clients' knowledge of their own lives.

Several basic factors that are helpful in understanding the family communication behavior of Asian and Pacific Islander families are outlined below. First, it is impossible not to communicate, as *all behavior is communication.* In an attempt to adjust to the cultural transitional process, an Asian or Pacific Islander child, due to his powerless status in the family, may choose physical symptoms to communicate his stress and resentment toward his parents' relocation. An Asian or Pacific Islander client's consistent absence from interviews may reflect his or her reluctance to engage in a more Westernized and Eurocentric style of problem solving. Asian American clients do communicate in their unique cultural ways, as discussed in detail at the beginning of this chapter. Prevailing Asian and Pacific Islander cultural norms, with reference to acceptable and idealized styles and modes of communication, are merely an extension of preferred cultural structural values (e.g., one should strive to exercise self-control; avoid confrontations that may shame family members or cause them to lose face; show humility, modesty, unselfishness, and *gaman* [patience, stoicism, tolerance for life's pain, and no complaints]; and *kenshin* [a primary concern for family interests above individual concerns]). A critical constructionist perspective, however, would warn family therapists not to be too aggressive or overly anxious to employ their own (culture- and class-bound) *globalized interpretations* of the meanings of the family's behaviors (White & Epston, 1990).

Second, communication not only conveys information but generally contains a command called *metacommunication* that is very relevant to Asian and Pacific Islander American families. Every relationship contains within it an implicit power struggle over who defines the nature of that relationship. Power struggle in the past was not a major problem within a traditional Asian family, in which each family member's position and status were well defined and rigidly enforced. The process of immigration, coupled with the infusion of Western cultural influence on individuals, can cause (cultural) confusion and intensify a power struggle within the family. Further, Asian and Pacific Islander family interaction takes into account a prescribed vertical hierarchical role structure that is determined by age, sex, generation, and birth order of family members. A family member's failure to identify and adhere to a metacommuncative pattern is sure to produce role conflicts and family problems. Because of the traditional vertical hierarchical structure of traditional Asian and Pacific Islander American families, which prohibits free verbal expression of emotions, especially true thoughts and negative feelings, family members may not be equipped with the communication skills to discuss problems and express themselves openly in a family group setting (Lee, 1997). Another important cultural consideration in attempting to enhance family communication among Asian and Pacific Islander family members is for parents to discuss their "adult" problems or to express their sadness in front of the children is considered culturally inappropriate and is viewed as losing control (Lee, 1997).

Cultural transition (whether voluntary or forced) may have had an extremely disruptive impact on the Asian or Pacific Islander family. Additionally family members may be suffering from posttraumatic effects from refugee resettlement. The family therapist can be helpful to Asian and Pacific Islander families by engaging them in what is referred to as *externalizing conversations,* wherein the family provides accounts of the effects of the migration experience and the experience of refugee resettlement on their lives (e.g., the state of their emotions, family, and peer group interactions). This assists in externalizing problems so that they are not nested in the individual or within the family (White & Epston, 1990). This concept is particularly important to the traditional Asian and Pacific Islander American family, with its emphasis on holding in feelings (as a courtesy and sign of respect for others). This cultural value renders Asian and Pacific Islander clients quite vulnerable to internalizing not only the stress of the problem, but the problem itself.

A third principle of communication relates to what Bateson (1972) refers to as the *punctuation of communicational sequences,* as exemplified in a parent-child relationship between an immigrant father and an American-born child. The father punctuates the sequence of communication thus: "I have to maintain authority over my undisciplined son." The son, on the other hand, defines the relationship differently; "I must emancipate myself from my overcontrolling father who refuses to allow me to grow up." Such a relationship can easily lead to an impasse in family transactions, resulting in child abuse, physical impairment on the part of the father or the son, or an *emotional cutoff* (Bowen, 1978; this concept will be formally presented and discussed in the next section of this chapter).

For an understanding of the nature of communication, it helps to recognize that there are two major types of communication: the *verbal content of communication* (what is being said) and the *nonverbal component of a message* (how it is said). Under most circumstances, human communication involves both verbal and nonverbal components in communication, and these components complement each other in the message. Asian and Pacific Islander cultures are described by anthropologist Edward Hall (1976) as being *high-context communication cultures.* This concept describes a culture that relies heavily on the nonverbal aspect of communication to relay some of the most important and powerful aspects of the message. Conversely, in a *low-context communication culture,* the most important and powerful aspects of a message are contained within the verbal component of a given communication—which is the case in Eurocentric cultures.

It is essential to determine the extent to which there is congruence between the message and the way it is delivered. Incongruity may take the form of inappropriateness, invalidation, or paradox. Virginia Satir (1986) specifically addresses the issue of *incongruous communication* in her timeless technique, the *human validation process approach* (discussed shortly). Again, the acculturation process between members of an Asian or Pacific Islander American family complicates these two aspects (congruence and delivery) of communication. Because various family members are often at a different of rate acculturation and value orientation, incongruous communication occurs more than is expected. It is extremely important that family therapists maintain a very low profile and take the role merely of facilitator, or at the very most a consultant (but not the expert), so as not to impose their own assumptions about Asian and Pacific Islander Americans onto the family's communication behavior. Additionally, family therapists are encouraged to pay special attention to the nonverbal content of family messages, given the high-context culture within more traditional Asian and Pacific Islander families. (The role of the family therapist as ethnographer and anthropologist will be discussed in detail in chapter 6.)

Only in a *congruent way of communication* does the person appear real and expressive of genuine feelings and sends out straight (not paradoxical or confusing) messages. We offer a caveat to non-Asian therapists and therapists that do not ascribe to traditional Asian and Pacific Islander ideals and ways of communicating (such as *filial piety* and an emphasis on interdependence and cooperation): Do not attempt to impose more Anglo-American, middle-class values onto Asian and Pacific Islander families (such as independence or individualism, competition, assertiveness, and directness in verbal communication.) There are ways in which family therapists can facilitate better communication within traditional Asian and Pacific Islander families that can lead toward problem resolution without violating or attempting to alter valued, functional, and adaptive cultural family behaviors. (These practice strategies will be discussed in more detail in the following section of this chapter.)

Due to changes that occur in the cultural transitional process and a weakened social support network, an Asian couple may experience difficulty in maintaining the traditional *complementary relationship,* in which the husband is the dominant and the wife is the submissive partner in the marriage. Furthermore, the same couple may also experience difficulty in a (competitive) *symmetrical relationship* that runs counter to traditional conjugal Asian and Pacific Islander values. Such a relationship may develop as the wife's financial earning power expands, coupled with her exposure to increased Western influences on egalitarian couple relationships. This delicate conjugal dilemma is particularly culture bound and deeply rooted in traditional hierarchical Asian and Pacific Islander family values; and the Westernized family therapist is severely cautioned not to exacerbate an already tense and troubling family situation. White (middle-class) feminist notions and ideals and other *dominating global-ized knowledge* (White & Epston, 1990) may have a deleterious and irreversible impact on the relationships of Asian and Pacific Islander couples. The couple needs to be encouraged to "find their own way," so to speak, to determine for themselves what blend (if any) of traditional versus more acculturated behaviors will work for them. The family therapist is advised to facilitate the couple to *reauthor the (ethnocultural) conjugal narrative* (Laird, 1993) that will help the couple to resolve the power issues and move past these dilemmas that they present in therapy.

Satir's (1986) classification of family behavior roles for a family member under stress has a great deal of usefulness in understanding Asian American families. The *placater* always agrees, apologizes, tries to please; the *blamer* dominates, finds fault, and accuses; the *super-reasonable* stance remains detached, calm, super cool, and not emotionally involved; the *irrelevant* stance distracts and seems unrelated to anything going on. Such distractions can take the form of physical illness, as is often the case with Asian Americans. These family communication roles are dysfunctional and do not contribute to the self-esteem of the individual. Within Virginia Satir's human validation approach to family therapy, she emphasizes above all else the centrality of all family behavior working toward the end result of fostering self-esteem within family members. Her philosophical bias is very consistent with traditional Asian and Pacific Islander values, in which consideration for the feelings of others and vigilance in monitoring rudeness, disrespect, or impolite behaviors that may cause a person to lose face (Satir would label this an attack on one's self-esteem) makes for a wonderful philosophical and existential fit within a critical constructionist framework for practice.

Finally, Satir's family assessment typically includes discovery, illumination, and discussion of *family secrets, myths,* and *rules.* These concepts may be problematic in the assessment process with very traditional Asian and Pacific Islander families within which family business (the family's "dirty laundry") is never disclosed to outsiders (i.e., non–family members). Additionally, in the long years of separation among the family members of immigrant and refugee families, there can be many family secrets and unresolved grief issues that members are not ready to share openly with each other. Family therapy may bring out "ghosts" from the past and can be overwhelming and at times damaging to family relationships. For these reasons, we have chosen to delay the discussion of the delicate subject of family secrets and myths to the next section on family structure theory, in light of the structural implications that communicating about these issues may have on Asian and Pacific Islander families.

Family Communication Practice Principles

The principles of behavior derived from family communication theory can contribute significantly to the understanding of the dynamics and interaction of an Asian and Pacific Islander American family. The following discussion aims to explicate the manner in which these family communication practice principles can be applied to actual work with an Asian and Pacific Islander American family.

*Family Communication Practice Principles as They Relate
to Work With Asian and Pacific Islander American Families*

Because the Asian and Pacific Islander American family interaction takes into account a prescribed vertical hierarchical role structure determined by age, sex, generation, and birth order of family members, infraction of such an interactive pattern is sure to produce role confusion, conflicts, and family problems. Insofar as family therapeutic goals are concerned, a therapist's first task is to engage the family members to alter the symmetrical (parallel or competitive) communication interchange and develop a complementary relationship (where one leads and the other follows) characteristic of the Asian and Pacific Islander American culture. However, due to the immigration process and the phases each family member may be experiencing at different times, complementary communication interchange within the family is bound to run into strong resistance and conflict. Family communication theory is very useful in assessing the family system and the interactive pattern, yet the therapist's role in engaging the family in renegotiation and redefinition of the power relationship will not be easy. The concept of power is too idiosyncratic, threatening, competitive, disrespectful, Western, and therefore foreign to the Asian and Pacific Islander American culture. However, Satir's approach, in which the therapist takes a great deal of time to help the family discover for itself when and how these relational changes occurred and what meanings each and every family member ascribes to this new (more acculturated) style of relating, can be extremely beneficial to the family's problem-solving and discovery processes in this regard.

The role of the therapist—initially defined by Haley (1963) in strategic family therapy, as well as other "paradoxical" family therapies, as that of a "metagovernor of the family system"—thus requires intense active participation and at times, manipulation. The therapist's active leadership role may easily be interpreted by the family as an unwelcome intrusion. Further, Haley's therapeutic tactics, such as paradoxical messages (double bind) and "prescribing the symptom" (encouraging the usual dysfunctional behavior) may be totally confusing and seem absurd to most Asian and Pacific Islander families. The techniques of *relabeling* and *reframing* (by emphasizing the positive) are more appropriate and relevant techniques, for they are more consistent with the traditional Asian and Pacific Islander cultural emphasis on respect and compassion for others.

While a communication or strategic therapist's emphasis on short-term time-limited behavioral change is an approach welcomed by traditional Asian and Pacific Islander families who operate on concreteness, a singular and persistent focus on power relationships may be a bit ambiguous, offensive, and intrusive. Most Asian and Pacific Islander Americans are taught that proper interaction should be guided by roles, duties, obligations, and deference to others.

Virginia Satir's (1967, 1986; Satir et al., 1991) cognitive-behavioral approach to *teach* family members to recognize the family's rules so that the rules and the interactional patterns may be changed has tremendous appeal. Her emphasis on *good feelings* within the family and among family members is consistent with the Buddhist teachings of harmonious living, compassion, selflessness, respect for life, and moderation in behavior. Satir's capitalization on family history, which she calls the *family life chronology* (Satir, 1967, 1986; Satir et al., 1975), can be an invaluable *narrative tool* in understanding the family system dynamics influenced by intergenerational immigration and acculturation processes.

In light of the high-context nature of communication in traditional Asian and Pacific Islander families, with an emphasis on the nonverbal aspect of the communication or message, *family sculpting* and *family choreography* can be extremely useful techniques. Further, the family therapist will be able to encourage elders to "sculpt" their perception of family problems without fear of shame or embarrassment when there are language barriers or communication difficulties between the therapist and the elders or between individual family members (who may be acculturated at different levels).

Family sculpting and family choreography techniques can be especially helpful in their potential to bridge communication difficulties that arise when members of the same Asian or Pacific Islander family do not speak the same dialect, or worse, the same language. Profound linguistic difficulties often are consequences of the result of different periods of immigration by family members to the United States and different rates of acculturation of these family members. It is not uncommon to find older members speaking only their native language and younger American-born members speaking only English. Because these family members may lack a common language by which they can communicate or share emotional exchanges, inappropriate, invalid, and confusing communicative exchanges are bound to occur.

Satir (1967, 1988, 1986; Satir et al., 1975) employs a rich array of experiential techniques (e.g., *sculpting, drama, communication stances, family stress ballet, ropes, parts party*) in her theory of family counseling. Although these techniques are invaluable in their own right, in that many of these family exercises do not heavily rely on verbal interchanges (as discussed earlier: when there are linguistic barriers, either between family members or between the family and the therapist), these strategies can be considered to be types of *nonverbal narratives* in that they encourage family members to tell their story their way. Family members are free to recreate their vision or perception of family relationships and family problems, as well as solutions to these problems.

Communication theory in work with Asian and Pacific Islander American families depends not so much on the theory itself but on "how," or the context (environment) in which it is used. Although generally it is true that effective family functioning depends on open, full, honest expression among all family members, for the therapist to encourage the younger members of an Asian or Pacific Islander American family to express openly and honestly their negative feelings in front of parents or elders would be totally insensitive and disrespectful. On the other hand, open expression of positive and respectful verbal and nonverbal behavior to older members of the family is expected and accepted. The use or misuse of conjoint family therapy (therapy with every family member present) is, clearly, extremely important. To express negative feelings honestly in front of others, especially those who are older, is not accepted by traditional Asian and Pacific Islander Americans and therefore is counterproductive. Behaving respectfully and deferentially to others will always bring honor and harmony in interpersonal interactions. A therapist's challenge, then, is how to promote respectful and appropriate behavior in resistive family members. Family members' perception of the therapist as a proper role model is significant, especially during the initial phase of therapist-family interaction; furthermore, *modeling* is an important practice technique for the therapist within Satir's (1986) human validation process approach.

In summary, communication family therapy, especially as developed by Virginia Satir (1986) and discussed in this section, is a family practice approach that shares the cultural values (assumptions), as well as the philosophical and existential position, of traditional Asian and Pacific Islander American family life. Communication family therapy is also philosophically and existentially compatible with social construction theory. Furthermore, the varied roles that are prescribed for the therapist within this family therapy model (namely, *educator or teacher, facilitator, mediator, advocate,* and *role model*) are important and viable roles for those persons who seek to enhance the communication process of Asian and Pacific Islander American families (including those who are foreign born, refugee, and U.S. born).

Family Structure Theory

The discussion that follows on family structure theory is divided into two sections. The first part examines behavioral principles and the second part examines family practice principles of structure family therapy as they relate to assessing and working with Asian and Pacific Islander clients.

Family Behavioral Principles of Structure Theory as They Relate to Understanding Asian and Pacific Islander American Families

The Asian or Pacific Islander American family is deeply immersed in a family system that does not stress individuality. The immense power of the family—parents, grandparents, ancestors, and extended kin—in shaping one's destiny is taken for granted and accepted as an implicit part of life. Who we are; how we think and communicate; what we choose to do and be; and whom we choose to be with, to love, and to marry are all functions of that complex family system that has developed over the generations. Murray Bowen (1978) is the person perhaps most closely identified with the intergenerational perspective. The central concept in Bowen's theory, the concept that links the generational and here-and-now perspectives, is *differentiation* as it relates to the intrapersonal, interpersonal, and intergenerational processes. In intrapersonal terms, *differentiation of self* and its opposite, *fusion,* refer to the relationship between the intellect and goal-directed activity, on one hand, and the emotions or feeling-directed activity, on the other. The well-differentiated person is provident, flexible, thoughtful, and autonomous in the face of stress. The less differentiated, more fused person is often trapped in a world of feelings, buffeted about by emotions, disinclined to providence, inclined to rigidity, and susceptible to dysfunction when confronted with stress.

In the sphere of interpersonal activities, differentiation means the ability to maintain a solid, nonnegotiable self in relationships within and outside the family; to take comfortable "I" positions; and not to forsake intellectual and emotional integrity to obtain approval, love, peace, or togetherness. Geographical and physical distances experienced by immigrating Asian and Pacific Islander Americans are not to be equated with differentiation. The differentiated person can leave the family to build his or her life without feeling disloyal and still remain emotionally close or can be geographically close without being trapped emotionally in intense family relationships.

In the sphere of family relationships, differentiation refers to the family's ability to accept change and difference from its members; such a family can allow its members to become autonomous. The concepts of differentiation and fusion not only apply to the existing family system but are also linked to the past through a process of *multigenerational transmission.* The *level of differentiation* in an individual, according to Bowen (1976, 1978), is determined by the differentiation level of one's parents and by sex, sibling position, quality of relationship, and environmental contingencies of developmental transition points.

Bowen's (1978) concept of *family projection process,* in which parental emotions help to shape and define what the child becomes, even though these definitions have little to do with the original realities of the child, closely apply to immigrant parents of American-born children in Asian and Pacific Islander American families. The *triangle,* or three-person system, which Bowen (1978) considers the basic building block of all emotional systems, has a different meaning in a traditional Asian and Pacific Islander family. Bowen (1976) believes that a two-person system may be stable as long as it is calm, but when anxiety increases, it immediately involves the most vulnerable other person to become a triangle. Due to male dominance and the unusually close mother–oldest son relationship in the Asian and Pacific Islander family, the two-person system (especially the husband-wife [spousal] and the mother-father [parental] systems) is seldom closed and solid. Hence the process of triangulation takes on a different meaning. In Bowen's (1978) view, the identification of these key triangles is a central assessment task in *detriangulating* key threesomes. The process of assessing the *intergenerational family system* and the use of that system as a resource for change is presented in Parts 2 and 3 of this chapter.

The term *invisible triangle* (Rasheed & Rasheed, 1999) is expanded from the concept of *triangles* in the family therapy literature (Bowen, 1978). We reconceptualize the concept of triangles and coin the term *invisible triangles* to refer to the existence of a third person, object, or event in a cultural system that exerts a powerful, but not always apparent, force on the systemic or dyadic relationship system (Rasheed & Rasheed, 1999). This concept has special relevance to the emphasis in traditional Asian and Pacific Islander families of carrying on family and cultural traditions, honoring ancestors, and the importance of the extended family. A more highly acculturated and assimilated Asian and Pacific Islander family member may feel obligated to continue on with a particular family legacy or family cultural tradition but may be conflicted due to his or her acquisition of more Western or Eurocentric cultural values. The invisible triangle can exact a deleterious emotional impact on such a family member until or unless some emotional resolution is achieved. It is quite possible that individual family members may come to family therapy not fully aware of or completely understanding the nature of the emotional turmoil or conflict that they bring to family therapy.

A related term (which we also coined) is the concept of *invisible cultural loyalties* (Rasheed & Rasheed, 1999). This concept is an expansion of the family therapy (intergenerational) concept of *invisible loyalties,* also referred to as *relational indebtedness* or *family ledgers,* as originally conceptualized by Ivan Boszormenyi-Nagy (1987). Invisible loyalties or family indebtedness can date back several generations and can also be a result of multigenerational and crossgenerational unresolved conflicts or unrealized goals with the family (Boszormenyi-Nagy, 1987). Given the importance of preserving family legacies, continuing family and cultural traditions, and honoring ancestors, as well as the importance of obeying and respecting elders within the family in traditional Asian and Pacific Islander families, one can easily imagine the emotional conflict that a more acculturated or assimilated family member might experience if this issue is not adequately addressed. Hence, family secrets, myths, and (powerful, but unspoken) family rules may serve to further complicate and exacerbate emotional turmoil if they operate in tangent with invisible cultural loyalties or with invisible cultural triangles.

Bowen's (1978) concept of *emotional cutoff* has particular relevance in work with Asian and Pacific Islander American families. According to Bowen (1978), everyone has some degree of unresolved emotional attachment to the previous generation. The lower the level of differentiation, the greater the degree of unresolved dependency to be dealt with in the person's own generation and/or marriage and to be passed on to the next generation in the (family) *projection process* previously discussed. The *emotional cutoff* consists of denial and isolation of the problem while living close to the parents, or by physically running away (as in the case of migration), or a combination of the two. Whatever the pattern, the person yearns for emotional closeness but is "allergic" to it. As a rule, the more a nuclear family maintains emotional contact with previous generations, the calmer, more orderly, and less problematic their lives will be. Conversely, the greater the degree of emotional cutoff, the more the nuclear family becomes a sort of emotional pressure cooker, with no escape valves or with attempted escapes that are far less effective than emotional contact with the extended family could be.

Having sketched in broad strokes some of the concepts and theories about the intergenerational family, we now turn to examine the present family system.

Family structure theory, which focuses on the family system's structural (contextual) dynamics, especially the creation, maintenance, and modification of those boundaries that are rules defining who participates and how (Minuchin, 1974), is useful in work with recent immigrant families. Because both husband and wife must often work outside the home, the couple (spouse) system within the immigrant family gradually shifts toward *disengagement* in those cases where a relationship is too rigid and distant. Such is also true for the parent-child subsystem. Because most immigrant couples' marriages depend on the approval and directives of the parents, the couple is often inadequately prepared to negotiate a series of mutually satisfying "patterned transactions." In addition, couples may also have difficulty in separating from their families of origin, which is considered essential in the maintenance of a spousal subsystem. Should the couple migrate with the extended family, their long work hours and the strange cultural environment may throw them into *enmeshment* (relationships that are overly close) with their parents and thus make the couple (spouse) subsystem extremely vulnerable.

Older siblings, because of economic necessity, may need to work. Long working hours may deprive them of their normal socialization and interaction with younger siblings, who may acculturate at a much faster pace in an American public school. A different pace of acculturation among sibling subsystems will tend to create tension and cultural value differences. The enmeshment created between the couple and their family and the disengagement of the couple's children can contribute to a large degree to the problem of immigrant families.

Normal family development is disrupted by cultural transition, and most immigrant families find adaptation to stress unbearable. In particular, "stressful contact of the whole family with extrafamilial forces" such as societal agencies

(Minuchin, 1974, p. 78) is more than the family can cope with. Other stresses at *transitional points* in a family's life, such as the birth of the first child, the emergence of the oldest child into adolescence, or the death of a loved one, will surely disrupt normal family functioning. Stress created by such *transitional points* can also be very problematic to immigrant American families (with foreign-born parents and American-born children) whose members experience different rates of acculturation. These differences in acculturation can led to *acculturative tensions* and *acculturative conflicts,* which can lead to even more emotional distance within families (Rasheed & Rasheed, 1999). If these tensions and conflicts are left unresolved, they can be primary contributing factors to emotional cutoffs and disengagement between family members.

Family Structure Practice Principles

Family Structure Practice Principles as They Relate to
Work With Asian and Pacific Islander American Families

Bowen's (1978) emphasis on differentiation of self (from the *family culture or ego mass*) as the primary goal of therapy has important implications and application in work with Asian and Pacific Islander families. Differentiation of self from family of origin is no easy task, for it contradicts Asian and Pacific Islander culture that places enormous value on the sensitivity of individuals to the opinions and expectations of others regarding their conduct. Externally derived evaluations become a part of one's system of self and form a significant basis for one's view of self (Norbeck & DeVos, 1972). Yet Bowen (1978) considers differentiation of self inevitable if one expects to function adequately in a rapidly changing bicultural environment.

Because of the traditional, highly structured family role system that does not encourage free expression and the language barrier within Asian and Pacific Islander families, conjoint family therapy as a treatment modality is neither feasible nor necessarily desirable. Bowen's family therapy techniques of focusing upon one individual, usually the most differentiated member of the family, is advantageous in work with the mixed acculturated Asian or Pacific Islander American family. This technique protects the dignity of the individual and honors the good name of the family. When the therapist works with an individual, the goal is to modify the structure of the emotional system of the family through that individual's change. At times, the specific individual may not necessarily be a member of the nuclear family. (A detailed description of this approach is presented in Part 2 of this chapter.)

The technique employed by Bowen (1978) to help a spouse define and clarify his or her relationship by speaking directly to the therapist instead of the husband and wife speaking to each other is also applicable to work with Asian and Pacific

Islander Americans. Bowen's detached but interested, intellectual, calm, low-key approach to problem solving again corresponds closely to Buddhism's teachings on moderation in behavior, self-discipline, patience, and modesty. Bowen's technique of actually teaching family members how to differentiate, clarify their values, and resolve family problems coincides with the family's expectation that the therapist is an expert, as well as with the philosophical stance of social construction theory. A therapist's efforts in taking a careful family history (*multigenerational transmission records*) reflect sensitivity to the immigration process, intergenerational perspective, and the need for individualizing each family.

Bowen's (1978) expression of the role of the therapist is that of a *coach, facilitator,* and *consultant,* which is very compatible with a social constructionist practice framework in that Bowen's primary goal in this therapy model is to coach the family and family members through a (self-) discovery process by constructing a narrative of the family's history, primarily through the use of the *genogram* (a multigenerational diagram of family information). In this model of family therapy, the client is the expert in charge of the data collection process. The therapist is merely there to help the family and its individual members sort through their emotional reaction to the meanings that the family and family members ascribe to various family information gathered about family relationships, family patterns, and family (emotional) processes. For the most part, the family and individual members set the goals and desired outcomes, as well as determining the direction that current family relationships will or will not go. Hence, in this approach, Bowenian family therapy does not rely upon or employ the therapist's *privileged ways of knowing* about the family. The family and its members are free to create or discover the *collective narrative of the family* as the therapist creates a space for multiple meanings of the families' experiences. (A lengthier discussion of Bowenian family therapy and its compatibility to social construction theory is presented in chapter 6.)

In light of the emphasis on the rich historical, cultural, and familial traditions of Asian and Pacific Islander cultures, it is especially important for the family therapist to empower Asian and Pacific Islander American families and family members to *locate the origins of individual personal narratives*—especially *debilitating, nonpotentiating narratives* (Young, 1996). The genogram can provide a way for the family therapist to help the family and its members *locate the origins of immobilizing, subjugating narratives* and their context and significance (e.g., historical, political, economic, sociocultural, familial). This discovery process may uncover family myths or secrets, derived from generations of dysfunctional family emotional processes, at the source of the emotional pain for the family or individual family member. The discovery process may also uncover societal prejudice, discrimination, and racism at the root of troubling *ethnic narratives* (*marginalized* or negative stereotypical *narratives*). Creating space for more *empowering, liberating narratives* may make it possible for the family and its members to revise and reconstruct these stories: a *reauthoring, restorying,* or even *racial restorying process* that can offer new information, new resources, and multiple opportunities (Freeman, 1992). It is also important to note that in light of the vertical hierarchical family structure of traditional Asian and Pacific Islander families (as well as other cultural values that avoid shaming confrontational power struggles), these reauthored stories can reflect each family member's unique emotional experience and, hence, unique interpretation. These collective narratives may help to maintain important close family ties as *multiple (emotional) meanings* are encouraged.

There are many advantages of the Bowenian family therapy approach in light of the traditional values of the Asian and Pacific Islander family. Family work can still occur even when families are separated by long distances as a result of migration and relocation to distant places. Because not all of the subsystems and dyads within the family are required to be present at the same time for family therapy to proceed, potentially explosive and volatile cross-generational tensions and conflicts need not be exacerbated. Family members can sort through issues such as *generational splits, acculturation tensions* and *conflicts,* and hierarchical concerns and begin to repair the damage that cultural transitioning may have had on family emotional relationships, in a much less emotionally charged atmosphere (hence allowing elders and parents to save face as they sort through complex family problems and emotions out of the presence of their children).

Minuchin's (1974) differential application of *joining techniques* is especially helpful during the beginning phase of treatment with an Asian or Pacific Islander American family. Much of the success in "joining" depends on therapists' ability to listen, their capacity for empathy, their genuine interest in clients' problems, and their sensitivity to feedback. According to Minuchin (1967), joining is not just the process of being accepted by the family, it is being accepted as a therapist and as one of the family leaders.

Maintenance is one technique used in joining. The therapist lets him- or herself be organized by the basic rules that regulate the transactional process in the specific family system. If a three-generation Asian or Pacific Islander American family demonstrates a rigid hierarchical structure, the therapist may find it advisable to approach the grandfather first and then to proceed downward. In so doing, the therapist may be resisting his or her first empathic wish—perhaps to rescue an identified patient from verbal abuse—but by respecting the ethnic-specific rules of the system, he or she will stand a better chance of penetrating a therapeutic impaction.

Maintenance concentrates on process, and the technique of *tracking* allows the therapist to examine the content of speech. In tracking, the therapist very closely follows the subjects discussed by family members. This not only enables the therapist to *join* the family culture (cultural joining); the therapist also has the opportunity to become acquainted with idiosyncratic idioms and metaphors that can later be used to help his or her directive statement carry (cultural) credibility.

Minuchin's (1974) *joining techniques* are generally helpful to a therapist working with an Asian and Pacific Islander family. His *disequilibration techniques* or *family restructuring techniques* generally do not share the same degree of effectiveness in working with this specific ethnic group. These techniques, including *enactment* and *boundary making, escalating stress* (by emphasizing differences), *physical movement, utilizing the symptom* (by exaggerating it), and *creating affective intensity* (by manipulating the mood and escalating emotional intensity) are much too abstract, challenging, and emotionally confrontive, and they are therefore antithetical to Asian and Pacific Islander culture and are sometimes counterproductive to therapy.

The preceding discussions aim to provide a framework within which to understand Asian and Pacific Islander American families of the past and the present. The family theories presented (communication, family structure and family of origin) can be applied in working with these families. Part 2 of this chapter discusses how to further integrate and apply these theories in therapy with Asian and Pacific Islander American families.

PART 2: CULTURALLY RELEVANT TECHNIQUES AND SKILLS IN DIFFERENT PHASES OF THERAPY

Beginning Phase

In view of Asian and Pacific Islander American clients' unfamiliarity with family therapy, the significance of the first-contact phase is obvious. If this beginning phase is not properly conducted, the first interview will most likely be the last time the therapist will have contact with the client or family. Four skills and techniques are essential in work with Asian and Pacific Islander Americans in the beginning therapy phase. These skills and techniques include engaging the client or family, cultural transitional mapping and data collection, mutual goal setting, and selecting a focus and system for therapy.

Engaging the Client or Family

Many Asian and Pacific Islander Americans do not understand the role of a family therapist and may confuse him or her with a physician. Regardless, they will perceive the therapist as the knowledgeable expert who will guide them in the proper course of action. Hence the family therapist is seen as an authority figure and expected to be more directive than passive. Being directive does not mean that the therapist will tell the family how to live their lives; rather, it involves directing the family therapy process. Minuchin's joining technique is most applicable because the therapist needs to be accepted as one of the family leaders. A family therapist needs to convey an air of confidence. When asked, he or she should not hesitate to disclose his or her educational background and work experience. Asian and Pacific Islander American clients need to be assured that their therapist is more powerful than their illness or family problems and that the therapist will "cure" them with competence and the necessary know-how.

Some Asian and Pacific Islander American clients may ask the therapist many personal questions about his or her family background, marital status, number of children, and so on. To gain an Asian and Pacific Islander client's trust and to establish rapport, the therapist will need to feel comfortable about answering personal questions. Once trust and rapport with the therapist are established, clients may form a dependency on the therapist. Such dependency patterns do not necessarily indicate transference or other psychodynamic difficulties. Given the interpersonal complexity of Asian and Pacific Islander cultures, forming relationships that mirror those found in family groups or in friendship networks may be helpful to the client as a means of guiding the interpersonal process with the therapist.

Due to the strong emphasis on obligation in Asian and Pacific Islander culture, clients may consider keeping appointments or following directives as doing something for the therapist in return for the therapist's concern. The therapist should neither condemn nor confront such client behavior but capitalize on it to help the client resolve his or her problem (Ho, 1982).

Additionally, a therapist needs to pay attention to "interpersonal grace" and show warm expression of acceptance, both verbally and nonverbally. The therapist can do this by, for instance, asking about the client's health, offering a cup of tea, suggesting the client remove his or her coat, or indicating a more comfortable chair. Such gestures serve to convey genuine concern and can tremendously contribute to beginning and maintaining a positive relationship—especially if the family enters therapy involuntarily, that is, via a court order or school recommendation.

Cultural Transitional Mapping and Data Collection

Relevant personal, familial, community information and cultural mapping are extremely helpful in the assessment of Asian and Pacific Islander American families who undergo rapid social change and cultural transition (Lee, 1997). Sluzki (1979) states that when working with migrant families, "in the course of the first interview, the therapist should establish which phase of the process of migration the family is currently in and how they have dealt (as a family and individually) with the vicissitudes of previous phases" (p. 389). Additionally, culturally specific factors relevant to each family member's life experiences must be ascertained. Personal data such as language and dialect spoken, physical health and medical history, foreign and/or Western medication used, work roles, help-seeking behavior patterns, and other significant demographic information (years in the United States, country of origin, immigration status, and so on) are helpful in assessment. Psychological data, including individual family members' process of adaptation and acculturation, past problem-solving abilities, and degree of life cycle interruption, can provide important clues to assessment and interventive goal formulation (Goldenberg & Goldenberg, 2002; Lee, 1997). Social and cultural data, which include the individual's immigration and relocation history, work hours, environment, and extent of contact with a human service network, will help the therapist to assess the degree of support or stress from the external environment.

A comprehensive map should also include the transitional position of the multigenerational family in society. Such a map may include the position of each individual and the family as a whole in life cycle stages, cultural origin, family form, and current status relative to other family members (Hartman, 1978; Lee, 1997). The map can provide insight to family members' intergenerational perspective and levels of differentiation (Bowen, 1978). Moreover, Bowen's concept of emotional cutoff can also be assessed by cultural mapping. Whenever differential rates of adaptation are found, the influence of transitional conflict may be presumed and relevant therapy applied. Lee (1982, 1997) has suggested four criteria to determine a family member's degree of acculturation: (a) years in the United States—as a whole, the longer the client lives in the United States, the more he or she is acculturated; (b) age at the time of immigration—an 8-year-old is more easily assimilated that an 80-year-old; (c) country of origin and political, economic, and educational background; (d) professional background—an English-speaking Japanese doctor is more easily assimilated than a Japanese cook.

Techniques in data collection require more than the usual question and answer form of interaction. The use of family photographs and albums, and paintings and music from the country of origin, can facilitate interaction and generate meaningful information (Ho & Settles, 1984). Although sharing feelings and family secrets with the therapist (who is an outsider) can provoke feelings of guilt and uneasiness, many Asian and Pacific Islander American clients are yearning for a close relationship with someone who is understanding and supportive. (Issues of mixed acculturation and bicultural ethnic identities within families will be addressed in greater detail in chapter 6.)

Mutual Goal Setting

Asian and Pacific Islander Americans, especially those who are from immigrant families and immigrant-American families, find it difficult to admit that they have emotional or psychological difficulties, because such problems arouse considerable shame and the feeling of having failed one's family. Here again, how the therapist presents interventive plans is especially important and relevant to Asian and Pacific Islander American culture. Families will respond more favorably if they perceive the intervention goal as an obligatory means to meet their concrete basic needs, such as employment, food, and shelter. Their acceptance of an interventive goal is consistent with their traditional social explanation of disorienting events. This type of explanation allows the individual to see him- or herself as a victim of some unfortunate but uncontrollable event, a result of "nonpersonal" determinants. Therapeutic goals emphasizing the rehabilitation of physical or organic illness also are acceptable to Asian and Pacific Islander American clients. An "impersonal" physical illness excuses the client from moral failure and familial irresponsibility. Minuchin's (1974) *maintenance technique* of following the client's basic rules in the transactional process greatly facilitates the mutual goal formulation process of therapy.

Asian and Pacific Islander clients may find loosely targeted and abstract long-term goals incomprehensible, unreachable, and impractical. They may prefer structured and goal-directed work with clear, realistic, concrete, and measurable objectives (Ho, 1976; Lee, 1997; Murase & Johnson, 1974). In many instances, a psychoeducational approach to family therapy may prove to be very important. Family therapists should be mindful of the fact that "talk therapy" alone isn't enough: Family therapists need to consider adopting other roles within the role of the "family helper" (e.g., *educator, social advocate, collaborator* with paraprofessionals or "therapist helpers," *role model*). This will enhance the therapist's ability to *mobilize and restructure the social and extended family networks.*

Family therapists should not rule out the possibility, however, that some Asian and Pacific Islander American families, especially immigrant-descendent families, may respond well to a very highly personalized, insightful therapy related to emotional cutoff or focusing on psychodynamic functions and difficulties. Families receiving this type of therapy should be carefully screened, and such therapy should not be attempted without a strong, trusting, therapist-client or therapist-family relationship. In any case, an integrative family therapy approach that borrows from the rich array of family therapy models available today is our preference when selecting an inter- or intrapersonal family therapy approach.

Selecting a Focus and System for Therapy

Prior to determining the focus of therapy, the therapist needs to assess the readiness of family members to communicate as a group. Minuchin's (1974) maintenance practice principle is helpful at this stage. The hierarchical and vertical structure of Asian and Pacific Islander American families does not allow all family members to share their true thoughts and negative feelings together. For parents to express fear or sadness openly in front of children indicates in Asian and Pacific Islander culture that parents are losing control and losing face, thus abdicating their authoritarian roles. Open expression of negative feelings by children might be interpreted as lack of respect and deference to parents. Such behavior might inflict shame on parents and guilt on the children. The therapist's decision about which family member to see and on which subsystem to focus must be based on the nature of the family problems, data derived from cultural mapping, and, perhaps most important, the readiness of the family for problem solving in a group or conjoint context.

Realistically, there are situations when the therapist will have access to only one family member, preferably the one who is the most acculturated, self-differentiated, and respected. Such cases reflect the usefulness of Bowen's (1976) family theory, which focuses on self-differentiation in actual application to Asian and Pacific Islander American families. Regardless of who is seen and what the focus of therapy may be, the therapist's beginning efforts must be directed toward resolving the external stress of the family. Further, the therapist's efforts have to be respectful but structured and active. Once the family experiences immediate concrete success, all family members develop more trust in the therapist and more hope of the family's ability to regain a harmonious lifestyle.

Most frequently in an Asian or Pacific Islander immigrant-American family experiencing multigenerational conflict, the respected subsystem in the family is the parents, who usually are less acculturated. In such cases, the parental subsystem usually is the focus selected by the therapist for therapy. Satir's (1967) theory that the parental subsystem is the axis around which all other family relationships are formed is very *culturally syntonic,* as the conjugal relationship is considered to be primary within the traditional Asian and Pacific Islander family culture. The parents are the architect of the family. The traditionalist attitude on the part of the father seldom allows the therapist to enter into the family system for therapy or restructuring. Hence help is often needed from a respected extended family member who is acculturated. The actual application of this "therapist helper" technique will be discussed more fully in the following section.

Problem-Solving Phase

Problem-resolution activities should be guided by the traditional cultural value system and current capacities of the Asian and Pacific Islander American family. Communication and structural practice principles no doubt have a great deal to offer a family therapist who is called upon to assist Asian and Pacific Islander American families. However, the degree of a therapist's effectiveness will depend on the differential application of these practice principles and how compatible they are with a traditional Asian cultural orientation. This direction requires different techniques and approaches than those usually used by family therapists. Eight skills and techniques of particular importance in the problem-solving phase of therapy include

1. Using indirectness in problem solving *Post-modern* problem-solving techniques:

2. Taking a narrative stance

3. Engaging in externalizing conversations

4. Engaging in a reflective dialogue

5. Critically reflecting on the multiple (emotional) meanings of messages

6. Promoting filial piety, obligation, and self-control

7. Restructuring the social support system

8. Employing a therapist helper

Each of these eight techniques and skills is discussed below.

The Use of Indirectness in Problem Solving

In view of Asian and Pacific Islander Americans' high regard and respect for authority (including the therapist's position of authority), the communication behavioral principle of complementarity needs to be observed. Direct confrontational techniques such as "Do you ever care about your family?" or "Tell your wife what you really think of her!" should be avoided. This directive communication style may be viewed as confrontational, disrespectful, and lacking moderation. Additionally, this message (style) may be viewed as criticism, a personal attack, unacceptable insult, and interpersonal rejection. Whenever an Asian and Pacific Islander client needs to be challenged about the impasse or persistent resistance that is responsible for his or her personal or familial functioning, the therapist is advised to use a more indirect means. For instance, "Do you ever care about your family?" (direct confrontation) could be changed to "We all have different ways of caring about our families—I would like to learn from you about your way of caring about your family" (polite, respectful, but more indirect). Similarly, "Tell your wife what you really think of her!" (direct confrontation) can be rephrased as "Please comment on the things your wife does that contribute to the family" (accentuating the positive indirectly).

Postmodern Problem-Solving Techniques

The meaning or interpretation that results when various family members take a *narrative stance* in attempts to sort out family problems may not be exact; hence the parties can be encouraged to engage in a *reflective dialogue* and *critically reflect* on the multiple emotional meanings that each family member has attached to the presenting problem, as reflected in the individual narratives (Rasheed & Rasheed, 1999). For example, stressful experiences of migration can be reflected upon to help family members become more attuned with how each family member uniquely experiences cultural transitions. Further exploration using this *reflective dialogue* can help the parties discover the positive feelings of concern, respect, and value that each places on his or her relationship with the others and the determination and desire of each family member for the family to survive stressful events such as migration, acculturation, and assimilation processes. Through the pragmatic aspects of traditional teachings of filial piety, mutual respect, and obligation, the family can resolve its own problems.

Promoting Filial Piety, Obligation, and Self-Control

The traditional Asian and Pacific Islander cultural emphasis on structure, authority, and hierarchy has continued to endure, even in the face of acculturation. An individual's worth is dependent upon how well she or he gets along with other family members and how other family members regard him or her. Children are expected to comply with parental and social authority; parents have the responsibility and obligation to perpetuate the family's good name. A therapist can facilitate the family's desire to maintain the family as a unit. Additionally, family members can be encouraged to render good deeds or favors to each other. They can be encouraged to do this as a means to fulfill their obligatory duties (filial piety) to make the family a harmonious place for the children and for themselves to live. A therapist's warm acceptance of a client is likely to encourage the client to be mutually accepting of that therapist as the family's therapist. The therapist needs to become comfortable with traditional Asian and Pacific Islander notions about and values regarding personal obligation, as this is the cornerstone upon which traditional Asian and Pacific Islander family life is built. Clients' feelings of obligation to return favors or to follow therapists' instructions or directives may in the end operate to help the family stay in therapy and resolve its problems.

Restructuring the Social Support System

Asian and Pacific Islander American families consist of strongly close-knit extended families and support systems. Members of the nuclear family or extended family are sometimes forced to interact to the extent that they become *fused* (Bowen, 1978). As a result of fusion, family members demand too much from each other and at times fail to meet their own individual needs or resolve family problems. This is more characteristic of newly arrived immigrant families than it is of other Asian and Pacific Islander American families. As soon as possible, the therapist should assist the family or the newly arrived members of the family in establishing a social support network whereby the family or the individual can reestablish a greater sense of *differentiation of self* (Bowen, 1978) and at the same time fulfill family expectations of a need for social belonging. A social support network can also provide the family or the individual with a way to bridge the ecological deficit, form friendships, ventilate frustrations, learn acculturated social skills, and enjoy recreational activities. Upon realizing that his or her situation is not unique, the individual can view his or her family problems from a more objective, less emotional, and more hopeful perspective. When the therapist tries to link the family with an existing social network, the concept of "balance" is vital. Factors essential for balance include matching the family or family member's age, country of origin, length of stay in this country, socioeconomic class, formal education, language, and religion with existing resources. In some instances, especially in areas where there is a scarcity of Asian and Pacific Islander American families, the therapist may need to identify, recruit, and organize such a social support network. Korean American families have built churches as a secondary network and as systems of social support (Daniel B. Lee, personal communication, January 28, 2003). It is imperative that family therapists avail themselves of the knowledge of local community agencies and special interest groups that address the social, cultural, and economic needs of Asian and Pacific Islander Americans (from the recently arrived immigrant or refugee to the highly acculturated U.S.-born Asian and Pacific Islander American).

Employing a Therapist Helper

In view of cultural shock, language difficulty, Asian and Pacific Islander American families' unfamiliarity with the concept of family therapy, family members' degree of *undifferentiation,* and families' overall resistance to therapy, the traditional therapist-family therapeutic approach may not be feasible. Instead, the strategic use of a therapist helper who is a family member, an extended family member, or a trusted family friend may be required to help the family solve its problems. The therapist helper approach is indicated when the family is persistently uncooperative and too emotional and when there is a definite language barrier between the therapist and the family. Although the therapist helper approach is often the last resort in family therapy, it can provide the family with a normal course of problem solving and assistance with acculturation dilemmas that are not influenced by the therapist. Because of the hierarchical, male-dominant culture of Asian and Pacific Islander Americans, the therapist helper normally will be male.

He should not be clearly identified as a traditionalist or as a Westerner. He needs to have the respect of both parties in conflict. For example, in the case of a father–youngest son conflict, the ideal therapist helper would be the oldest son. In the case of a husband-wife conflict, the therapist helper may need to be an uncle or an individual whom both spouses respect. In some instances, if extended family members cannot be found, an individual who has a bicultural background and reputation (someone who is foreign born but is adjusting well in the United States) can be asked to be a therapist helper.

For the therapist helper approach to work, the family in conflict needs to agree that the therapist helper will be visiting with them for the purpose of problem solving. Additionally, the therapist helper needs regular coaching and supervision from the therapist.

Evaluation and Termination

The collectivist values of Asian and Pacific Islander American culture need to be considered during the evaluation process. It is unrealistic to expect Asian and Pacific Islander clients to provide spontaneous and honest feedback to their therapy, in light of their cultural values, which emphasize deference to authority figures. An innovative method of assessment that takes into consideration the family's cultural background is best for Asian and Pacific Islander clients. Evaluation methods should be systematic but anonymous, focusing on the therapist's employment of relevant means or procedures in helping the family and its members resolve relevant individual and family group goals and problems (Ho, 1980).

In view of traditional Asian and Pacific Islander clients' reliance on social, moral, and physical illness to explain their interpersonal and psychological problems, the therapist should not emphasize the dysfunctional state of the family's problem in attempting to help family members evaluate their progress. Traditional Asian and Pacific Islander clients' adherence to modesty and moderation in behavior will not allow them to credit themselves individually or publicly. Instead, they may attribute family improvement to their ancestors, who continue to look after them. As a means to honor their ancestors and the therapist, the family may invite the therapist to a feast. The therapist should feel comfortable in complying with the family's obligation.

Considering traditional Asian and Pacific Islander clients' capacity for self-control and their unwillingness to be a burden to others, especially to authority figures, therapists need to guard against premature termination initiated by clients. Hence evaluation depending only on clients' self-report may be inaccurate and inappropriate. Instead, therapists need to make home visits and engage in a variety of informal activities and rituals, such as a tea party or festival celebrations within the client's own home environment and community. Through informal interactions with the clients and the family, the therapist can obtain first-hand information pertaining to the overall functioning of the family.

The process of termination should take into consideration the Asian and Pacific Islander cultural concept of time and space in a relationship. The client may regard the therapist as a family member and may want to maintain contact with the therapist even after the successful achievement of treatment goals. For many Asian and Pacific Islander American families, a good relationship is a permanent one that is to be treasured. If a good relationship is allowed to continue in a natural course, the traditional psychodynamic therapeutic concept of separation anxiety during the termination phase may not apply in work with Asian and Pacific Islander families or family members.

The preceding discussion applies to existing family theoretical perspectives and emic-based practice principles in therapy with Asian and Pacific Islander American families. Part 3 of this chapter will further explicate and delineate how these theoretical perspectives and practice principles can be integrated in actual therapy with Asian and Pacific Islander American families.

PART 3: CASE ILLUSTRATION

The following case illustration describes a 65-year-old Chinese widow whose husband died while they lived in Hong Kong. The issues revolved around her coming to live with her son in the United States. This case illustrates how one of the authors, a Chinese therapist, was attuned to and addressed the cultural issues unique to Asian and Pacific Islander American families.

Mental health service is totally new to Mrs. Chan.	Mrs. Chan, a 65-year-old Chinese widow, was referred to me by a community mental health treatment center worker. The worker declared that she was no longer able or willing to work with the client, who spoke very little English and had displayed *limited cooperation.*
Emotional problems manifest themselves in physical symptoms. Problems related to husband's death, immigration process, and present rejection by son's family. An ecological conception of presenting problem.	According to the mental health worker, Mrs. Chan was first referred to her by family physician, who had been unable to correct Mrs. Chan's *insomnia and weight loss* through medication. In addition to her physical problems, Mrs. Chan's symptoms included depression and lack of appetite and energy. She spent her time *gazing motionlessly out the front window* of her apartment.

Social isolation and disengagement: desire for contact.

Therapist being Chinese caused Mrs. Chan to lose face but to gain hope and understanding. Mrs. Chan's deference to authority (therapist). Therapist's deference to Mrs. Chan (her age). A mutual practice of ritual.

When the mental health worker first introduced me to Mrs. Chan, Mrs. Chan's reaction was mixed, with *shame* and *hopefulness.* She remarked that she feared losing face because of her situation and regretted greatly that she had been a *"burden"* to me. I replied that I considered it a *privilege* and a rare opportunity to be of assistance to her.

To establish family ties and obligation, to convey social grace, and to apply joining techniques.

I added that my deceased *mother's maiden name was the same as her last name.*

Her communication conveys acceptance of me as a helper.

Mrs. Chan relaxed and remarked that my mother must be very *proud of me.* I thanked her for her indirect compliment.

An indirect signal to the mental health worker that I needed privacy with Mrs. Chan.

I then *thanked* the mental health worker for introducing me to Mrs. Chan.

To convey social grace and to create a natural atmosphere for sharing.

As soon as the mental health worker departed, Mrs. Chan began to *prepare tea for me.*

Therapist exercises ritual to show respect for and deference to the client.

I *immediately volunteered* to help her.

Indirect means to vent hostility toward son and emotional cutoff.

Mrs. Chan sighed and remarked that she wished her son was *as respectful* as I was toward her.

Therapist's ritualistic behavior consistent with Chinese practice. Use of nonverbal communication as a means to "track down" client's problem.

To help Mrs. Chan ease her pain and disappointment, I intentionally avoided *looking her in the eye*: instead, I helped her with her tea.

Mrs. Chan volunteered that the last several months had been very painful for her.

Country of origin.

Eight months ago, her husband died in *Hong Kong,* where she used to live.

Five months ago, her *only son* had invited her to live with him and his family in the United States. [The family's transitional cultural map is described in Figure 2.1]

Implication of close mother-son dyadic relationship.

It is considered a disgrace for a widow to live alone.

To protect her son's reputation and to save face for herself. Revelation of family paradigm.

Mrs. Chan was apprehensive at first about leaving her home, close friends, and relatives living in Hong Kong, but due to Chinese *social pressures and customs*, she yielded to the idea of living with her son. She did not wish her relatives and friends to *suspect* that her son *did not want to take care of her.*

Different rates of acculturation and generational conflict. Family subsystem boundary is threatened.

Unfortunately, living with her son and his family did not work well for her. Mrs. Chan and her daughter-in-law, an *American-born Chinese*, never seemed to get along with each other. They had an *open conflict* about the *role* of a wife and the manner in which young children should be disciplined.

Example of (cultural) triangulation; intergenerational conflict manifests in physical symptom. Problems caused by transactional dysfunction.

Mrs. Chan's son, *caught in the middle*, developed a severe case of sleep disturbance.

Her difficulty was perceived as deficits in the environment and adaptive strategy. Intervention efforts were directed to multivariable systems, an ecosystem practice principle.

To protect her son's health, Mrs. Chan agreed to live in an apartment by herself. Mrs. Chan explained that the idea of living away from her son was *difficult* for her. She would never have conceded to his idea if she still *lived in Hong Kong*.

I then visited Mrs. Chan's son at *his home*. He and his wife seemed most uncomfortable in my presence. To put the couple at ease, I empathized by saying that I could easily understand the potential conflict the couple might have had with a mother *they hardly knew*. Mr. Chan responded that he really had no choice, for his primary *responsibility* was to his wife and two children.

To ease guilt. To join with the spouse system. To relabel the problem; socially, emphasis on nuclear family and an indication of Western values.

To "track down" and promote filial piety sentiment. To open up space for alternative actions.

I commented that I could appreciate the dilemma he was in, but I *suspected* that he was not *totally satisfied with his mother living alone.*

His mother is perceived as external threat. Nuclear family becomes "enmeshed."

" Not at all, not at all," Mr. Chan continued, shaking his head, "but I cannot let her [his mother] *disrupt my family!*"

Treatment goal responsive to cultural orientation—harmony within the family.

"It would be *ideal* if both your *immediate family* and your *mother* could be *taken care* of equally well," I challenged.

"It would be nice, but I don't know how," Mr. Chan responded despondently.

Capitalizing on Mr. Chan's wife's egalitarian role in mutual goal formulation. Using the family as a resource for problem solving.

I *asked Mrs.* Chan (Mr. Chan's wife) if she had any suggestions.

Mrs. Chan first responded by regretting the situation. Then she suggested that perhaps her mother-in-law could have *limited visits with the family* and the children. We all agreed to give this idea a try.

Negotiating and stabilizing the new structure based on redefined roles of family members.

In the next 2 months, the senior Mrs. Chan enjoyed her *regular visits with her son* and his family. Between regularly scheduled visits, Mrs. Chan had several opportunities *to babysit* for her grandchildren, who had grown fond of her.

Individual therapy is used to assist self-differentiation and to augment family transactions.

During this 2-month period, I visited Mrs. Chan weekly and helped in her *adjustment* to her husband's death, to a new culture and environment, to her son, whom she had not previously seen for 10 years, and to her son's wife and children.

To reestablish social support system as a supplementary intervention effort.

To help her construct a new, more potentiating (self) narrative that expands her previous notion of (family) responsibility to the wider Chinese community.

To satisfy her altruistic need and obligation (social). To complete the therapist's effort in enhancing relationships between systems.

To encourage Mrs. Chan to be a part of the community, I *introduced her* to several Chinese families. On several occasions, she *participated* in activities of the Chinese foreign student organization. She assumed the role of an *"away-from-home mother"* to some of the Chinese students from Hong Kong. Mrs. Chan's ailments subsided. Her son and his family soon planned to invite her to live with them.

Figure 2.1   Family Cultural Transition Map and Genogram

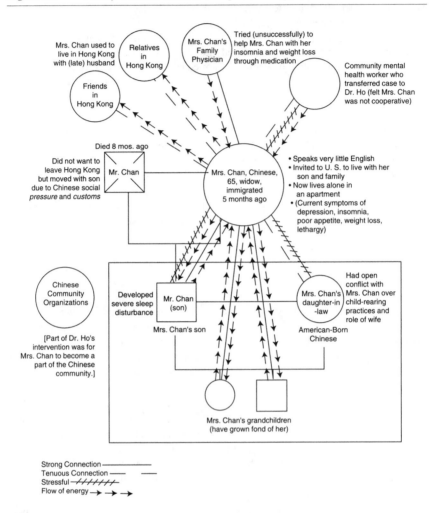

Strong Connection ————
Tenuous Connection —— ——
Stressful ✗✗✗✗✗✗✗
Flow of energy → → →

PART 4: CULTURALLY RELEVANT TECHNIQUES AND SKILLS FOR SPECIFIC THERAPEUTIC MODALITIES

Couple Therapy

Traditionally, when a couple experiences marital discord to a degree that requires outside help, members of the extended family, especially the husband's parents, are the ones to provide assistance. The process of immigration often separates the couple from the extended family. Similarly, the process of acculturation and the changed roles and status of both husband and wife make marital adjustments necessary but difficult, and hence the dyad becomes vulnerable due to the adjustments that must be made. In most instances, the process of acculturation brings about a shift in the power differential between men and women that may be prompted by women's access to alternatives for self-sufficiency and changes in attitudes toward marriage and partnerships (Bradshaw, 1994; Brown & Shallett, 1997). These factors, in addition to the couple's unfamiliarity with and distrust of mental health services, leaves the married pair with practically no resources for securing help with their marital conflict. Within the couple (this is especially true of the wife), discord and unhappiness are generally turned inward toward the self and are reflected in frequent psychosomatic complaints and a high suicide rate. Asian and Pacific Islander couples seldom seek couple therapy. The following guidelines are suggested for therapists providing marital therapy to an Asian or Pacific Islander couple.

Assessing the Couple's Readiness for Conjoint Marital Therapy

Asian and Pacific Islander clients, especially males, may need to safeguard respected roles and save face. A husband may be unwilling to admit publicly, both to his wife and the therapist, that he fails as the responsible head of the family. He often may not disclose intimate information about the couple's sex life or potential physical spouse abuse. Likewise, a traditional Asian and Pacific Islander wife may not express openly how she actually feels toward her husband. If either spouse is not ready for a conjoint session, couple therapy can best be conducted by a therapist assisting the husband and wife privately and individually to understand and gain empathy for each other. An approach that is calm and unemotional but interested may be most effective in assisting the individuals in the couple to gain a cognitive understanding of the problem. Through a *cultural restorying process* (in which a *new ethnocultural conjugal identity* is explored), the couple may alter those rigid roles and expectations toward each other that may no longer be functional or adaptive in the new surroundings.

Reauthoring the (Ethnocultural) Conjugal Narrative

Focus on the affective aspect of the couple's relationship, which generally is emotional in nature, is discouraged. The therapist should emphasize the new role or behavior each spouse needs to assume to solve specific problems, whether they be disciplining a child, financial management, or taking care of the couple's parents. Again, the couple should be encouraged to reauthor a new ethnocultural conjugal narrative, which will assist the couple in modifying their behavior and opening up space for alternative conjugal behaviors that will remedy the current situation. The concept of family is very important in traditional Asian and Pacific Islander culture. This emphasis on family cohesiveness is very motivating and can be a definitive strength that can facilitate the clinical process.

Challenging the Couple's Willingness and Ability to Collaborate

A couple experiencing marital discord usually feels confused, frustrated, and shameful because of their inability to improve the situation. The couple may feel worse if they attribute the present difficulty to their selfishness and lack of consideration for others. The therapist's task is to relabel the presenting power-struggle problem as a system transactional problem and provide the couple with the opportunity and know-how to regain feelings of obligation and self-worth.

Teaching the Couple Skills for Negotiation

The key to problem solving in marital conflict is full and open communication and skill in negotiation. However, negotiation in marriage is a Western concept that is not emphasized in traditional Asian and Pacific Islander culture. This low priority may render some husbands and wives inexperienced in negotiating with their spouses, especially in light of traditional highly structured role expectations and dyadic complementary styles of communication. The therapist's task is to assist the couple in learning to negotiate in a symmetrical fashion. Should one of the partners (particularly the husband) attempt to influence the therapist to adapt to a Western style of behavior, the therapist should gently remind the couple of the presenting problem that brought them in for therapy. Without engaging in further debate or intellectualization about the wisdom of Western or Eastern lifestyles, the therapist can redirect the couple to focus on the immediate problem and the common goal of recreating a harmonious home environment that will benefit the couple's children and honor their ancestors. The concept of biculturalism is applicable for use during therapy, for it provides the couple with a tool by which to negotiate privately in an egalitarian fashion. At the same time, the couple can interact with each other in a more traditional way when they are with others within their ethnic community. Although the focus in couple therapy generally is interpersonal, the presenting here-and-now couple conflict may or may not be resolved if one spouse or both partners remain *undifferentiated.* The Bowenian approach to differentiating the individual can be very helpful to emotionally laden couples.

Divorce Counseling

The divorce rate among Asian and Pacific Islander Americans is relatively low. However, there is concern about the increasing divorce rate among younger, more acculturated Asian and Pacific Islander Americans who believe in the American ideal of romantic love and personal happiness in marriage (Benokraitis, 1993). In addition to the cultural values that prohibit the breakdown of a family in general and divorce in particular, most Asian and Pacific Islander Americans with a traditional orientation are not familiar with legal divorce proceedings. Those who decide to end their marriage may not wish to discuss it with a therapist whose experience is unknown to them. Hence divorce therapy usually is indicated after the client has obtained medical treatment for physical symptoms, or after the client has established a trusting relationship with the therapist through different presenting problems. Because divorce is a very serious step for Asian and Pacific Islander clients, the following recommendations are suggested to ensure that the clients receive appropriate help and services.

Exploring the Consequences of Divorce

Given that divorce is regarded as socially unacceptable within traditional Asian and Pacific Islander culture, therapists need to help clients anticipate the possible ostracism that they may face. Regardless of an individual client's unique need and reason for the divorce, other relatives and close friends may view the client's behavior as immature and impulsive. The client may be labeled as lacking compassion, tolerance, and self-control. The therapist needs to assess the client's strength to withstand the painful and punitive consequences without resorting to physical maladies or suicide. In cases of constant physical abuse, the therapist must intervene appropriately to ensure the physical safety of the client. In those situations in which there is prolonged emotional suffering due to unresolved conflicts, the therapist may introduce an analogous concept such as temporary separation as a means to dilute the tension between a husband and wife. Only as a last resort should the idea of divorce be discussed as a possible alternative. The untimely and premature introduction of the idea of divorce may hasten the termination process of therapy or it may render a disservice to clients whose problems would be compounded by the lack of familial and social support resulting from divorce.

Providing the Client With Legal and Social Support at the Time of Divorce

If divorce is the alternative chosen by the client, the therapist's role is to provide the client with the best possible legal assistance through securing a lawyer who is not only proficient in divorce proceedings but sensitive to the client's cultural orientation and background. In addition, the therapist should help the client secure a support system consisting of the client's relatives and close friends. The client may also need additional help with child care and other daily tasks during critical unsettling periods. Again, the ecosystem approach to divorce, along with the concept of *family equilibrium,* should be considered. Precautions against clients potentially attempting suicide also need to be considered at this stage. In attempting to provide the client with rationalization and emotional support, the therapist needs to help the client understand that the decision to divorce is not necessarily a result of immaturity or lack of self-control and self-discipline. The divorce can be interpreted as the client's desire to discontinue indignities and defacing the family's name. It is sometimes helpful to use the explanation that the wife and husband were not meant for each other in the first place.

A husband or wife's decision to endure the suffering inherent in divorce can also be relabeled as their devotion to the children who no longer need to be subjected to the disharmony of unending marital discord. The therapist's respect and acceptance of the client's decision to continue the marriage or divorce can be most comforting to the client during a very emotionally upsetting period.

Empowering More Liberating Narratives: Helping Clients Cope With Postdivorce Adjustment

Considering the relative lack of importance placed on romantic involvement in traditional Asian and Pacific Islander marriages, emotional termination and adjustment toward the ex-spouse after divorce may not be as traumatic as in more Westernized "romantic" marriages. However, for some clients, divorce can trigger previous unresolved multigenerational emotions and problems. The Bowenian intergenerational perspective and the calm "coaching" role on the part of the therapist can be used effectively with many divorced clients. The necessity for the client to assume new roles after divorce especially that of breadwinner and disciplinarian for the children, may present difficulties for Asian and Pacific

Islander women. Minuchin's (1974) *restructuring perspective* should help the divorcee cope with the time after the crisis. To compensate for her guilt and to save face and reaffirm her decision to divorce, an Asian or Pacific Islander divorcee may be reluctant to seek and receive help from relatives and close friends. Furthermore, she may decide to put her stoicism to a real test, rationalizing her suffering as a natural and fair consequence of her "misbehavior" (divorce).

Postdivorce counseling should, then, focus on assisting the client to deconstruct these debilitating and depotentiating narratives and empower the client to construct more liberating narratives of the divorce experience. This process may be of particular use in the face of relatives and close friends who may not agree with the client's decision to divorce. They may withdraw support and sympathy for the client; the therapist's task will then be to help the client secure new support systems, preferably with other divorcees who share similar experiences.

Asian and Pacific Islander clients who choose divorce usually consider it the last resort and are quite resourceful in adjusting to postdivorce problems. As discussed previously, highly traditional Asian and Pacific Islander American males may be highly prejudiced against divorcees, especially those who have children by a previous marriage. As a result, some divorcees may choose to intermarry; others may elect to remain single and devote their full attention to their children. The latter decision can potentially produce *enmeshment* in the mother-child relationship. A therapist's task is to assure the divorcee that she does have options after divorce and that divorce, despite being a critical moment, consist of both danger (*ngi*) and opportunity (*gee*), components of the Chinese character for crisis. The therapist's task in postdivorce counseling is to help the client focus upon the opportunity component of the crisis.

Single-Parent Therapy

Traditional Asian and Pacific Islander American cultural objections to divorce and the strong kinship support system make single parenthood a new phenomenon. Special considerations are recommended in working with this client population.

Mobilizing the Support System

In view of Asian and Pacific Islander American close-knit family ties, a divorcee seldom finds herself taking care of children without (at the same time) receiving some means of assistance from relatives or close friends. For recently arrived immigrants, support systems may not be as readily available as for second- or third- generation clients. The therapist's primary task in single-parent therapy is to assess the extent to which the client is using or under using the existing support system.

Liaisons Between the Client and Relatives

In situations when divorce is too much a stigma for the relatives, the therapist's task is to be a systems broker between the client and her relatives. The therapist needs to clarify for the relatives the reasons for the client's divorce. Again, the therapist's use of social, moral, and physical relabeling as a way to understand divorce may help to reduce the relative's misunderstanding, guilt, and resentment toward the divorcee. Additionally, the therapist needs to sensitize the relatives to the various needs of a single parent who may be reluctant to seek help from them actively. The needs of the single parent obviously are the primary concern, but the therapist should never lose sight of the fact that the single parent's relatives also feel ambivalent and may have unmet needs. The therapist needs to be supportive and patient with the relatives, who may choose to vent their disappointment, anger, and resentment toward the single parent. Should the relatives persist in rejecting the single parent, the therapist then can gently remind the relatives of their responsibilities for and obligation to the single parent and her children. The therapist's accepting attitude toward the single parent can be a consoling force to a relative who may have feared the stigma others would attach to a divorced family member.

Assisting the Single Parent to Restructure the Family

Due to past rigid social parental roles and expectations and responsibilities, coupled with guilt and embarrassment, some Asian and Pacific Islander American single parents refuse to seek help from outside the family or from their older children. Thus a single parent may expect to function both as father and mother to the children, without support from relatives. Many parent-child conflicts occur as the single parent "burns out" physically and emotionally. The therapist's task is to assess the single parent's level of differentiation, motivation, and knowledge of parenting and to support the single parent's desire to be a responsible parent whose duties include ensuring that the children get the best possible care. With trust and positive rapport, the therapist can gently guide the single parent to restructure and divide tasks, responsibilities, and functions within the family. To be the head and authority figure of a family is a totally new concept to many female Asian and Pacific Islander single parents. The therapist's task is to educate the client to assume the dual role of disciplinarian and nurturer in the family.

The relationship between the mother and the oldest son traditionally is very close. The father's absence due to divorce may further reinforce this natural enmeshment or fusion between the mother and her oldest son. Therapists need to be cognizant of such cultural familial structural phenomenon. Constructive suggestions to ensure both the mother's love and the oldest son's developmental needs usually are welcomed, but any criticism regarding the potential enmeshment between mother and son will be rejected as culturally insensitive.

Assisting Single Parents to Define and Meet Own Their Needs

To assume the role of a single parent successfully, clients may need help in defining and meeting their own needs. Their failure to meet their own needs may be related to their level of differentiation, and it can be detrimental to their physical and mental health as well as jeopardizing the children's freedom and opportunity to meet their developmental needs. Yet, single parents may not be receptive to suggestions to meet their own needs at a time when they perceive that their problems were caused by their own egotism and selfishness. Hence a therapist should employ the ecosystem approach by capitalizing upon community resources, such as educational and recreational opportunities for the children. When the children are constructively and productively occupied, single parents can take pride in their accomplishments as responsible parents. They may then relax their guilt feelings about the divorce. Subsequently, they may come to realize that they are competent and also have individual needs.

Whether single parents can successfully meet their needs or not also depends on their children's cooperation and acceptance of the parent's needs. Because most children of divorced parents harbor feelings of ambivalence, children may fear that their inattention and insensitivity may further alienate their parent. As a result, they become overly attentive and protective toward the parent. Their inability to let go also limits their parent's opportunity to be free and to attend to personal needs and to help facilitate these needs whenever possible. Again, the Bowenian theoretical perspectives on family organization and structuring are very applicable in work with a single parent and children.

Therapy With a Reconstituted Family

In view of the relatively low divorce rate among Asian and Pacific Islander families, therapy with reconstituted families is not expected to be in great demand.

Should such therapy be needed, the highly structure familial roles in traditional Asian and Pacific Islander families may make negotiation and final accommodation within the reconstituted family extremely difficult. The following suggestions are provided for family therapy with a reconstituted Asian or Pacific Islander family.

Focusing on Parental Coalition

Problems in a reconstituted family may manifest themselves in parent-child conflicts through a child bearing the symptoms of the family. The therapist's initial and primary focus should be on assessing and repairing the parental subsystem (Satir, 1967). One factor among the many that are identified as important for the success of these families is a viable parental coalition (Benokraitis, 1993). A mutually supportive couple relationship seems to influence the success of the relationship with the children. As a means of repairing the parental subsystem, the therapist needs to sensitize the couple to structural concepts, such as new boundaries and roles, which are required in the functioning of a reconstituted family. Should the husband and wife experience an impasse in their negotiations, the therapist may need to capitalize on existing resources by introducing the couple and the children to another well-functioning reconstituted Asian and Pacific Islander American family. The problem family is thus provided with an accepted role model to emulate.

Help the Family to Change Existing
Family Narratives Through Restorying

If an Asian or Pacific Islander family is very traditional, then filial piety toward one's natural parents should not be challenged. For a child to respect another adult as a natural parent is disloyal and therefore forbidden. Moreover, many of the social definitions of stepparent roles have traditionally been derogatory, and myths about wicked stepparents abound. The therapist's task is to encourage the children to vent and to dispel such myths, thus disempowering immobilizing sociocultural narratives. Some children may never love or respect their stepparent as they do their natural parent, but they still have a responsibility to honor their mother or father and make the home environment a harmonious setting. In view of a more traditional Asian or Pacific Islander client's emphasis on blood ties and ancestral worship, the therapist should never attempt to persuade the children to "replace" their natural parent with their stepparent. Rather, children can be encouraged to broaden their traditional definition of family and encouraged to find a new (albeit appropriate and respectful) family role or position for the stepparent outside of that of "parent."

Work With the Relatives and
Grandparents of the Reconstituted Family

The work of the reconstituted family in boundary definitions will never be complete if the network of relatives is uninvolved. The degree to which the kin network needs to be involved varies with different families. The reconstituted family needs to be cognizant of the effects of relatives and grandparents on the family members' interaction with each other. The ecosystem approach can be useful to the therapist at this stage.

During periods of single parenthood, many Asian and Pacific Islander grand-parents assume a major role in the family, especially if the parent and children return to the parental home. Some grandparents retain the parent-child role with their own children despite the fact that the child is now a parent. This often results in grandparents usurping the authority of the natural parent or stepparent with their grandchildren (Weiss, 1979). Structurally, grandparents and relatives of both former spouses need to reestablish new boundaries for themselves with the family members of the new marriage so that they can serve as a source of support rather than pose potential conflict. If the parents of a reconstituted family are willing to express their concern directly to the children's grandparents, the therapist's task is to be a liaison who can tactfully convince the grandparents that their best assistance to their children and grandchildren at the present is noninterference.

PART 5: CONCLUSION

The family is the central unit of social organization for Asian and Pacific Islander Americans. Due to a vastly different cultural orientation, English-language limitations, separation from friends and extended kin, and other isolating environmental factors, the family often provides the only means of interaction, socialization, validation, and stabilization for this ethnic group. The Asian and Pacific Islander American family is shaped not only by past traditions and current life experiences but by the ongoing political and economic events in Asian and Pacific countries, as well as in the United States. Many migration-related and environmental stresses, such as poor housing, underemployment, discriminatory laws, and individual and institutional racism, exert a disorganizing influence on the Asian and Pacific Islander American family system. A critical perspective enables the therapist to understand these multiple disorganizing influences.

The continued underutilization of mental health services indicates Asian and Pacific Islander Americans' tradition and strong reliance on the dictum that personal and interpersonal problems should be kept within the family and solved there. Hence family therapy remains the most pertinent problem-solving approach and modality for Asian and Pacific Islander American clients. Therapy with Asian and Pacific Islander American families requires taking a holistic view of health and a critical, interactive, and contextual perspective of behavior. This chapter has focused on the holistic view and the integration of historical, economic, social, political, psychological, physical, and cultural phenomena during different phases of (ecosystemically based) family therapy with Asian and Pacific Islander American families using a critical constructionist perspective.

3

Family Therapy With First Nations Peoples

PART 1: PRETHERAPY PHASE CONSIDERATIONS: A CRITICAL PERSPECTIVE

Names and Images

There are multiple designations for the ethnic and racial group originally labeled *Indians* or *American Indians* and *Alaskan Natives.* Though the term American Indian is no longer considered appropriate by many, one or more of the following generic designations, *Native Americans, Native people, First Nations peoples, or indigenous peoples,* are currently used in North America to replace the term American Indians (Weaver, 2003; Yellow Bird, 2001). There is no consensus about which term is best, yet some Native people have strong preferences for one term over the others (Weaver, 2003). Each of these labels attempts to encompass a diversity of languages, lifestyles, and kinship systems and organizations (McGoldrick, Giordano, & Pearce, 1996; Polacca, 1995). However, each label has significant sociopolitical implications. As Yellow Bird (1999, 2001) points out in discussing the significance of some of these terms,

> Many Indigenous Peoples are mistakenly called *Indians, American Indians,* or *Native Americans.* They are not Indians or American Indians because they are not from India. They are not Native Americans because Indigenous Peoples did not refer to their lands as America until Europeans arrived and imposed this name on the land. Indians, American Indians, and Native Americans are "colonized" and "inaccurate" names that oppress the identities of First Nations Peoples. (Yellow Bird, 2001, p. 61)

The implication of Yellow Bird's words (although obviously he does not speak for all indigenous persons) underscores the tumultuous and tragic history of a group of people who have struggled to maintain a cultural and ethnic identity and the integrity of their (ethnocultural) heritage. Furthermore, these struggles have provided the cultural and historical context for the families of Native people; their family life has been dramatically shaped and altered by historical and contemporary experiences and events. The first section of this chapter will address the impact of these historical experiences on the family life and family structure of First Nations peoples.

It is important to note that each of these terms, although representing the diversity of a group of people, is still generic. To honor their own unique culture and traditions, First Nations peoples would rather self-identify and hence be referred to by their specific indigenous sociopolitical and cultural group or nation—for example, Navaho, Apache, or Chippewa.

We acknowledge, from a critical constructionist perspective, that ethnic identities are political constructs and *collective ethnic identity narratives* and their productions are affected by power relationships in terms of who gets to narrate whose ethnic identity and whose version of an identity gains public recognition in a particular sociopolitical context (Cornell, 2000). In an attempt to be sensitive to how the ethnic identity narrative has been constructed for this group of people, the authors will use the terms *First Nations peoples, indigenous peoples,* and *Native people* interchangeably. Other terms will be used only in direct quotes or when those terms are used in major documents or studies, such as census data.

Demographics

In the continental United States and Alaska, there are over 550 distinct Native tribes. Historically, the term *tribe* has been used in an ethnological sense and in an official, political sense. Prior to the official federal definition of a Native tribe, this term specifically referred to a "group of indigenous people bound together by blood ties, who were socially, politically, and religiously organized to the tenet of their own culture, who lived together, occupied a definite territory, and who spoke a common language or dialect" (Utter, 2001, p. 57).

Over the course of U.S. history, the United States government has determined which indigenous groups were tribal "political entities" so that federal officials could negotiate peace treaties, grant land acquisitions, regulate Native affairs, permit claims by First Nations peoples against the government, and determine which indigenous groups were affected by particular statutes (Cohen, 1982). Many First Nations peoples were relegated to reservations, and there were situations in which ethnologically autonomous groups were bound together on one reservation or split up and spread over two or more reservations to be absorbed into a "tribe" for governmental political designations. Though a definition for the term *tribe* does not exist in the U.S. Constitution, this term is specifically found in numerous treaties, legislative agreements, statues, and even presidential executive orders (Cohen, 1982).

Native "tribes" are as ethnically differentiated as the "tribe" of Europeans and are far more diverse—culturally and linguistically (Lum, 2002). Some of the tribes are small, with fewer than 100 members; the Cherokee, Choctaw, Sioux, Navajo (Dîné), Chippewa (Ojibway), and Latin American Indians have populations of more than 100,000 (U.S. Census Bureau, 2000). According to the 2000 U.S. Census, 43% of First Nations peoples live in the Western United States. About half of the total number of Native people lives in urban areas (Sutton & Broken Nose, 1996). For example, in New York City and Los Angeles, there are approximately 100,000 indigenous people. Other non-urban indigenous people are very traditional, live in isolated rural areas on reservations, and may know very little English. Many others have been raised in urban areas and have had little or no contact with their Native heritage. Regardless of their location, many First Nations peoples experience continual struggle and conflict in attempting to achieve a balance between their Native values and those of the dominant society.

One hundred years ago, the population of U.S. Native people was about 250,000. In the 1990 U.S. Census, approximately 2 million Native people were counted. In the 2000 U.S. Census, persons were allowed to indicate one or more racial or ethnic identities. Data from this census revealed that out of the total U.S. population of 281.4 million, 4.1 million (1.5%) reported "American Indian" and "Alaskan Native" as their ethnic identity. This figure includes the 2.5 million people (0.9%) who reported only "American Indian" and "Alaskan Native" as their racial or ethnic identity. An additional 1.6 million reported their racial identity as "American Indian" and reported at least one other racial identity. Given the fact that the 2000 U.S. Census, for the first time, permitted respondents to report one or more races or ethnicities if they considered themselves as such, the 2000 census data are not directly comparable to earlier census data. In the 1990 U.S. Census, only 2 million Native people identified themselves as "American Indian." Comparing this number with those individuals who self-identified in 2000 *only* as "American Indian," the increase between 1990 and 2000 is 26%. If one were to combine the number of "American Indians" who reported only one race with the "American Indian" individuals who reported more than one race, the population increase would be 110%.

In contrast to any other ethnic minority group in the United States, a person is not a "real" or "authentic" Native unless he or she fits into categories defined by the federal government, including blood degree and tribal status. To be eligible for federal Native programs, a person must be able to prove that he or she has at least one-quarter Native "blood," as recognized by the federal government. The fact is that over 60% of First Nations peoples are of mixed heritage, having African American, white, and Hispanic backgrounds (Sue & Sue, 1999).

First Nations peoples are generally perceived as a homogenous group, a composite of certain physical and personality characteristics that have become stereotypes reinforced by the media. As Deloria (1969) says, "People can tell just by looking at us what we want, what should be done to help us, how we feel and what a 'real' Indian is like" (p. 9). Obviously, the idea that there is an "Indian" stereotype that could fit all or even most First Nations peoples today is naïve and simplistic. Like other clients, the Native client wishes to be recognized as a person, a human being, and not as a category. To recognize the Native client as a person, the family therapist must understand and respect the unique cultural family background and rich heritage of the indigenous client.

Cultural Values in Relation to Family Structure

Although no Native tribes are identical in their cultural beliefs and practices, there are some unifying concepts that set them apart from the dominant society. The following list is not meant to be exhaustive but rather illustrative of some of the ways First Nations peoples' values differ from the values of white Americans. It is not meant to apply rigidly to all indigenous peoples because of the individual differences noted previously.

Table 3.1 summarizes and contrasts cultural values between the dominant society (white, middle class) and indigenous people.

Harmony with nature. First Nations peoples hold nature as extremely important, for they realize that they are but one part of a greater whole. Their sense of humanity's integral relationship with its environment is clearly grounded in an ecological framework. There are many rituals and ceremonies among the tribes that express both their reverence for nature's forces and their observance of the balance that must be maintained between them and all other living and nonliving things. They believe that growing things of the earth and all animals have spirits or souls and that they should be treated as humanely as possible, with respect and appreciation for the contributions they make to people's life cycles. Indigenous peoples' need for keeping in harmony with nature has often been negatively misinterpreted as "laziness" or "inactivity." Family therapists are warned not to negatively interpret a client's lack of interest in changing his or her personal environment with a lack of interest in resolving presenting problems. Rather, a more *culturally syntonic* (culturally compatible) interventive goal may be to alter the way a Native family copes with environmental challenges. (This is not to say that matters of social justice, for example, should be shrugged off as a fact of life by Native peoples; absolutely not! Social justice issues are man-made problems and are not endemic to the natural environment.)

Present-time orientation. Native persons are very much grounded in what is happening in their lives at the moment; they are less interested in making specific

Table 3.1 Cultural Value Preferences of Middle-Class White Americans and First Nations Peoples: A Comparative Summary

Areas of Relationships	Middle-Class, White Americans	First Nations Peoples
Man to nature, environment	Control over	Harmony with
Time orientation	Future	Present
Relations with people	Individual	Collateral
Preferred mode of activity	Doing	Being-in-becoming
Nature of man	Good and bad	Good

Sources: Data on white, middle-class American values are based on the work of Papajohn and Speigel (1975); Native cultural data are taken from studies and observations of Zintz (1963), Bryde (1971), Attneave (1982), Lewis and Ho (1975), and Sue and Sue (1999).

plans for future endeavors. They are busy living their lives rather than preparing for them. In contrast to the general belief that they have no concept of time, Native people are indeed time conscious. They deal, however, with natural phenomena—mornings, days, nights, months in terms of moons, and years in terms of seasons or winters (Tracks, 1973). This time orientation may be partially related to the nature of traditional Native economies and the need to focus on daily survival, and it is also related to the Native worldview of events moving through time in a rhythmic, circular pattern. Artificial imposition of schedules disrupts the natural pattern.

The contemporary Native family may have maintained some of this naturalness of rhythm. Hence use of "Native time" can be both a tool for passive-aggressive resistance to mechanistic inhumane ways and a way of expressing contrasting priorities. In the course of family therapy, concrete immediate problems and their solutions may be more relevant than future-oriented, abstract, philosophical goals.

Collateral relationship with others. First Nations peoples believe in working together and getting along with each other; the family and the group take precedence over the individual. The concept of collateral relationship reflects the integrated view of the universe wherein all people, animals, plants, and objects in nature have their place in creating a harmonious whole. In emergencies, but only for a brief period, an authoritative leader, who is usually an elder with demonstrated expertise and problem-solving skills, may be permitted to take charge, but this is clearly a second choice. The impatient solution of majority vote revered by democracies seldom takes place; instead, long and arduous discussions are generally held until a group decision can be reached. The implication here for family practice with Native families is that the family therapist should not expect important decisions to be made quickly or by majority desire; rather, the therapist should more likely anticipate that the Native family will need to consult with extended family members—possibly even community or tribal members. Westernized family therapists will need to replace their culturally based internal clock (preconceived notions of when certain clinical processes should occur) with the culturally based internal clock of First Nations families.

Closely related to the concept of collateral relationship is the traditional practice of "giveaway" that still persists in almost all tribes. All forms of belongings are given ritually to honor others for their help or their achievement or to acknowledge kinship ties. The practice of "giveaway" serves as a means of recycling goods, honoring one's ancestors, and showing respect to the living (Momaday, 1974).

Native people's adherence to collateral relationships is sure to conflict with the dominant culture's stress on individuality and competition. Native children in public schools are often mistakenly seen as unmotivated due to their reluctance to compete with their peers in the classroom or on the playground. Native workers may also be mistakenly labeled as lazy or unproductive. However, the cooperative spirit can be revitalized and capitalized on in problem-solving processes during a family crisis or imbalance.

Being-in-becoming as preferred mode of activity. The dominant culture has repeatedly demonstrated a value system that seeks to control and be in charge and that often destroys the balance of nature. This is done with the view that human beings are superior to all other forms of life and have, therefore, the right to manipulate nature and situations for their comfort, convenience, and economic gain. In contrast, the Native person is taught to endure all natural and unnatural happenings that he or she will encounter during life. First Nations peoples believe that to attain maturity, which entails learning to live with life-its evil as well as its good, one must face genuine suffering. Hence First Nations clients may appear pessimistic, downtrodden, low-spirited, unhappy, and without hope for the future. However, as one looks deeper into their personality, another perspective is visible. In the midst of abject poverty comes *the courage to be*—to face life as it is while maintaining a tremendous sense of humor (Huffaker, 1967).

A Native person's *courage to be* may also be misinterpreted as stoicism, lack of emotion, and vulnerability. The Native person is alone, not only with others but also to him- or herself. Native people control their emotions, allowing themselves no passionate outbursts over small matters. Their habitual mien is one of poise, self-containment, and aloofness, which may result from a fear and mistrust of non-Native persons. This worldview translates to a person with amazing resilience, and it is imperative that family therapists understand this mode of being. (We have long speculated that in mainstream American culture, one is taught that life should be without pain [emotional, psychological or physical] and without obstacles—at all times. It is thus no small coincidence that depression is epidemic in this society;

as the nature of life [the true nature of life] is not a perennial state of bliss, joy, and happiness. Americans spend a tremendous amount of their time, effort, and resources in attempting to achieve this utopian state. This is not to imply that First Nations peoples thrive on pain, problems, and obstacles, nor are we implying that Native persons make no effort to create a more comfortable existence for themselves. Rather, the implication here is that the Native way teaches one to expect life's unpleasant events, to learn and grow from these events, and to gain honor from being able to survive the inevitable trials and tribulations of life.)

As Native persons value their own right to be, so do they value and respect others' rights to be and to do their own thing. Traditionally, Native people are raised not to interfere with others (Sue & Sue, 1999). From childhood, they learn to observe rather than to react impulsively to situations. They learn to respect the rights of others to do as they will and not to meddle in their affairs. This philosophical stance, as interpreted in child-rearing practices, may be viewed negatively by those who hold a different worldview. It is important for family therapists to understand that to purposely allow children to learn from their own experiences and mistakes is a far cry from ignoring and neglecting children. Rather, Native families may allow the environment to do the disciplining, at times and within reason.

The nature of man is seen as good. One of the most central elements of the worldview of indigenous peoples is the orientation toward human nature as essentially and generally good. Human misbehavior is thought to result from a lack of opportunity to be and to develop fully. There are always some people or things that are bad and deceitful. A Native person believes, however, that in the end, good people will triumph just because they are good. This belief is seen repeatedly in Native folktales about Iktomi the spider. He is a tricky fellow who is out to fool, cheat, and take advantage of good people. However, Iktomi usually loses in the end, reflecting the Native person's view that the good person succeeds and the bad person loses (Bryde, 1971).

First Nations peoples' tribal and Christian religions. Both Native tribal and Christian religion play important parts in the lives of Native people. Religion is incorporated into their being from the time of conception, when many tribes perform rites and rituals to ensure the delivery of a healthy baby, to the death ceremonies, wherein great care is taken to promote the return of the person's spirit to the life after this one. In view of the diversity of Native tribes, considerable variation in the practice of Native religions is to be expected. It is not unusual for Native people to participate in ceremonies and rituals within the Native religions and also to attend and hold membership in Christian religions. Native people who speak native languages tend to maintain their religious ceremonies, customs, and traditions. They also have more trust in their native "medicine people" for physical and mental health needs than in the non-Native medical doctor or family therapist. Solutions to some family problems may require services from both cultural perspectives.

With the knowledge of these selected (Native) cultural values, family therapists may be expected to understand and appreciate the traditional cultural values and worldview of First Nations peoples. Next we explore the family structure and the contemporary scene of the Native family.

Extended Family Ties

The failure of providing effective family service to First Nations peoples lies primarily within the therapist's misuse of the nuclear family conceptual framework in organizing service delivery. Consequently the Native family may become a unit of analysis with specified household parameters. Household units of both nuclear and extended family models can be found in Native family systems (Red Horse, 1980b).

Native family systems are extended networks, characteristically including several households. The Native family is an active kinship system inclusive of parents, children, aunts, uncles, cousins, and grandparents (Wahrhaftig, 1969). In addition, nonkin can also become family members through naming ceremonies in which a child is named after them. This individual then assumes family obligations and major responsibilities for child rearing and as a role model for the child.

Due to historical tribal mobility and the force of American governmental policy, many family systems extend over broad geographical regions and assume interstate dimensions (Red Horse, 1980b). The notion of a multiple family household provides family members with a strong sense of belonging along both vertical and horizontal extensions. Grandparents and older namesakes serve as role models for younger family members. They provide examples for spousal interaction and child-rearing guidelines.

Thomas (1969), in an attempt to illustrate how the vertical family structure is reinforced with horizontal organization, describes the important roles of uncles and aunts in Oklahoma Cherokee families. The authority structure of the extended family system could be arranged in a variety of ways, with an administrative focus on the oldest man or woman. The specific patterning of an extended family again varies according to tribal differences, yet in each, the basic outline follows the structure of three or more generations in each household.

Native family networks adhere to what has been identified as an open family–closed community pattern (Mouseau, 1975). Outsiders, including the family therapist, do not gain entrance easily. The extended family network represents a relations field characterized by intense personal exchanges that have lasting effects upon one's life and behavior (Speck & Attneave, 1974).

Mate Selection and Husband-Wife Relationship

In view of the important influence of extended family ties, many tribes strongly encourage their young people to marry within their tribal group. Contact between young men and women is controlled by clan mores and systems. Traditionally, most marriages are arranged, and couples enter into the marital relationship with some feeling of apprehension. In the Apache tribe, male relatives of widows are expected to marry the widow. If this cannot be done, the widow is free to marry whomever she chooses (Brown & Shaughnessy, 1982).

The traditional marital practice of Native people is basically monogamous. Men join their wives' household and economically support their wives but retain ritual, leadership, and disciplinary roles in their natal households (Brown & Shaughnessy, 1982). Thus a husband may discipline his sister's children and play only a passive role in his wife's household. The Hopi say that "the man's place is on the outside of the house." The disharmony created in these contrasting roles contributes to a high divorce rate among the Hopi (Eggan, 1966).

Partly due to the extended family system household and partly due to the man's role as a hunter whose work takes him outside of the home for extended periods, open display of emotions and affection between the husband and wife rarely exist, although the mutual bond may in fact be close, affectionate, and satisfying. Traditionally, Inuit men treated their wives as inferior and were reluctant to have close interpersonal contacts (Hippler, 1974). Couples rarely went visiting together or entertained friends together, and nonkin adult social gatherings were usually of the same sex only. Within the Navajo tribe, traditionally, the sons-in-law were not permitted to speak to or to look at their mothers-in-law (Brown & Shaughnessy, 1982). Such practice was regarded as a sign of respect for the mother-in-law–son-in-law relationship.

Native women, independent for the most part, play a submissive, supportive role to their husbands (Hanson, 1980). Traditionally, the wife would observe her husband constantly, looking for signs and opportunities to please him. In some instances, it was customary for the Lakota husband to take additional wives to assist in household chores.

Although traditionally Native wives had a position of low prestige, they had far more freedom and latitude in their roles than men did. As observed by Spindler and Spindler (1971), "The disruptions created in rapid cultural change hit the men more directly, leaving the women less changed and less anxious— Menomini women continue to play the affective, supportive, 'expressive' role of wife, mother and social participant in a more or less traditional fashion, unhampered by rigid role prescriptions" (p. 398). Today, Native women have two primary chores: to survive and to keep their families intact (Medicine, 1978). Their experience at hard seasonal labor has made them more employable than their husbands. This sometimes causes conflict in the marriage.

Parent-Child Relationship

Traditionally, the parents in a First Nations family were occupied with basic survival needs, such as hunting, providing shelter, gathering or cultivating crops, and preserving food. Because the basic parental disciplinary role is shared among relatives of several generations, biological parents are afforded the opportunity to engage in fun-oriented activities with their children. Hence the Native parent-child relationship is less pressured and more egalitarian that that of the dominant culture. When children are infants, they experience intense, warm, maternal care from the mother. They may be carried in a parka hood on the mother's back with skin-to-skin contact much of the time. This kind of extreme nurturance generates a strong sense of security in the child, who is most likely to be egocentric but optimistic, friendly but ambivalent about violence (Hippler, 1974).

Among all tribes, children are of utmost importance, for they represent the renewal of life. Native children are not seen as entirely dependent beings but rather as individuals who can, within a short time after birth, make important decisions regarding the kind of person that they will become. Traditionally, the belief in the rightness of the child's choice results in discouragement of adults giving them orders and physical punishments to force specific behaviors (Lewis, 1970; Morey & Gilliam, 1974; Vidal de Haymes et al., 2002). Children are disciplined and taught by numerous caretakers other than the biological parents. They are expected to respond to the appropriate behavior passed on by generations. Native children are not taught to have guilt, for parents believe they have no control over others or their own environment (Attneave, 1982).

In some tribes, the mother and the daughter may be referred to by the same term (Brown & Shaughenessy, 1982). A daughter would properly address her mother as "mother-sister," and the mother would properly address the child as "child-sister." This again emphasizes the high status that the child is afforded in Native families.

Because the Native parent is only one of the "instructors" in the child's life, parental instruction usually takes the form of observation and participation. A child is seldom told directly what to do and is often left to his or her own devices and decisions. This brand of freedom is not experienced in a vacuum, however, but rather in concert with the felt expectations from many significant adults, including grandparents (Red Horse, 1980b). These expectations serve as an important support with which to make the right choice.

Parent-child interaction among Native families is often determined by sex role. For example, it was common for Lakota women to instruct their daughters and granddaughters in proper conduct throughout adulthood. Sons, on the other hand, after the age of 10 years old, were the primary responsibility of the father. Unfortunately, in fatherless homes, young sons are often without guidance due to the mother's reluctance to assume this responsibility for fear of creating a "winkle" or "sissy" (Hanson, 1980). Further, traditional parent-child interaction is greatly diminished by the fact that about 20% to 25% of Native children grow up outside of their parents' home (Brown & Shaughnessy, 1982).

Sibling Relationship

The strong extended family ties and the clan system of Native culture provide a child with many siblings. In addition to biological brothers and sisters, a Native child traditionally is brought up with many cousins. They have close interaction with each other through early childhood. The particular supportive patterns between brothers and sisters usually begin in adolescence when they are expected to help in the material support of the tribe and in religious activities. The similarity of cousin relationships and the brother-sister relationship allows a Native child the nurturance and support she or he needs to grow up as an adult (Blanchard, 1983).

Because observation and participation are a major part of a Native child's socialization and development, younger siblings receive encouragement from their older siblings to behave appropriately. Often the older siblings provide the first demonstration of a behavior, and it is part of their responsibility to assist in the formation of certain behaviors.

Due to the different matrilineal and patrilineal patterns among the tribes, there is no distinct favoritism offered to any specific sex or gender. The particular economic and social system dictates the more desired sexual identity of the child for the tribal group. For example, among the Southwest Pueblos, girls are often preferred over boys, but in other tribes, boys are preferred. Similarly, cultural traits of noninterference, non-competition, and interdependence render the ordering position of siblings less of a significant factor within First Nations families. However, Native people's cultural emphasis upon sexual identity and development strongly encourages children to participate in sex-role–appropriate activities. Hence, at the age of 8 or 10, siblings of the same sex form a closer relationship with each other than with siblings of the opposite sex. Such close relationships last until adulthood.

Intermarriages

Traditionally, Native marriages are more in the nature of a contract between kin groups. With the influx of Europeans in the early 1800s and the more recent Relocation Act (Stuart, 1977) endorsed by the Bureau of Indian Affairs to assimilate the Native people into the mainstream of the population in the cities, there is a gradual increase in intermarriages among Native people of different tribes, as well as between Native people and other racial groups.

Differences between Europeans who arrive in the New World play an important role in determining the nature of First Nations–European intermarriage. For example, the French, Spanish, and Portuguese are more tolerant of intermarriages with indigenous people than are northern Europeans. Thus, since colonial times, there have been significant populations of Spanish-Indian *mestizos* and French-Indian *métis* but few British-Native interracial marriages.

The exact number of intermarriages in previous centuries between Native people and non-Native ethnic groups, including intermarriage between Native people and African slaves, is difficult to ascertain, especially in territories bordering the early colonies and slave states (Green, 1999; Katz, 1997). Yet authorities speculate that over half of those who identify themselves as Native are married to non-Natives (Greenbaum, 1991). Because groups in the Southwest are more isolated, members tend to "marry out" less; Native people in the South, East, and Midwest, however, have long histories of intermarriage with Filipinos and other Asian immigrants (Green, 1999). In terms of intermarriage between Native tribes, Churchill (1999) points out that First Nations peoples have for the most part maintained a relatively high degree of sociocultural inclusiveness and consequently high reproductive interactivity. For example, the Cheyenne have intermarried with Arapaho, Ojibwa with Cree, Cayuga with Onondaga, Yaquis with Turamara, and Choctaw with Chickasaw.

Divorce and Remarriage

In view of the diversity of tribal cultures and customs and the vast cultural differences between Native people and the dominant culture, marriages between tribes and other ethnic groups are destined to run into great difficulties. Marriages within the tribe also are negatively influenced by the dominant societal value of individualism and competitiveness. According to data from the 1980 U.S. Census, of women who had married for the first time 10 to 14 years before 1980, divorce or separation had occurred for 53% of African American women, 48% of "Native American" women, and 37% of non-Hispanic white women (Demo, Allen, & Fine, 2000; Sweet & Bumpass, 1987). We can expect the rate of divorce and remarriage to be higher among urban Native people who intermarry and lack the support of the extended family system.

Divorce and remarriage are more acceptable within First Nations families than in the dominant American society (Price, 1981). Such acceptance may be related to Native people's cultural traits of collateral relations, being-in-becoming, rightness of choice, and noninterference. The strong support system consisting of extended family ties and multiple households reaffirms the place of the divorced person in his or her family. As an example of the permissiveness of remarriage, some indigenous tribes of the Great Plains and Coastal Northwest still practice polyandry, or multiple husbands. This occurs only in special circumstances, such as the crippling of an older married brother and the subsequent additional marriage of the younger brother to the older brother's wife. This tolerance of diversity within First Nations societies tends to be greater than in the dominant society, which has a rather limited set of familial rules that emphasize permanent, monogamous marriage.

Impact of Migration and Cultural Adjustments

The breakdown of First Nations cultural traditions and family customs began in the early 1800s. In 1815, the United States government coerced tribal leaders into signing treaties they could not read and thus could not understand (Costa & Henry, 1977). These treaties opened the door for a greater influx of European homesteaders and miners. As the influx of whites continued, and they eventually became the politically dominant group, Native people were restricted to reservation areas. By 1849, the Bureau of Indian Affairs was given full authority to oversee the activities of First Nations peoples. The sacred Black Hills were taken by an illegal treaty, the buffalo were destroyed, and First Nations languages and religious practices were forbidden by missionary schools (Merian, 1977). It was during this period that First Nations children were taken away from their parents with the intention of educating them in the white man's mold. These children's placements later included boarding schools, religious institutions, foster care, and adoption. These practices severed the links of the support system that centers on children and thus encouraged the destruction of the basic tenets of tribal life. Fortunately, these practices were corrected in 1978 with the Federal Indian Child Welfare Act. This act was created (a) to reduce the large number of Native children put in foster care by placing jurisdictional control of child welfare cases in the hands of tribal courts for children domiciled and residing on reservations and (b) to ensure that Native children remain with their parents whenever possible. The intent of the Child Welfare Act was to preserve First Nations culture. Before the Indian Child Welfare Act, one in four Native children was being removed from his or her home and placed into boarding school, a residential home, or a non-Native foster home.

The Dawes Act of 1887 (Merian, 1977), which divided reservation land into allotments and individual ownership, forced Native men and women to become farmers and ranchers. With the shift in occupational skills and requirements, Native men were no longer recognized as brave warriors or hunters. Native women were also traumatized, as they painfully watched their children taken away and witnessed the gradual psychological deterioration of their husbands.

Following World War II, the unemployment rate soared for First Nations peoples returning to their reservations. In 1952, the Bureau of Indian Affairs sought to relieve the high unemployment problem by finding jobs for Native people in urban areas (Stuart, 1977). This program was considered as yet another attempt by the government to destroy the Native culture and family structure by encouraging assimilation into the urban environment rather than attempting to strengthen First Nations ways of life by developing more work opportunities on reservations (Farris, 1973). Between 1952, and 1968, some 67,522 First Nations peoples who were heads of households were relocated through this direct employment program (Bureau of Indian Affairs, 1971).

From the above historical overview, it can be seen that although Native people are diverse, they in fact share a common history of oppression and colonialization (Yellow Bird, 2001). This history chronicles the first contact with Europeans, which resulted in First Nations peoples being systematically destroyed through genocidal military actions (Duran, Duran, Brave Heart, & Yellow Horse-Davis, 1998). From that first contact came, over time, the following periods of exploitation and oppression of indigenous peoples:

- *Economic competition*—land, wildlife, and lifestyle were taken or destroyed by European settlers
- *Invasion and war*—the U.S. government carried out a policy of extermination through military action, and many Native people were killed or forced to leave their homelands
- *Subjugation and reservation*—Indigenous people were forced to live within the confines of reservations and were often relocated to unfamiliar lands
- *Boarding school*—Native children were forcibly removed from their homes and placed into boarding schools often hundreds of miles away. Inspired by the motto "Kill the Indian, Save the Man," the boarding schools implemented a systematic plan of destroying Native culture (cultural genocide) by forcing the children to cut their hair, forbidding them to speak their own language, forcing them to adopt European dress, and using physical punishment to enforce compliance to these expectations
- *Forced relocation and termination*—Many First Nations peoples were relocated from reservations into large metropolitan areas

This history of struggle and oppression and the experiences of colonialization and cultural genocide have a multigenerational impact on the contemporary experiences of Native people and their families (Yellow Bird, 2001). The grief, trauma, and oppression experienced by their ancestors are ever present in the lives of Native people and within the historical and emotional matrix of the family (Brave Heart-Jordan & DeBruyn, 1995). The grief and unresolved trauma resulting from these historical events in turn contribute to the array of current social difficulties faced by First Nations people.

The statistics for income, education, and mental health among Native people present a bleak picture. In discussing the array of social and economic problems facing First Nations peoples, Karger and Stoesz (2002) presented the following data:

- In 1990, more than 16% of Native males living on reservations were unemployed, compared to 6.4% of the total population
- In 1990, 33% of the Native population lived below the poverty line, compared to 14.5% of whites
- Sixty-five percent of Native people on reservations are high school graduates
- Sixteen percent of Native homes are without electricity; the U.S. average is 0.1
- Roughly 43% of Native people who live beyond infancy die before age 55, compared to slightly more than 16% for the general population
- Native people have a maternal death rate 20% higher than the national average
- The death rate for tuberculosis is six times higher among Native people than that for the population as a whole; chronic liver disease is four times the norm; diabetes, influenza, and pneumonia are two times the norm
- Suicide rates among Native people are twice the national average, with rates highest among young people
- Native people have the highest rate of alcoholism of any ethnic group in the United States (pp. 67-68)

Living against such ecological stress and daily threats to survival, the life of a First Nations family is certain to deteriorate rapidly. Additionally, children of urban Native families are being raised with fewer contacts with traditional life. Their peers are often non-Natives, and they increasingly grow up to marry non-Natives, further diluting their indigenous heritage (Price, 1981). Yet, despite a multitude of adversities, First Nations families have a long history of durability and persistence in survival.

Family Help-Seeking Patterns and Behaviors

The indigenous culture emphasizes harmony with nature, endurance of suffering, respect and noninterference toward others, a strong belief that man is inherently good and that he should be respected for his decisions, and similar ideas and beliefs. Such traits make a family in difficulty very reluctant to seek help. Their fear and mistrust toward non-Natives, caused by past oppression and discrimination, make it almost impossible for a non-Native family therapist to gain entry into the family system. Native families experience several similar stages in their attempt to assist their members, but different families may have different service needs and help-seeking patterns. Judging by family lifestyle patterns, contemporary Native families can be classified into three types (Red Horse, 1980b).

1. The *traditional* family overtly adheres to culturally defined styles of living. The parents and grandparents speak the native language. The family practices tribal religion, customs, and mores and has an extended family network.

2. The *nontraditional* or *bicultural* family appears to have adopted many aspects of nontraditional styles of living. Although the parents or grandparents are bilingual, English constitutes conversational language at home. The family adopts the Anglo belief system and actively takes part in social activities with groups and individuals from the dominant culture. The structure of the family is extended and lies with kin from reservations and across states.

3. The *pantraditional* family overtly struggles to redefine and reconfirm previously lost cultural lifestyles. Both English and the native language are spoken in the pantraditional family. This kind of family practices a modified tribal belief system and struggles to maintain the traditional extended family network, as well as cultural activities.

As would be expected, traditional families generally would not seek help or willingly receive help from a family therapist. In their attempt to recapture and redefine cultural lifestyles, pantraditional families also may not be receptive to the idea of family therapy. Bicultural families are the ones most likely to be receptive to family therapy, for they have adopted the dominant culture and its mores.

The different family lifestyle patterns among First Nations peoples do not imply an ongoing erosion of cultural values. Studies suggest, however, that Native core values are retained and remain as a constant, regardless of family lifestyle patterns (Weaver, 2001; Yellow Bird, 2001). The extended family network maintained by all three family lifestyle patterns is one good example that reflects the Native family's resistance to cultural assimilation. In an attempt to organize indigenous people's help-seeking patterns schematically, Lewis (1984) further confirmed the extended network behavior characteristic of Native families. When a family needs help, the extended family network is the first source to be contacted. Second, a religious leader may be consulted to resolve problems plaguing the family. Third, if the problem is unresolved, the family will contact the tribal community elders. Last, when all these fail, the family *may* seek help from the mainstream family and healthcare system.

Often, when the family has contact with the therapist, the family is not psychologically or emotionally ready for help. Some families see a therapist only when ordered to do so by a court. Such contacts usually result in failure of service delivery, and they further reinforce the Native family's distrust of family service providers.

Applying Culturally Sensitive
Family Theories, Models, and Approaches

Cultural and Political Factors Relevant to
Family Therapy With First Nations Families

First Nations families have endured some of the most horrific experiences known to humanity. Present-day First Nations families are still dealing daily with the consequences of attempts at racial and cultural genocide, which will undoubtedly have a multigenerational impact. We decided to begin this section (about family practice) a bit differently than the other chapters. There are many factors that led us to this decision, the first of which is that a majority of family therapists faced with a Native family are likely never to have met or even spoken to a First Nations person. (This would be very unlikely in the case of the other three racial minority groups examined in this volume. It is hard to imagine a family therapist—even one that has been reared and educated in the most racially homogenous white environment—never having seen or at least spoken to or been around an African American, Asian or Pacific Islander American, or a Latino, however limited or superficial this interaction may have been.) Second, Native communities and their social issues have remained very much in the margins of practice within the various helping professions, and education about First Nations families continues to be shamefully and conspicuously absent from the therapy curriculums of professional schools of helping. One would be hard pressed to argue against the sad fact that the average family therapist knows less about Native families than any other ethnic minority family group.

Third, negative cultural stereotypes about First Nations peoples still abound in mainstream culture and in the mass media today. A case in point is the ongoing struggle of Native people in fighting to rid our society of some of the last vestiges of these despicable and offensive racial caricatures: sports mascots. One of the authors read some training literature (Vidal de Haymes et al., 2002) that was trying to drive home the point of how hurtful, harmful, and downright neglectful our American society continues to be in allowing these racial mascots to continue. The cartoon pictured a Native male, with an extremely exaggerated smile, a very pronounced nose, and a feather stuck on top of his head. The caption read: "The Cleveland Indians." However, there were other racial and ethnic groups featured with similarly exaggerated (racial) facial features and accompanying cultural stereotypical clothing. Their captions read: "The Cleveland Chinese," "The Cleveland African Americans," "The Cleveland Jews," and so on.

The point is that due to these and a host of other factors, we felt it important (as our discussion of family therapy begins) to highlight core cultural values, worldview issues, and political factors relevant to First Nations peoples as they (directly) relate to family therapy, even at the risk of some repetition. Our contention is this: *You must learn about the family's tribe, the family's relationship with that tribe, and their tribe's relationship with other tribes. There is no substitute.*[5]

Family Therapy Considerations

There are a myriad of cultural and political factors affecting members of a First Nations family in regard to their ability to communicate openly and effectively with others. These factors also have important implications for multigenerational (emotional) family processes and the family structure (in terms of strengths and vulnerabilities) of Native families. These factors include, but are not limited to, the following concerns.

1. Effective communication among Native family members is made difficult and challenging by the diversity of tribal languages, traditional (Native) communication styles that rely more on the use of rich metaphors (in contrast with the dominant American communication approach, which values a much more direct communication style and does not rely on nonverbal communication), and the fact that members of the younger generation are more likely to be much more highly acculturated and hence more likely to use a more dominant American communication style and more likely to employ English as their first language (if they know the tribal language at all).

2. Native family members are encouraged to place the needs of others above their own and are therefore encouraged to withhold verbalization of their needs, wants, and feelings. Mainstream family therapy goals and processes (e.g., unbridled, free-ranging directive verbal expression of feelings and the pursuit of individual agendas over that of the family) will need to be modified in family therapy with Native families.

3. Some of the central "threads" of child rearing (non-Natives may refer to these threads as principles or philosophies) are that Native children are expected to learn through observation and experience and are afforded the opportunity to make many of their own decisions at an early age. The Native culture places children at the center of the Nation and shows a great deal of respect and faith in a child's inherent ability to make good choices. The concept of self-determination is truly celebrated in Native cultures and is very much in line with the professional ethos of the various disciplines of family therapists, as well as being consistent with the value assumptions of many of today's family therapy models. Natural consequences are viewed as the primary managers of behavior. (Family therapists are cautioned not to view this child-rearing style as permissive, unstructured, or lacking in guidelines when Native parents seek assistance with child-centered concerns.) Additionally, children

are expected to take their decision making seriously and make decisions that are not just in keeping with their own individual wants and needs but are made with the next seven generations in mind. Inter- and multigenerational issues (loyalties and conflicts) should be anticipated as important family concerns.

4. Native extended family ties and multiple households allow individual family members a great deal of latitude in vertical and horizontal interaction with family members of different generations, ages, and sexes. *Mixed acculturative patterns* within today's Native family will (at times) present challenges to these traditions. When the extended family household is forced to become a nuclear household, as in the case of urban living (and in the case of families not living on reservations or areas not highly populated with other Native families), family members who are more accustomed to interacting and resolving problems in concert with a rich array of blood and nonblood relatives and fellow tribal members are forced to find (and are in need of) new ways of communicating and problem solving with only a limited number of family members available.

5. Indigenous people are the poorest and most oppressed ethnocultural group in the United States. Their struggle to survive and to meet such basic needs as housing, food, and healthcare may leave family members bereft of energy needed for communication and problem solving of their family's social and emotional concerns. Native families may thus have grown accustomed to putting off these activities.

6. The oral tradition of storytelling is seen as a means by which to pass on and teach values and religious beliefs; within this tradition, there is a reliance on the use of metaphors to drive home the essential points to be learned from the story. The use of *metaphors* and *narratives* in family intervention plans is encouraged as a *culturally syntonic* mode of practice with Native families.

7. Elders play an important role in passing on values to children and are seen as wise and helpful in decision making (hence their presence in families is viewed as critical to family life.) The absence of Elders may leave a Native family feeling incomplete and lacking direction. Assistance in relocating Elders with their families (whenever possible) is desirable. New traditions may need to be established by Native families in the absence of Elders.

8. Life span phases are not necessarily controlled according to age; rather, family or cultural role may be more of a determining factor in role behavior (within and outside the family; e.g., an indigenous healer or helper may be very young and yet may assume care for others in a family, clan, or tribe.) *Role strain* and *role conflict* may result as a consequence of *mixed acculturative patterns*.

9. Life-span development, as a process, serves to identify the primacy of family roles through behavioral activity at each phase. Marginalized, isolated, and *biculturally conflicted* families are at greatest risk for *role confusion*.

10. Interdependence in social (especially familial) relationships is encouraged. That is, self-reliance is immersed in a complex web of interdependent, relational behavior (this idea contrasts with that of individualism as a central, dominant, American cultural value).

11. First Nations families today live in widely varying family structures (nuclear, extended, augmented by blood and nonblood relatives, single parent, divorced, blended or step, matriarchal, matrilineal, patriarchal, patrilineal, and a few are uniarchal.) However, traditional Native values and family life are based on the ideal of an extended or augmented family, with the (tribal) community also being seen as a kind of family. Additionally, communal living is highly valued. Important systems of social support and indigenous social networks may be absent in the lives of many of today's First Nations families living away from reservations. These families will need help is establishing supportive networks and help in attempts to reconnect with indigenous support systems.

12. In traditional Native culture, group effort, cooperative spirit, and community action and decision making are valued within social relationships. Sharing is seen as the goal versus hoarding or conspicuous consumption of material goods. One example of this sharing is exemplified in the Seven Laws of the Lakota, which guides their social behavior (*Woope Sakowin*): generosity, compassion, humility, interdependence, respect (for all of creation), noninterference, and tolerance. Intergenerational (and internal individual) conflict is likely to occur as First Nations families absorb individuals in different phases of assimilation and acculturation.

13. In Native cultures, communication is indirect and direct criticism is to be avoided. Instead, the message should be conveyed through nonverbal (more gentle) means or verbally through another group member. Listening is an extremely valued skill and shows respect for others. Gloating and boisterous behavior are seen as reprehensible; modesty is valued. Communication should be nonintrusive, not aggressive and direct. Thus direct eye contact and firm (as opposed to gentle) handshaking are seen as impolite behavior. Mainstream family therapists or family therapists holding mainstream values will need to revisit their behaviors and values and reconsider goals for therapy, as well as considering carefully how they will attempt to structure communication in family therapy with Native families.

14. Knowledge is gained through listening, observing, and emulating Elders, family members, and community (tribal) members, as well as via experience. Ways of reinforcing these important cultural values in the family therapy process with Native families should be identified.

15. In the light of varying rates of acculturation and assimilation between family members, conflicts arise from biculturalism versus traditionalism between

family members (and bicultural conflict within the individual, who is pulled in two different directions between traditional tribal culture and mainstream culture); the growing rates of mixed marriages and inter-tribal marriages, which may expose conflicting values and family structures (e.g., matriarchal/lineal versus patriarchal/lineal). Today's indigenous families thus face more internal strife and tensions than ever before. Along with a high level of acculturation comes a greater threat of generational removal from the reservation (hence *generational cutoffs*). These factors pose serious problems to the healthy emotional family life of Native families.

16. The multigenerational impact of many of today's First Nations parents having been reared in boarding schools, without emotional nurturing and positive (or even appropriate) parental role modeling, presents monumental obstacles for those Native parents who were victims of boarding school atrocities and are now struggling to provide a healthy family life for their own children.

17. The marginalization of indigenous families and their members who experience difficulty coping as a result of their movement back and forth between the reservation and urban life is an additional burden that Native families face in family life.

18. Religion is seen as a way of life and is extremely important, as is spirituality. The circle of life is a holistic idea: Parts work for the whole, versus a linear notion or subsystems that operate separately. Illness affects the mind, spirit, and body negatively—these parts are intricately intertwined. The Creator speaks to humans in dreams, visions, and through life experiences. Fragmentation of (social and mental health) services and diagnostic efforts that compartmentalize family problems (rather than viewing these problems and concerns holistically) is not *culturally syntonic* with traditional Native values and philosophies.

19. The idea of respect for the environment, that nature is beautiful and one should strive for harmony with nature (life's forces), is valued over attempts to change the essence of nature, life, the environment, and the natural world. Family therapy goals that violate these principles should be considered *culturally dystonic* to traditional Native family life.

20. The Native approach to life is pragmatic. The purpose of today is to enjoy and to work for current needs. The goal of a good work ethic is to take care of needs, so that one can enjoy life. Hence a practical view is taken of work, wealth, and material goods; acquisition of material goods is not meant to be an end unto itself, but rather a means to an end. The goals of therapy (desired behavioral and material outcomes) will need to take this philosophy of life into account in establishing an intervention plan with Native families.[6]

21. Tribal identity gives structure, meaning, direction, and purpose to the individual's life; it provides a sense of belonging. Separation from the tribe

(whether intended or not, voluntary or involuntary—forced via extermination, termination, or relocation of one's tribe) thus has major implications for its impact on the spiritual and emotional life and health of Native individuals and their families.

22. *Environmental racism* (pollution of air and water on or near reservations) must be considered an important ecological practice issue in work with First Nations peoples.

23. The cultural identity of many First Nations peoples has been undermined by the cumulative effects of racial and cultural genocide, forced relocation, the termination of some tribes, and a back-and-forth connection to the reservation. Individuals thus do not feel really accepted in either cultural world. These factors have contributed to a "pancultural movement" among indigenous peoples in an attempt to reestablish lost traditions and tribal associations. This movement is a way in which to encompass tribal variation as a sort of reformation of Native traditions. Within this movement, multitribal groups are more likely to accept the rituals of other tribes. Therapists should anticipate that there will be residual unresolved emotional issues of loss and adjustment to this new "tribal association" for Native families. Additionally, family therapists should also anticipate the need to address *invisible family loyalties* (unresolved family debts or *family ledgers*) and *invisible cultural loyalties* (unresolved feelings or guilty feelings of indebtedness to the tribe, nation, or clan of origin to continue and uphold its cultural traditions and values).

24. The experiences of *historical trauma* and *tiers of trauma* (colonialism, socioeconomic and political dependency on the U.S. government, boarding school experiences, and the current cumulative effects of these traumas), as well as additional trauma (including forced sterilization; coerced relocation or forced migration; compulsory assimilation, such as in mission schools and child welfare placements of Native children; and U.S. policies aimed at the assimilation, genocide, and extermination of First Nations peoples; cultural bereavement; and intergenerational post-traumatic stress disorder) all create an enormous need for First Nations peoples to grieve their many losses. Leading scholars in the field of study of Native cultures agree that Native individuals and families have never been able to adequately mourn the events that have happened to their ancestors. This unresolved grief (a result of *intergenerational trauma*) is considered to be the root of many contemporary social problems of First Nations peoples, and it will be emphasized as a central family therapy concern throughout the remainder of this chapter (Brave Heart, 1999, 2000, 2001, in press; Brave Heart-Jordan, 1995; Brave Heart-Jordan & DeBruyn, 1995, 1998; Duran & Duran, 1995; Duran et al., 1998; Hall, 1986; Johnson & Johnson, 1998; Kuerschner, 1997; Lum, 2002; Red Horse, 1980a, 1980b, 1982; Red Horse, Lewis, Feit, & Decker, 1978; Sue & Sue, 1999; Williams & Ellison, 1996).

All these factors take on a great deal of significance as family therapists begin to apply family theory and family therapy models in practice with First Nations families. Let us move now to the application of specific family theories and family therapy approaches, keeping the listed factors in mind to give shape and direction to clinical interventions so as to inform a more *Nativecentric* approach to family therapy with First Nations families. A Nativecentric orientation or worldview can provide for a sort of *cultural holding environment* (a more culturally nurturing and supportive setting) to protect Native families from further psychocultural assaults within the context of the therapy process.

Family Communication Theory

Family communication theory pertaining to daily interactions among family members has a great deal of relevance and applicability in family therapy with First Nations peoples. The following discussion focuses on family communication theories and family therapy approaches and is organized into two parts. The first section describes principles of family behavior from the perspective of family communication theory. The second section describes practice principles derived from the family communication therapy model. These sections will take into account political factors, cultural values, worldview, and family structure of First Nations peoples as previously discussed and articulated in this chapter.

Communication Principles of Family Behavior as They Relate to Understanding First Nations Families

Discussion of the major principles of family communication theory will rely primarily on the works of Virginia Satir (1986; Satir et al., 1975). Satir, known to many as the "grandmother" of family therapy, originally constructed her family therapy model with a focus on communication and problem solving (Duhl, 1989). During the course of her career, she experienced a shift of emphasis in her philosophy and began to incorporate existentialist philosophical notions into her already well-established and well-received family communication approach. Her revised family therapy model came to be known as *the human validation process approach* (Satir, 1986). Satir's revised approach retained important basic tenets of family communication behavior, such as the value of open and honest communication among family members and clarity of roles. However, her revised model also began to incorporate, in a very significant way, a *humanistic* focus. The end result is a family communication model of therapy that is an excellent philosophical fit with the cultural values of First Nations peoples. The underlying value and theoretical assumptions of Satir's communication family model is also an excellent theoretical and philosophical fit with the critical constructionist perspective, as outlined and conceptualized in this volume (see chapter 1).

Specifically, Satir's revised human validation model emphasizes the growth potential of all individuals. This value assumption is extremely consonant with traditional Native families' approach to child rearing, in which a great deal of faith is placed on the child's inherent ability to evolve into a good decision maker if encouraged and allowed to flourish. Satir places great value on the therapist's roles of *observer, role model,* and *educator.* The therapist's role as the Elder, so to speak, within these family sessions is also consistent with Native families' expectations that family members will derive a great deal of their learning through listening, observation, and emulation of Elders and family members, who are seen as role models and teachers.

Satir's conceptualization of key therapist tasks takes on a decidedly social constructionist flavor in that she views these tasks as to *observe* and *describe* what is going on inside the family system from a position outside of the system—an idea central to the postmodernists. That is, the postmodernist approach is to *facilitate* a better understanding of the meanings behind communication and to *empower* the family to discover new ways of coping by *opening up spaces for alternative stories or actions.* Satir has always believed in the growth potential of individuals, their ability to make their own choices, and has clearly displayed within her family practice model how much she values clients' knowledge of their own lives.

Native families and family members' use of silence can evoke misconceptions. It is true that sometimes silence is used as a safe response to defend against outsiders who are considered intruders. However, silence is also a customary practice among First Nations peoples, especially during the beginning phase of a social contact. There is no urgent need to jump into conversation; that may be offensive to the other person. Prolonged silence may also be due to a Native family or family member taking time to reflect before responding, as a sign of respect for the listener. Silence can be comforting to Native family members, so mainstream family therapists will need to become more comfortable with extended periods of silence. There is something about time and silence among Native people that creates *oneness of spirit,* and this must take place before a meaningful conversation or relationship can occur. *Reflective dialogue* could provide for a quiet, culturally syntonic forum in which the Native family or family member can *critically reflect* on his or her experiences and *restory painful or debilitating experiences* so as to find or create new ways of coping with experiences of historical trauma (Rasheed & Rasheed, 1999).

Satir believes that as a person experiences successes in good communication and problem solving, *self-esteem* is enhanced. She believes that family problems are a result of poor coping; and poor coping is a result of low self-esteem. She states, "The person is not the problem, the coping is the problem" (Satir, 1986). Satir believes that good communication and problem-solving skills are essential elements for a satisfying family life. Furthermore, she believes that families under stress (such as Native families) may, over time, adapt dysfunctional (family) roles that do not serve them well. The *blamer, super-reasonable,* and *irrelevant* roles may be especially dysfunctional for Native families and family members, in view of prevailing traditional cultural values. For example, the blamer stance dominates, finds fault, and accuses; the super-reasonable stance remains detached, not emotionally involved in family processes; and the irrelevant stance serves to distract family members from the task at hand and seems to be unrelated to and disinterested in anything that is going on in the family. Clearly, any of these stances would be diametrically opposed to traditional Native cultural values of tolerance, compassion, respect, avoidance of direct criticism, group decision making, cooperative spirit, and collectivity. These values are but a few of the core cultural values that are violated by these dysfunctional family stances, and they should be viewed by the family therapist as serious threats to harmonious family life within First Nations families.

Other role conflicts may present themselves as challenges to Native families. *Role strain* and *role conflict* may result as a consequence of *mixed acculturative patterns,* resulting in *acculturative tensions and conflicts* (both between and within Native family members). Traditional roles that formerly helped to establish and define important developmental milestones for age, gender, community, or family roles may no longer be available to isolated, marginalized, or biculturally conflicted families living away from reservations or disconnected from a Native community and extended family members. First Nations families will need assistance in communicating about these painful issues and will need even greater assistance to move toward problem resolution.

The human validation process model advocates for clear and direct communication but not directive communication (Satir, 1986). The difference is this: *Directive* communication is an "in your face" communicative style, whereas *direct* communication conveys a clear message that is not ambiguous, dishonest, or vague. Native family members show respect for each other in their use of indirectness. Direct criticism is to be avoided and is preferably placed within the *metacommunication* of a message (the message about the message) along with more powerful nonverbal cues. This more indirect style of communication is viewed as being more polite and respectful and less aggressive. There is more reliance on nonverbal cues to relate a message; hence traditional Native families are considered to be more of a *high-context communication culture* (Hall, 1976). This concept describes a culture that relies heavily on the nonverbal aspect of a message (how it is said) to relay some of the most important and powerful aspects of a message. Conversely, in a *low-context communication culture,* the most important and powerful aspect of a message is contained within the verbal component of a given communication—as in the case in Eurocentric cultures.

Communication theorists agree that *all behavior is communication.* Additionally, within all human communication there is the *verbal component of a message* (what is being said) and the *nonverbal component of a message* (how it is being said). Native families view communication as an opportunity to affirm concern for others and to convey respect for others. Hence, relationships are seen as being an opportunity to develop and establish one's character and integrity as a person, which is vastly more important within First Nations cultures than the purpose of establishing who holds the power in the relationship, which is important in Eurocentric communication styles. This cultural value is precisely the reasoning behind Native cultural dislike of the preferred firm American handshake and direct eye contact. These nonverbal behaviors, as well as the *meta-communication* embedded within the messages they convey, are "power moves" that are devalued by First Nations peoples. Some communication theorists posit that every relationship contains within it an implicit power struggle over who defines the nature of that relationship (Haley, 1963). Native families and family members' interaction with others is more *collateral* (cooperative versus competitive) in nature, and the use of covert power (via verbal or nonverbal means) to manipulate a relationship is shunned. Hence the stark contrast between varying worldviews.

Linguistic obstacles may undermine family communication processes; that is, indigenous family members may speak different native languages or dialects. Linguistically, family members may be at different levels of acculturation and assimilation, rendering family sessions much more difficult to conduct. Additionally, varying *levels of acculturation* within the same family can create acculturative tensions within First Nations families. Differences in acculturative behaviors (especially within the realm of communicative behaviors) may complicate the communication process for Native families. Specifically, incongruous communication could occur and might take the form of inappropriate communication or behavior that is (however unintentionally) invalidating to other family members (Satir, 1986). The family therapist is encouraged to pay special attention to the nonverbal content of family messages, given the high-context culture of more traditional Native families.

The effects of acculturation and assimilation, as well as the effects of migration on the family life cycle, have forced Native couples to renegotiate their relationship. Traditionally, Native couples have had a much more egalitarian relationship than other ethnocultural groups. Their need for economic survival in a hostile environment has forced their relationship to shift more from a symmetrical (similar) to complementary (dominant/submissive) relationship. This shift often complicates the couple's relationship and family life, as this relational shift occurs at a time when the family's emotional support system has been weakened and the demands for meeting basic family needs such as food, housing, and healthcare are even greater. Native couples (especially those couples that have varying acculturative behaviors or are from different tribes, with different conjugal structures) need to be helped to "find their own way" so to speak, to determine for them what blend (if any) of traditional tribal versus acculturated conjugal behaviors will work for them. The family therapist is advised to facilitate the couple to *reauthor their (ethnocultural) conjugal narrative*, which will help them to resolve the power issues and move past these dilemmas.

The problem of internalized racism, that is, viewing oneself in the same negative light as does one's oppressor, is of particular concern and relevance in practice with Native families in view of pervasive and enduring negative and destructive societal racial stereotypes that continue to be perpetuated upon First Nations peoples. This internalized oppression (accepting the negative messages and stereotypical images of others) is no doubt the psychological result of hundreds of years of racial and cultural genocide. The vestiges of racism continue to persist today, as in the case of the previously referenced "Indian" sports mascots. Indigenous family members need to be empowered to challenge these *globalized interpretations* of their culture and *deconstruct debilitating and nonpotentiating ethnocultural metanarratives* so as to enable their families to *reconstruct new, more potentiating narratives* for themselves.

Other painful (perhaps even taboo) subjects, such as "historical trauma" (coerced relocation; forced migration; loss of tribal affiliation either through extermination, termination, or relocation; relatives' experiences with boarding and mission schools; compulsory assimilation; child welfare experiences; forced sterilization; and the cumulative effects of attempts at racial and cultural genocide), are emotionally intense and painful subjects for First Nations peoples. These emotionally laden issues may have become the source of *family secrets, myths* and *rules* governing family and individual behavior. There are many potential areas of unresolved grief that may have become forbidden subjects for family discussion. Native families and family members may be suffering from post-traumatic stress syndrome, and the family therapist can be helpful by engaging the family in *externalizing conversations* wherein family members provide accounts of the historical traumas in their lives (emotional state, familial, peer), making it possible to externalize the problem so that is not nested in the individual or within the family (Laird, 1993; White & Epston, 1990). Families can also be encouraged to *restory* some of these traumatic experiences, to allow the family and its members an opportunity to locate the (specific) *origins of immobilizing aspects* of these experiences and losses (Laird, 1993). First Nations families and family members should then be encouraged to *reconstruct a narration of oppression and resilience* that *challenges disempowering sociopolitical and sociocultural metanarratives*. The family therapist will need to take great care and caution in approaching these subjects, especially as an outsider.

The principles of behavior derived from family communication theory can contribute significantly to understanding the dynamics and interaction of a First Nations family. The following discussion aims to further explicate the matter in which these family communication principles can be applied to actual work with Native families.

Communication Practice Principles as They Relate to Work With First Nations Families

First Nations families' experience with public institutions has historically been that of deception and betrayal. This unfortunate history explains in part why Native families prefer Native therapists and why they seek help from mainstream societal agencies only as a last resort. The challenge on the part of the therapist working with Native families is to "join" the family and be accepted by them. Specifically, *cultural joining* (Rasheed & Rasheed, 1999) is the technique of exploring ways to make changes that are the most culturally syntonic to the family by including important cultural, religious, and/or civic leaders from the Native community. These persons can also serve as expert cultural consultants to the therapist and thus lend credibility to the therapy process. (A more detailed discussion of the clinical issue of engagement of Native families will be presented in Part 2 of this chapter.)

The communication theory is very useful in assessing the family system and interactive pattern, yet a therapist's role in engaging the family in renegotiation and redefinition of the power relationship is not an easy task. The concept of power is too controlling, interfering, noncollateral, disrespectful, and foreign to Native culture. In light of the history of exploitation, colonialism, and paternalism, family therapists' active leadership role prior to their acceptance by a First Nations family may easily be interpreted by the family as an unwelcome intrusion. The role of the therapist, as defined by some streams of family therapy, is that of a "metagovernor" or director of the family system, thus requiring intense active participation and at times manipulation (Haley, 1963). Therapeutic tactics such as *paradoxical messages* (*double bind*) and *prescribing the symptom* (encouraging the usually dysfunctional behavior) may be perplexing and appear disrespectful to most Native families. Rather, to begin the family therapy process slowly, expecting a longer period for engagement and assessment, while one assists the family with concrete needs such as transportation, food, housing, healthcare, and assistance with legal problems, is recommended instead. (We will return to this subject later in the chapter, in Part 2.)

The technique of relabeling or reframing (by emphasizing the positive) is more in congruence with the Native cultural emphasis on respect and individuality. A family communication therapist's emphasis on relieving concrete problems or suffering may be welcomed by the First Nations family, however, a rigid adherence to time-limited behavioral change may be offensive to the family's traditional time orientation.

Satir et al.'s (1975) cognitive approach, to teach family members to recognize family roles so that the family rules and interactional patterns may be changed for the sake of benefiting the entire family system, has great appeal in the light of Native cultural values with their emphasis on cooperative group effort. Such cognitive understanding should not be attempted until a trusting relationship is developed between the therapist and the family. Understanding and changing interactional patterns require the therapist to acknowledge the extended family ties and multiple-household framework. Native families may also require help in the constant renegotiation of expectations of roles within the family, given a constantly changing environment and forces of acculturation and assimilation within the family. Additionally, with the increase of intermarriage between tribes and with non-Native persons, there will be even more of a need for the family to possess sound communication and problem-solving skills.

Satir's (1967, 1986) emphasis on "good feelings" within and among family members is consistent with Native teachings of harmony, collaterality, and the general goodness of man. Her use of family history, which she calls "family life chronology" (Satir, 1967), can be an invaluable *narrative tool* in helping the family reminisce and value its past, as well as work through the tremendous number of losses (historical trauma) experienced by First Nations families. This discussion can also lead to the exploration of the influences of intergenerational migration and tribal and community dislocation and acculturation, and it may be critical to helping the current family members better understand new family system dynamics.

Native peoples' reliance on the *use of metaphors and storytelling* (to pass on cultural values and religious beliefs and to transmit and punctuate specific messages) is a natural fit with the critical constructionist view. The pancultural (Native) movement, wherein new tribal affiliations are formed along with new traditions, may pose new challenges for Native families who have joined this movement in an attempt to reclaim and restructure tribal heritage. Native families and family members can be encouraged to relive important aspects of their original traditional tribal heritage by storytelling, which may serve two purposes: It can reinforce positive self-images (or *build potentiating ethnic narratives*) to combat what many feel to be a deterioration of all that once was sacred and important, and it may serve to pass on important cultural images and memories toward the nurturing of positive ethnic identities (narratives) in children. To this same end, First Nations families should be encouraged to perform or reenact missed rituals (e.g., naming ceremonies, drumming circles, talking circles, releasing the spirits, wiping the tears (Brave Heart, 1999, 2000,

2001, in press; Brave Heart-Jordan, 1995; Brave Heart-Jordan & DeBruyn, 1995, 1998; Duran & Duran, 1995; Duran et al., 1998; Hall, 1986; Johnson & Johnson, 1998; Kuerschner, 1997; Lum, 2002; Red Horse, 1980a, 1980b, 1982; Red Horse, Lewis, Feit, & Decker, 1978; Sue & Sue, 1999; Williams & Ellison, 1996).

Family therapists need to proceed with caution in implementing some of Satir's (1967, 1986, 1988) experiential techniques such as *family sculpting, family choreography, drama, communication stances, family stress ballet, ropes,* and *parts party.* These techniques may be potentially very helpful in family therapy with Native families who emphasize learning by observation and participation and a reliance on rich metaphors to impart important messages and teaching, but family therapists must take great care not to intrude and otherwise impose their own "sculpting suggestions" (asking family members to take certain positions, etc.), because these may violate (sex role and family) cultural norms and ideals of polite, respectful, and appropriate behavior. For example, among the Lakota, there has been strict regulation of cross-gender interaction patterns between siblings and males with their mothers-in-law (limited direct verbal communication in both directions), as well as other cultural taboos concerning direct eye contact and the expression of overt physical affection in front of outsiders, particularly non-Natives (Wintemute & Messer, 1982; Brave Heart, 2001). On the other hand, open expression of positive and respectful verbal and nonverbal communication among older family members are expected and accepted (Wintemute & Messer, 1982).

To communicate effectively with First Nations families, family therapists need to consider modifying their behavior, such as limiting verbosity, slowing speech, and lowering their voice. Therapists should not rush to speak after posing questions (unless they are asked to), as silence may be a period of thoughtful reflection on questions asked. They can communicate by paying attention to family members' needs and by respecting them as worthy, good individuals. Therapists can communicate effectively by not being overly dependent on the verbal mode of interaction; instead, family and family members' use of metaphors in story telling and within other oral Native traditions, poetry, journals, artistic ability, musical talents, and other natural assets can be used to facilitate communication. A more varied use of untapped clinical data and sources is very much a postmodernist notion (Rasheed, 1998). Native families should be encouraged not to strive for consensus but to *explore the multiple (emotional) meanings* of important historical and cultural events and experiences. Family members then become empowered to take from these experiences what is most meaningful and helpful to them (Laird, 1993).

Family Structure Theory

The discussion of family structure theory here centers on behavioral principles and family practice principles. The first section examines family behavioral principles of family structure theory. The second section presents family practice principles of structure family theory as they relate to assessment and therapy with First Nations families.

Family Behavioral Principles of Family Structure Theory as They Relate to Understanding First Nations Families

The family structure theory strongly adheres to the system outlook and was primarily developed and advanced by Minuchin (1974) and Bowen (1978). Murray Bowen is the person perhaps most closely identified with the intergenerational perspective. Rather than observe the basic elements in a family transaction, the structuralists are interested in how the family is organized or structured. Although it stresses the importance of the individual's right to make his or her own decisions, the Native family is deeply immersed in a family system that extends beyond kin to nonkin (as in namesakes) and beyond the nuclear parameter to include multiple households. The central concept in Bowen's theory is *differentiation* as it relates to the interpersonal, intrapersonal, and intergenerational process. Bowen's concept of a *differentiated person* (and the opposite concept, *fusion*) in intrapersonal terms appears to apply to Native People's idealization of a well-adjusted person who knows when and how to use his or her "head" as well as how to express emotions. In the sphere of interpersonal activities, this same person is able to maintain a *solid* (nonnegotiable) *self* in relationships within and outside the family and to take comfortable "I" positions. He or she does not forsake intellectual and emotional integrity to obtain approval, love, peace, or togetherness. In the sphere of family relationships, differentiation refers to the family's ability to accept change and difference in its members. The less differentiated, more fused person is often trapped in a world of feelings, buffeted about by emotions or emotionally directed activity, and is more susceptible to dysfunction when confronted with stress. The respect that Native culture bestows upon each family member should make Bowen's theory extremely (philosophically) compatible. The actualization of the differentiation concept may be difficult for a Native family whose children do not grow up in their own family with the support and teaching from the traditional extended family. It is estimated that 20% to 25% of First Nations children are raised outside their natural family network (Vidal de Haymes et al., 2002).

In general, it is true that the process of *multigenerational transmission* is linked to the family of the past, but the level of differentiation in an individual may not be closely determined by the differentiation level of one's parents, by sex, or by sibling position, as advocated by Bowen (1978). The rationale behind such uncertainty is that the typical Native child experiences a broader sphere of interaction with extended family members in many households, as compared to an Anglo child's limited interaction with only nuclear family members. Thus in the assessment of a First Nations family's relationships, greater attention should be devoted to the extended family relationship and framework.

Similarly, Bowen's (1978) concept of *family projection process,* in which parental emotions help to shape and define what the child becomes even though the shapes and definitions may have little to do with the original realities of the child's environment, may not be applicable to traditional Native families, in which child rearing is not the sole responsibility of the biological parents but a common, shared duty of the extended family. A close relationship between child and grandparents (or the person for whom the child was named) may have more to do with the family projection process than the relationship between the child and the biological parents within traditional Native families.

The *triangle,* or three-person system, which Bowen (1978) considers the "basic building block" of all emotional systems, also has a different meaning when applied to a traditional indigenous family. In a multiple household with extended family, the parental or spousal system is seldom as central (meaning the only other emotional subsystem or emotional dyad present in the household, outside of the sibling subsystem) as it is in a single nuclear household system. In fact, the conjugal dyad may play a minor role in the overall parental subsystem, depending on family circumstances. If the spousal system is under stress, such individuals as the person for whom the child is named, cousins, aunts, uncles, or even non-blood relatives can become the vulnerable other person in the (emotional) *triangle.* Relationships between grandparent and grandchild, the person for whom the child was named, an older sibling, an aunt or uncle, or other relationships may run the risk of *triangulation* in times of stress; again, the grandparent spousal system in a traditional Native family is also not as intense as it is in the Anglo grandparent system.

We introduced the concept of *invisible cultural triangles* (Rasheed & Rasheed, 1999) as an expansion of Bowen's triangle concept. We reconceptualized the concept of triangles to refer to the existence of a third person, object, or event in the cultural system that exerts a powerful but not always apparent force on the systemic or dyadic relationship system. Historically traumatic events and experiences (as in the case of the Native holocaust or painful assimilation experiences) can become *triangled* into the emotional system of Native families and *create immobilizing and debilitating ethnocultural (family, community, tribal or clan) narratives.* These *sociopolitical narratives* can take on a life of their own; hence the family members or family can become victims of a *collective narrativized past* or at least a *narrative stance* that does not work for them (or their family).

A related term also coined by the authors is the concept of *invisible cultural loyalties* (Rasheed & Rasheed, 1999). This concept is an expansion of the family therapy (intergenerational) concept of *invisible loyalties,* also referred to as *relational indebtedness* or *family ledgers,* as originally conceptualized by

Ivan Boszormenyi-Nagy (1987). Invisible loyalties or *family indebtedness* can date back several generations and can also be a result of *multigenerational* and *cross-generational unresolved conflicts* or unrealized goals within the family (or tribal group; Boszormenyi-Nagy, 1987). Given the importance of preserving family legacies, continuing family cultural traditions, and attempting to preserve Native tribal customs, it is easy to imagine the emotional conflict that an indigenous family member may feel if this issue is not adequately addressed. Hence, *family secrets, family myths,* and (powerful, but unspoken) *family rules* may serve to further complicate and exacerbate emotional turmoil if they operate in tangent with invisible cultural loyalties or with invisible cultural triangles.

Bowen's (1978) concept of *emotional cutoff* has significant application in work with First Nations families. According to Bowen (1978), everyone has some degree of unresolved emotional attachment to the previous generation. The lower the level of differentiation, the greater the degree of unresolved dependency to be dealt with in the person's own generation and/or passed onto the next generation in the *family projection process.* The "cutoff" consists of denial and isolation of the problem while living close to the parents or by physically running away, as in the case of (voluntary) migration, or a combination of the two. Bowenian theory (1978) postulates that as a rule, the more a nuclear family maintains emotional contact with previous generations, the calmer, more orderly, and less problematic family members' lives will be. Conversely, the greater the degree of cutoff, the more the nuclear family becomes a sort of emotional "pressure cooker." This concept indicates the importance of First Nations peoples being able to maintain consistent contact with members of their extended family system.

Family structure theory focusing on the family system's structural (contextual) dynamics, especially the *creation, maintenance, and modification of boundaries,* which are rules defining who participates and how (Minuchin, 1974), is useful in work with Native families. In an extended family system with multiple households, the subsystem boundaries between spouses, grandparents, parents and children, and siblings seldom are closed or rigid. These subsystems are functional historically because of cultural value reinforcements. As times change and as First Nations families continue to migrate to urban areas (with fewer and fewer families living on reservations), the original extended family ties may have broken down. These factors, coupled with racial and cultural oppression and discrimination, financial problems, and poor healthcare, make it difficult for individuals in the traditional Native family to retain culturally adaptive, functional family roles and traditional boundaries.

The family system concepts of *boundaries, multigenerational transmission* (of family and cultural values), the *family projection process,* and *emotional cutoff* have important implications for First Nations parents (and their children) who grew up in boarding schools away from home. The fact that these schools were erected for the purpose of cultural genocide (forced assimilation), combined with the severely (physical, emotional, and sexual) abusive conditions endemic to all of these institutions, have profound multigenerational implications for today's First Nations families. The absence of parents, grandparents, the sibling subsystem, or any extended family in these horrific boarding schools profoundly deprived the children (now parents) of functional knowledge of their culture. As a consequence of the abusive treatment by the adults who ran these cultural prisons, those people who spent most of their childhood and adolescence in them were consequently left with little or no knowledge of appropriate and healthy parenting. They were left bereft of important parenting skills they needed as adults and as parents of their own children.

The family's ability to maintain traditional parent-child roles is further handicapped by the fact that both parents, and sometimes older siblings, have to work outside the home. Long working hours and different working schedules can create interactional problems and difficulty within a subsystem and between subsystems. For example, if the father (or even both parents) works a night shift, both parents will have little time to interact with each other to maintain and solidify their spousal subsystem. The parents may also have too little time with their children, and older siblings may have to assume parenting responsibilities in the family (boundary rupture).

Such a scenario traditionally would not have posed much of a problem, because First Nations families were able to maintain the larger parental subsystem typical of traditional culture. However, with increasing migration and relocation to secure employment, the Native family structure is becoming increasingly nuclear, single parent, and divorced. A ruptured system boundary requires that family members use a great deal of sensitivity, effort, and energy to repair it. Raising the issue of boundary conflicts and subsequent repair can disrupt harmony within the family and is discouraged by the traditional culture. However, this "boundary work" is becoming a growing concern and issue in family therapy with Native families. Finally, *boundary modification and repair* require that family therapists possess sufficient interpersonal communication skills to work with Native families in these areas.

Family Structure Practice Principles and Work With First Nations Families

Bowen's emphasis on differentiation of self (from the family "culture mass") as the primary goal of therapy has important implications and applications in work with First Nations families. Extended family ties are extremely important to a Native family. To some extent, a family framework can be used as a guide for assessment, for formulating therapy goals, and for the therapy itself. Bowen's concept of "self-determination" should not be misconstrued as individualism or narcissism; instead, it coincides with the Native concept of individuality. Individualism requires that uniqueness be deviation from the "normal." Individuality allows uniqueness to become the refinement of life, and it requires a philosophy that can give understanding and meaning to the world. Hence, a differentiated person is not a self-centered person but an individual who knows and values his or her past, including ethnic heritage and family background. A self-differentiated person is not only responsible for him- or herself but also responsible for others, especially family members and relatives. Yet sometimes there exist components of one's family background and structure that are dysfunctional and thus create or perpetuate disharmony within the entire family system. This culture mass, or *family ego mass,* to which Bowen refers is a condition that requires a family to disengage or engage differently to ameliorate present family problems.

Family group interaction characteristic of Native culture should be conducive to conjoint family therapy (with every family member present). However, the format and structure of conjoint family therapy with the therapist in charge may be too rigid and, therefore, unnatural to the Native way of interaction. Instead, the therapist may need to capitalize upon the ceremonial feasts and encourage families to perform or reenact missed cultural rituals (Brave Heart, 2001; Lum, 2002; Red Horse, 1980b, 1982; Sutton & Broken Nose, 1996) as a means to facilitate family interaction.

Again, due to the unnaturalness of the formal family therapy format (as well as the history of oppression that First Nations peoples have experienced in contact with institutions), some family members may not feel comfortable and may remain unavailable for conjoint therapy. Bowen's (1978) technique of focusing upon one individual, usually the more differentiated or respected member in the family (or whoever is willing to come), should be useful. In any case, this individual could be a grandparent, older sibling, or other extended family (or tribal member) of either sex, depending upon the tribal affiliation of the family. Although the therapist will be working with an individual, the goal is to modify the structure of the emotional system of the family through that individual's change and effort.

Bowen's (1978) detached but interested, rational, calm, low-key approach to problem solving again corresponds closely to the Native cultural emphasis on moderation, patience, and self-discipline. His efforts in taking careful family history (multigenerational transmission records) reflect his sensitivity and respect for the cultural nurturance system, migration process, intergenerational perspective, and the need for individualizing each family.

Bowen's (1978) belief is that the therapist should be a *coach, facilitator,* and *consultant.* This therapeutic style is very compatible with a social constructionist practice framework in that Bowen's primary goal in this therapy model is to coach the family and family members through a self-discovery process by constructing a narrative of the family's history, primarily through the use of the *genogram* (a multigenerational diagram of family information). In this model of family therapy, the client is the expert in charge of the data collection process. The therapist is merely there to help the family and its members sort through their emotional reaction to the meanings that the family and family members ascribe to various family information gathered about family relationships, family patterns, and family (emotional) processes. For the most part, the family or family member sets the goals and desired outcomes, as well as determining how current family relationships will or will not change. Hence, Bowenian family therapy does not rely upon or employ the therapists' *privileged ways of knowing* about the family in this approach. The family or family member is free to create or discover the *collective narrative of the family* as the therapist creates *a space for multiple meanings* of the family's experience.

In light of the emphasis on the rich historical, cultural, and familial traditions of indigenous cultures, it is especially important for the family therapist to empower the Native family and its members to *locate the origins of individual personal narratives*—especially those that are *debilitating* and *nonpotentiating* (Young, 1996). The genogram can provide a way for the family therapist to help the family and its members *locate the origins of immobilizing, subjugating narratives* and their context and significance (e.g., historical, political, economic, sociocultural, familial). This discovery process may uncover family myths and family secrets derived from generations of dysfunctional family emotional processes and show them to be the source of the emotional pain for the family or individual family members. The discovery process may uncover societal prejudice, discrimination, and racism at the root of troubling *ethnic narratives* (*marginalized* and *negative stereotypical narratives*). Creating space for more *empowering liberating narratives* makes it possible for the family and family members to revise and reconstruct these stories (a *reauthoring, restorying,* or even *racial restorying process*) that can offer new information, new resources, and multiple opportunities (Freeman, 1992). It is also important to note that in light of the cultural value of indirect communication (which avoids confrontational power struggles), these reauthored stories can reflect each family member's unique emotional experience and hence unique interpretation, thus helping to maintain important close family ties as *multiple (emotional) meanings* are encouraged.

There are many advantages to the Bowenian family therapy approach in light of the traditional values of the Native family. Family work can still be conducted even when families are separated by long distances as a result of migration and relocation (on or off the reservation) or relocation to other states or cities. Because all of the subsystems and dyads within the family are not required to be present at the same time for family therapy to proceed, potentially explosive and volatile *cross-generational tensions* and *conflicts* need not be exacerbated. Family members can sort through issues such as *generational splits* and acculturation tensions and conflicts. Family members can then repair emotional cutoffs (caused either by forced physical separation or via emotional detachment that acculturative conflicts may have exacerbated) and begin to repair other (emotional) damage that *cultural transitioning* may have created in family emotional relationships, in a much less emotionally charged atmosphere.

First Nations families can be encouraged to seek out "new family members" by creating new families, as in the case of *hunka* (the making of relatives), which results in a sort of surrogate family for clients who may be estranged from family members. Through a ceremony binding the participants' spirits—a condition considered more sacred than biological kinship—this ritual creates a potentially powerful support system and may provide alternative psychological resources if immediate kin are too far away, emotionally unavailable, or embroiled in dysfunctional family patterns (Brave Heart, 2001).

Minuchin's (1974) differential applications of *joining techniques,* which focus on the beginning phase of therapy, reflect his sensitivity to individual family differences and the understanding that structural change in a family usually requires time and patience. His *maintenance technique,* whereby the therapist is organized by the basic rules that regulate the transactional process in a specific family system, goes a long way toward helping to establish mutual respect and trust with the family.

Although Minuchin's (1974) joining and maintenance techniques are compatible with Native family values and structure, his *disequilibration techniques,* or *family restructuring techniques,* generally do not share the same degree of congruence and effectiveness with this specific ethnic group. These techniques, including *enactment* and *boundary marking, escalating stress* (by emphasizing differences), *physical movement, utilizing the symptom* (by exaggerating it), and *manipulating the mood* (by escalating the emotional intensity), are much too esoteric (not practical or immediately useful), too directive, disrespectful of harmony and balance, and emotionally confrontive, and they are therefore antithetical to Native culture. With modification, however, these techniques may work with bicultural or highly acculturated Native families and family members.

The concept of *soul wound* has been an integral part of the knowledge of First Nations peoples ever since Columbus landed in this hemisphere and Cortez arrived in Vera Cruz, Mexico (Duran et al., 1998). Today's scholars of First Nations peoples have come to refer to the soul wound as "historical trauma"; and "healing the soul wound" of Native people is seen as one of the most important clinical tasks for those working with Native clients (Brave Heart-Jordan & DeBruyn, 1995). Bringing validation to a community and providing a clinical context in which Native people can grieve the many losses that they have experienced as a result of the Native holocaust has critical mental health implications for many generations of families to come. The critical constructionist perspective, along with an integrative approach to family therapy as articulated and advanced in this book, is offered as an approach for healing the soul wound of First Nations peoples. An ethnohistorical approach to family therapy with First Nations peoples, wherein a meticulous, detailed, narrative account of each person's (unique) emotional experience of the many losses and tragedies endured by First Nations peoples has the ability to complement existing intergenerational approaches that focus primarily on intra- and interfamilial issues and events. Taking an ethnohistorical account of how Native families and family members have come to construct their own *individual narrative,* thus allowing for a *reflective dialogue* that can lead first to a *deconstruction of marginalizing, immobilizing, ethnic narratives* (as well as *deconstructing negative sociocultural metanarratives* of the family group) and then empower Native clients to *reconstruct more liberating and potentiating narratives* of a tragic past, has the potential (we think) to allow the healing process of the soul wounds of First Nations peoples to begin.

The preceding discussion on applying culturally sensitive family theories aimed to provide a framework within which First Nations families may be understood and served. The communication and structure theories can be differentially applied in therapy with these families. Part 2 of this chapter explains how to integrate and apply these theories in actual work with indigenous families.

PART 2: CULTURALLY RELEVANT TECHNIQUES AND SKILLS IN DIFFERENT PHASES OF THERAPY

Beginning Phase of Therapy

The beginning phase of treatment in work with a First Nations family or family member is of paramount importance. This may be attributed to several factors. First Nations culture emphasizes self-determination and respects individuality. A family therapist will be consulted only if all other help-seeking attempts have failed. Further, First Nations peoples' unfamiliarity with family therapy and their lack of knowledge about what a family therapist can do makes the first-contact phase extremely precarious. As Sutton and Broken Nose (1996) have pointed out, studies show that First Nations people who do come to therapy hope that the therapist is an expert who can give them concrete, practical advice about their problems and be sensitive to their cultural beliefs and differences (Attneave, 1982; DuBray, 1993; LaFramboise, Trimble, & Mohatt, 1990; Polacca, 1995).

Therapists must also be cognizant of the historically racist relationship between First Nations peoples and the helping professions. Help has historically been rendered by missionaries, teachers, and social workers who have tried to "help" indigenous people by changing their value system, taking their children, and alienating them from the strength and support of their own people and heritage (LaFramboise et al., 1990; Sutton & Broken Nose, 1996). These experiences have led many Native people to distrust therapists and therapy.

In an attempt to make the family's first visit meaningful, a family therapist should be knowledgeable about First Nations peoples' central cultural themes, their historical experiences with helping professionals, and the theoretical concepts from communication and structure theories. This knowledge base can serve as a guide to interacting with the family from a *Nativecentric* perspective. Four specific skills and techniques are essential in work with a Native family in the beginning phase of therapy. These skills and techniques include (a) engaging the client or family, (b) cultural transitional mapping and data collection, (c) mutual goal setting, and (d) selecting a focus and system for therapy.

Relationship Skills and Techniques in Engaging the Client or Family

Engaging a Native family for therapy begins with understanding why the contact is taking place. Generally, rapport with a Native family should not be too difficult to establish if the initial contact to see the therapist is made by a member of the family concerned, especially if it is made by the head of the household, often the grandparent. Such a family usually is bicultural and has some knowledge and appreciation of family therapy. However, more typically, contact with family therapist occurs during a family crisis or when a member of the family runs into difficulty with such mainstream societal agencies as public schools, courts, public health, or human service institutions. In these cases, the family's mistrust level will be particularly high during the first contact with the therapist.

Therapists who understand the anxiety level of the family may still need to be reminded that Native families do not wish others to meddle in their private affairs. Furthermore, the family may have limited prior knowledge of what family therapy is and what a family therapist can do. The most familiar role in which the family can place the therapist is that of an indigenous healer (medicine man), who usually performs the service in a short time, with little involvement or participation by the family members. The family members are primarily observers of the ritualistic healing and helping service performed by the medicine man. Therefore, during the initial contact with the family, therapists need to be active and directive so that they can be accepted with a "quota of leadership" (Minuchin, 1974) similar to that of an indigenous healer. Unlike the indigenous healer, the family therapist begins a process of engaging the family members in the therapy process. The therapist must be aware that building credibility and trust with the family will be a very slow process.

Sensitivity is respected; uncertainty, insecurity, artificiality, and insincerity are unacceptable to a Native family. Although they may avoid eye contact as a means to convey mistrust or respect, Native clients are very observing. They have been long-time victims of oppression and exploitation and do not want to be gullible or taken advantage of again. It is important to note that the *character* of the therapist is as important as his or her professional credentials.

If contact has been initiated by the therapist, he or she needs to explain calmly and openly to the family who the therapist is, what the therapist's role is with the agency, and the reason for the interview. This kind of straightforwardness may be a breath of fresh air for the family, and they may be relieved to find hope for solving their long suffering with problems.

Open, caring, and congruent communication with the family on the part of the therapist should also be simple, precise, slow, and calm. The therapist's attention and concern for other extended members of the household will help the family feel that they are in good company with a stranger. There may be periods of silence, especially when the therapist introduces disturbing information or emotionally laden material. Therapists should allow themselves and the family time to gather their thoughts and emotions before pressing on to a new topic. Due to other stress factors in daily life, family members' testing period with the therapist, and the family's uncertainty as to how to resolve the family problem, the contact phase of therapy with a Native family may take longer than with a family from the dominant culture. It is important for therapists to respect the time differential and not overtly or covertly pressure Native families for activity. Should the therapist fail to stay abreast of the client's position, the family may adopt a passive-aggressive approach and agree with everything suggested by the therapist but do nothing afterward.

To minimize the unnaturalness of the initial therapist-family contact, Minuchin's (1974) maintenance technique is helpful. This "requires the therapist to be organized by the basic rules that regulate the transactional process in a specific family system" (p. 175). To do this, a therapist needs to be attentive, talk less, observe more, and listen actively. This approach is congruent with First Nations families' style of communication.

As a means to sustain the family for longer term therapy, therapists need to promote the sense that they are available at all times, including times of crisis. Thus, therapist-family contact should not be limited to weekly 1-hour sessions in the office. Therapists should also be flexible with appointment times. Some sessions can be conducted at the family home, and the sessions' duration may range from 20 minutes to 2 or 3 hours. Consistent with the First Nations peoples' cultural characteristic of giveaway, a family may give the therapist a gift at the end of a session to demonstrate their appreciation of friendship and collaterality. The therapist should receive it without worrying about potential client manipulation. The family does not expect the reciprocity of gift exchange, for they interpret the therapist's warm and helpful visit as a gift to them.

Skills and Techniques in Cultural Transitional Mapping and Data Collection

Despite Native families' continual efforts to resist acculturation, each family member is influenced to a certain degree by dominant cultural views. All family problems can, to some extent, be attributed to the family and the family members' coping mechanisms with the external world as it is controlled by the dominant culture. Therefore, it is vitally important in the course of the first stage of therapy that the therapist establish which phase of the process of acculturation the family is currently experiencing and how they have dealt with the vicissitudes of previous phases (Sluzki, 1979). Viewing the outside world with distrust and hostility, a First Nations family may maintain no meaningful contact with mainstream societal agencies, such as healthcare agencies. Such data need to be collected for future therapy purposes. Therapists should be prepared for an *elongated assessment phase* (Rasheed & Rasheed, 1999) because of the unique and complex societal factors affecting the lives of Native families. Family therapists are encouraged to use an *ethnographic* (anthropological) *approach* to assessing families (Rasheed & Rasheed, 1999) and to "view the family as tiny societies that over time, seem to develop their own systems of meaning and beliefs, their own mythologies, and ritual practices, and their own cultures" (Laird, 1993, p. 80).

Family data such as tribal identity and heritage, language spoken, physical health history, life-span and developmental history of family members, boarding school experiences, and migration process are critical in assessment. Considering the importance of extended family ties, a therapist needs to assess the strength or potential dilution of the present household boundary and support system. A sociocultural map should also include the transitional position of the multigenerational family. Bowen's (1978) concepts of differentiation, triangulation, and emotional cutoff can also be assessed by such cultural mapping. The technique of cultural mapping is very similar to the technique of constructing a *genogram* (Pendagast & Sherman, 1977). In making a genogram, a therapist inquires systematically into family patterns among aunts, uncles, siblings, cousins, grandparents, and so on in an attempt to gather information about patterns of closeness, distance, and conflict. A genogram generally assists the therapist in understanding multigenerational patterns and influences, that is, the history of the presenting family's difficulties, and can also provide the therapist and the family with some insights into how the family wishes the problem to be resolved (Wachtel, 1982). The projective nature of this technique makes it culturally relevant and compatible in work with indigenous families who wish to resolve their family problem in accordance with traditional cultural values.

However, in constructing a genogram, the therapist needs to phrase highly structured questions such as "How did your grandparents get along?" or "Who did your mother go to when she got mad at your father [triangulation]?" carefully and, if possible, spontaneously. To be less formal and structured but more flexible and creative, the therapist should not take notes during the interview. The family should be encouraged to share background information with pride and not simply as a means to disentangle present family problems. To this end, family members should be encouraged to tell "stories" of their family's experiences, paying special attention to oral stories about relatives, family traditions, customs, rituals, and folklore (Laird, 1993). This may be a more culturally sensitive and nondirective approach to obtaining information for the genogram.

To collect information on structural and communicative interaction, a therapist needs to visit the family at home and attend ceremonies where extended family members and multiple household members gather. The creative use of family photographs, indigenous crafts, poetry, and music (Ho & Settles, 1984) can go a long way toward collecting invaluable data regarding individual and family functioning. The technique of *cultural mapping* will be illustrated in detail in Part 3.

Skills and Techniques in Mutual Goal Setting

Minuchin's (1974) adaptation categories of family stress also are pertinent to First Nations families. These stresses include (a) stressful contact of one member or the whole family with extrafamiliar forces, such as work or migration; (b) transitional points in the family, including the death or birth of a new baby; and (c) idiosyncratic problems, such as a physical or mental handicap on the part of a family member. What should be added to Minuchin's list are those stressors associated with acculturative tensions, racism, and poverty. These additional stressors can create biculturally conflicted families who are at the greatest risk of role confusion.

Many clients' family problems are caused by the family's inability to provide basic needs such as food, shelter, and proper healthcare. Therefore, in the process of mutual goal setting, a therapist needs to be cognizant of the family's fundamental struggle for survival and satisfaction of basic human needs. Family therapists will do a Native family a disservice if they are overly concerned with psychodynamic structure and negligent of the family's basic needs. As the primary goal is met, more basic family systemic problems may emerge. Sensitive, effective, and speedy delivery of concrete services will contribute to a trusting relationship between therapist and family.

The process of mutual goal formulation should take into consideration First Nations peoples' cultural trait of interdependence. Group decisions take precedence over individual choice. Therefore, whenever possible, a therapist needs to involve all family members, even extended family members, in selecting a therapy goal. Sometimes the process of involving all relevant family members (and other tribal members) can be so therapeutic that further intervention by the therapist is unnecessary. This can be considered as a form of tribal network therapy (Speck & Attneave, 1974), in that the larger social network of the Native family is enlisted as a part of the therapeutic process.

As can be expected, group consensus in goal setting is time consuming, but a Native family has a flexible time orientation. The family can wait patiently for a group decision and will experience no urgency in completing certain tasks required of each family member for change. Hence, the time-limited and goal-directed mentality of the therapist may need moderation when working with a First Nations family.

For a therapeutic goal to have a chance for completion, it has to be realistic, comprehensible, and defined in concrete terms (Edwards & Edwards, 1984). Further, therapy goals have to be within the capacity of the client or family.

Skills and Techniques in Selecting a Focus and System for Therapy

The Native family nurturance system consists of extended family ties. The presenting family problem may involve an individual member of a subsystem, such as a spouse. Extended family relationships should always be kept in focus, especially during the assessment period. In work with a more traditional Native couple who are physically and emotionally neglecting their child, a family therapist's suggestion to see the couple as the targeted therapy focus, with the goal of repairing the spousal subsystem, may be confusing and offensive to the couple. This would totally neglect the dynamic function of extended family ties. If the grandparents of the child are contacted, they could either temporarily assume the child-rearing role, or they could remind the child's parents of their respective roles. Thus what is now considered as "kinship care" within contemporary child welfare literature is an integral part of Native culture. If the grandparents' marriage is matrilineal, the system unit to be selected for therapy should be the grandmother, because she is the most respected member of the extended family. Hence selecting a focus or system for therapy depends on the nature of the problem, the common and specific structure of the extended family, the acculturation level of the family, and the motivation and capacity of the subsystem unit selected. For instance, in the above family situation, should the grandmother refuse to work with the therapist or not speak English and no other interpreter is available, the therapist may need to consult with other respected family members. Perhaps a great-aunt can assume the role of the grandmother. On the other hand, if the couple is bicultural and the partners wish to improve their marital relationship as a means to provide better care for their child, couple therapy may be in order.

Realistically, there are situations when the therapist will have access to only one family member, preferably the one who is the most acculturated, self-differentiated, and respected. Bowen's (1978) family therapy theory, which focuses on self-differentiation, can be most helpful. Again, in applying the concept of differentiation, the family sphere of differentiation needs to be the starting point. Lack of differentiation can manifest itself in *enmeshment* or isolation (Minuchin, 1974), as in the case of emotional cutoff. Once the emotional cutoff is dealt with, the client can begin working on interpersonal and intrapersonal differentiation. Regardless of which family member is seen and what the focus of therapy may be, the therapist's beginning efforts must be directed toward resolving the external stress or meeting the basic unmet needs of the family.

Problem-Solving Phase of Therapy

In view of First Nations families' holistic, interdependent view of the world and their close interpersonal relationships, their interpretation of family problems and how these problems should be solved are important factors. The specific approach and direction adopted by the Native family for problem solving are guided naturally by their traditional value system and current capacities. Communication and structure practice principles no doubt have a great deal to offer a family therapist who is called upon to assist First Nations families. However, the degree of a therapist's effectiveness will depend on the differential application of these practice principles and how compatible they are with a First Nations cultural orientation. Eight skills and techniques of particular relevance in the problem-solving phase of therapy with First Nations include the following:

1. Restorying the narrativized past

2. Engaging in externalizing conversations

3. Reconstructing a cultural narrative of oppression and resiliency

4. Mobilizing and restructuring the extended family network

5. Promoting interdependence as a family restructuring technique

6. Employing role model and educator and advocate roles

7. Constructing new sociocultural metanarratives

8. Collaborative work with an indigenous healer or helper, paraprofessional, or therapist helper

Skills and Techniques in Problem Solving

The environment in which therapy takes place should not become another vehicle for forced assimilation or psychological racism and evolve into (yet another) imperialist, paternalistic, victimizing, traumatizing experience for First Nations families. Relabeling and reframing as interventive techniques serve as important practice skills. However, within the relabeling process, it is the therapist who is redefining the presenting problem for the family. These reframes certainly can and should encompass those external forces of families' life space that are really at the core of the presenting problem and that become entrapping niches for families and family members. However, the critical aspect of this particular technique is that it is, indeed, the therapist deciding or determining how problems should and can be interpreted. We contend that it is a much more empowering (and appropriate) experience for the Native family and its members to be accorded the respect and opportunity necessary to interpret their condition for themselves, using their own worldview perspective and cultural lens. By approaching the problem-solving phase in this manner, the therapist coveys a "critical consciousness" and a message of respect and sensitivity. It is then that the family and family members can become empowered by *restorying the narrativized past* in a way that acknowledges ecosystemically based obstacles the family has faced and endured, applying their own meanings and interpretations to their plight.

Indigenous families and family members should then be empowered to *reconstruct a cultural narrative*—not only of oppression (hence externalizing the problem), but also of *resilience*. The meaning or interpretation resulting from this *restorying process* may vary among family members. However, the important metacommunication conveyed by this process is that all family members, including the therapist, respect and value the individual (a core Native cultural value), as *multiple (emotional) meanings of historical trauma* are restoried by individual family members. Each individual is free to reconstruct his or her own (cultural) narrative of oppression and resilience. Hence individual family members are free to give voice to their own unique experiences (ethnic themes) and are not constrained by the metanarrative of their family or ethnocultural group.

Mobilizing and Reconstructing the Extended Family Network

One of the factors plaguing the Native family is the lack of extended family support due to the family's having migrated out of its native environment, where mutual inter- and intrafamily support was strong. This, coupled with the different acculturation rates of family members, make decision making and problem solving within the family extremely difficult. If parents defend against contamination by the dominant culture through totally retreating from the community at large, a

Native family can easily become *enmeshed*. This state of sociocultural isolation has been a contributing factor to many of the domestic violence and child abuse cases within Native families (Lewis, 1984). The skills and techniques used to mobilize the extended family network should be consistent with First Nations peoples' nurturance system, wherein family integration is not made rigid by a closed system. The following case vignette addresses the impact of social isolation on Native families.

Although a good student in the past, Debbie, the teenage daughter of the Tiger family, has been missing school recently. When the parents were informed of this, they displayed no surprise but expressed willingness to cooperate with the school official in getting Debbie back to school regularly. The school social worker, who served as family therapist, happened to live in the same neighborhood as the Tigers, and she volunteered to transport Debbie back and forth to school. Through this consistent relationship, the therapist became a trusted friend of the Tiger family. To express the family's gratitude and friendship, Mrs. Tiger provided the therapist with a regular supply of home-grown vegetables. Through this informal exchange, the therapist learned that the Tigers were totally shut off from the community, which Mr. Tiger labeled as "crazy" and "not to be trusted." Mr. Tiger did not have a regular job. "On his days off, he managed to get drunk," according to Mrs. Tiger. Although Mrs. Tiger was willing to get some therapy for their family problems, Mr. Tiger insisted that he would not have any of "that stuff" (therapy). After learning that the Tigers are religious individuals who attend church regularly, the therapist referred the Tigers to a minister for consultation. The minister, although a non-Native, was highly respected by the Native people in the community. The minister later introduced the Tigers to other Native people who attended the same church but belonged to different tribes. Through such extended interaction with other Native people, Mrs. Tiger became more relaxed and paid more attention to Debbie, who managed to attend school regularly without the family therapist's assistance.

As is clear in this example, a therapist's skills in mobilizing a social support network hinges upon familiarity with and respect for the Native person's need for safety and social belonging. Additionally, therapists need to familiarize themselves with available community resources, both informal as well as formal, and to make proper referrals as needed. Proper referrals, as indicated by the above case example, require a trusting relationship between the therapist and the family, the correct referral source, and the right timing.

Promoting Interdependence as a Family Restructuring Technique

Traditionally, First Nations family members grew up in a secure, comfortable environment wherein each individual knew the proper form of interactive behavior.

Because of changing times, the negative influences of public boarding schools, and the pressing demands of urban living, some Native families are caught in a bind, within the family as well as outside of the family. In addition to their lack of early role models and inadequate coping skills in a hostile environment, family members still retain such traditional practices as noninterference, leaving others alone, and allowing individuals to make their own decisions. Many Native families endure suffering as a way of life. A therapist can assist these families by encouraging them to reminisce about the interdependent qualities of traditional Native living.

First Nations people are not selfish or self-centered individuals; they are considerate and pay attention to others' needs, especially to the needs of other family members. Disillusionment stemming from contemporary life, acculturative tensions and conflicts, and basic survival demands to provide for the family can leave parents with no energy or resources. They need an impetus and, at times, a role model. A family therapist who respects First Nations culture can provide this and assist the families in interdependent living.

To effectively implement the technique of interdependence promotion, therapists need to serve as a role model. They need to spend time, however slow the process may be, involving everybody in the (extended) family in a *critically reflective* and collaborative problem assessment and solution formulation. Using the strategy of *cultural* or *therapeutic joining,* the therapist, along with the family, can determine what changes are more culturally syntonic to the family system (Rasheed & Rasheed, 1999). The therapist's knowledge and skills in group-work practice, including group structure, group membership, leadership, decision making, and dynamic communication, will be valuable in promoting interdependence within the family.

Employing Role Models, Educator Roles, and Advocate Roles

Many First Nations people grew up and were educated in boarding schools and out-of-home placements. In some tribes, there is a long history of intermarriage. Thus many Native people internalized parental role models that were incongruent with their tribal or Native cultural models. The child-rearing influence of the dominant culture and the different acculturation rates of family members compound the problem. Parents may lack the knowledge or skills to manage household tasks and educate their children to survive in a bicultural world. A therapist should be supportive in empowering the parents to develop the skills to survive in a bicultural world and maintain (and possibly enrich and deepen) their connection to their Native heritage.

A word of caution must be given at this point. In working in a supportive capacity with Native clients, therapists must keep alert to avoid reproducing in their interventions the paternalistic and racist orientation reflected in the boarding school movement. What should be kept in mind is that the goal of interventions grounded in an ecosystemic and critical constructionist perspective must be strengths based and empowerment oriented. The interlocking dimensions of empowerment are (a) the development of a more positive and potent sense of self, (b) the construction of knowledge and the capacity for a more critical comprehension of the web of social and political realities in one's environment, and (c) the cultivation of resources and strategies or more functional competence for the attainment of personal and collective goals (Lee, 1987).

At times, the therapist may need to function as a strong advocate for Native clients. This should be a form of advocacy that involves the client in the process. Because Native people often learn best by observation and participation, the therapist should talk less and do more when it comes to advocacy issues. For example, the therapist may need to accompany the parent, along with the child (or children), for healthcare and to pay utility bills before service is terminated. Some parents have no prior experience in dealing with community agencies or resources external to the family and need support in navigating through such bureaucracies. Because many Native families are the victims of societal lags and intentional or unintentional indifference by agencies and institutions essential to their survival and well-being, the therapist may have to serve as an *advocate* for the family. The role of an advocate is not an unbiased one. The therapist should collaborate with the family, as well as with other families experiencing similar problems. The success derived from advocacy can boost family morale in areas where, in the past, they had experienced only hopelessness and defeat. Through example, the therapist can teach, support, and thus empower the parents to develop a more potent sense of self, to understand the sociopolitical realities of their environment, and to obtain resources to support their personal goals.

As therapists assume the teacher role, their interaction with the family must be guided by both First Nations cultural values and communication and structure theories. They should explain to the family that some new skills they are advocating may conflict with the family's indigenous cultural traits but that these skills are essential for survival in the social and economic world of the dominant culture. Therapists should explain that the survival of the family is at stake and that family members' development of skills for coping and adapting in a dominant society does not entail forsaking Native culture. In taking this stance, therapists must take a *nonhierarchical position* with the Native family and become more of a *cultural consultant* in terms of articulating what the appropriate skills for survival are in the social and economic world of the dominant culture (Rasheed & Rasheed, 1999).

In the family's attempt to remobilize or restructure its extended family ties, it may also need skills essential for functioning as a nuclear family. Members may need help in strengthening subsystem boundaries, especially that of the spousal subsystem. Without the benefit of traditional extended family ties, parents may require assistance with assuming the executive role in a household. They may need to integrate some components of child-rearing practices from the dominant society so their children can succeed in public schools.

Constructing New Sociocultural Metanarratives

With the rate of tribal intermarriage increasing, it will become more important for indigenous couples to construct new *sociocultural metanarratives* that create new cultural traditions that are more functional for their particular marital union. Intertribal indigenous couples and couples within which partners are at different levels of acculturation may need to consider a cultural shift from one that espouses the traditional family to one of a pantraditional family. (See the earlier section on "Family Help-Seeking Patterns and Behaviors" for a review of the definitions of these terms.) Even in circumstances wherein both parties have become aware of conflicting tribal (cultural) traditions or different levels of acculturation or biculturalism that are exacerbating the conflict, the renegotiation process requires a great deal of skill on the part of the family therapist. Therapists must be careful to move slowly enough to allow the couple's relationship to survive these changes. Hence, a great deal of attention needs to be paid to feelings of anger, resentment, and loss; these issues and feelings must be resolved before proceeding with negotiations toward a new sociocultural metanarrative (which, hopefully, will be more functional for the intermarried or even mixed acculturated couple).

Mr. Dancewell belonged to a tribe that required the husband to move into his wife's household. The wife, in this particular tribe, had the primary responsibility for child rearing. The husband's responsibility was to raise his sister's children, especially the male children.

Mr. Dancewell moved with his parents to a large city when he was 15. When he was 20, he married his present wife, who was from a different tribe. His wife was impressed with Mr. Dancewell's interest and concern for young children, especially his sister's children. After Mr. and Mrs. Dancewell had a child of their own, Mrs. Dancewell was disappointed with the apathy her husband showed toward the new baby. She rationalized her husband's apathy by saying he did not relate to infants. She later discovered that Mr. Dancewell's behavior did not change as the child grew older, and this began to create problems in the marriage. After consulting with an elder from his own tribe, Mr. Dancewell realized that his tribe's sociocultural metanarrative was one of shared parental responsibility for his (biological) child. Because his wife was from a different tribe, she held a much different sociocultural metanarrative.

The circumstances in this example occur more frequently than most family therapists realize. When they happen, they should not be categorically labeled as client resistance. They should be carefully examined and respected. Often the therapist may need to explore with and seek help from tribal leaders, including the Elders and the indigenous tribal healer. Timely consultation and collaboration with indigenous healers is consistent with the ecosystemic principles of equifinality, meaning that a number of different interventions may, owing to the complexity of systems, produce similar effects or outcomes.

Collaborative Work With Indigenous Healers, Paraprofessionals, and Therapist Helpers

Indigenous healers, shamans, and spiritual leaders play a vital role in the lives of many First Nations families, especially those who have successfully held on to their rich tradition. Even for bicultural families, there still may be a need for an indigenous healer and spiritual leader, especially when a family member experiences grief that connects with early childhood experiences (Hanson, 1981). A family therapist should not hesitate to consult with a spiritual leader when the need arises. The leader should always be treated with professional integrity and respect. The useful technique of strategic collaboration with an indigenous healer or spiritual leader points out once again the important need for the therapist to view the family in a holistic fashion.

Native culture is diverse, and many families may resist certain aspects of the dominant culture, particularly a healthcare provider or family therapist. It is sometimes necessary to help the family without direct face-to-face involvement. When this is necessary, a *therapist helper* or *link therapist* (Landau, 1981) can be used. Such a person may be able to help the family resolve its problems according to its own customs and traditions. Ideally, the therapist helper is an Elder or grandparent who is highly respected by the extended family. When such a person is unavailable, another family member who sees the value of family therapy can assume the role of therapist helper. In some instances, the therapist helper does not need to be a member of the extended family but could be a highly trusted and respected individual. Once the therapist helper is selected, he or she needs to have coaching sessions with the therapist to determine an assessment and therapy plan for the family. The therapist needs to be open and to learn from the helper the family's strengths and problems and which direction to proceed in accordance with specific tribal beliefs and family behavior. The therapist provides the helper with professional knowledge regarding family structure, intergenerational perspective, and communication dynamics and skills essential to resolving family problems. Planned intermittent consultative sessions between the therapist and the helper are needed to monitor and stabilize change in the family. Because this technique aims at problem solving that is short term (four to eight sessions) in nature, it differs with Bowen's (1978) "coach approach," which is directed at multigenerational family systemic change. Bowen's approach usually requires a longer duration and a more intensive training and consultation for the "coach."

Evaluation and Termination Phase of Therapy

Family therapy with First Nations people is a continuous process that starts slowly and also ends slowly. The usual therapeutic mentality that assumes time-limited therapy with clear-cut, successful outcomes may not be applicable in work with this group. Rosen and Proctor's (1978) model for specifying and evaluating therapy outcomes is relevant in work with Native families. In evaluating therapy progress with Native families, three types of outcomes are to be expected. First are the *intermediate* outcomes, which contribute to or create a climate for continued therapy. Some families will only allow the therapist to help them with basic needs problems. When this is accomplished, therapy terminates. The therapist should not be discouraged that the family has decided not to work on their relationship problems, for this may happen later.

Second are the *instrumental* outcomes. When achieved, these are assumed to lead to the achievement of the ultimate outcomes without further therapy. This is particularly true with First Nations families whose basic needs are unmet or unattained. However, once those basic needs are met, the therapist could go on with the task of repairing relational bonds with the family. Third are the *ultimate outcomes,* which constitute the reasons for which therapy was undertaken. Examples of these outcomes include resolution of a child's adjustment problem in school or at home or problems with the marital relationship, alcoholism, and physical illness that are caused by family relationship disturbances.

Therapists may need to maximize their observational skills when evaluating a family's progress. They will need to ascertain whether further therapy is required. A therapist should participate in and be a part of the family's activities, including making home visits and participating in seasonal ceremonies and other rituals. Whenever the family can maintain an open system within the extended family, renew relationships with relatives, and deal effectively with societal agencies and resources, termination of therapy is in order. The intense interactive subsystem relationship characteristic of a nuclear family in a dominant society should not be used as a yardstick in evaluating a Native family. Instead, the inclusive, extended-family framework should always be kept in mind in the evaluation of a family's functioning.

Some family members are so psychologically isolated and emotionally deprived that the relationship with the therapist may represent the first stable, nurturing relationship they have ever experienced. They may interpret termination as a major loss in their lives. Therapists need to be comfortable with this type of client-therapist connection and not view such behavior as deceptive manipulation. The termination process should take into consideration the Native client's concept of time and space in a relationship. Because the relationship has taken a long time to build, it will also take a long time to end. Some families may never want to end a good relationship. They learn to respect and love the therapist as a member of their family, and they may wish to maintain contact with the therapist even after the successful achievement of therapy goals. Therapists should learn to treasure such a natural relationship and not allow their "professionalism" (or rather, differences in how boundaries between family helpers and families are drawn due to differences in culture value orientation and worldview) to spoil a genuine human sharing.

The preceding discussion should be helpful in understanding First Nations families and applying family structure and communication theoretical perspectives and (emic-based) *Nativecentric* practice principles using a critical constructionist perspective. Part 3 of this chapter will present a case example to explicate and delineate how these family theoretical perspectives and emic-based practice principles can be integrated into actual work with a Native family.

PART 3: CASE ILLUSTRATION

The Redthunder family was referred (to Dr. Ho) by a school counselor who claimed that 13-year-old Ron Redthunder was "beside himself." According to the counselor, Ron had been a quiet, "well-behaved" student and a good athlete. Over the past 3 months, Ron had "changed." He now attended school irregularly, with dirty clothes; exhibited destructive behavior in class; and refused to speak to anybody.

Convey interest in client.

Convey sensitivity and respect for client as an individual.

Create comfortable environment for client.

Convey Native time orientation.

To shift power position and to help client feel relaxed.
Client shows beginning of trust.

When Ron showed up in my office, I immediately told him that *I had wanted to come by his school* to visit with him but changed my mind, for I did not *want his classmates* to think that he was in trouble. Ron glanced at me and said nothing. He then glanced at some *Native art and craftwork* in my office. These had been given to me by my former clients. I asked him to feel free to take time to look at them. Ron was also interested in the wall poster with pictures of Navajo people. I asked *Ron to explain to me* what these symbols on the picture meant. Ron smiled and said that he wished he knew.

To establish "family" ties.

Then, hesitantly, Ron asked if I was *Indian.* I replied smilingly, "No, but *I feel we are cousins,* for history tells us that thousands of years ago, Native people migrated from China." Ron was very interested in my explanation and my ethnic background.

Client shows sign of trust.	He *volunteered* that he once heard a similar story from his grandmother, who died 3 months ago. I responded that I was sorry to learn about the death of his grandmother. Ron commented, "*It* [death of grandmother] *hit my mother real hard.*" I responded that his mother and grandmother must have been *very close emotionally.* Ron replied sadly with his eyes down, "Yes!"
Sharing family secret.	
Constructing a partial genogram.	
Respect client's time orientation and premature self-disclosure.	I did not wish to rush Ron at our first meeting, so I expressed pleasure at meeting him and talking with him. I briefly explained the agency (Transcultural Family Center) and my role as a therapist.
Entering into the client's space.	Because I was *interested in meeting his family,* with his permission, we arranged our next meeting at his home. As he parted he quipped, "Do you know karate?" I quipped back, "*Yes, I do know 'Hai-Karate.'*" We both laughed.
Use of humor.	
Flexibility with time.	My next visit with Ron and his mother, Mrs. Redthunder (R), took place at their home and *lasted 4 hours.* The first hour, Mrs. R *explained to me how to grow vegetables.* We visited the home vegetable garden. As Mrs. R became comfortable with me, she began to talk about her family background. She and her husband (Mr. R) met in Phoenix, Arizona, 15 years ago when both worked for a meat company. Mrs. R, a *Hopi* from New Mexico, grew up *on a reservation* with both parents, one brother, two sisters, and one male cousin. She recalled many *good times while growing up.* Five years ago, her mother's health began to deteriorate. Mrs. R invited her to live with the family. "I needed my mother as much as she needed me," Mrs. R stated.
Joining technique.	
Cultural mapping.	
Matrilineal family background, multiple household.	
Growing up with traditional values.	
Security of extended family ties.	

Depression caused by grief and disconnection.

Cultural taboo.

Allow client to gather her spirits without interruption.

Mother-son enmeshment, cause for Ron's school problem.

Less traditional, more acculturated.

Isolation partly caused by Hopi tribal practice, excluding husband from child rearing.

Weak spouse subsystem partly caused by triangulation.

Circular repercussion.

Systemic diagnosis.

Mrs. R volunteered that her mother's recent death was by no means a surprise, but it did immobilize her to the point that she *could not eat, sleep, or do her regular chores.* She felt that all her energy had "gone out" of her and that her financial inability to return her mother's body to the reservation for burial was something "that I couldn't live with. All this doesn't help my high blood pressure and dental problems," Mrs. R continued.

After a *long pause* (about 2 minutes), Mrs. R volunteered that if it had not been for her son, Ron, she could never have continued to live. I inquired to what extent Ron had comforted and assisted her. *"He* [Ron] *is the only person I talk to,"* replied Mrs. R.

In my next visit with the family, I had an opportunity to talk with Mr. R. He is a 41-year-old Pueblo who grew up in Los Angeles. His parents had died when he was young, and he had *limited knowledge of his tribal background.*

Mr. R. is a truck driver, on the road 3 weeks out of a month. He often expressed feelings about the road and complained, "I feel a *total stranger at home."* Mr. R elaborated that his wife would not involve him in the care of their son, and that the *marital relationship* had deteriorated. *"My being gone* so much of the time *didn't help,"* volunteered Mr. R.
The family's transitional cultural map is described in Figure 3.1.

Structurally, it is apparent that there is a cross-generational coalition between the mother and the son that excludes the father. This phenomenon was created partly due to cross-tribal child-rearing practices, the death of Mrs. R's mother, the husband's job, a general lack of extended family support, and the closed system that the family had with the community at large.

The enmeshment between the mother and son temporarily crippled the normal development of the acculturated adolescent son, whose need to individuate triggered his depression, which was manifested in problems at school.

Concrete service to meet basic needs; technique of joining.

As the first step to therapy, I took Mrs. R to *a free health and dental clinic* (the family was in a poor financial situation). Once the working relationship was secured, I involved the family in restructuring therapy through repairing the spousal relationship. This was hampered by Mr. R's consistent absence from the family because of his job. When Mr. R was available for couple interaction, Mrs. R had great difficulty in relinquishing her power role (a trait she had inherited from the Hopi tradition). When the couple bogged down and was frustrated with their instructed ways of interaction, they vented, *"Our folk did not talk to each other this way."* I was empathic with their concerns but challenged them to build an interdependent relationship and work for the well-being of the family.

Expected resistance due to cultural residues.

Technique of promoting interdependency.

Restructured extended family ties.

Aware of the influence of extended family ties, *I introduced the family to a pancultural First Nations organization.* There, Mrs. R met a distant cousin of her mother. Two months later, Mrs. R's cousin helped her secure a part-time job at the same place where the cousin worked. They later managed to take a trip back to the Hopi reservation. Mrs. R had an opportunity to participate in a burial ceremony and to *grieve over her mother's death.*

Created an open system external to family.

A traditional grief process.

Improved spouse relational subsystem.

The Redthunders' *couple relationship* progressed to a point where Mr. R. was willing to spend more time at home. He began to develop and enjoy *a new relationship with his son.* Ron no longer had difficulties at school.

Restructured father-son relationship.

Problem solving through system change.

Therapist as family member.

Good relationship never ends.

Giveaway practice.

Over a 6-month period, I had 14 contacts with the family. Most meetings took place in the family home. Some contacts lasted only 20 minutes; others lasted 1 to 4 hours. At the beginning phase of therapy, I *gave the family my home telephone number* to let them know I was always available. Since the therapy terminated, the family has continued to invite me to ceremonial feasts. Occasionally, they still supply me with home-grown vegetables.

Figure 3.1   Redthunder Family Transitional Cultural Map

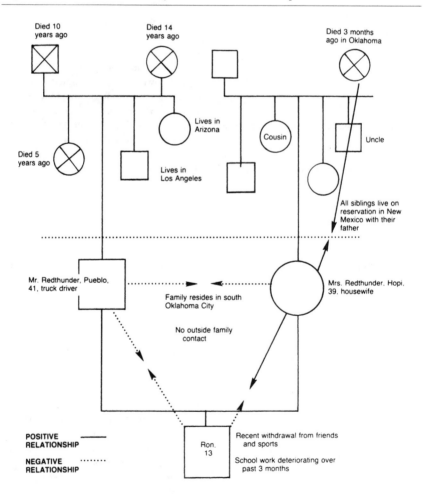

PART 4: CULTURALLY RELEVANT TECHNIQUES AND SKILLS FOR SPECIFIC THERAPEUTIC MODALITIES

Couple Therapy

Historically, when Native families resided with their clan and extended family members, there was less marital discord due to clear role expectations and a strong familial support system. As times change, Native families, like families of the dominant society and other ethnic groups, are subjected to rapid political and social change and ever-increasing demands within and outside the family. Native families gradually are forced to shift from inclusive extended family ties to an exclusive nuclear family system. Losing the support of the extended family network makes this change difficult. Another factor creating stress in couple relationships is the increasing rate of intermarriages (both intertribal and interracial). Intertribal marriages, as reflected in the Redthunder family, bring together different tribal cultures and customs, which can affect gender relationships and child-rearing practices. This factor, coupled with the varying degrees of acculturation (mixed acculturation patterns) among the partners, can affect the couple's relationship and their ability to resolve marital difficulties. Likewise, interracial marriages can create the need for the couple to negotiate different cultural values and worldviews presented by each partner to create a mutually satisfying *conjugal narrative*. If such negotiations are not done successfully and in a manner that meets the lifestyle goals and personal needs of each, the couple may encounter major difficulties in the marital relationship. High rates of divorce, along with other social indicators, further reflect difficulties in coping with traumatic historical and contemporary social forces that have been and continue to be disruptive of Native family life. When a couple experiences marital discord, other unresolved problems often appear, including domestic violence, alcoholism, suicide, and unemployment. Marital discord can also be reflected in parent-child conflicts, with the child bearing the parental marital symptoms, as reflected in the Redthunder family case illustration. Obviously, couple therapy constitutes one of the most important therapeutic modalities for the prevention of family breakdown and erosion. The following guidelines are suggested when providing couple therapy to a First Nations couple.

Assessing the Need for Couple Therapy

The focus of couple therapy must shift when working with Native couples. The primary focus of most clinical models of couple therapy is on the dynamic interpersonal relationship between husband and wife. The importance of this relationship centers on a nuclear family system framework, with the implication that the family has only nuclear family members to interact with and to meet the family's needs. However, such is not the case within a First Nations extended family system. Individual members grew up traditionally in an extended family clan system, and children tend to maintain such a system when they grow up, marry, and have children and grandchildren. This system provides them with security, hope, and the necessary means to meet their needs for problem solving, including marital problems. Hence it is vital that a couples therapist keep this emic, *Nativecentric* cultural framework in perspective when recommending couple therapy for problem solving with a Native couple. Therapists who neglect this framework may find it impossible to mobilize couples for problem solving.

Incorporating the Extended Family System in Couple Therapy

Using the extended family system framework, a therapist can assess marital problems according to the relational transaction the couple has with extended family members. Minuchin's (1974) system boundaries concept can be extremely helpful in assessing the degree of *enmeshment* or *disengagement* experienced by the couple. Couple enmeshment can take the form of excessive interaction between the partners and exclusion of other subsystems, such as children and other relatives. However, couple enmeshment within Native families may take place between one partner with members of his or her family of origin, such as a grandparent, father, mother, aunt, uncle, or cousin. Bowen's (1978) intergenerational perspective can be used to assist the enmeshed partner to redefine and restructure a new relational boundary.

Couple disengagement occurs most frequently among urban Native families who are burdened by different working hours, the rapid pace of urban life, and total isolation from the extended family and from the community at large. Often the solution to couple disengagement is mobilization and restructuring of extended family ties; when this is done, the couple can regain a support system. To do less means that the therapist may exacerbate further the couple's conflict and cause a breakdown of the marriage. At times, the general unavailability of extended family ties and the high percentage of intermarriage among urban First Nations peoples may leave couple therapy as the best viable alternative for resolving marital problems. Couple therapy can often be used to teach problem-solving skills, family development task skills, child-rearing skills, financial management, and sexual adjustment.

Assessing the Couple's Readiness for Couple Therapy

Couple therapy for problem solving with the family can be a totally new concept to many Native couples. In the past, couple conflicts were resolved within the extended family system or clan, with the Elders prescribing proper directions. Because self-disclosure is not a cultural ideal or goal within First Nations culture, disclosure of unpleasant marital secrets to a stranger may become totally unbearable. However, situations do develop in which a family therapist is called in for assistance. Such situations normally develop when the couple's child experiences behavioral problems at school or in the community, when a family member becomes seriously ill, or when a family member faces legal problems resulting from alcoholism, domestic violence, or other causes.

As First Nations peoples become increasingly acculturated and involved in intermarriages, more are seeking couple therapy to help resolve their problems. The therapist should first assess how ready each partner is for couple therapy. Factors involved in assessing the couple's readiness include (a) motivation (what brings the couple in for therapy), (b) each partner's level of acculturation, (c) the partners' ability to interact verbally in conjoint therapy, (d) traditional tribal practices relating to the husband-wife relationship, and (e) the level of realistic expectations by the couple of the therapist. Generally, the couple is ready and can benefit from couple therapy if the couple seeks it and both partners are committed to working toward improving their situation. The more acculturated the husband and wife are, the less resistive they will be in therapy.

Couple therapy will be valuable only if the couple can interact with each other and with the therapist. This can be difficult to assess initially because the cultural mandate of many Native individuals is to withhold verbalization of needs, wants, and feelings. Each partner may belong to a different tribe, each prescribing different sex-role relationships with children, in-laws, and relatives. The use of a genogram to sort out these differences at the beginning of a couple's therapy session can help the couple obtain a visual picture of these differences. Discussion around the data uncovered in the genogram can further facilitate interaction between the partners and interaction between the couple and the therapist.

Teaching Communication Skills to the Couple

Native couples, like married couples of other ethnocultural groups, wish to live in a harmonious relationship with each other. The nuclear family system created by the process of migration and cultural change forces them to interact intimately for daily problem solving. Often, couples lack the requisite experience, knowledge, and skill to manage the level of intimacy inherent in a nuclear family system. In addition, if the husband and/or wife grew up in boarding schools or away from home, they were deprived of a functional interactive couple model. Specifically, the couple needs to learn that conflict is an inherent part of an intimate couple relationship. The couple should learn how to detect conjugal problems before they escalate into an unmanageable situation. The partners need to develop these skills along with a sense of comfort in relating their feelings and intentions to each other. The couple needs to learn effective communication feedback skills and techniques so each partner can be listened to without disruption and distortion. To resolve a difficult problem in which both partners have a deep emotional investment, a structure for effective sharing is needed. In such a structure, a mutually agreeable time, place, and energy are reserved for problem solving. The couple needs to realize that although other basic needs of daily living, such as cooking, washing, and child rearing, are important and should take precedence, an effective couple relationship at times can be as important as or more important than taking care of those daily chores. If the couple's conflict remains unresolved, it drains their energies and effectiveness in performing the necessary daily family and household maintenance tasks. At times, one partner or the other can become physically ill and incapacitated because of continued unresolved marital strife.

First Nations people respect others and value egalitarian interdependent relationships. One strategy that can promote this sense of respect is *exception, survival, or possibility questions* (Saleeby, 1997). Through this form of questioning, the partners are encouraged to search for strengths within each other's parenting or other couple- or family-related tasks. They could be encouraged to amplify situations in which the partners perform in some outstanding manner in fulfilling their family responsibilities (Rasheed & Rasheed, 1999). Couple therapy can provide the missing link for their realization of a harmonious relationship and for understanding the strengths each brings to the relationship.

In the case of interracial marriages, which, depending on the level of acculturation of the Native person, may be bicultural as well, a couple may need to develop a communication format that allows them to articulate multiple meanings of their experience of culture in an interracial and bicultural relationship (White & Epston, 1990). The meanings that the couple attributes to their cultural experience will be shaped by their own culture of origin. A white partner will have different experiences than an African American partner or an Asian American partner. The therapist must be especially attentive to both invisible family loyalties and invisible cultural loyalties with an interracial couple. To the extent that these multiple loyalties negatively affect the relationship, it will be necessary for the couple to reauthor a new (ethnocultural) conjugal narrative that reflects both the merging of and the uniqueness of each cultural and family-of-origin perspective. The therapist can facilitate this process.

Using Cotherapists as Interactive Models

Consistent with First Nations peoples' learning style (observation and active participation), a cotherapist model can be ideal in couple therapy with Native couples (Norlin & Ho, 1974). Preferably, the composition of the cotherapist team should be male-female. The leadership style of the cotherapist team should be guided according to the tribal customs of the husband and wife. For example, if the wife came from a matrilineal tribe, the female cotherapist may need to be more assertive, at least at the onset of the therapy session. Leadership style on the part of a cotherapist team changes according to the needs presented by the couple in therapy. The cotherapist team approach provides a Native couple with many advantages, including (a) an effective interactive model for the couple to emulate, (b) a therapy process that resembles a natural extended family system interaction, and (c) a secure learning environment in which the couple can observe another couple (therapist team) disagreeing. It also serves as an educative and experiential tool to teach the couple how to express warm and supportive feelings.

Divorce Therapy

The divorce rate among Native couples is very high. This is to be expected, as many political and social factors are working against these married couples. These factors include the breakdown of extended family ties, highest rates of unemployment, unmet physical and economic needs, poor physical and mental health, and highest rates of alcoholism and attempted suicides. First Nations peoples' traditional respect for individuality and a person's right to make his or her own decisions, as well as their strong belief in noninterference, make divorce a socially acceptable behavior, and there is no negative stigma attached. Further, the unconditional acceptance of a divorcee by the extended family and the practice of multiple households facilitate postdivorce adjustment and greatly reduce the burden that a divorcee normally experiences. Even though divorce is fairly common among First Nations peoples, some divorcees have difficulties and need therapy. The following recommendations are provided to ensure that such clients receive services responsive to their needs.

Exploring the Divorce Experience and Its Consequences

Some Native individuals experiencing divorce harbor guilt feelings. Such guilt feelings may occur when individuals think they have behaved irresponsibly and that this behavior adversely affects their children. Early experiences in boarding schools and Christian religious teachings may also arouse guilt feelings about divorce. Individuals who lacked a warm, secure, home environment to grow up in as children may project that their primary mission in life is to provide a stable home environment for their children. Attempting to correct earlier childhood experiences with one's own children has the potential of generating disappointment, feelings of lack of fulfillment, and depression. A couple's depressive symptoms, in turn, can affect both partners' normal functioning.

Traditionally, when an individual experienced divorce, he or she had the blessings and the support of the extended family, which usually lived nearby. Because of migration and other factors related to job opportunity, divorcees may be far away physically and emotionally from their original extended family. The vacuum created by divorce can throw divorcees into a state of total frustration and desperation. This crisis can be compounded when a divorcee has no prior knowledge of or experience in using community health and social services. The role of the therapist is to assess the client's needs and act quickly to help the client resolve them.

Providing the Client With Extended Family and Social Support

Divorce can be especially traumatic if the decision to end the marriage is not mutual and if the divorced partner (typically the female) has no employable skills. Further, the divorcee may be left with several children to support. The therapist's first task is to assess structurally the extent of the divorcee's extended family support system. Should the divorcee's extended family system be unavailable due to geographical distance or emotional cutoff, the next best possible extended family system for the divorcee may be a pancultural First Nations organization or a First Nations church group. The divorcee also needs to be informed of public health and social agencies that can provide temporary relief for her and her family.

Whenever a divorcee is temporarily incapacitated by divorce, the therapist needs to become a mediator, broker, or advocate for the family. This involves finding a means to meet the family's basic needs and to provide the divorcee with concrete and emotional support. Concrete support may include transporting her to a health clinic and helping her shop for food. Some clients, during this critical stage, find it very difficult to cope with the experience of divorce and manage the tasks of daily living. The therapist should anticipate these reactions and be comfortable with assisting with concrete support, while at the same time helping and empowering the divorcee to become interdependent with other support groups.

Postdivorce Adjustment and Building New Relationships

Once the critical stage of divorce is stabilized and the family's basic needs are being met, the therapist's next task is to engage the divorcee in assessing her emotional feelings about her ex-husband. Some clients find it difficult to acknowledge the finality of the divorce. The former spouse, after all, remains her children's father. The therapist's role is to sensitize the client to the possible negative effects this emotional tie may have on her and her children if it prevails. Such indecision and unfinished business with her ex-husband may also prevent her from entering into a new relationship that could be enriching to her and her children.

Similarly, some divorcees experience difficulty with the loss associated with divorce. A client may become temporarily immobilized, physically and emotionally. Such incapacitation may be related to the activation of invisible cultural loyalties due to the discontinuance of certain traditional tribal practices. As in the case of the Redthunder family, a client's previous experience of the loss of a significant family member may further contribute to this sense of incapacitation. Finally, a family therapist must be sensitive to the cumulative trauma and loss experienced by indigenous people. This factor may give shape and contour to a divorcee's lived experience of divorce. In other words, there may be a heightened sensitivity to loss, with subsequent difficulties in managing the grieving process. The use of a genogram as a means to track down the client's past relationships and losses, along with an understanding of tribal practices and the tribe's experiences with loss and trauma, may help the client in the grief process.

Single-Parent Therapy

Traditionally, the single-parent family structure did not exist in First Nations culture, in which multiple households were the rule rather than the exception. This has changed, due to the increased number of nuclear families in urban areas and nonreservation settings. However, the continued traditional practice of extended family ties across city and state lines (Red Horse, 1980b) makes the adjustment of a single-parent family somewhat easier. In some tribes, a single parent and her children can always return to her parents' household after the divorce (Brown & Shaughnessy, 1982).

Due to unemployment and other factors, there is an increased number of single parents who choose not to return to their parents after divorce. Consequently, these single parents may find themselves physically alone and emotionally isolated in a hostile environment populated by non-Native people. The following suggestions aim to assist these families in resolving problems characteristic of single-parent households.

Mobilizing the Support System

Although First Nations women are known for their hardworking attitude and resourcefulness (Hanson, 1980), the demands of single-parenthood may far exceed the single parent's ability to cope. The primary task of the therapist is to determine whether the basic needs of the family are being met. Those needs include adequate food, housing, and healthcare. With the permission and cooperation of the single parent, the therapist needs to help the family make the necessary connections so that the family's basic needs are secure. When there are no extended family ties available, the therapist should help the family establish new ties by contacting First Nations social service agencies, church groups, and neighborhood organizations. The family may also need assistance in securing public financial assistance and using public healthcare facilities. Such activities may be foreign and unfamiliar to a new single parent.

Restructuring the Family

Being a single parent requires the rearrangement of daily chores and emotional relationships among different family members. Partly because of the single parent's need to prove that she is self-sufficient and partly because of her unfamiliarity with outside resources, the single parent–child relationship is frequently thrown into a state of confusion and enmeshment. After the divorce, the children and the mother realize that each has to contribute extra to compensate for the absence of the father. Some single parents suffer the "super-mother" syndrome and burn out easily and quickly. Because the children are expected to contribute more to the care of the household, they may be forced to grow up prematurely, without the benefit of normal play and socialization with other children of their age. In a condition not unique to First Nations single mothers, some single parents abdicate their role as mother due to past unmet childhood needs or needs to feel attractive and to be loved by another person. When this happens, the family is thrown into a state of disengagement, often with no organization or relational bonding among family members. In the therapist's attempt to introduce structure to the family, efforts should be devoted to encouraging the single parent to assume a parental role. Skills required in appropriate parenting are usually compatible with Native culture. Dual and bicultural perspectives help ensure the children's developmental needs in a changing world.

Identifying and Meeting Personal Needs

Single parenthood is a difficult family experience to adjust to, yet it provides an opportunistic condition of opportunity in which an individual may reflect and grow. Some single parents go from childhood to early adulthood to marriage and never experience single independence. They often have no self-identity, and their happiness in life is dependent on their close associates. Such "being-in-becoming" and "let-live" attitudes may be difficult for the client who lives outside her own cultural group. Single parents need to realize that they do have some control of their own lives and of their children's destiny. Single parents must learn what they need in life and how to go about getting it. These characteristics should not be misconstrued as competitiveness and aggression, which are antithetical to

First Nations culture. Instead, they are essential qualities necessary to living responsibly with oneself and others.

Therapy With a Reconstituted Family

Because of First Nations peoples' past and present experience in living in multiple households, the reconstituted family phenomenon should present less of a problem to them than it does for dominant culture families whose past references are limited to the single-household nuclear family. The prevalence of traditional couple-headed households with children is higher among First Nations peoples than in African American and white families, attesting to the fact that in spite of high divorce rates, couple-headed families are valued among Native people (Benokraitis, 1993, p. 338). Yet a Native family's composition, its past relationships, and loyalties with previous marriages make life in a reconstituted family potentially conflicted. The following practice techniques are suggested when providing family therapy for reconstituted First Nations families.

Focusing on Parental Coalition

As with people of all ethnicities, many First Nations people remarry because of their love and affection and because they believe it will be best for their children. First Nations people are not used to living on their own, nor do they choose to live by themselves. When an opportunity arises to share a household with another single parent or family, they may choose to do so for the sake of the whole family. Problems arise when the children encounter conflicts with their stepparent or stepbrothers or stepsisters. If children are no longer happy, as originally expected by the parents, the couple may want to end the marriage.

Minuchin's (1974) structural theory has a great deal of appeal in terms of helping Native couples solidify their marital relationship and new family structure. This is the primary step to ensuring good functioning of the reconstituted family. A mutually supportive couple relationship influences the success of the parents' relationship with the children (Benokraitis, 1993). First Nations parents may not be accustomed to focusing on themselves. However, solidification of the spousal subsystem boundary has to be developed. Therapists can motivate couples to work on their relationship as a means to ensure their children's happiness in the reconstituted family.

As with any couple in a reconstituted family, Native couples in a reconstituted family may carry with them unrealistic expectations from previous marriages. Such expectations are usually distorted and fantasy based. These expectations can be detrimental to the present marriage and should be explored and examined in therapy. The goal of such examination is to prevent these expectations from affecting the current reconstituted family.

Clear Role Definition and Expectations of Family Members

Mutual expectations of the reconstituted couple need clarification. Other family members, including siblings, cousins, aunts, and uncles who may live in the same household, also need a clear understanding of their roles and functions in the reconstituted family. It is not unusual for First Nations people to grow up in groups and therefore be familiar with group discussion for problem solving. It is vital that each family member's role be clearly spelled out and understood so that unnecessary misunderstandings are avoided and potential conflicts have a base for satisfactory resolution.

Expectations must be carefully negotiated. Tribal differences, acculturation differences, varied backgrounds within reconstituted families, and past experiences with previous spouses and family all complicate the negotiation process. Newly reconstituted families will need to learn negotiation and problem-solving skills that require assertive effort and readjustment of traditional time orientation. They need to learn that constant negotiation among family members is integral to family well-being, including the reconstituted family.

Involving Extended Family Members

The well-being of a reconstituted family depends on the family's relationship with its extended family members. This is particularly true with First Nations families, in which the strong influence of the extended family is deeply felt by every family member from the moment of birth. If the interface between the reconstituted family and the extended family is strained, the former will run the risk of becoming enmeshed. The emotional cutoff from extended family members is so costly that it is bound to have a negative effect on the reconstituted family. If the influence is strong, the therapist may need to involve extended family members in therapy sessions. The therapist should never assume that the interface between the reconstituted family and the extended family naturally constitutes an enmeshment. In First Nations culture, such close relationships generally characterize strength and should be respected and capitalized on in therapy, particularly with reconstituted families.

PART 5: CONCLUSION

This chapter has focused on a holistic view (an integration of historical, economic, social, political, psychological, physical, and cultural phenomena) and a

Nativecentric (emic-insider and culture-specific) approach in work with First Nations families during different phases of (ecosystemically based) family therapy, using a critical constructivist perspective. First Nations families have endured intergenerational historical trauma (cultural and racial genocide) and have experienced rapid social change. Today, they continue to be treated like immigrants in their own native land. To survive, they are forced to adopt economic and political skills from the dominant culture and yet tenaciously and courageously try to preserve their own (Native) culture.

The strength of the Native family lies with its strong extended family ties and multiple household systems. Within this interdependent framework, a family finds its place and derives its worth. This same traditional system provides a family with problem-solving strengths. The family therapist can serve First Nations families only if he or she recognizes the strength of the extended family system and respects the individual and the traditional culture.

4

Family Therapy With Latinos

PART 1: PRETHERAPY PHASE CONSIDERATIONS: A CRITICAL PERSPECTIVE

Since the original publication of this book in 1987, the Latino population has more than tripled, from a total population of 12 million (U.S. Census Bureau, 1980) to a total population of 37 million as of 2001 (U.S. Census Bureau, 2001b). Without a doubt, Latinos, as a group, are one of the fastest growing ethnic populations living in the United States. Once considered the second largest ethnic minority group in the United States (second in number to African Americans), the U.S. Census Bureau reports that as of July 2001, Latinos have surged past African Americans as the country's largest ethnic minority group population. (The 2000 census data indicate that the African American population ranges between 34.7 million and 36.7 million persons—depending on whether the "black" category is the only one marked versus marking "black" and another race [U.S. Census Bureau, 2001b].) Census projections estimate that the Latino population will continue to grow to more than 59 million persons by the year 2025 and to more than 133 million persons by the year 2050 (U.S. Census Bureau, 1993). At that point, it is estimated, one in five people in the United States will be of Latino heritage (U.S. Census Bureau, 1993). At this growth rate, it becomes even more likely that American family therapists will be working with Latino families. These demographic changes make the need for more relevant and more reliable information on working with the Latino family even more of a critical professional concern; however, the marriage and family literature is generally lacking in this area.

Latinos are a population that can be understood only in terms of increasing heterogeneity; they are very diverse in terms of national origin, level of acculturation, length of U.S. residency, social class, and other demographic factors. The three largest Latino groups are Mexican, Puerto Rican, and Cuban. Mexican Americans represent approximately 59% of the total Latino population in the United States, Puerto Ricans make up approximately 10%, and Cubans constitute only 3%. Latinos from the Dominican Republic (one of the newer Latino immigrant groups) are the fastest growing Latino group in the United States, constituting about 2% of the Latino population. Latinos from Central America (whose countries of origin are Belize, Guatemala, El Salvador, Honduras, Nicaragua, Panama, and Costa Rica) and South America (whose countries of origin are Argentina, Bolivia, Chile, Colombia, Ecuador, Paraguay, Peru, Uruguay, and Venezuela)—combined—make up about 9% of the total Latino population. Several factors are said to have contributed to this rapid increase in the Latino population. One notable factor is the increased influx of immigrants, especially from Mexico. Another factor is the relatively high fertility rate of Latinas. A third contributing factor to this increase in the Latino population reflects the initiative and mandate of the U.S. Census Bureau to count previously undocumented immigrants, which brings up the question of how much of the increase in the number of Latinos is an increase in the official number of persons documented versus an actual increase within the Latino population.

Such an aggressive effort to count undocumented Latinos in the United States has at least two ramifications. One ramification is evident in the increased number of Latinos in America and the possible social, economic, and political presence Latinos can garner due to the increased population numbers. The most ominous ramification is whether the increased number of Latinos will also increase the potential for confrontations between Latinos and other ethnic groups around limited and/or shared social, economic, and political resources. Without a doubt, such a formidable presence with the United States is likely to gain Latinos increased visibility within American society.

Mexican Americans have continued to make up by far the largest segment of the U.S. Latino population (59%), so it should come as no surprise that a significant portion of the research and publication of professional social science literature dealing with Latinos includes only Mexican-origin groups (Demo et al., 2000; Massey, Zambrana, & Bell, 1995). Unfortunately, as is the case with other racially oppressed ethnic minority groups, the outcomes of studies on Mexican-origin groups have been generalized to other Latino populations. The homogenization of ethnic minority groups is not a new phenomenon. We challenge family therapists working with Latino families to strive to culturally tailor their interventions within this population and take time to better understand important differences between and among Latino families.

Names and Images: Ethnic Identity—Hispanic or Latino?

Ethnic identity is a narrative identity that is often reflective of an ethnic group's sociopolitical struggle for self-determination. A group's right to establish its own identity is based on how the group interprets its collective history and the efforts of the group to create and maintain sociopolitical consciousness and ethnic pride. In this context, the use of the term *Hispanic* has raised questions as to whether it adequately meets the previously stated requirement as a designation of ethnic identity. The term Hispanic, which has been used to define Spanish-speaking immigrants, was introduced by the U.S. Office of Management and Budget in 1978. The rationale for the use of this term was to aid census takers who needed a term for whites (and others) who claimed some degree of Spanish language or cultural affiliation. As a result, the Federal Registry defined a "Hispanic" as a person of Mexican, Puerto Rican, Cuban, Central or South American or other "Spanish" origin, regardless of race (Green, 1999).

The term Hispanic has increasingly come under criticism; some consider it offensive, whereas others merely see it as a bureaucratic term with very little personal significance. Falicov (1998) states that the term *Latino* more accurately describes the sense of linguistic and cultural affiliation of those persons of Mexican, Puerto Rican, Cuban, Central or South American or other Spanish origin:

> [It] affirms their native pre-Hispanic identity. . . . "Latino" is a more democratic alternative to "Hispanic" because Hispanic is a term strongly supported by politically conservative groups that regard their Spanish heritage as superior to the "conquered" indigenous groups of the Americas. Latino is also geographically more accurate, since it refers to people from Latin America rather than to people from Spain. (p. 34)

However, even the term Latino, progressive as some may consider it to be, should not be used as a personal cultural or ethnic descriptor for those with Latin cultural and possibly (Spanish) linguistic affiliation: Not all so-called Latinos (e.g., Brazilians, Latin American *Indios*, persons from Belize) have Spanish as their native language. Persons of this origin may more likely describe themselves in terms of their country of origin rather than as Latino. Thus they may describe themselves as Cuban, Mexican, Puerto Rican, Dominican, Nicaraguan, or another nationality that resides within Central or South America (Garcia-Preto, 1996a). In spite of the preference to use country of origin as the basis for ethnic identification, the term Latino is viewed as reflective of a proud yet general sense of cultural and linguistic connection between persons from various countries in the Americas wherein a Latin-based language is spoken.

Language as a Shared Identity

The Latino population in the United States is heterogeneous in its ethnicity, physical appearance, cultural practices, traditions, and Spanish language dialects. These populations represent a diverse group of multigenerational immigrants from different Spanish-speaking countries as well as long-term residents of the

Southwest United States (Santiago-Rivera, Arredondo, & Gallardo-Cooper, 2002). The Spanish language binds Latinos in a sense of cultural connectedness and "anchors" their shared identity (Falicov, 1998). Although the Spanish language may represent this sense of cultural affinity, each group or nationality may speak Spanish with a cultural style that highlights group differences by using idioms and metaphors that are unique to that group (Arredondo & Perez, 2003; Zuniga, 2001). The same word or term may vary in meaning between, for example, Cubans and Puerto Ricans.

In spite of the shared identity through the Spanish language, Arredondo and Perez (2003) point out that the use of the Spanish language in the United States is shaped by its sociopolitical context. The use of Spanish in the English-speaking United States has clear social, cultural, and political ramifications, causing some Latinos to prefer to speak English rather than Spanish. Arredondo and Perez (2003) state the following reasons for this preference:

- Language can be associated with the time of immigration in the United States, with recent immigrants possibly being more monolingual Spanish speakers who have English as a second language. As one becomes more assimilated one may prefer the use of English over Spanish.
- Many Latinos, particularly Mexican Americans, do not speak Spanish at all, as they may have been taught by their parents that to become assimilated and to avoid punishment for speaking Spanish, as their parents experienced, they (the children) should not learn Spanish.
- Although being bilingual or speaking Spanish whenever possible could be an indication of comfort for the Latino immigrant, speaking Spanish in the workplace is often discouraged so as not to make non–Spanish speakers feel uncomfortable.
- "Code-switching," or using Spanish and English in the same sentence, may be used to emphasize a point with a particular English or Spanish word even though the primary and accepted language for discourse remains English.
- Being bilingual is an academic, psychological, social, and economic asset for those in bicultural and bilingual settings (Arredondo & Perez, 2003). Still, English remains the accepted language for discourse.

The preference for English over Spanish can more fully be understood within the context of an antibilingual movement within the United States that culminated in antibilingual legislation in Arizona in 2000 and in California in 1995 (Arredondo & Perez, 2003). This type of public reaction to an integral part of one's cultural identity such as one's language has implications for the sociopolitical realities and reactions to Latinos in the United States. These negative reactions can further create a sense of conflicted cultural and linguistic loyalty for Spanish-speaking immigrants. The linguistic dilemma—To what extent can or should they refrain from speaking their language of origin? To what extent do they compromise their language in the act of assimilation into an English-speaking culture?—certainly has psychological implications for the Latino sense of self-esteem.

The History of Social Oppression

While Mexican American, Puerto Rican, Cuban, and other Spanish-speaking minorities in the United States share a cultural and linguistic background, there are also shared legacies of historical colonization, oppression, and marginalization in relation to the United States. This history began with the European explorers and their arrival in the Americas—the "New World." Their arrival was to be marked by a history of conquest and slavery through the establishment of the slave trade from Africa to the "New World."

Mexico

In Mexico, prior to the arrival of the European explorers, the indigenous people had achieved a high degree of civilization. Upon the arrival of the explorers and, later, the conquistadors, the indigenous people were subjugated by the Spaniards. From this experience of subjugation emerged the Mexican culture, which represents a blend of the indigenous and Spanish cultures. This blending of cultures has a distinct cultural presence in parts of what is now the Southwest United States. In 1848, the Mexican-American War led to the defeat of Mexico and the subsequent acquisition by the United States of the territories of most of what is now California, Arizona, New Mexico, Colorado, Texas, and Utah. The war resulted in extensive negative feelings between the original Mexican residents and the U.S. pioneers (Zuniga, 2001).

These feelings are still evident in the response of U.S. citizens to Mexican immigrants who currently reside in the United States without legal documentation. Proposition 187, which passed in California in 1994, clearly expressed the sentiments of California citizens toward this population and spawned an anti-immigration movement. Under this proposition, undocumented residents, mainly Mexican immigrants, were restricted from receiving public health services, social services, public education, and welfare benefits (Cowan, Martinez, & Mendiola, 1997; Zuniga, 2001). The passage of this proposition corresponded with the increase in hate crimes toward Mexican immigrants (Coalition for Humane Immigrant Rights of Los Angeles, 1995).

As many Mexicans are typically darker skinned (than other Latino groups), they further experience discrimination in housing, education, and jobs and are deported more readily than other Latino immigrants (Falicov, 1996). Mexicans are the largest Latino group in the United States; 6 out of 10 Latinos are of Mexican origin. This group has low family incomes but high labor force participation rates for men and increasing rates for women (U.S. Census Bureau, 1996). Mexicans have the lowest educational attainment of all Latino groups (U.S. Census Bureau, 1996).

Puerto Rico

In Puerto Rico, the indigenous people were virtually eradicated by the Spaniards, who were replaced with African slaves (Fitzpatrick, 1981). Today's Puerto Rican culture reflects that blend of African, Native, and persons of European heritage. Puerto Rico became an unincorporated territory of the United States as result of the Spanish American War, which ended 400 years of Spanish rule in 1898. In 1900, the U.S. government appointed a governor (from the United States) and a civil government composed of island residents. The United States had veto power over any legislation passed by this civil government, and their representative to the U.S. House of Representatives had no vote in Congress.

In 1917, a Bill of Rights was established in Puerto Rico, and the United States granted citizenship to all Puerto Ricans. In addition, military service became obligatory for all eligible males. With an elected U.S. governor in 1948, Puerto Rico became a commonwealth in 1952. Political power still resides with the U.S. House Committee on Insular Affairs and the Senate Committee of Territorial and Insular Affairs. Puerto Ricans cannot vote in U.S. elections and have little power over the fate of their own island (Garcia-Preto, 1996b).

Puerto Ricans are able to travel back and forth between Puerto Rico and the United States ("the mainland") without a visa. This back-and-forth migration may "represent a solution to the problems they face here (on the mainland), as an oasis from the prejudice, discrimination and isolation that plagues their lives" (Garcia-Preto, 1996b, p. 190). This (*circular*) migration back and forth from Puerto Rico to the mainland also has the negative impact of repeated disruptions and renewal of family ties (Garcia-Preto, 1996b).

The factors of "prejudice, discrimination and isolation" may also be particularly salient for darker skinned Puerto Ricans, who may be more exposed to racism and prejudice in the United States. Puerto Ricans are the most economically disadvantaged of all Latino groups. Compared to Mexicans and Cubans, Puerto Ricans have the lowest median family income and the highest unemployment and poverty rates (U.S. Census Bureau, 1996). Puerto Ricans also have the highest rate of female-headed households of all Latino groups (U.S. Census Bureau, 1996).

Cuba

The Cuban culture is a blending of Spanish and African cultures (Bustamante & Santa Cruz, 1975; Ortiz, 1972). Cuba's unique historical connection to powerful nations such as Spain, the United States, and the Soviet Union distinguishes Cubans from other Latin countries. Cuba's current socialist ideological stance gives it a unique position in relationship to the United States and in many ways overshadows the early history of Cuba in the historical and political memory of the United States.

The largest Cuban immigration occurred following the Cuban revolution in 1959. Those who migrated during the 1960s were primarily the white, educated, and upper and middle class professionals who could not adapt to the revolutionary changes in Cuba (Bernal & Shapiro, 1996). Subsequent waves of migration occurred between 1965 and 1973-were groups of Cubans who came in search of economic freedom; and in 1980 they were working class or unemployed Cubans, mostly Afro-Cubans, who came to the United States. In 1990 Cubans risked their lives to come to the United States by makeshift rafts to escape extreme economic hardship in Cuba, when the Soviet Union ended their aid to Cuba (Bernal & Shapiro, 1996). The *Cubanization* of cities in Florida resulted in anti-Cuban sentiments, with emerging concerns about maintaining English as the state's official language (Zuniga, 2001).

Cuban families have higher incomes and far lower poverty rates than do other major Latino groups (U.S. Census Bureau, 1996). Cubans are the highest educated major Latino group in the United States (U.S. Census Bureau, 1996). However, the Cuban workforce is polarized, with one segment moving into higher wage work and the other remaining locked in low-wage employment (Perez-Stable & Uriarte, 1993).

Other Latino Groups

Political repression, civil war, and their accompanying economic dislocations have fueled the immigration of a substantial number of Salvadorans, Nicaraguans, and Guatemalans since the mid-1970s (Hamilton & Chinchilla, 1997). The U.S. population of Central Americans more than doubled between the 1980 and 1990 censuses and now outnumbers Cubans (U.S. Census Bureau, 1993). These Latinos migrated under difficult circumstances and face a set of serious challenges in the United Stated (Dorrington, 1995). A high percentage of them are undocumented (estimates range from 40%-49%), they have marginal employment and high poverty rates, and they are not recognized by the U.S. government as political refugees (Lopez, Popkin, & Telles, 1996). Central Americans, especially undocumented persons, who fear deportation, often occupy a low-wage niche in private service (e.g., as domestic workers in private homes).

With the end of Trujillo's 30-year dictatorship and the political uncertainties that ensued, there was a "massive displacement" of Dominicans from their homeland as a significant number began migrating to the United States in the mid-1960s (Grasmuck & Pessar, 1996). Even though the Dominican immigrants have urban middle class origins, their middle class aspirations remain largely unfulfilled, in part due to their lack of advanced educational credentials and lack of competence in the English language. They occupy low-wage, marginal, and mostly dead-end employment for individuals with advanced education (Torres & Bonilla, 1993). Dominicans have high rates of poverty and female-headed families. Approximately four out of ten Dominican family households are headed by women.

Latinos: A Racially Mixed Ethnic Group

The Latino population as a whole is considered a racially mixed group. From this historical and cultural blending of African, indigenous, and European heritage in countries such as Mexico, Puerto Rico, Cuba, and Central and South American countries, one finds within the heterogeneous Latino cultures the presence of *mestizos*—persons of blended indigenous and European heritages—and *criollos* or *mulattos*—persons of blended indigenous, African, and European heritages. Not only are there different national groups, there are issues of racial phenotype, for example, color, which may range from very pale to very dark within one family. Those darker colored Latinos may find themselves subjected to stereotyping and color-based discrimination within the United States. Those with lighter skinned complexions may become an "invisible minority" (Montalvo, 1991) by blending into the white melting pot (Flores, 2000). These factors contribute to the degree of biracial and bicultural experiences within the Latino population in the United States.

Arredondo and Perez (2003) suggest that any clinical approach to Latinos must take into account these bicultural and biracial experiences though a mestizo- (and mulatto-) based orientation, which can provide an understanding of current psychosocial experiences of Latinos in the following contexts:

- The survival of Latino people in new environments in spite of a history of colonization, invasions, conquest, and marginalization
- The survival of Latino people through cooperation, collaboration, and learning of new skills in new environments
- The intermarriage between indigenous peoples, European settlers, and Africans (slaves)
- The synthesis of indigenous, African, and European religious practices
- The revolutions against European domination, leading to Latino culturally based ideologies

Through mestizo- and mulatto-based orientations, there can be an appreciation of the heterogeneity of Latino people as well as a sense of the strength of their shared identity. Mestizo and mulatto lenses or theories and models of clinical family interventions can be shaped to be culturally responsive to the needs of Latino families.

Socioeconomic Status

Many Latinos have relatively low educational achievement and tend to lag behind other ethnocultural groups on overall educational attainment. For example, 27% of Latinos have less than a 9th grade education, compared to only 4% of non-Latino whites (U.S. Census Bureau, 2001b). Latinos are less likely to enter college and complete a bachelor's degree, although there have been some gains made between 1980 and 1990. In 1980, 54% of the Latino population did not have a high school diploma, and only 8% held a college degree. Ten years later in 1990, 50% of the Latino population did not have a high school diploma, and 9% held college degrees. Mexican Americans have the highest percentage of people with less than a 9th grade education, whereas Cubans and Central and South Americans have had the most gains in education, particularly at the bachelor's and advanced degree levels (U.S. Census Bureau, 2001b).

The poverty status of Latinos worsened in the 1980s and 1990s in comparison to other groups. Although the poverty rate for African Americans declined from 33% to 29.3% from 1992 to 1995, the poverty rate for Latinos rose from 23% to 30.3% during this same period, surpassing the African American poverty rate for the first time (Karger & Stoesz, 2002; U.S. Census Bureau, 2001b). Wages remain low for Mexicans and Puerto Ricans, for they tend to live in states with large concentrations of Latinos where there is increased competition for low-wage jobs. About 44% of the Latino population is earning $19,000 or less, compared to about 19% for non-Latino whites. Among higher income levels, only 24% of the Latino population earns $35,000 or more, compared to 50% of the non-Latino population. Cubans have the highest income level of all Latino groups (U.S. Census Bureau, 2001b). The 1999 income figures show that 30% of Latino children under the age of 18 live in poverty, compared to only 9% of non-Latino white children (U.S. Census Bureau, 2001b). These figures reflect an increasing number of women heading households (especially Puerto Rican women), a situation that creates a declining economic condition for the family and thus a decline in the well-being of the family (Santiago-Rivera et al., 2002).

Cultural Values in Relation to Family Structure

The traditional Latino family unit has changed; recent data show that the percentage of children living in intact Latino families in the United States has declined from 74% in 1980 to 64% in 1995 (Estrada, 2000). This statistic is very significant in that the Latino family structure plays a very vital role in the lives of this large ethnic group. The following discussion is an overview of the cultural values and the family structure of Latinos. The heritage of Latinos is rich and diverse. However, some commonalities do exist, such as a shared lineage with Spanish, African, and indigenous Native cultures. Certain unifying cultural concepts also distinguish Latinos from the dominant society. The cultural concepts that form the foundation for the Latino-American family structure and relationships include *familismo, marianismo, personalismo, dignidad, respeto, machismo, hierarchy, spiritualism,* and *fatalism.* These common cultural Latino values significantly influence Latino family life, organization, and structure. Each of these cultural values is described, and a discussion of how these values affect family subsystems and overall family interaction follows.

Familismo. In general, Latinos have a strong family orientation in that they value close relationships and stress interdependence, cohesiveness, and cooperation among family members. Latinos have a very deep awareness of and pride in membership in the family. Familismo stems from a collectivistic or allocentric worldview in which there is a willingness to sacrifice for the welfare of the group (Marin & Triandis, 1985). This worldview is manifested in a shared sense of responsibility to care for children, provide financial and emotional support, and participate in decision-making efforts that involve one or more members of the family (Falicov, 1998; Marin & Marin, 1991; Moore & Pachon, 1985; Santiago-Rivera et al., 2002). The importance of family membership and a strong sense of belonging cut across caste lines and socioeconomic conditions. Individuals' self-confidence, worth, security, and identity are determined by their relationship to other family members. The importance of family is evident in the cultural use of family names (Fitzpatrick, 1981). The man generally uses both his father's and mother's name together with his given name; for example, José Garcia Rivera. Garcia is his father's family name and Rivera is his mother's family name. If the man is to be addressed by only one name, the father's family name is used. This reflects the patriarchal pattern of the Latino family.

Because the family is of great importance to the individual, each member has a deep sense of family obligation. The needs of the family (collectively) may supersede individual needs. The family is the strongest area of life activities. It is a closely knit group in which all members enjoy status and esteem (Ulibarri, 1970). During good times or during crisis, the family's name and family members' welfare always come first. It is this sense of family obligation that should be encouraged during therapy. Unfortunately, the concept of familismo has been pathologized. Diagnostic labels such as *enmeshed* and *codependent* have been widely used to describe Latino families. On the contrary, familismo is one of the strengths of Latino culture. Falicov (1998) urges clinicians to "examine their own personal and professional values and philosophies about family structure and connectedness, while exploring the specific meanings of closeness and attachment for each family" (p.164).

Personalismo. Along with the concept of *familismo,* Latinos define their self-worth in terms of those inner qualities that give them self-respect and earn them the respect of others. They feel an inner dignity (*dignidad*) and expect others to show respect (*respeto*) for that dignidad. Personalismo is also a cultural trait that reflects a collectivistic worldview (Levine & Padilla, 1980) in which there is a great deal of emotional investment in the family. Positive interpersonal interaction will help to maintain mutual dependency and closeness for a lifetime. Hence, great importance is given to those positive interpersonal and social skills to facilitate warm, close relationships.

Machismo. Closely related to the concept of personalismo is the quality *machismo,* literally, maleness. Machismo is referred to as a quality of personal magnetism that impresses and influences others. It is a style of personal daring by which one faces challenges, danger, and threats with calmness and self-possession. More centrally, machismo encompasses a man's responsibility to be a good provider, protector, and defender for his family (Morales, 1996). Loyalty and responsibility to family and community is what makes a man a good man. The Latino meaning of machismo has been confused with the Anglo definition of "macho" that describes sexist, male chauvinist behavior (Morales, 1996). The Latino meaning of machismo should not be pathologized and erroneously equated with what Americans have come to (more negatively) understand as macho (men who are insensitive, domineering, and certainly do not manifest a protective family function). The Latino meaning of machismo conveys the notions of an "honorable and responsible man" (Morales, 1996).

White, middle-class Americans stress individualism and emphasize the individual's ability to compete for higher social and economic status. The Latino culture values those inner qualities that constitute the uniqueness of the person and his or her goodness. Latinos believe that every individual who has some sense of personal dignity will be sensitive about showing proper respect (respeto) to others and demand respect for self as well. This expectation is intensified when a Latino first encounters a non-Latino and interprets the latter's insensitivity as personal insult or disdain. Contrarily, if personalismo is reciprocated in a social or professional interaction, trust is developed and so is obligation. Hence a Latino family may seek and perhaps benefit from family therapy not because of agency affiliation or the professional reputation of the therapist but simply because of the therapist's skill and ability to convey personalismo when dealing with the family.

Sense of hierarchy. Historically, Latinos lived in a world of two class systems: high and low. Members rarely conceived the possibility of moving out of the class into which they were born. Social class position was as fixed and natural as the parts of their bodies. The Latino sense of hierarchy is further manifested in the leadership structure of the family, wherein the father occupies the role of superior authority and the mother's role is to follow. In addition to gender hierarchy, there is also generational hierarchy, in which parents expect to be obeyed when they advise their children. Younger children are expected to obey older children, who serve as role models. The Latino has a distinct concept of personal worth from an individual's position in the social structure. The concept of hierarchy has great therapeutic implications for family therapy and in the dynamics of family communication and the problem-solving process.

Spirituality and spiritualism. In the Latino cultural orientation, there is a clear interrelationship between faith, religion, spirituality, and spiritualism (Flores & Carey, 2000; Santiago-Rivera et al., 2002). Latinos emphasize spiritual values and are willing to sacrifice material satisfaction for spiritual goals. Catholicism is the predominant religion for Latinos (Santiago-Rivera et al., 2002). Their ways of worship, however, differ from other predominantly Roman Catholic ethnic groups, such as the Irish. In the Latino culture, there is the belief that one can make direct contact with God and the supernatural, without the assistance of intervention of the clergy. A significant part of the Latino population, especially Puerto Ricans, believes in spiritualism. The belief is that the visible world is surrounded by an invisible world inhabited by good and evil spirits who influence human behavior (Delgado, 1978; Falicov, 1998). Thus spirits can either protect or harm and can prevent or cause illness. To be protected by good spirits, an individual is expected to perform good and charitable deeds in the secular world.

Folklore that combines the heritage of Spanish, Catholic, medical, and religious practices with African and indigenous belief systems is common among many Latinos. For example, the practice of *Santeria* (an indigenous Cuban healing tradition), which combines Catholicism with Yoruban (African) beliefs; the practice of *espiritismo* (an indigenous Puerto Rican healing tradition); and *curanderismo* (an indigenous Mexican healing tradition) are prevalent throughout Latino communities in the United States (Gonzalez-Wippler, 1996; Morales-Dorta, 1976). With certain families, mobilizing the support systems available through these folk traditions can augment family therapy; this combination of services has been documented as having very powerful therapeutic effects (Garrison, 1977). It is important, however, to ensure that the family and its members are indeed working with a bonafide culturally indigenous folk healer, as opposed to quacks and charlatans who engage in exploitative and destructive practices, as in the case of the eclectic (typically commercialized) "reader/adviser" who professes to use such devices as tarot cards, crystal balls, ESP, and the like. Research has shown that culturally sanctioned and culturally indigenous folk healers do not use mass media (television, newspaper advertising, radio, etc.) to attract clients; people know where they are and the community's natural system of sanctioning is a client-based (word of mouth) referral system (Garrison, 1977).

Fatalism. Latino culture values the spirit and soul as much as it values the body and perhaps less than it values worldly materialism. Latino culture emphasizes transcendent qualities such as justice, loyalty, and love. This worldview teaches that one should not be preoccupied with mastering the world. There is a keen sense of destiny (partly related to fundamental fears of the sacred) and a sense of divine providence governing the world. The popular songs "Que Sera, Sera" (what will be, will be) and "Si Dios Quiere" (If God wills) reflect the Latino cultural expression of *fatalism.* According to Falicov (1998), therapists working with Latinos must distinguish between a "deficit-oriented" fatalism and the "resource-oriented" kind. A deficit understanding may disempower an individual. On the other hand, the fatalistic attitude can serve as a functional quality, leading to the acceptance of many tragic and unfortunate events as beyond one's control. Furthermore, it softens the sense of despair or personal failure that is the common by-product of the middle class American value system. American family therapists are strongly cautioned not to pathologize the concept of Latino fatalism or view it as a negativistic, fatalistic, "doomsday" perspective. This interpretation is a gross misunderstanding of the true essence of this very functional, adaptive cultural concept; it should not be confused with the American notion of fatalism.

Traditional Family Structure and Extended Family Ties

Immigration contributes to the proliferation of family forms and a variety of household arrangements among Latinos (Vega, 1995). Chavez (1990, 1992) identified *transnational* families (families with members who have dual citizenship), *binational* families (families with members who are undocumented and members who are citizens or legal residents), extended families, multiple-household families, blended and stepparent families, single-parent families, and other arrangements among Mexican and Central American immigrants. The Latino nuclear family is embedded in an extended family network that includes such relatives as grandparents, uncles, aunts, and cousins (Madsen, 1964). The extended family often includes lifelong friends and godparents created through Catholic baptism. This selection of godparents, through the process known as *compadrazco* (godparentage), has historical significance and is an important tradition among Latinos (Santiago-Rivera et al., 2002). By this process, children acquire a godmother (*madrina*) and godfather (*padrino*) who directly share responsibility for the child's welfare and thus form co-parent bonds with the child's parents. The function of godparents within the family is to provide security, guidance, and love for the godchild. They may be chosen from among members of the extended family or from outside the family. Reasons for selecting a particular godparent may include proximity, friendship, wealth, and social or political status. The two most important types of godparents are those selected at baptism and marriage. The godparents of baptism assume responsibility for the child if birth parents become unable to fulfill their duties. Godparents of marriage contribute to the expense of the wedding and may function as mediators between the couple in case of quarrels or separations (Abad, Ramos, & Boyce, 1974). During times of crisis, transferring children from one nuclear family to another within the extended family system is a common practice among Latinos. Unless the practice is regarded as a problem by the family, a therapist working with the family should not criticize or attempt to alter such arrangements. Interdependence, both inter-generational and lateral, characterizes the Latino extended family supportive network. Falicov (1998) uses the concept of familismo to describe this system of extended kinship ties and its interdependence beyond the nuclear family. These family connections and the frequency of contact among members tend to be greater than those of Anglo-Americans (Padilla, Carlos, & Keefe, 1976).

Mate Selection and the Husband-Wife Relationship

Traditionally, intermingling and dating among young Latinos was much more restricted than it is today. A young man interested in a young woman was expected to speak to the parents of the girl, particularly the father, to declare his intentions. No serious courtship could even begin if the families disapproved. When a marriage materialized, Latinos might practice a *patrilocal* residence pattern, wherein a young bride lives with her husband's family. The traditional ideal prescribes that the daughter-in-law has the same obligations as a daughter and, therefore, performs many domestic chores under the supervision of her mother-in-law.

The hierarchal role of male dominance and female submission rooted in Spanish customs defines the husband and wife relationship. The husband assumes the instrumental role of provider and protector of the family and the wife the expressive role of homemaker and caretaker. The Latino (male) is expected to be dignified and hardworking. Because it is the wife's responsibility to care for the home and keep the family together, the husband is not expected to assume household tasks or help care for the children. This arrangement results in wives assuming power behind the scene but overtly supporting their husband's authority (Stevens, 1973). Because it is the existence of children that validates and cements the marriage, "motherly love" (*el amor de madre*) is considered to be a much greater force than "wifely love."

Corresponding to the male gender role of machismo for men is the cultural value of *marianismo,* which defines the gender role ideal for the traditional Latina (female). *Marianismo* has religious associations to the Virgin Mary, for as girls grow to be women and mothers they are expected to honor the model of the Virgin Mary in terms of purity, self-sacrifice, nurturance, piety, virtue, and humility. In their roles as wives and mothers, their behavior should exemplify these traits. What is implicit in this role expectation is that women are expected to be spiritually stronger than men (Lopez-Baez, 1999; Santiago-Rivera et al., 2002). The marianismo role supports the ideal of male dominance and female submission.

The outward compliance with the cultural ideal of male dominance (machismo) and female submission (marianismo) may be more social fiction than actuality. In reality, Latino families may include husbands who are domineering and patriarchal (Penalosa, 1968), who are submissive and dependent on their wives for major decisions, or who follow a more egalitarian power struggle (Hawkes & Taylor, 1975). As Latinos move up the socioeconomic ladder to more middle class levels, assimilation of Anglo-American lifestyles occurs, and husband-wife sex-role delineations become less strict.

Among recent immigrants, there may be attempts to maintain traditional gender role expectations. Reflecting this concern, Espin (1999) points out that although men may have freedom to develop new identities in the new country, women may continue to be constricted to traditional gender role expectations for their sex. However, more women are becoming single parents and must take on roles traditionally held by men (this situation will be discussed later in the chapter). Thus the role behaviors reflecting marianismo are not evident in the single parent, although individuals may have some internal conflict regarding not being able to fulfill these traditional expectations (Santiago-Rivera et al., 2002).

Parent-Child Relationship

The parental functions of Latinos follow the cultural prescriptions for the husband-wife relationship. The Latino father disciplines and controls the children and the mother provides nurturance and support. Consistent with the Latino hierarchical cultural orientation, the (authoritative) status of parents is high and that of children low. In this sense, Latino parents are seen as authoritarian parents who exert clear control over children (Falicov, 1998; Garcia-Preto, 1996b, 1998). Parents engender the respeto (respect) of children through complementary transactions. Most parents would not expect or want to be friends with their children.

The role of the mother is idealized and equated with self-denial and abnegation. Although traditionally the father generally is not as directly involved in the children's care as the mother, he protects the mother and demands that the children obey her. He is relaxed and playful with younger children and more stern and strict with older children, especially daughters (Fitzpatrick, 1981). The father's disciplinary role reduces his direct involvement with the children and reinforces the mother's centrality in the family. Such a coalition between mother and children is fairly typical among Latino families and should not be labeled as "pathological triangulation" in need of change or therapy.

Although Latino families today may reside in single households, extended family members, such as grandparents, uncles, aunts, and godparents, perform many parental functions. They provide nurturance, support, guidance, and a controlling influence for the children. Child-rearing practices that reflect Latino parental attitudes have been described as using the dimensions of cooperation over that of competition and achievement aspirations. Anglo-American children show greater competitiveness and achievement aspirations and Latino children show greater cooperation (Kagan & Buriel, 1977).

Sibling Relationship

The sibling relationship within a Latino family is characterized by a large size (relatively large numbers of children in the family), vertical hierarchal structure, and male sex-role dominance. Relationships between cousins are often close, especially between *primos hermanos* (first cousins), and may resemble a sibling relationship. Due to parental encouragement to form close kinship bonds within the family, it is common for Latino children to have few peers or friends other than their siblings and cousins.

Early in life, siblings are assigned real responsibilities necessary for the functioning of the household (Murillo, 1971). They are expected to get along with each other, with older children taking care of younger ones and brothers protecting their sisters. Latino parents typically accord authority to older siblings and delegate supervisory and caretaking functions to them. This subordinates the younger children to the older children and makes all of them responsible for household chores.

Cross-sex sibling companionship is curtailed at adolescence and is replaced by complementary functions such as girls doing household chores and boys chaperoning and protecting girls. Female siblings learn their proper role early in life. A girl is afforded less freedom than her brothers. She begins to play the role of mother and homemaker by caring for younger brothers and sisters and by helping with the housework. Because children are taught respect, cooperation, and control of aggression (Rothenburg, 1964) at an early age, there is typically little sibling rivalry. Even during adulthood, emotional support, guidance, and practical help among siblings is usual. Male dominance and sibling order remain the compelling factors in adult-sibling relationships and interactions.

Intermarriage

Latinos have a long history of intermarriage, and this trend seems to be continuing. Recent statistics show that Latinos have the highest rate of intermarriage of all ethnic minority groups in the United States, with Latino men intermarrying more than Latinas (Santiago-Rivera et al., 2002). More than 57% of third-generation Latinos will intermarry (Santiago-Rivera et al., 2002; Suro, 1999). Two thirds of the Latino population will marry European Americans.

Heubusch and Dortch (Santiago-Rivera et al., 2002) indicate that gender, nationality, and generational levels further influence Latino intermarriage rates. Factors that predispose a Latino toward intermarriage are having a partial or complete college education, hoping to gain a higher socioeconomic status, and age younger than 35 years. Latinos born in the United States are also more likely to intermarry than are immigrants. Latino cross-cultural marriages are twice as high in states with low Latino populations.

In situations of intermarriage, many couples may have a different experience of maintaining contact with their family of origin due to different cultures, customs, values, beliefs, and role expectations (Santiago-Rivera et al., 2002). For example, one member of the couple may feel that the other gives too much time, energy, or attention (or too little) to the family of origin, not recognizing that such giving may be reflective of family and *invisible cultural loyalties*. Marital conflict can further arise when a non-Latina wife is not as husband and family oriented as a Latino husband might expect her to be. For these reasons, greater stability is predicted for non-Latino/Latina types of intermarriage than for Latino/non-Latina marriages (Muguia, 1982).

Given the heterogeneity of the Latino population, there is a great potential for marriages between different Latino ethnic groups. These unions create *cross-cultural bicultural families*. In these types of intragroup unions, the couple may share similar ethnic and cultural values and language but have distinct differences in life experiences, unique ethnic identity, and degree of contact with U.S. culture (Santiago-Rivera et al., 2002).

Divorce and Remarriage

Although the Latino divorce rate is lower than for other ethnic groups, in recent years there has been an increase in the divorced, separated, or widowed population, with Puerto Ricans being more affected by the trend (U.S. Census Bureau, 2001b). Puerto Ricans represent the lowest percentage of people married with spouse present and highest percentage of people never married; Cubans, on the other hand, have higher percentages of people who are married with spouse present than do non-Latino whites (U.S. Census Bureau, 2001b). Yet Cubans also have the highest percentage of divorced individuals compared to non-Latino whites (U.S. Census Bureau, 2001b).

Most Latino families remain two-parent families throughout the lifetime of the parents, despite a higher unemployment rate, poorer health, lower socioeconomic conditions, and stresses inherent in immigration and acculturation. The previous low divorce rate of Latino families may be closely related to their cultural value of familismo, in which self-worth is dependent upon belonging to and obligation to the family. The Latino vertical family structure, with its emphasis on male dominance, conflicts with the egalitarian concept of the dominant society, but it clearly explicates the role definition in marriages. Spousal relationships are reinforced by cultural traditions and by extended family ties. The Latina's realistic expectation of the wife's role may help to reduce the frustration and disappointment generally associated with romantic love as cherished in the egalitarian relationships of the dominant culture.

The predominant religion of Latinos is Catholicism, which has a strong prohibition against divorce, and this also is likely to be a contributing factor to the low rate of divorce among Latinos. Marriage is very much a two-family affair, and a marriage can be dissolved easily if it does not have the sanction of both families. When divorce does occur, the parent granted custody of the children usually has the moral and the practical support of the extended family.

Immigration and Acculturation

For Latinos, migration may involve a search for better economic and educational opportunities or an escape from political changes in their country of origin (Falicov, 1998). In understanding the impact of migration, Zuniga (1992) and Falicov (1998) describe the migration process as it affects individuals and families. From their perspective, the immigration experience involves the following stages.

1. The preparatory stage reflects the decision to migrate, coping with the sociocultural factors prompting the emigration, and saying good-bye to family, friends, the support network, and the country and culture of origin.

2. The second stage is the act of migration, which refers to the migration experience itself. This experience may be coupled with trauma, stress, and moving into "uncharted territories."

3. The third stage may find the family dealing with dramatic shifts in their cultural "bearings" as they cope with acculturative stresses in the new culture and attempt to navigate or alternate between the host culture and the culture of origin. This stage may reflect a *transgenerational* struggle in which different values between younger generations and older generations may arise.

4. The fourth stage may reflect a shift in roles, behaviors, and expectations that make it possible to develop a sense of biculturalism, which may result in role conflicts but does present a wider range of coping behaviors in the new environment.

The issue for Latino families is how and to what extent the migrant process affects them. Membership change within the family during migration necessitates family restructuring of roles and functions and transactions. The traditional hierarchical role structure may run into conflict when the husband and father becomes unemployed. The acculturation rate for the children can threaten authoritarian parents who may have to depend on their children to translate for them when dealing with community agencies, immigration authorities, and healthcare services. The faster rate of acculturation for young Latinos (Szapocznik, Scopetta, & Tillman, 1978) has increased stresses and conflicts in many families. Lack of support outside the family system and fears of crime, drug addiction, and more accepting sexual mores often cause parents to be strict and overprotective with adolescents, especially daughters (Badillo-Ghali, 1974). Children often rebel against their parents' rigid discipline and reject traditional customs that they consider inferior to American mores.

Members are faced with learning a new language and new social and political ways of life. Feelings of isolation and despair are common among new immigrants. To ascertain the impact of immigration and political and cultural adjustment on a Latino family, the therapist should start out by identifying the family's original birthplace(s). Not all Latinos are immigrants. For example, many Mexican Americans who reside in the southwestern United States were born in the United States (as in the case of second-generation Mexican Americans and New Mexicans). Due to political agreements between the United States, Mexico, and Puerto Rico, immigrants enjoy freedom of travel back and forth to visit relatives. Such visits reduce the emotional cutoff normally associated with relocation and immigration. On the other hand, until just recently, Cuban immigrants were not allowed to visit their relatives in Cuba.

The timing of migration is another factor affecting the adjustment rate of Latinos. For example, as described earlier, the Cuban migration of the 1960s was overrepresented by whites, disproportionately composed of the upper and middle classes, and heavily aided by major (U.S.) federal programs. Conversely, the 1980 influx of Cuban immigrants was found to consist of 40% nonwhites, who were poorly educated and likely to be sociopolitical dissidents (Spencer, Szapocznik, Santisteban, & Rodrigues, 1981). The new arrivals are destined to encounter more severe immigration and adjustment problems than the 1960 group of immigrants. There are also the undocumented immigrants who take the risk of entering the United States illegally to work and finance their families and in the process encounter poor living conditions, economic exploitation, and racist treatment (Perez Foster, 2001; Zuniga, 2001).

Latinas appear to require more time to acculturate than men. This may be due to the passive-submissive role of women in their traditional culture (Szapocznik et al., 1978). If women must work outside of the home to help support the family, they frequently suffer role confusion and conflict. Use of the wife's employable status and earning power may be essential for the economic survival of the family, but it threatens the superior role of the husband and father. The wife's long working hours outside the home can affect her satisfaction and self-image as a good mother. Poor economic conditions and the frustration and stress inherent in the acculturation process can result in mental health problems for Latinos (Ruiz, 1977).

Help-Seeking Patterns

Studies indicate that Latinos do not consider mental health services a solution to their emotional and family problems (Green, 1999). Acosta et al. (1982) gave the following reasons for Latinos' underutilization of health and mental health services: (a) language barriers, (b) cultural and social class differences between therapists and patients, (c) insufficient number of mental health facilities, (d) overuse or misuse of physicians for psychological problems, (e) reluctance to recognize the urgency for help, and (f) lack of awareness of the existence of mental health clinics.

Latinos consider the family their primary source of support. It is difficult for a husband and father who is the head of the family to admit that he is not fulfilling his leadership role of providing for the family. Before outside help is solicited, godparents or *compadres* may be consulted. If the family problem involves marital discord, the *compadre* of the marriage may function as mediator for the couple (Falicov, 1982; Sue & Sue, 1999). In a Puerto Rican family, the *padrino* also is used to mediate intrafamily conflict and act as an advocate for the family (Fitzpatrick, 1981). The *padrino* is an individual in one of the higher positions of the family structure who has a personal relationship with the family, for whom he provides material needs and emotional guidance.

Because Catholicism plays a vital role in the life of Latino Americans, in times of stress and illness, priests, folk healers, and religious leaders can be strong family resources. It is not unusual for a Latino to equate the role of the family therapist with that of a priest and to expect some immediate help from the therapist. At other times, the Latino family and family members may see the family therapist as a physician from whom they traditionally seek help for emotional and psychological problems (Padilla et al., 1976).

Mexican Americans attribute their emotional problems to two main causes: family conflicts and financial difficulty (Moll, Rueda, Reza, Herrera, & Vasquez,

1976). Among this group, family therapy is fairly well accepted as a methodology for family problem solving, as well as for individual symptoms. Further, the therapist is respected as an individual who possesses authoritative knowledge about human interaction.

In terms of family service needs, Latino families can be categorized into three types (Casas & Keefe, 1980; Padilla et al., 1976): (a) newly arrived immigrant families, (b) immigrant-American families, and (c) immigrant-descent families. Newly arrived immigrant families need information, referral, advocacy, and such concrete services as English-language instruction. Due to cultural and language barriers, they seldom seek personal or family therapy. Immigrant-American families are characterized by cultural conflict between foreign-born parents and American-born children. They need help in resolving generational conflicts, communication problems, role clarification, and renegotiation. Native or immigrant-descent families usually are acculturated, speak both languages at home, and can seek help from mainstream social services, including family therapists in private practice.

Within these broad service-needs classifications, Latino families also need to be understood from the perspective of their (family) developmental life-cycle tasks, in light of the constant need for change and adaptation to their new environment. Falicov (1999) identifies eight stages of Latino family life cycle. This paradigm allows for an understanding of expected transitions in the life of Latinos based on culturally relevant periods of expected change. Lyle and Faure (2000) expand upon Falicov's (1999) model to incorporate unexpected real-life crisis or transitions encountered by Latino families, such as geographical separations, early deaths, divorce, and stepfamilies. Within all these perspectives, Santiago-Rivera et al. (2002) conceptualize four different Latino family realities (the intact *familia,* the single-parent *familia,* the bicultural-biracial *familia,* and the immigrant *familia*) that need to be considered in work with Latino families.[7] This chapter will use these perspectives in guiding family therapy assessments and interventions with Latino families.

Applying Culturally Sensitive
Family Theories, Models, and Approaches

Cultural and Political Factors
Relevant in Family Therapy With Latino Families

The first part of this chapter presented important ecological factors (historical, social, economic, political, psychological and cultural) that operate to profoundly influence family life, structure, functioning, and processes. Below is a summary of key factors to consider in working with Latino families. These factors include

- Discrimination in education, employment, healthcare, and housing that compounds the external stressors of Latino families
- Poverty and other economic issues
- Migratory experiences (stress; culture shock; "crisis of loss," including possible post-traumatic stress in persons from war-torn countries; unresolved grief; a "circular" or back-and-forth migration pattern that may create dislocation or disconnection to family members; inability to return to war-torn countries [*emotional cutoff*])
- Acculturation stress and assimilation processes (generational gaps, intergenerational conflicts and issues, acculturation differences, tensions and conflicts between and within different family members, and special issues of acculturated bicultural families [intergenerational and intercultural conflicts due to different levels of acculturation] and cross-cultural biculturated families [Latinos have the highest rate of intermarriage in the United States; slightly more than half (57%) of third-generation Latinos cross-marry (Santiago-Rivera et al., 2002)])
- Language barriers (e.g., English-only classrooms) and linguistic considerations (English proficiency, bilingualism, language switching, "code switching," language barriers between family members that create family hierarchy problems)
- Immigration status and lack of documentation (discrimination and poverty, including tensions and other problems created by having documented and undocumented persons in the same family [binational families] and issues of transnational families)
- Cultural and racial and ethnic identity issues (as a mixed-race ethnic group heritage, i.e., mestizo and mulatto), as well as biracial and bicultural ethnic minority identity issues
- Changing and more varied Latino family structure and Latino family roles and values
- Latino spirituality, spiritualism, and religion
- Traditional beliefs concerning illnesses and health and understanding their role in coping patterns and implications for family therapy; understanding, respecting, and working with indigenous folk healers
- Contemporary urban social problems (such as gangs, teen pregnancy, drug abuse, high school drop-out or "push out," and welfare reform in which undocumented persons are rendered ineligible)
- Latino cultural values and worldview orientation
- Identify and focus on coping strengths: Although it is important to identify many of the previously listed factors that polarize the family, healing takes place through the identification and nurturance of strengths in the family

. Behavioral principles of family communication theory and family structure theory are discussed in this section. Practice principles derived from these theories will be reviewed also. Family communication theory and family structure theory are useful to therapists preparing to work with Latino families.

Family Communication Theory

Family communication theory and practice offers enormous potential for family therapy with Latino families. The following discussion focuses on family communication theories and therapy approaches and is organized into two parts. The first section describes principles of family communication behavior from the perspective of family communication theory. The second section describes practice principles derived from family communication therapy models.

Theory about communication has been an essential part of understanding families since the early days of some of the very first pioneers of family therapy (Duhl, 1989). Much of the following discussion about family communication theory and practice relies on the work of Virginia Satir (1967, 1986, 1988). Satir is acknowledged by family therapy historians as being the very first woman pioneer in family therapy (Duhl, 1989). Known to many as the "grandmother" of family therapy, she originally constructed her family therapy model with a focus on communication and problem solving (Duhl, 1989). During the course of her career, she experienced a shift of emphasis in her philosophy and began to incorporate existentialist philosophical notions into her already well-established and well-received family communication approach. Her revised family therapy model came to be known as the human validation process approach (Satir, 1986). Satir's revised approach retained important basic tenets of family communication behavior, such as the value of open and honest communication among family members and clarity of roles. However, her revised model also began to incorporate, in a very significant way, a *humanistic* focus. The end result is a family communication model of therapy that is an excellent philosophical fit with the cultural values of Latino families.

Specifically, Satir's revised human validation model emphasizes the growth potential of all individuals. Satir believes that one of the family's central and most critical functions is the enhancement of the self-esteem of its members. To this end, Satir focuses on facilitating communication in the family that will enhance the self-esteem of individuals in the family. This value assumption is extremely consonant with the traditional Latino value of respeto (respect) for the individual. Some of the most prominent Latino value orientations in interpersonal relationships are personalismo, respeto, dignidad, *simpatia, confianza,* and *carino.* These values correlate with each other and often are difficult to identify separately. Satir's trademark style of "making personal small talk" (which Latinos would designate *platicar*) before attempting to gain central assessment information, exemplifies the Latino value orientation of personalismo: The person is always more important than the task at hand, including the time factor. Satir is also very purposeful in addressing each and every family member by name and family position; being very careful to honor the position of heads of household represents her sensitivity (respeto) to each individual's position in the family as she strives to enhance a sense of pride, regardless of the individual's family position (dignidad). Satir's conversational, friendly, easy-going, sometimes humorous style (*simpatia*) helps her to gain approval of Latino families and family members. In our experience, when teaching Satir's model of family therapy it is not unusual to find students initially impatient with Satir's lengthy introductions and initial conversations before direct questioning begins. However, Satir's informal interpersonal style facilitates the development of trust, intimacy, and familiarity with family members (*confianza*) in establishing a therapeutic alliance. Satir follows a hierarchical approach to greeting family members, starting with males or elders and adults before children (appealing to the Latino families' *sense of hierarchy*). Probably one of the behaviors most uniquely attributable to Satir is her use of physical touch while talking to the person—her nonverbal expression of affection and genuine concern for the family and family members (*carino*).

Satir places a great deal of value on her roles as *observer, role model, advocate, culture broker,* and *educator.* Her role as the "elder," so to speak, within these family sessions is also consistent with Latino families' sense of hierarchy and expectations that family members will derive a great deal of their learning through listening, observation, and emulation of elders and family members who are seen as role models and teachers. Falicov (1998) cautions therapists to assume a "humble expert" approach with the Latino family. A balance must be maintained between humility and openness ("not knowing" to prevent stereotyping) and demonstrating expertise. Being direct but humble is interpreted as awareness of the limitations of the therapist's knowledge but with a genuine respect (respeto) for the family (Santiago-Rivera et al., 2002).

The underlying values and theoretical assumptions of Satir's communication family therapy are not only an excellent philosophical and existential fit with the critical constructionist practice perspective, her techniques are, as well, extremely compatible with social construction theory. (See chapter 1 for a discussion of social construction theory and the critical constructionist practice perspective.) Satir conceptualizes the therapist as having many important tasks. These tasks take on a decidedly social constructionist flavor. She views the tasks of the therapist as to *observe* and *describe* what is going on inside the family system from a position outside of the system—a belief central to the postmodernists—to *facilitate* a better understanding of the meanings behind communication and to *empower* the family to discover new ways of coping by *opening up space for alternative stories or* _actions._ Satir has always believed in the growth potential of individuals, their ability to make their own choices, and has clearly displayed within her practice model how much she values clients' knowledge of their own lives.

Satir believes that as a person experiences successes in good communication and problem solving, _self-esteem_ is enhanced. She believes that family problems are a result of poor coping, and poor coping is a result of low self-esteem. She states, "The person is not the problem, the coping is the problem" (American Association of Marriage and Family Therapists, 1986). Satir believes that good communication and problem-solving skills are essential elements for a satisfying family life. Furthermore, she believes that families under stress (such as Latino families) may, over time, adapt dysfunctional (family) roles that do not serve them well. The _blamer, super-reasonable,_ and _irrelevant_ roles may be especially dysfunctional for Latino family members, in view of prevailing collectivist cultural values that emphasize family cohesiveness. For example, a family member taking the blamer stance dominates, finds fault, and accuses; one taking the super-reasonable stance remains detached, not emotionally involved in family processes; and one adopting the irrelevant stance serves to distract family members from the task at hand and seems to be unrelated to and disinterested in anything that is going on in the family. Clearly, any of these stances would be diametrically opposed to traditional Latino cultural values of personalismo, respeto, dignidad, simpatia, confianza, and cariño. These values are but a few of the core cultural values that are violated by these dysfunctional family stances, and they should be viewed by the family therapist as serious threats to harmonious family life within Latino families.

Other role conflicts may present themselves as challenges to Latino families. _Role strain_ and _role conflict_ may result as a consequence of _mixed acculturative patterns,_ resulting in _acculturative tensions and conflicts_ (both between and within Latino family members, especially in the case of binational, transnational, bicultural, biracial, and cross-cultural families.) Traditional roles that formerly helped to establish and define important developmental milestones for age, gender, community, or family roles may no longer be available to isolated, marginalized, or biculturally conflicted families living away from or disconnected from Latino communities and extended family members. Latino families will need assistance in communicating about these painful issues and will need even greater assistance to move toward problem resolution.

The human validation process model advocates for clear and direct communication but not directive communication (Satir, 1986). The difference is this: Directive communication is an "in-your-face" communicative style, whereas direct communication conveys a clear message that is neither ambiguous, dishonest, nor vague. Latinos show respect for each other in their use of indirectness and may find direct communication methods rude or insensitive. Highly sensitive family issues should be presented first with an apology or recognition that the message could be interpreted as rude or offensive.

Direct criticism is to be avoided and is preferably placed within the *metacommunication* of a message (the message about the message) along with more powerful nonverbal cues. This more indirect style of communication is viewed as being more polite, respectful, and less aggressive. There is more reliance on nonverbal cues to relate a message; hence traditional Latino families are considered to be more of a *high-context communication culture* (Hall, 1976). This concept describes a culture that relies heavily on the nonverbal aspect of a message (how it is said) to relay some of the most important and powerful aspects of a message. Conversely, in a *low-context communication culture,* the most important and powerful aspect of a message is contained within the verbal component of a given communication—as is the case in Eurocentric cultures.

Communication theorists agree that *all behavior is communication.* Additionally, within all human communication there is the *verbal component of a message* (what is being said), and the *nonverbal component of a message* (how it is being said). Latino families view communication as an opportunity to affirm one's concern for others and to convey respect (respeto) for others. Hence, relationships are seen as an opportunity to develop and establish one's character and integrity as a person (dignidad).

Linguistic obstacles may undermine family communication processes; that is, some Latino family members may be bilingual, others may speak only (or primarily) English, and still others may speak only (or primarily) Spanish. Family members may be at different levels of acculturation or assimilation, rendering family sessions much more difficult to conduct. Additionally, varying *levels of acculturation* within the same family can create "acculturative tensions" within Latino families. Differences in acculturative behaviors (especially within the realm of communicative behaviors) may complicate the communication process for Latino families. Specifically, incongruous communication could occur and might take the form of inappropriateness of communication to other family members or behavior that (however unintentionally) appears invalidating to other family members (Satir, 1986). The family therapist is encouraged to pay special attention to the nonverbal content of family messages, given the high-context culture of more traditional Latino families.

The effects of acculturation and assimilation, as well as the effects of immigration on the family life cycle, may have forced Latino couples to renegotiate their relationship. Their need for economic survival in a hostile environment (wherein all family members who are employable, including elder children, have to take on employment when available) may force their relationships to shift—upsetting the traditional hierarchy in the family system and subsystems especially in the conjugal dyad, which may shift from a complementary (dominant-submissive) relationship to a symmetrical (similar) conjugal relationship. This shift often complicates the couple's relationship and family life, as it is likely to occur at a time when the family's emotional support system has been weakened and the demands for meeting basic family needs such as food, housing, and healthcare are greatest. Latino couples (especially those couples that have varying acculturative behaviors) need to be helped to "find their own way," to determine for themselves what blend (if any) of traditional versus acculturated conjugal behaviors will work for them. The family therapist is advised to facilitate couples to *reauthor their (ethnocultural) conjugal narrative,* which will help them to resolve power issues and move past these dilemmas.

The problem of internalized racism, that is, viewing oneself in the same negative light as one's oppressor, is of concern and relevance in practice with Latino families. This internalized oppression (accepting the negative messages and stereotypical images of others) is of general concern to all people of color, and family members need to be empowered to challenge these *globalized interpretations* of their culture and *deconstruct these debilitating and nonpotentiating ethnocultural metanarratives* to enable themselves to *reconstruct new, more potentiating narratives.*

People who have undergone painful migratory experiences and those from war-torn countries may need help in dealing with these traumatic experiences (coerced relocation, forced immigration, loss of national affiliation, relatives who were left behind and still remain in politically volatile countries), which can be emotionally intense and painful subjects. These emotionally laden issues may have become the source of *family secrets, myths,* and *rules* governing family and individual behavior. There are many potential areas of unresolved grief that may have become forbidden subjects for family discussion. Latino families and family members may be suffering from post-traumatic stress syndrome; and the family therapist can be helpful by engaging the family in *externalizing conversations,* wherein the family provides accounts of trauma in their lives (emotional state, familial, peer) to externalize the problem so that it is not nested in the individual or within the family (Laird, 1993; White & Epston, 1990). Families can also be encouraged to *restory* some of these traumatic experiences, to allow the family and its members an opportunity to locate the (specific) *origins of immobilizing aspects* of these experiences and losses (Laird, 1993). Latino families and family members should then be encouraged to *reconstruct a narration of oppression and resiliency* that *challenges disempowering sociopolitical and sociocultural metanarratives. Reflective dialogue* could provide for a quiet, *culturally syntonic* forum in which the Latino family and family members can *critically reflect* on their experiences and *restory painful or debilitating experiences* to find or create new ways of coping with experiences of migratory trauma (Rasheed & Rasheed, 1999). The family therapist will need to take great care and caution in approaching these subjects, especially as an outsider.

The principles of behavior derived from family communication theory can contribute significantly to understanding the dynamics and interaction of a Latino family. The following discussion aims to further explicate the manner in which these family communication principles can be applied to actual work with Latino families.

Communication Practice Principles

Communication Practice Principles as
They Relate to Work With Latino Families

Latino families may be very reluctant to seek help from cold, impersonal institutions, and this, in part, may be why Latino families seek help from mainstream social agencies only as a last resort. The challenge on the part of the therapist, when working with Latino families, is to "join" the family and to be accepted by them. Specifically, *cultural joining* (Rasheed & Rasheed, 1999) is the technique of exploring ways to make changes that are the most culturally syntonic to the family by including important cultural, religious, and/or civic leaders or even folk healers from the Latino community. These persons can also serve as expert cultural consultants to the therapist and thus lend credibility to the therapy process, as well as serving as additional systems of social support to families in counseling.

Because all behavior is communication of one kind or another, it is impossible not to communicate. The Latino style of communication is often governed by traditional hierarchical structure, which may result in communication that is more formal, indirect, and even guarded in public, especially when dealing with a (probably Anglo) therapist who is considered an authority figure (Falicov, 1982). If there are profound (communication) differences in style, Latinos may endure the first encounter with a therapist without displaying signs of displeasure, but they may not return for the next scheduled session.

To ensure that the therapy continues, the therapist should solicit feedback from the Latino family and family members and should state clearly that clients will not be contacted again if they fail to meet the next appointment. The concept of *metacommunication* (in this case, the "message within the message" is that of a command) is highly relevant to Latino families. According to Haley (1963), every relationship contains within it an implicit power struggle over who defines the nature of that relationship. The traditional hierarchical structure of the Latino family means that these families experience limited power struggles, because each family member knows his or her position and status in relation to other family members. The infusion of dominant cultural influences on individualism, the process of immigration, and family life-cycle adjustment may have greatly altered the traditionally prescribed vertical and hierarchical role structure determined by age, sex, generation, and birth order of family members. One of the preliminary challenges for the therapist may be to help the family rework its metacommunication process for problem-solving purposes.

Latino family interaction revolves around a prescribed vertical and hierarchical role structure determined by age, sex, and professional authority. Because of the authoritative role of the therapist, family members often find it impolite or inappropriate to disagree during a therapy session. It is important that the therapist actively encourage family members to express their positive and negative reactions to the therapy goal and process. The hierarchical role structure places the father in a spokesman role, and his position as head of the family should never be challenged with attempts to influence the family communication system, especially by his own children, with mainstream cultural ideals of democratic family decision making. It is advisable that beginning family therapy sessions be divided between spouse subsystem and sibling subsystem. Further, to respect the authoritarian parental position, parents should be interviewed first and children second. When the parents are ready to be interviewed with their children (assuming the therapist is bilingual), Spanish can be used to communicate with the parents and English can be used with the children. An interchange of languages is useful in delineating blurred generational boundaries (Falicov, 1982). Should the therapist need a translator (this is not an ideal situation, as the presence of a translator may change the counseling structure and dynamics [Bamford, 1991; Bradford & Munoz, 1993; Seijo, Gomez, & Freidenberg, 1991]), it is highly recommended that Spanish-speaking professionals be used instead of family members or friends of the family.

To maintain a good therapeutic working relationship with the Latino family, especially the father, the therapist's communicative style should be less direct and less confrontational. Satir's use of humor, allusions, and diminutives may soften the directness; these are often more effective forms of communication with Latinos, as they are consistent with Latino cultural transactional styles.

Communication theory is helpful when assisting the family in problem solving, renegotiation, and redefinition of power relationships. Latinos may find the concept of power idiosyncratic, threatening, competitive, disrespectful, Western, and, therefore, foreign. The role of the therapist should be guided by the cultural values of the family. For example, the therapist should use the polite form of the pronoun "you" (*usted*) with adults to indicate respect. Children can be addressed in the familiar form (*tu*) (Bernal & Flores-Ortiz, 1982). Haley's therapeutic tactics, such as prescribing the symptom (encouraging the usual dysfunctional behavior), may be confusing and disrespectful to Latino families. Haley's technique of *relabeling* or *reframing* (by emphasizing the positive) is consistent with the Latino culture's emphasis on respect and interdependence. The relabeling technique also can help the family shift from the disease model to an interpersonal and social justice perspective, such as intergenerational conflict experienced among family members.

Virginia Satir's (1967) communication theory can be used to help Latino family members recognize the dysfunctional roles they sometimes assume as a maladaptation to cultural transition and acculturative stresses. She also challenges family members to be compassionate toward each other and to help each other to feel good and "respected." Familismo is very important, and Latinos are taught to sacrifice self-interest to better other family members and the family as a whole. Satir's theory focusing on the "feeling good" (1967, 1986) component of each individual and the entire family should greatly appeal to Latino families and family members, as it is consistent with Latino cultural values of harmony, collaterality, collectivity, and cooperation. Her use of family history, which she calls the "family life chronology" (Satir, 1967), can be an invaluable *narrative tool* in helping the family reminisce and value its past, as well as working through those losses especially experienced by immigrant Latino families. This discussion can also lead to the exploration of the influences of acculturation and may be critical to helping the current family members better understand new family system dynamics.

The reliance on the use of *storytelling techniques* using native culture stories and characters to deal with the adjustment issues of children, also called *cuento* therapy (Constantino, Malgady, & Rogler, 1986; Ramos-McKay, Comas-Diaz, & Rivera, 1988); *metaphors and images; narratives* incorporating culture value orientation, short stories, and religious icons to address Latino issues, oppression, and abuse (Bracero, 1998); and *dichos* (Spanish proverbs, sayings, and words interjected to convey a client's behavior, thoughts, conflicts, and so on in storytelling or self-disclosure style; Zuniga, 1992) are *culturally syntonic* and a natural fit with critical constructionist perspectives and techniques. Latino families and family members can be encouraged to relive important aspects of their original traditions and ethnic and cultural heritage by storytelling and the use of dichos, metaphors, and narratives, which may serve two purposes: reinforce positive self-images (or *build potentiating ethnic narratives*) to combat what individuals may feel is forever lost to them and their families and passing on important cultural images and memories to nurture positive ethnic identities (narratives) in children.

In light of the high-context nature of communication, with an emphasis on the nonverbal aspect of the communication or message in traditional Latino families, *family sculpting* and *family choreography* can be extremely useful techniques. Further, the family therapist will be able to encourage parents to "sculpt" their perception of family problems without fear of shame or embarrassment when there are language barriers or communication difficulties between the therapist and the parents and children (who may be acculturated at different levels).

Family sculpting and family choreography techniques can be especially helpful in their potential to bridge communication difficulties that arise when members of the same family do not have the same command of English or, worse, not all family members speak either English or Spanish. Profound linguistic difficulties often are consequences of the result of different periods of immigration by family members to the United States and different rates of acculturation of these family members. It is not uncommon to find older members speaking only their native language and younger American-born members speaking only English. Because these family members may lack a common language by which they can communicate or share emotional exchanges, inappropriate, invalid, and confusing communicative exchanges are bound to occur.

Satir (1967, 1986, 1988; Satir et al., 1975, 1991) employs a rich array of experiential techniques (e.g., *sculpting, drama, communication stances, family stress ballet, ropes, parts party*). Although these techniques are invaluable in their own right, in that many of these family exercises do not heavily rely on verbal interchanges (as discussed earlier as useful when there are linguistic barriers, either between family members or between the family and the therapist), these strategies can be considered *nonverbal narratives* in that they encourage family members to tell their story—their way. Family members are free to recreate their vision or perception of family relationships and family problems, as well as solutions to these problems.

Family therapists need to proceed with caution in implementing some of Satir's (Satir et al., 1991) experiential techniques, such as *family sculpting, family choreography, drama, communication stances, family stress ballet, ropes,* and *parts party*, even though these techniques may be potentially very helpful in family therapy with Latino families, who emphasize learning by observation and participation, as well as a reliance on rich metaphors to impart important messages and teaching. Family therapists must take great care not to intrude and otherwise impose their own "sculpting suggestions" (asking family members to take certain positions, etc.), which may violate (sex role and family) cultural norms and ideals of polite, respectful, and appropriate behavior.

To communicate effectively with a Latino family, family therapists need to consider modifying their behavior, such as limiting verbosity, slowing speech, and lowering the voice. They can communicate by paying attention to family members' needs and by respecting them as worthy, good individuals. Therapists can communicate effectively by not being overly dependent on the verbal mode of interaction; instead, family and family members' use of metaphors in story telling and within other oral Latin traditions, poetry, journals, artistic and musical efforts, or other natural assets can be used to facilitate communication. A more varied use of untapped clinical data and sources is very much a postmodernist notion (Rasheed, 1998). Latino families should be encouraged not to strive for consensus and to *explore the multiple (emotional) meanings* of important historical and cultural events and experiences. Family members then become empowered to take from these experiences what is most meaningful and helpful to them (Laird, 1993).

Interacting harmoniously during times of transition and crisis requires communicative skills, including effective styles. Traditionally, Latinos are taught to be cooperative and "other centered" in interpersonal relationships. An exchange of real feelings and intentions among all individuals at the early stage of therapy, therefore, may not be conducive to problem solving.

In summary, communication family therapy, especially as developed by Virginia Satir (1986) and discussed in this section, is a family practice approach that shares the cultural value assumptions and philosophical and existential positions of traditional Latino family life. Communication family therapy is also philosophically and existentially compatible with social construction theory. Furthermore, the varied roles that are prescribed for the therapist within this family therapy model (namely, *educator and teacher, facilitator, mediator, advocate,* and *role model*) are important and viable roles for those persons who seek to enhance the communication process of Latino families (whether foreign born, refugee, or U.S. born).

Family Structure Theory

This discussion of family structure theory centers on work developed and advanced by Bowen (1978) and Minuchin (1974). Reviewed here are behavioral principles and practice principles of structural family theory as they relate to assessment and therapy with Latino families.

Bowen was trained as a psychoanalyst. He based his theory on a clinical study of schizophrenia at the Menninger Clinic in the early 1950s and at the National Institute for Mental Health in the early 1960s. Specifically, Bowen was impressed with the "emotional stuck togetherness" (*emotional fusion*) and the intensely transactional nature of the nuclear family system (Bowen, 1978, p. 207). Bowen did not specify the ethnic composition of the "sick" families under study, so one must assume his family sample represents Anglo middle-class American families. Bowen bases his concept of *differentiation of self* on this intense emotional "stuck togetherness" characteristic of a nuclear family. The concept may not have the same degree of relevance to Latino families, whose strong sense of familismo extends beyond the nuclear family to include extended family members (*compadres*). Because of the inclusive relationship with extended family members, interaction within the nuclear family is seldom so close and intense.

Latino husband and wife interaction is not always based on romanticism, as is common in egalitarian relationships where there is more "emotional stuck togetherness." Because the spousal system boundary may not be as emotionally close, it may not be so susceptible to the *process of triangulation,* a three-person system that Bowen considers the "building block of all emotional systems" in and outside the family. The central nurturing role of the Latina mother and the disciplinarian role of the father may create an alliance between mother and children that will exclude the father. Such a structural coalition is well accepted within the Latino family structure, as opposed to Anglo family culture, which views this situation negatively. Further, the Latina wife's sense of familismo, hierarchy, and family obligation discourages her from subverting her husband's relationship with her or sabotaging her child's relationship with his father. Under normal circumstances, Latinos usually conducts themselves according to what is best for the whole family, even if this requires self-sacrifices. However, during moments of crisis triggered by acculturation, triangulation may develop.

While the cultural practice of familismo with extended family members makes the nuclear emotional system less intense and triangulation less likely, it may weaken the *family projection process* and the *multigenerational transmission process* described in Bowen's theory. Bowen (1978) defines the concept of *emotional cutoff* as unresolved emotional attachment to parents. This scenario may be more prevalent among newly arrived Latino immigrants, particularly the 1980 wave of Cuban refugees. The immigrants' inability to return for home visits further compounds their adjustment problems and feelings of isolation.

Bowenian family therapy incorporates important intergenerational processes, allowing family therapists to explore critical historical events and intergenerational patterns affecting current functioning. Bowen's theory conceptualizes family change in a nonpathological framework as the family adapts to a stage in the life cycle such as marriage, birth of a child, departure of each child, retirement, aging, and death (Santiago-Rivera et al., 2002).

Structural family therapy is highly recommended with Latino families because it incorporates a generational view; focuses on balancing the structure of the family; and uses a direct, concrete, here-and-now approach to problem solving (Wilson et al., 2000). The model's hierarchical parent-child relational position parallels Latinos' vertical communication style and reinforces the expected boundaries within the family (Santiago-Rivera et al., 2002). Similarly, the broad family framework, with a direct, no-nonsense, problem-solving approach, agrees with the preferred style of intervention among Latinos.

Minuchin (1974) looks at the structure of the Latino family system. It is characterized by its clear hierarchical role structure, which is determined by age, sex, generation, and birth order of family members. The authority distribution within the family is clearly defined: The father acts as head of the household; the mother acts as mediator between the children and their father; and older children, especially males, exert authority over younger siblings. The dominant culture family structure gives husband and wife different levels of authority over their children (Minuchin, 1974).

A therapist working with a Latino family should not assume that the spouse boundary is *diffuse* (too open to outside interference or intrusion, not well defined, or not intact) just because the spousal system of the Latino family is structured differently (hierarchical instead of egalitarian). It is also important to keep in mind that although the Latino father acts as spokesman for the entire family, in actuality the mother may be the true power behind the surface of the family structure (Garcia-Preto, 1996a).

The Latino family is typically large, and it is not unusual, therefore, for the older sibling to have the responsibility of caring for younger children and assisting with other household duties normally performed by adults while both parents work outside of the home. A therapist should avoid interpreting this as *boundary diffusion* and should not label an older child as "parentified child" (Minuchin, 1974, p. 53). This complementary accommodation between spouses and between parents and children characterizes the strength of the Latino American family structure.

Immigration, acculturation, and the family life cycle transition sometimes undermine the Latino father's authoritarian position. The children's acculturation rate is often faster than the parents'. The parents may have to rely on their children as interpreters, given that children often learn English faster than their parents. The Latino father may be unable to find a job in the United States. If the mother does find a job outside the home, she may seek a more egalitarian relationship with her husband. She may also be torn between performing her traditional wife and mother role and working to support the family economically. The entire situation can create a state of *enmeshment* characterized by the *diffusion of intergenerational boundaries* (Minuchin, 1974).

We have introduced the concept of *invisible cultural triangles* (Rasheed & Rasheed, 1999) as an expansion of Bowen's triangle concept, reconceptualizing the concept of triangles to refer to the existence of a third person, object, or event in a cultural system that exerts a powerful but not always apparent force on the systemic or dyadic relationship system. Historically, traumatic events and experiences (as in the case of Central Americans from war-torn countries or Latinos with painful immigration experiences) can become *triangled* into the emotional system of Latino families and *create immobilizing and debilitating ethnocultural (family, community, tribal, or clan) narratives*. These *sociopolitical narratives* can take on a life of their own; hence the person or family can become a victim of a *collective narrativized past* or at least a *narrative stance* that does not work for them (or their family).

A related term also coined by us is that of *invisible cultural loyalties* (Rasheed & Rasheed, 1999). This concept is an expansion of the family therapy (intergenerational) concept of *invisible loyalties,* also referred to as *relational indebtedness* or *family ledgers,* as originally conceptualized by Ivan Boszormenyi-Nagy (1987). Invisible loyalties or *family indebtedness* can date back several generations and can also be a result of *multigenerational* and *cross-generational unresolved conflicts* or unrealized goals within the family or tribal group (Boszormenyi-Nagy, 1987). Within cross-cultural, bicultural or biracial, and binational or transnational families, it is not hard to imagine that it might become difficult to preserve family legacies and continue family cultural traditions. It is easy to imagine the emotional conflict that family members may feel if these issues are not adequately addressed. Hence, *family secrets, myths,* and (powerful, but unspoken) *family rules* may serve to further complicate and exacerbate emotional turmoil if they operate in tangent with invisible cultural loyalties or with *invisible cultural triangles.*

Bowen's concept of *emotional cutoff* has significant application in work with Latino families. According to Bowen, everyone has some degree of unresolved emotional attachment to the previous generation. The lower the level of differentiation, the greater the degree of unresolved dependency to be dealt with in the person's own generation and that can be passed onto the next generation in the *family projection process.* The cutoff consists of denial and isolation of the problem when living close to the parents or by physically running away, as in the case of (voluntary) immigration, or a combination of the two. As a rule, the more a nuclear family maintains emotional contact with the previous generations, the calmer, more orderly, and less problematic their lives will be. Conversely, the greater the degree of cutoff, the more the nuclear family becomes a sort of emotional "pressure cooker." This concept indicates the importance of the extended family system, within which Latinos are able to maintain consistent contact with each other.

A different pace or level of acculturation between family members will tend to create tension and cultural value differences. Younger children may become acculturated at a much faster pace in an American public school. These differences in acculturation can lead to *acculturative tensions* and *acculturative conflicts,* which can lead to even more emotional distance within families (Rasheed & Rasheed, 1999) and, if left unresolved, can be primary contributing factors to emotional cutoff or *disengagement* between family members.

Family structure theory focusing on the family system's structural (contextual) dynamics, especially the *creation, maintenance,* and *modification* of *boundaries,* which are rules defining who participates and how (Minuchin, 1974), is useful in work with Latino families. In an extended family system with multiple households, the subsystem boundaries between spouses, grandparents, parents and children, and siblings seldom are closed or rigid. These subsystems are functional historically because of cultural value reinforcements. As times change and as

Latino families continue to migrate to areas in which fewer and fewer Latino families live in or near them, the original extended family ties may break down. These factors, coupled with racial and cultural oppression and discrimination, make it difficult for Latino individuals to retain culturally adaptive, functional family roles and traditional boundaries.

The family's ability to maintain traditional parent-child roles is further handicapped by the fact that both parents, and sometimes older siblings, have to work outside the home. Long working hours and different working schedules can create interactional problems and difficulty within a subsystem and between subsystems. For example, if the father (or even both parents) works a night shift, the parents will have little time to interact with each other and maintain and solidify their spousal subsystem. The parents may also have too little time with their children, and older siblings may have to assume parenting responsibilities in the family (boundary rupture).

The above scenario will not pose much of a problem if Latino families are able to maintain the larger parental subsystem typical of traditional Latin culture (as in the case of *compadrazco*). However, with increasing migration and relocation to secure employment, the Latino family is becoming increasingly nuclear, single parent, and divorced in structure. A ruptured system boundary requires that family members use a great deal of sensitivity, effort, and energy to repair it. Raising the issue of boundary conflicts and subsequent repair can disrupt harmony within the family and is discouraged by the traditional culture. However, this "boundary work" is increasingly becoming a growing concern and issue in family therapy with Latino families. Finally, *boundary modification and repair* require that family therapists working with these families possess sufficient and appropriate interpersonal communication skills.

Minuchin's (1974) concept of different sources of stress reflecting the family system and its structure is relevant to work with Latino families. His emphasis on the "stressful contact of the whole family with extrafamilial forces" (p. 63) sets him apart from other theorists, whose major concerns are confined to the extended family or the nuclear family system. By focusing on the extrafamilial forces, Minuchin is sensitive to the political, social, and cross-cultural processes of poverty and discrimination that many Latino families face after arriving to the United States. Minuchin advocates that family therapists assume the role of an *ombudsman*. They can then assist the family in reorganizing various social institutions and structures for its own benefit.

Family Structure Practice Principles

"Differentiation of self" is a universal process, varying only in quantity and quality among different cultures. For example, Anglo-Americans may believe that sending an adolescent to work outside the home encourages the adolescent's differentiation of self. The same behavior should not be expected of a Latino adolescent whose parents need him to assist with daily house chores. Furthermore, his ethnicity and lack of fluency in English may prevent his finding and keeping a job. Instead of self-differentiation, the general rule among Latino families is not to separate but to maintain connectedness; the "we" takes precedence over the "I." The relational and interdependent nature of Latino families corresponds to an understanding of the self-construct as a collective developmental process instead of a process in which the object is a differentiated individualist self (Santiago-Rivera et al., 2002). Terms generated among Latinos to replace the dominant culture's construct of the differentiated self are the *familial self* (Falicov, 1998) and the *cultural self* (Romero, 2000). Different cultures define and facilitate the process of differentiation of self differently. It is the responsibility of each therapist to learn about the specifics of the Latino culture and to assist clients to differentiate accordingly.

Bowen's (1978) coaching process of obtaining, organizing, and understanding the family's history makes sense in terms of accurate assessment of individual and family needs. The process, however, may be antithetical to the Latino's "present" orientation. Newly arrived Latinos may be reluctant to invest energy, time, and financial resources to find out what is wrong with their parents, relatives, and ancestors. The research process may be a more viable therapeutic tool with acculturated, middle class Latino families.

Bowen's (1978) premise that parental relationship dictates the entire nuclear family's emotional system is logical. His preference for singling out the couple relationship as a therapeutic target may alienate the parents. The mother often feels more challenged to perform as a good mother than as a wife. Bowen's emphasis on concentrating on the individual in family therapy can be applicable in dealing with an authoritative, rigid Latino father who does not tolerate family members challenging him. In defending this one-to-one therapeutic technique, Bowen (1978) writes: "From my orientation, a theoretical system that 'thinks' in terms of family and works toward improving the family system is family psychotherapy" (p. 157). The one-to-one therapeutic modality may be the only workable resolution for many Latino families. This is the preferred modality when interaction is rigidified by traditional role structure and the family as a whole is not amenable to family therapy because of mistrust, inadequate resources, or language barriers.

Some (less acculturated or non-English speaking) family members may not feel comfortable and may remain unavailable for conjoint therapy. Bowen's (1978) technique of focusing upon one individual, usually the more acculturated or respected member in the family (or whoever is willing to come), should be useful. In any case, this individual could be a grandparent, older sibling, other extended family (e.g., madrina/padrino or compadrazco). Although the therapist may work with an individual, the goal is to modify the structure of the emotional system of the family through that individual's change and effort.

Bowen's (1978) detached but interested, low-key approach to problem solving, during which he takes a careful family history (multigenerational transmission records or ethnohistory), reflects his sensitivity and respect for the cultural nurturance system, immigration and migration processes, intergenerational perspective, and the need for individualizing each family.

Bowen's (1978) belief is that the therapist's roles include those of *coach, facilitator,* and *consultant.* This therapeutic style is very compatible with a social constructionist practice framework, in that Bowen's primary goal in this therapy model is to coach the family and family members through a (self) discovery process by constructing a narrative of the family's history, primarily through the use of the *genogram* (a multigenerational diagram of family information). In this model of family therapy, the client is the expert in charge of the data collection process. The therapist is merely there to help the family and its members sort through their emotional reaction to the meanings that they ascribe to various family information gathered about family relationships, family patterns, and family (emotional) processes. For the most part, the family and its members set the goals and desired outcomes, as well as determining how or whether current family relationships will or will not change. Hence, Bowenian family therapy does not rely upon or employ the therapists' *privileged ways of knowing* about the family. The family and its members are free to create and discover the *collective narrative of the family* as the therapist creates *a space for multiple meanings* of the family's experiences.

In light of the emphasis on the rich historical, cultural, and familial traditions of Latino cultures, it is especially important for the family therapist to empower the Latino family and family members to *locate the origins of individual personal narratives*—especially *debilitating, nonpotentiating narratives* (Young, 1996). The genogram can provide a way for the family therapist to help the family and its member *locate the origins of immobilizing, subjugating narratives* and their context and significance (e.g., historical, political, economic, sociocultural, familial). This discovery process may uncover family myths or secrets derived from generations of dysfunctional family emotional processes as the source of the emotional pain for the family or individual family member. The discovery process may uncover societal prejudice, discrimination, and racism to be at the root of troubling *ethnic narratives* (*marginalized* or *negative stereotypical narratives*). Creating space for more *empowering, liberating narratives* makes it possible for the family and its members to revise and reconstruct these stories (a *reauthoring, restorying,* or even *racial restorying process*), which can offer new information, new resources, and multiple opportunities (Freeman, 1992). It is also important to note that in light of the cultural value of indirect communication (which avoids confrontational power struggles) these reauthored stories can reflect each family member's unique emotional experience and unique interpretation. Helping to maintain important close family ties as *multiple (emotional) meanings* is encouraged.

There are many advantages of the Bowenian family therapy approach in light of the traditional values of the Latino family. Family work can still be conducted even when families are separated by long distances as a result of immigration or migration or relocation to other states or cities. Because not all of the subsystems and dyads within the family are required to be present at the same time for family therapy to proceed, potentially explosive and volatile *cross-generational tensions* and *conflicts* need not be exacerbated. Family members can sort through issues such as *generational splits* and acculturation tensions and conflicts. Family members can then repair emotional cutoffs (caused either by forced physical separation or via emotional detachment that acculturative conflicts may have exacerbated) and begin to repair other (emotional) damage that *cultural transitioning* may have had on family emotional relationships, in a much less emotionally charged atmosphere.

Minuchin's (1974) differential applications of *joining techniques* that focus on the beginning phase of therapy reflect his sensitivity to individual family differences and the wisdom that structural change in a family usually requires time and patience. His *maintenance technique,* whereby therapists allow themselves to be governed by the basic rules that regulate the transactional process in a specific family system, goes a long way toward helping to establish mutual respect and trust with the family.

Minuchin's (1974) joining and maintenance techniques are compatible with Latino family values and structure, but his *disequilibration techniques* or *family restructuring techniques* generally do not share the same degree of congruence and effectiveness with this specific ethnic group. These techniques, including *enactment* and *boundary marking, escalating stress* (by emphasizing differences), *physical movement, utilizing the symptom* (by exaggerating it), and *creating affective intensity* (by manipulating the mood and escalating the emotional intensity), are much too esoteric (not practical or immediately useful), too directive, disrespectful of harmony and balance, emotionally confrontive, and, therefore, antithetical to Latino culture. With modification, however, these techniques may work with bicultural or highly acculturated Latino families and family members.

In an *ethnohistorical* approach to family therapy with Latinos, a meticulous, detailed narrative account of each person's (unique) emotional experience of the many losses and painful experiences has the ability to complement existing intergenerational approaches that focus primarily on intra- and interfamilial issues and events. Taking an ethnohistorical account of how Latino families and family members have come to construct their own *individual narrative* thus allows for a *reflective dialogue* that can lead to first a *deconstructive of marginalizing, immobilizing ethnic narratives* (as well as *deconstructing negative sociocultural metanarratives* of the family group) and then empowering Latino clients to *reconstruct more liberating and potentiating narratives* and begin the healing process.

Bowen's (1978) definition of the role of a therapist is that of a *culture broker*. This is consistent with the emic approach to work with Latinos. His heavy reliance on the client to be active and to implement the research, assessment, and differentiation processes may not be congruent with the Latino's perception of the therapist as an expert. Hence the therapist's roles of teacher, research, strategist, supporter, and cheerleader should be conducted with a greater degree of activity, especially at the onset of therapy with Latino families and family members.

Minuchin's differential applications of joining techniques are especially helpful during the engagement phase of therapy with a Latino family (Bernal & Flores-Ortiz, 1982). The strategic use of the maintenance technique enables the therapist to organize therapy by the basic rules that regulate the transactional process of a Latino family system. By following the transactional process of a specific family, the therapist can capitalize on the personalismo quality essential for establishing a working relationship with the family. In work with a three-generation Latino family presenting a rigid hierarchical structure, the therapist may find it advisable to address the grandfather first. Adherence to the family transactional process may perpetuate the pathogenic structure of the family, but such a *transitional joining technique* is essential if the therapist is to have any impact on the family. Once personalismo is cultivated and trust is developed, the therapist can use his or her role as "padrino" to unstructure and restructure the family.

The technique of tracking may help the therapist examine the content of family interaction and analyze family structure. The therapist should keep in mind that Latino family structure differs from that of the dominant culture, and the degree of intensity within each subsystem varies as compared to the dominant culture. For instance, although the Latino spousal subsystem is not as emotionally intense as that of the dominant culture, the Latino sibling subsystem and the extended family subsystem are much stronger and more involved. Minuchin's (1974) boundary-making and restructuring techniques are helpful, provided they are adapted to the Latino family structure framework.

In applying Minuchin's (1974) disequilibration (of boundary) technique, the therapist can use different modalities, including interviewing the parents separately, using Spanish to communicate with the parents, and using English when speaking to children.

Minuchin's joining techniques are generally sensitive to the Latino family structure, but his family restructuring techniques, such as *escalating stress* (by emphasizing differences), *utilizing the symptom* (by exaggerating it), and *manipulating mood or creating affective intensity* (by escalating the emotional intensity) are highly confrontational. They should not be used prior to developing a trusting relationship. The strategic application of these techniques will be illustrated in the case illustration in Part 3 of this chapter.

The preceding discussions aim at presenting a clear picture of the cultural values and family structure of the Latino family structure. Communication and structure family therapy theories have been reviewed, along with their application in therapy with Latino families and family members. Attention will now be directed to culturally relevant techniques and skills in three phases of treatment: beginning, problem solving, and termination-evaluation.

PART 2: CULTURALLY RELEVANT TECHNIQUES AND SKILLS IN DIFFERENT PHASES OF THERAPY

Beginning Phase

The engagement phase of therapy is a critical period for Latino clients. Therapists must recognize its importance and be cognizant of the traditional help-seeking patterns of this group. Such patterns include the Latino's under use of therapy, high dropout rate, language barrier, lack of financial resources, and unfamiliarity with family therapy as a viable therapeutic modality for family problem solving.

The following discussion attempts to apply and integrate the cultural knowledge of Latinos and communication and family structure theories used during the beginning phase of a family therapy. Specifically, four major skills and techniques are considered essential in therapy with a Latino family in the beginning therapy phase. These skills and techniques are (a) engaging the client or family, (b) cultural transitional mapping and data collection, (c) mutual goal setting, and (d) selecting a focus or system for therapy.

Engaging the Client or Family

There exists a long history of discrimination against Latinos. Clients who have experienced such discrimination find it difficult to trust a family therapist who is perceived as representative of the majority system. The level of mistrust is compounded by the fact that some Latinos do not have the proper documents to reside in this country. It is important that therapists define their role early with the client and disassociate themselves from any connection to immigration authorities. To develop an element of trust, a therapist can help the client feel comfortable by displaying in her office objects, pictures, or symbols from Latino culture. Because the social interaction of the Latino is governed by hierarchical role structure, the therapist needs to address the father or grandfather first. To convey a sense of respect, the therapist is advised to use the polite form of the pronoun "you" (*usted*) with adults. A tone of acceptance that avoids confrontation is especially essential during this period.

The language factor is most important during the engagement phase with a family who is unable to speak English (Gonzales, 1978). It can be humiliating, especially for older Latinos who try to speak English but are unable to be understood. Using children as translators immediately reverses the authority structure of the family, and it may further alienate the parental subsystem, especially the father. When there are no Spanish-speaking therapists available, it is advisable to use Latino adults as interpreters. However, Abad and Boyce (1979) found that the use of translators produced distortions that resulted in limitations and frustrations for both therapist and client. On the other hand, a study by Kline, Austin, and Acosta (1980) indicated that the use of translators did not have an adverse effect. Rather, Spanish-speaking clients felt greatly understood and were positive about their treatment experiences.

Latino families may expect the therapist to act as a medical doctor. The therapist needs to be active, polite, and willing to give advice. The family may have experienced past discrimination. The therapist is advised, therefore, to acknowledge these family experiences as a means to "join" the family emotional process. In addition, therapists need to create good feelings (Satir, 1967) within the family by praising their efforts to confront the difficult problems of daily living.

The application of relationship skills in the process of joining takes into consideration the differences between each Latino subgroup. For instance, in engaging Cuban families in therapy, attention needs to be devoted to empathizing with the family's defensive element myths about returning to Cuba (Bernal & Flores-Ortiz, 1982). A third-generation Puerto Rican family, however, may be more concerned with respect and disrespect. To maintain the Latino family's "present" and "doing" orientation, therapists should provide the family with personal observation, positive feedback, and concrete suggestions. The therapist's acknowledgment of the important contributions made by various family members can revitalize the familismo cherished by the family. Therapists' relabeling of family difficulties as family transactional issues provides the family with hope and concrete solutions to their problems.

Skills and Techniques in Cultural Transition

Mapping and Data Collection

The therapist should demonstrate personal interest in the family to be consistent with the Latino orientation of personalismo. This can be accomplished by first determining the cultural background of the family and inquiring about it. This shifts the focus of the therapy session away from the "problem" of the "identified patient" and provides the family with an opportunity to educate the therapist, who plays the role of cultural broker. As the therapist assumes the role of a researcher, Minuchin's (1974) tracking technique is helpful. It allows the therapist to follow the subjects discussed by family members like a "needle follows the record groove" (p. 176).

Once the preliminary problem has been identified, the therapist proceeds to obtain information essential to understanding the family system and its content. The frameworks of Boszormenyi-Nagy and Krasner (1980) are helpful in ascertaining the family's connectedness with their birthplace, culture, or roots:

> Having roots and legacies in common is a nonsubstitutive bond among people that not only outlasts physical and geographical separations from family of origin, but also influences the degree to which offspring can be free to commit themselves to relationships outside of the original ties, including marriage and parenthood of their own. (p. 768)

To ascertain the migration phase of the family, the therapist needs to inquire how long the family has lived in the United States. Families, as well as individuals within the family, acculturate at different rates. This can cause added stress and problems with each other in family transactions (Szapocznik et al., 1978). The therapist can assess the degree of connectedness to the culture of origin by asking the reason behind the family's immigration. The therapist should also inquire who initiated the move, and what connection the family already had in the United States; other questions pertaining to the political, social, and family pressures preceding the move; and which family members remain in the homeland. These questions can generate important information with which to ascertain "invisible obligations" (Boszormenyi-Nagy & Krasner, 1980). An assessment of a Latino family's connectedness to its culture is critical, for it leads to "identifying cultural and relational resources; understanding of loyalty conflicts; obtaining a broader contextual view; and developing legacy-based therapeutic strategies" (Bernal & Flores-Ortiz, 1982, p. 363).

Considering the importance of extended family ties, a therapist needs to assess the strength or potential dysfunction of the present household boundary and support system. The technique of cultural mapping and the use of a genogram are helpful in assessing multigenerational patterns and influences. They also provide some insight into how different Latino groups wish to resolve their family problems in accordance with traditional values.

To some extent, all family problems can be attributed to the family and the family members' coping mechanisms with that world controlled by the dominant culture. Therefore, it is vitally important in the course of the first therapy stage that the therapist establish which phase of the process of acculturation the family is currently experiencing and how they have dealt with the vicissitudes of previous phases (Sluzki, 1979). Viewing the outside world with distrust and hostility, Latino families (especially those families that may have undocumented family members) may maintain no meaningful contact with mainstream societal agencies such as healthcare agencies. Such data need to be collected for future therapy purposes. Therapists should be prepared for an *elongated assessment phase* (Rasheed & Rasheed, 1999) because of the unique and complex societal factors affecting the lives of Latino families. Family therapists are encouraged to use an *ethnographic* (anthropological) *approach* to assessing families (Rasheed & Rasheed, 1999) and to "view the family as tiny societies that over time, seem to develop their own systems of meaning and beliefs, their own mythologies, and ritual practices, and their own cultures" (Laird, 1993, p. 80).

Mutual Goal Setting

The basic problem inherent in the process of mutual goal setting stems from the different perceptions of the therapist and the family. Again, the therapist's knowledge and receptivity toward Latino culture is valuable not only in the problem identification process but also later at the implementation stage. Many of the problems experienced by Latino families, especially newly arrived families and families of lower socioeconomic class, are basically social and involve learning to cope with environmental stresses. The therapist's responsiveness to the family's request for immediate, concrete services and to act occasionally as the family's advocate helps to open up other problems plaguing the family (Mizio, 1979).

Falicov (1982, 1998) further divides therapeutic goals with Latino families into three categories: (a) the therapeutic goal related to situational stress, (b) the therapeutic goal related to dysfunctional patterns of cultural transition, and (c) the therapeutic goal related to transcultural dysfunctional patterns. Situational stress occurs at the interface between the family and the new environment. Problems may include social isolation, unfamiliarity with community resources, or poverty. Dysfunctional patterns of cultural transition are interactional patterns that were once adaptive to cultural transition but later became rigid in the family's functioning. An example of dysfunctional patterns is a parent-child role reversal due to different rates of acculturation. Transcultural dysfunctional patterns are basically universal and are characterized by a limited range of repetitive interactional behaviors, hierarchical imbalance with rigid coalitions, developmental impasses, and other family-system boundary problems.

The process of mutual goal formulation requires that the therapist be cognizant of the conflicting value orientations many Latino families face. For instance,

Latinos may be brought up with interdependence values that conflict sharply with the independence values held by the dominant culture, including the therapist (Acosta et al., 1982). A Latino client is not likely to formulate therapy goals that will benefit him- or herself only. Similarly, the significance attached to the parent-child, especially mother-child, dyad is much greater than that attached to the marital dyad in Latino culture. Although the child's presenting problem may be attributed to the parents' dysfunctional marital relationship, therapy goals put forward by the therapist at the onset of therapy that focus on repairing the marital subsystem will be strongly resisted. Another therapy goal emphasizing the parents' families of origin or multigenerational transmission may also be too threatening, too time consuming, and antithetical to Latinos' "present" and "doing" orientations. Conversely, therapy goals focusing on the parent-child relationship challenge the wife's desire to be a good mother. Through learning how to perform dutifully in a mother-child relationship, the mother may learn how to interact differently with her husband. Until the family as a unit can experience success in the parent-child relationship, other goals involving individual family members in differentiating or facilitating the marital subsystem for boundary repair may never materialize.

The Latino culture emphasizes a strong "present" orientation. Therapy goals may need to be specific, concrete, practical, and short term (Acosta et al., 1982). They should be formulated without undermining the hierarchical structure role of the family.

Selecting a Focus or System for Therapy

Understanding and respecting the Latino family's cultural norms and present social context are perhaps the therapist's most important skills when defining the family's problem and selecting a focus or family subsystem unit for therapy. For example, a Latino's obligation to family is so strong that it is not uncommon for a nuclear family to involve the extended family as their major locus of social activities. Such intense, frequent, extrafamilial contacts are uncommon according to Anglo family norms and should not be misconstrued as a symptom of enmeshment.

When situational stress involving the whole family or some individual family members occurs, a therapist needs to adhere to the hierarchical structure of the family by consulting with the father prior to implementing any therapeutic strategy. The closeness of the mother-child relationship makes it necessary to consult with the mother before intervention focusing on the child.

Occasionally, the dysfunctional family pattern may involve diffuse marital subsystem boundaries. Conjoint couple therapy is not recommended as a therapeutic modality. The husband's sense of authority and defense may intensify in the presence of an outsider, that is, the family therapist. Similarly, the wife's passive role structure may cause her confusion and ambivalence toward her husband to intensify during dyadic marital therapy. Whenever marital therapy is conducted with a more acculturated Latino couple, Bowen's (1978) detached, calm, and intellectual approach is helpful. It is particularly useful in terms of diffusing the emotionality of the marital relationship and guiding marital interaction according to cultural norms.

As a sign of fulfilling familial obligations, Latino children may refrain from openly challenging their parents in the therapist's presence. A separate session with children may be in order for negotiating issues they may not normally discuss in their parents' presence. Through structured sibling therapy, the diffuse boundary of sibling relationships is solidified. Such a restructuring of the sibling subsystem can, in turn, extricate an overprotected child from the parental subsystem.

Considering the importance machismo plays in the father's role as head of the family, conjoint family sessions with every family member present may be disrespectful to the father. Hence Bowen's (1978) therapeutic strategy of focusing on the self-differentiation of one person (preferably the father) may be most appropriate. With this one-to-one therapeutic modality, the father no longer needs to be concerned with his traditional obligatory authoritarian role. Instead, with the help of a therapist who listens to him empathetically, the father can examine different alternatives that will facilitate his role as the family head.

On the opposite end of the target-focus continuum, therapeutic activities involving the extended family can be used to deal with developmental impasses connected to cultural transition. Such activities may include initiation rites or fiestas such as weddings, baptisms, and graduations. These can facilitate the smooth transition marking the traditional family life cycle.

Problem-Solving Phase

The following discussion focusing on the problem-solving phase of therapy with Latino families considers the cultural norm, family structure, traditional help-seeking behavior, and capacities of this particular population. In addition, the application of communication and family structure theories has been integrated into the therapeutic process. Seven skills and techniques of particular importance in the problem-solving phase of therapy include the following:

1. Employing home visits as problem-solving tools
2. Postmodern problem-solving techniques: taking a narrative stance, engaging in a reflective dialogue, and critically reflecting on the multiple (emotional) meanings of messages

3. Skills and techniques involved in reframing and relabeling

4. Mobilizing and restructuring the social and extended family network

5. Promoting familial obligation as a family restructuring technique

6. Employing role models and the educator and advocate roles

7. Collaborative work with a folk healer, paraprofessional, or therapist helper

Home Visits

Latino families may lack specific knowledge about health and mental health services. They also may have limited financial resources and transportation, and may be unfamiliar with family therapy as a viable resource for problem solving within the family. Home visits should be a logical therapeutic tool for reaching this particular ethnic group. In some instances, home visits may be the *only* way of initiating or maintaining a relationship with a Latino family (Mizio, 1979). Thomas and Carter (1971) also have stressed the significance of reaching out to the family and seeing the family in their natural environment, that is, their home.

With Latino families, home visits can be used effectively by therapists to personalize their relationship with the family. The fact that the therapist spends time and effort to visit with the family helps the family to perceive the therapist as genuine and trustworthy. The therapist's impact on the family system will automatically increase if the family is able to relate to him or her as they would to a compadre. The effectiveness of home visits has been proven in family therapy with Puerto Rican families (Hardy-Fanta & MacMahon-Herrera, 1981).

Postmodern Problem-Solving Techniques

The meaning or interpretation that results when various family members take a *narrative stance* in attempts to sort out family problems may not be exact, but the parties can be encouraged to engage in a *reflective dialogue* and *critically reflect* on the *multiple emotional meanings* that each family member has attached to the presenting problem, as reflected in the individual narratives (Rasheed & Rasheed, 1999). For example, stressful experiences of migration can be reflected up to help family members become more attuned with how each family member uniquely experiences cultural transitions. Further exploration using this *reflective dialogue* can help the parties discover the positive feelings of concern, respect, and value that each places on his or her relationship with the others and the degree of personal determination and desire for the family to survive stressful events such as immigration, migration, acculturation, and assimilation processes.

Reframing and Relabeling

Latino families' interaction is guided by hierarchical role structure and interdependence. Haley (1976) and Minuchin's (1974) reframing and relabeling techniques can be effective with this group. By using these techniques, the therapist acknowledges the (negative) influence of the ecological context on the family's life, function, and processes by emphasizing the positive aspects of (adaptive) behavior and redefining or emphasizing negative elements in the family's life space.

Rolando, a 15-year-old, was referred by his father, who claimed that the boy was totally "out of control." The family had migrated from Mexico City 8 years earlier. Rolando spoke fluent English and occasionally served as interpreter for the family. According to the father, Rolando's problem started about 1 year ago when he began to stay out late and to skip school frequently. The father was employed as a carpenter but was laid off intermittently. Rolando's complaint was that he was tired of having no money to spend and that he wished he were allowed to get a job. After father and son had repeatedly exchanged words of conflict, the therapist reframed Rolando's rebelliousness as a way to express his family obligation, that is, to help the family financially by getting a job. The therapist further reinforced the father by commenting that Rolando's concern and obligation for the family was learned from the father. The therapist's reframing helped both the father and son to view their behavior in a more positive vein and establish a more open line of communication.

During the process of relabeling, the therapist should be sensitive to complementary roles with the Latino family. For example, a wife's accusatory remark to her husband, "You never come home," can be relabeled (to the husband) as "Your wife enjoys your company very much. She wants to know what she can do to influence you to want to spend more time with her." A therapist's relabeling may not accurately reflect the true meaning of what was said, but the important underlying message that relabeling can help to convey to the family is that all family members respect each other and harmonious living is the primary family concern.

Social and Extended Family Network

Latino families are well known for their emphasis on familismo. Studies have indicated that Latinos make use of the extended family network much more extensively than Anglos (Mindel, 1980). A social support network is essential for the newly arrived Latino, who needs a place and a way to bridge the ecological deficit, to ventilate frustration, to learn acculturated social skills, and to form friendships. In addition, the extended family or social network helps the individual or the family to reconnect with the culture of origin.

Latino families may feel a strong tendency toward reconnection with their culture of origin, but not all Latino ethnic subgroups have the same degree of access to their home country (Bernal & Flores-Ortiz, 1982). Puerto Ricans have the best access to their cultural roots because of the historical antecedents, relative proximity, cost of travel to the island, and legal status. Conversely, because of political pressures and an economic blockade, Cuban Americans are the most disconnected group from their country of origin. Despite the close proximity to the frontier, Mexican Americans often have not had access to their native roots because of immigration impositions.

In an effort to mobilize social networks, the therapist's role may become that of a social intermediary or "matchmaker." Minuchin (1974) has described specific strategies geared toward the alleviation of environmental stress and the cultural adaptation process. One immediate resource for communal activities is the parish or the parochial school. Some priests, if sensitive to the problems of acculturation, can offer significant spiritual support, especially when dealing with physical illness, old age, and death (Falicov, 1982).

Familial Obligation

The process of acculturation has not diminished the Latino's need to be valued by others, especially by family members. A person's worth is dependent upon the quality and nature of his or her relationship with other family members. A Latino father may feel multiple threats to his integrity. As a result, he may show reluctance, especially at the engagement phase of therapy. Therapists should examine the positive cultural meanings of the Latino father's machismo. Such factors can include loyalty, fairness, responsibility, and family centrality. These qualities can bridge, rather than bar, the way to engaging a Latino father in family therapy (Ramirez, 1979). Thus a therapist needs to reconsider the negative stereotype of machismo and appeal to the father on the basis of his importance to the well-being of his family.

Roberto, the second son of Mr. Ruiz, a Puerto Rican, has been in trouble with the school authorities because of a disciplinary problem. The school principal's efforts to meet with Mr. Ruiz failed when Mr. Ruiz would not respond to the principal's request for a conference. The school principal informed Roberto that he would remain suspended until his father came in for a conference. The Ruiz family did not respond for a week. The school social worker wrote to inform Mr. Ruiz of her desire to meet with him at his home regarding Roberto. In the letter, the worker mentioned that Mr. Ruiz might be very busy and have difficulty scheduling an appointment. She said that she needed his guidance in how best to work with his son. The worker also proposed a time and date for the home visit.

When the home visit actually occurred, Mr. Ruiz was apologetic about the inconvenience his family problem might have caused the worker. In addition, Mr. Ruiz was hospitable and expressed great appreciation for the worker's visit. He vowed that he would do whatever was needed to help his son.

Promoting familial obligation as a means of resolving family problems can also be used in other situations. A Latina wife publicly assumes the supportive role to her husband, but privately or covertly she may undermine his authority, especially in regard to child-rearing practices. To be consistent with traditional Latino communication interactional patterns, the therapist should not encourage the wife to express openly her hostility toward her husband. Instead, the therapist needs to encourage the wife to suggest openly and publicly to her husband other alternatives in child rearing. The public support that the husband is receiving from his wife can reinforce his powerful role as patriarch, and, at the same time, he may become more receptive to new ways of child rearing.

More than anything else, a Latino wishes to get along with others (interdependence), especially family members. The therapist's task is to promote this essential quality and capitalize on its strength.

Role Models, Educator Role, and Advocate Role

The process of migration and acculturation often creates confusion and disorganization for individual members as well as for the whole family. Latino families that have experienced loss due to transcultural migration must be concerned with *entrapping niches* (debilitating and nonsupportive environments), which can threaten the basic survival of the family. The therapist's role as cultural translator, mediator, and model (DeAnda, 1984; Minuchin, 1974) is vital to help the family form an open system with available community resources. The newly established network based on mutual aid can provide needed economic, emotional, and educational assistance to families in cultural transition.

Being sensitive to the Latino culture does not preclude the therapist's attempting to produce change in areas that restrict the family's ability to alter their circumstances or solve their problems. A therapist's task is not to change the Latino patterns of family interaction but to alter those specific patterns that are dysfunctional within the family (Miller, 1959). For example, a Latino couple experiencing acculturation conflict and tension but desiring harmonious family living may need to learn a more egalitarian model of male-female relationship. The power of alignment that characterized the family is challenged by the presentation of a model of transaction in which the husband pays attention to what the wife has to say, in which there is give and take, and in which each partner has a voice in decision making. Particularly helpful, according to Satir (1967) and Miller, Nunnally, and Wackman (1975), are family communication skills that include mutual reinforcement, methods of constructive disagreement, the use of feedback, brainstorming, and decision-making options.

Many Latino families, especially those in the lower social economic class and those without legal immigration documents, are the victims of societal lags and intentional or unintentional indifference by agencies. The therapist at times may need to assume an advocate role for the family. Because these families do not wish to draw public attention to themselves, it is important that the therapist's biased advocacy on their behalf not subject them to further agency humiliation or discrimination.

Collaborative Work With a Folk Healer, Paraprofessional, or Therapist Helper

In the not-too-distant past, folk-healing practices among Latinos were misunderstood. Labeled as "dangerous prognostic signs and as evidence of reliance on primitive defense mechanisms, which if they persisted were ultimately destructive to the integrative functions of the ego" (Douglas, 1974), for example, the phenomenon of espiritismo has been diagnosed as hallucinatory or psychotic thought processes (Purdy, Pellman, Flores, & Bluestone, 1970). However, many Latino clinicians and cultural anthropologists have refuted such claims and concluded that folk practitioners are appropriate within their respective cultural contexts (Douglas, 1974; Garrison, 1977). For example, espiritismo has been found to provide integrative and identity factors to migrant minorities in their acculturation process (Douglas, 1974). It has helped to discharge tension and anxieties generated in social life as well as providing face-to-face contact and interpersonal intimacy (Rogler & Hollingshead, 1965). The practice of Santeria helps to delineate the explanation of the irrational, problem-solving skills, and regression "in the service of the ego" (De La Cancela, 1978). Curanderismo has been identified as providing a Catholic therapeutic method of confession and reassurance (Kiev, 1968). De La Cancela (1978) has identified some similarities between Western psychotherapy and folk healing. Such similarities include the admission of unacceptable impulses and emotions and their displacement to culturally acceptable outlets, practitioners' acceptance and tolerance of deviance, the use of introspection and identification as therapeutic process, and the amount of training required of a practitioner. In view of the functional similarities between folk healers and family therapists, the necessity and wisdom in the integration of these two practices is obvious. The actual collaborative work between the family therapist and the spiritualist will be illustrated by a case example in Part 3 of this chapter.

Mixed acculturative patterns within some Latino families may render them unreceptive to family therapy or unresponsive to conjoint family therapy in which all family members are present for problem solving. In these cases, the therapist may need to adopt the therapist-helper concept (Landau, 1981). Through this approach, the therapist does not have to have face-to-face direct contact or confrontation with the family. The chosen therapist-helper, an extended family member (e.g., padrino) or a nuclear family member, can act as a therapeutic agent with the guidance and consultation of the therapist. Such a therapist-helper could possibly reduce outside intrusion; eliminate language barriers; and alleviate transportation, cultural, and financial difficulties. This approach can ensure that the change direction goes according the needs and cultural norms of the family.

Evaluation and Termination Phase

In view of the Latino family and family members' value of spontaneity in interpersonal relationships, any rigid scheduling or objective criteria for evaluating the therapeutic outcome may meet with resistance. Therefore, it is important that a therapist respect what the family has to say about the progress or improvement of its situation. One example would be the family's emphasis on the welfare of the child. A therapist can evaluate the strength of the spousal subsystem by inquiring about the transformation of the parent-child subsystem. By listening to each parent describe his or her interaction with the child, the therapist can obtain a clearer picture of how the parents interact.

The assessment of family therapy progress should also be guided by the therapy goal. If the therapeutic goal relates to situational stress, the therapist's evaluation should be directed to the interface between the family and the new environment only. Any evaluation of intrafamilial functioning is inappropriate except to establish a new contract involving a different therapeutic goal. In assessing therapeutic goals relating to dysfunctional patterns of cultural transition or transcultural dysfunctional patterns, therapists need to be cognizant of the unique cultural perspective of the Latino culture. Latino culture views family structure, differentiation of self, emotional cutoff, and so on differently than Anglo culture. Unless the family interactive pattern is detrimental to the growth and development of family members, any suggestion for its repair may run the risk of misjudgment of evaluation.

Latinos have strong feelings of obligation, interdependence, and collectivity. Because of this, a family may tend to deemphasize the extent of its family problem. The family may be so considerate of the therapist's time and effort that they prefer not to burden the therapist but to terminate therapy prematurely. It is important that therapists use home visits or become a part of the family's social environment so that they may evaluate firsthand how well the family is progressing.

Generally, therapeutic goals will relate to situational stress and will be short term. Accomplishment of therapeutic goals is assessed according to whether the family is able to obtain concrete services, including community resources, essential financial help, and healthcare services. Therapeutic goals related to transcultural dysfunctional patterns usually involve role conflict or role reversal between parent and child or husband and wife. Accomplishment of these therapeutic goals is measured in terms of compatibility of roles and reduced situational stress. For instance, when the Latino husband secures gainful employment, this may reverse the role conflict he felt when he was unemployed. Therapeutic goals related to transcultural dysfunctional patterns involving intergenerational transmission or idiosyncratic problems (Minuchin, 1974) may require longer term therapy.

The Latino client's values concerning interpersonal relationships and family ties may make the process of termination more foreign to them. The enabling role that the therapist plays in the therapeutic process will win trust for the therapist: The family will truly trust and accept the therapist as a member of its extended family. Termination, on the other hand, can be a big loss, especially to some families who are culturally and emotionally cut off. Therefore, it is important that a therapist be comfortable with this element of human relationships and not feel threatened by the family's interdependent behavior, seeing it as deceptive manipulation.

The preceding discussion should be helpful in understanding Latino families and applying family structure and communication theories and (emic-based) *Latincentric* practice principles using a critical constructionist perspective. Part 3 of this chapter offers a case example to explicate and delineate how these family theoretical perspectives and emic-based practice principles can be integrated in actual therapy with a Latino family.

PART 3: CASE ILLUSTRATION

Mrs. Herrara, a 46-year-old Puerto Rican widow, was referred to us (the Transcultural Family Study Center) by the community mental health center. She was hospitalized there for 3 days because of an "unexplainable" seizure she suffered. Mrs. Herrara refused to be hospitalized any longer but did agree to seek help from our center. According to Mrs. Herrera, her 15-year-old daughter Graciela was "driving her crazy."

The family's cultural transitional map and genogram is described in Figure 4.1.

During my first meeting with Mrs. Herrera, she was very inquisitive about my [Dr. Ho's] ethnic background and asked if Convey respect to client's culture.   I spoke Spanish. "*I wish I could,*" I replied spontaneously. Mrs. Herrara volunteered that she used to frequent one Chinese restaurant in Puerto Rico and knew several Chinese waiters who spoke Spanish. I told

Use personalismo to establish common ties.

Mrs. Herrara that *my maternal grandmother used to work in a Chinese restaurant* in Panama and learned to speak Spanish there. Mrs. Herrara asked if I had emigrated from Panama. I told her that I *came from Hong Kong when I was 19 years old.* Mrs. Herrara volunteered that she had come from Puerto Rico 25 years ago with her husband and 2-year-old daughter, Fanta, who now lives in New York City. Her second daughter, Graciela, was born in New York City, where they have close extended family ties. The family moved to Oklahoma City 6 years ago when the oil business was booming. Mr. Herrara suffered a head injury at work and died 2 years after the incident.

To establish common ground (immigrant experience) with the client.

Migration background.

According to Mrs. Herrera, her husband "was not much of a husband," for he got drunk and "chased after women all the time." Due to her husband's job-related death, Mrs. Herrera receives a pension from the company for which he had worked. I responded to Mrs. Herrera's family background information with great interest and empathy and I *inquired how she managed the family after her husband's death.*

Problem identification.

Presenting problem.

Mrs. Herrera sighed, *"This explains what I am here* to see you about." Mrs. Herrera continued that right after her husband's death 4 years ago, her first daughter, Fanta, returned to New York City to marry her old boyfriend, leaving Mrs. Herrera to take care of Graciela by herself. Mrs. Herrera has thought about returning to New York City, but her present job as an office clerk has prevented her making a major career move. "I am no college graduate, and *I like my present job real well.* Besides, I *cannot stand my mother-in-law,* who lives in New York City," continued Mrs. Herrera.

Loyalty and security to employment.

Intergenerational emotional system.

Then Mrs. Herrera proceeded to inform me that lately she had had some vigorous hyperkinetic trances that had caused her to miss work and led her to hospitalization. "That clinic and the medication did me no

	good," complained Mrs. Herrera. *When asked to elaborate on her trance*, Mrs. Herrera broke down crying. She reflected
Specification of problem single-parent nuclear emotional system; failed to fulfill familial obligation.	that perhaps the trance was related to *her difficulties with Graciela, who would not mind her*. Mrs. Herrera recalled that the last two seizures happened right after Graciela walked out on her during an argument. *I*
Joining the client.	*empathized by saying that* she felt she had no control over the situation. Mrs. Herrera agreed and elaborated that when she was Graciela's age, she also *had great difficulty*
Multigenerational emotional transmission.	*with her father*, who would not allow her to have boyfriends. "I wish I had listened to my father. Instead I got myself pregnant and had to have an abortion," continued Mrs. Herrera. "Before my husband died, he asked me to promise him that I would *take good care of Graciela*," Mrs. Herrera cried
Familial obligation.	again. "You feel you have failed your husband," I empathized. Mrs. Herrera nodded and *cried louder*. Before the
Encourage the client to grieve.	session ended, I asked if she could bring Graciela with her for the next session. Mrs. Herrera replied that Graciela told her that she would never come to "no agency to see no shrink." I arranged a date to *visit*
The necessity for and value of home visits.	*with her and Graciela at their home*. Mrs. Herrera thanked me for listening to her problem.
	At the home visit, Mrs. Herrera had arranged for Graciela to meet me. The Herreras lived in a predominately white
Joining the family.	neighborhood. They decorated their home neatly. I *was inquisitive about the wall posters* showing scenery of Puerto Rico. I asked Graciela if she had been to Puerto
Joining and establishing rapport with Graciela and cultural mapping.	Rico. She replied only once the year before her father died. I *asked if she could show me pictures of her father* and other relatives who live in Puerto Rico and in the states. Graciela was cooperative and relieved that I did not focus immediately on her
Cultural mapping.	relationship with her mother. *While going over the family photo albums* and listening
Need to be in touch with family of origin. Social isolation.	to both Mrs. Herrera and Graciela, I commented how *much they must miss their*

Lack of cultural and religious contact.

Reestablish cultural and religious ties.

relatives. Mrs. Herrera sighed, and said "We have nothing to do with anybody anymore!" Mrs. Herrera continued that lately they *had not been to Mass* and that they just did not feel comfortable attending the white Catholic Church. I asked *if they knew of a Hispanic Catholic Church* nearby. Mrs. Herrera replied that she did but she never inquired more about it. I told her that I knew the pastor of that church. With their permission, I would ask the pastor to visit with them. Mrs. Herrera nodded and said, "Of course."

I then directed my attention to Graciela, who at this time was preparing herself a sandwich. She *asked me if I wanted one,* and I said, "yes." Meanwhile, *I encouraged Graciela to share with me* things that interested her, including her daily activities.

Client shows sign of acceptance.

Therapist's use of accommodation technique.
Show interest and assess Graciela's social functioning.

Recognizing client's strengths.

After listening to Graciela's description of her school and social activities, I *complimented her for being a good student* academically and for being popular among her peers. Graciela was quite apologetic about the problems she might have caused her mother, but insisted that *"I must live my own life."* Mrs. Herrera interrupted by saying, *"As long as you are my daughter* and live with me in the same house, you ought to let me know when and where you are going." Graciela capitalized on the situation to point out to me, "You see, this is what I have to put up with all the time." She left hurriedly and walked toward the kitchen.

Sign of acculturation and individualism.

Family life cycle adjustment.

I commented that I *could see how each of them showed caring* toward each other differently. Before I left, we *exchanged appreciation for the time spent with* each other. We also agreed on the time of my next visit. I reminded them that a *Catholic priest might* be visiting with them. Mrs. Herrera was concerned that the next time she had a seizure, she might be "put in the hospital for good." I comforted her by letting her know

Reframing from negative to positive.

Personalismo.

Collaborative work with priest.

Collaborative work with folk healer.

that I would *consult with my Hispanic colleague*, who was also a folk healer, and that he might be of assistance to her in regard to her seizure. Before my next visit with the Herreras, the Hispanic priest visited the family. Mrs. Herrera was thrilled to inform me that *Graciela went to Mass with her for the first time in 6 months*. Mrs. Herrera was also glad to share with me her visit with the folk healer I had recommended. Mrs. Herrera informed me that the folk healer explained to her that her seizure was a *form of "despojo"*—a cleansing of her spirit. Her seizure served the function of letting her know that something was wrong in her life. A malevolent spirit, imposing itself for whatever purpose, was the cause, and a despojo was part of the cure.

Sign of improved relationship.

Puerto Rican spiritualism.

Collaborative work with folk healer.

When I consulted with the folk healer, he confirmed what Mrs. Herrera had already told me. The folk healer also informed me that he intended to treat Mrs. Herrera with traditional rituals involving the despojo, with herbal remedies and baths, and perhaps exorcisms. The folk healer also confirmed that Mrs. Herrera's difficulty with her daughter definitely was related to the evil spirit that was plaguing her. When I asked Mrs. Herrera about her relationship with her daughter, Mrs. Herrera *warned that Graciela was her primary* responsibility and that no *counselor from the school or the mental health clinic was* going to tell her that she should leave her daughter alone. Mrs. Herrera's behavior was a product of her culture, her own teenage pregnancy, her injunction from her deceased husband, life-cycle adjustment to a teenage daughter, and her emo-tional enmeshment with Graciela, who represented the only person with whom she interacted in her immediate environment.

A sign of Mrs. Herrera's emotional "stuckness."
Implying to worker that he should not interfere.

Joining with the client's resistance or emotional "stuckness."

I *empathized by* stating that I could understand and appreciate her position and that *Graciela should feel fortunate to have a mother who really cared about* her. Mrs. Herrera asked if I had any suggestion

Reinforcing cultural norm and reframing.

Paradoxical intervention.

in regard to her dealing with Graciela. I *encouraged Mrs. Herrera to keep close* tabs on Graciela's whereabouts and to telephone Graciela occasionally at a previously arranged time. Graciela rejected my proposal immediately, but Mrs. Herrera compromised by stating, "If I could keep track of you, then I would be willing to let you go out with your friends more often." After a short pause for consideration, Graciela agreed. As a reward, I suggested that once a week both of them spend one fun evening together outside of the house.

An elaborate system was arranged for Mrs. Herrera to keep track of Graciela. For instance, on Saturday evening, Mrs. Herrera was to call Graciela at 10 p.m., 12 midnight, and 1 a.m. Sunday morning before Graciela returned home. Because the purpose of the telephone calls was to ensure Graciela's safety, the call was intended to be brief. However, it was Mrs. *Herrera's responsibility to call on time.* After the first week, Mrs. Herrera was successful in fulfilling her end of the agreement. At the end of the second week, Mrs. Herrera complained that she got tired, especially on Saturday evenings doing nothing but waiting to call Graciela. She volunteered that her weekly *outing with Graciela had been enjoyable* and that her overall *relationship with Graciela seemed* to have improved. Mrs. Herrera asked if it was "okay" if she discontinued calling Graciela on her night out. I replied, "Who is going to take care of Graciela?" "She [Graciela] is a big girl now, and *besides I trust her,*" replied Mrs. Herrera.

The task was arranged intentionally so it had little chance for success.

Repair of parent-child subsystem.

Result of paradoxical intervention.

As Mrs. Herrera's relationship with her daughter improved, the seizures stopped. The family had *increased its involvement* with the Church. Through church activities, Mrs. Herrera made friends with several *Hispanic single parents.* "When Graciela had a night out with her friends, I gave myself a night out with my friends, too," quipped Mrs. Herrera.

Removal of presenting problem.

Family "closed" system became an "open" system.

Reconstruct extended family and support system.

I had seen the family a total of 13 times, which covered a time span of 4 months. Six sessions were held conjointly with both Mrs. Herrera and Graciela. Five sessions were held with Mrs. Herrera alone, and two sessions were spent individually with Graciela. Two months after the termination, Mrs. Herrera twice referred two Hispanic American families to our agency for service. She made these families *promise to say "hi" to me* when they saw me.

Therapist became a compadre to the family.

Figure 4.1   Herrera Family Cultural Transitional Map and Genogram

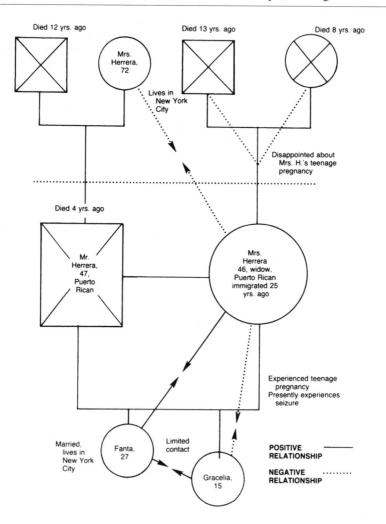

PART 4: CULTURALLY RELEVANT TECHNIQUES AND SKILLS FOR SPECIFIC THERAPEUTIC MODALITIES

Couple Therapy

The traditional Latino cultural values of familismo, personalismo, and hierarchy, as well as Catholicism, may be responsible for the low Latino divorce rate. The conjugal dyad is an integral factor in the overall functioning of a family; hence the couple's conflict is typically reflected elsewhere in the family system. Such conflicts are further exacerbated by the immigration and acculturation process. The process of acculturation and the changed roles and status of both husband and wife make marital adjustments extremely vulnerable. In most instances, the process of acculturation brings about a shift in the power differential between men and women prompted by women's access to alternatives for self-sufficiency and changes in attitudes toward marriage and partnerships (Bradshaw, 1994; Brown & Shallet, 1997). The increase of interracial and intercultural Latino marriages can also be another stress for the couple. Intermarriage among Latino subgroups and marriage to non-Latino partners can also create the need for the couple to negotiate different cultural values and worldviews. Couples may need help in creating a new *ethnocultural conjugal narrative.* However, traditional Latino health-seeking behavior may inhibit couples from seeking help for their problems, especially those family problems that center on sensitive marital relationships. Only the middle class and more acculturated couples may seek marital therapy for their family problems (Falicov, 1982, 1998). The couple's unfamiliarity and reluctance to improve their marital relationship may result in a host of other family problems involving alcohol, drug abuse, psychosomatic illnesses, and children acting out. Because of the couple's conscientious role as parents, they may be more receptive to seeking therapy for their child. The therapist should not prematurely and openly confront the couple about the real nature of their couple relationship or the cause of their child's problem. Instead, the therapist needs to adopt Minuchin's (1974) joining technique and use the parent-child focus as an entrée into the dyadic system. The following specific guidelines are suggested for therapists providing marital therapy to a Latino couple.

Incorporating the Extended Family System

The traditional closeness in a parent-child relationship can be a source of marital conflict. Minuchin's (1974) system boundaries concept relating to *enmeshment* and *disengagement* is helpful in assessing and restructuring the spousal relationship. Because of the hierarchical role structure of the Latino couple relationship, the therapist should not assume that the egalitarian relationship framework can serve as a guide or standard for Latino couple performance. The important focus here is to rectify the problem for which the family came and is willing to cooperate. What constitutes an appropriate level of self-differentiation or couple subsystem differentiation is culture specific and highly idiosyncratic. *Respeto* for the individual and couple's dignity is vital, especially in the assessment stage of couple therapy.

If the couple or one of the partners refuses to cooperate, the therapist again can mobilize extended family members to help. The *padrino,* a godparent, is often an ideal person with whom the therapist can work collaboratively to improve the couple's conflict. Working collaboratively with the padrino, in addition to sometimes being the only way to get the couple to cooperate, offers the following advantages: (a) It enables the couple to resolve conflict in a culturally relevant and natural fashion, (b) it reduces cultural and language barriers, (c) it mobilizes the natural source of the problem-solving approach, and (d) it reinforces the client's extended family system ties. The specifics of working with a padrino who serves as a therapist-helper is described in Landau's (1981) work with immigrants.

Strategic Use of Individual Interviews

The Latino husband may have difficulty openly admitting that marital conflicts exist. His wife may be reluctant to openly challenge her husband in the therapist's presence. Under such circumstances, individual interviews can be used as a tool to bridge the gap. The individual interview is particularly beneficial at the beginning phase of therapy. First, it promotes the development of rapport or personalismo. The one-to-one interview contact facilitates the development in each spouse of the secure feeling that the therapist understands and is concerned about the individual, not just the marriage. The therapeutic context facilitated by the one-to-one interview fosters trust and diminishes cognitive distortion detrimental to problem solving. Second, the individual interview provides an opportunity for the disclosure of intimate information that spouses are often reluctant to disclose in the conjoint couple interview. Examples of such information include extramarital affairs, incest, or thoughts of divorce. This information is vital to understanding the couple's problem, as well as their motivations and capacity for resolving marital conflicts.

To rectify the confidentiality, secrets, and triangulation issues prevalent in couple therapy, the therapist should inform the couple at the beginning of the individual interview that confidentiality will be maintained. The therapist may also suggest disclosure of some specific information considered essential to resolving the couple's conflict. Again, disclosure of particular information should be mutually agreed upon between the individual and the therapist, with the individual client assuming the disclosing role. In view of Latino culture's emphasis on familismo and familial obligations, the therapist can expect to find the couple cooperative and willing to do whatever is necessary to resolve their conflicts.

Teaching Communication and Problem-Solving Skills

Traditional Latino cultural upbringing prescribes how a couple should interact. As the nature of a couple's relationship shifts from hierarchical to egalitarian (perhaps as a result of the acculturation process), the traditional mode of couple interaction, especially for sensitive problem-solving issues, may no longer be functional for them. Thus the couple will need to learn new ways of relating to each other on both the cognitive and affective levels. On the cognitive level, the couple is advised to specify their expectations of each other and of their marriage. The use of exception survival or possibility questions can encourage the couple to search for strengths within each other and in their relationship (Saleeby, 1997).

In addition, the couple needs to be sensitized to realize that their ability to communicate openly and directly on the cognitive level is influenced by their ability to empathize with each other's feelings. To teach a spouse to communicate empathetically, the therapist can request that both the husband and wife think about and then communicate (either to the therapist or to the spouse) his or her understanding of the feelings and viewpoint of the other. Such understandings are then checked out with the other spouse and inaccuracies are corrected (Guerney, 1977). Particular attention should be given to each spouse's understanding of (a) what he or she has done or said that has aroused hurt feelings in the other and (b) what the other wishes had happened instead of what did happen (desired alternative behavior).

In the case of interracial or intercultural marriages that, depending on the level of acculturation of the Latino partner, may be bicultural as well, a couple may need to develop a communication format that allows them to articulate *multiple (emotional) meanings* of their experience of culture in an interracial and bicultural relationship (White & Epston, 1990). The meanings that the couple attributes to their cultural experience will be shaped by their own culture of origin. An Anglo partner will have different experiences than an African American partner or an Asian American partner. The therapist must be especially attentive to both *invisible family loyalties* and *invisible cultural loyalties* with interracial couples. To the extent that these multiple loyalties negatively affect the relationship, it will be necessary for the couple to *reauthor a new (ethnocultural) conjugal narrative* that reflects both the merging of, and the uniqueness of, each cultural and family-of-origin perspective. The therapist can facilitate this process.

Divorce Therapy

The divorce rate among the Latino American population remains relatively low in comparison to the Anglo population (Falicov, 1982; Zinn & Well, 2003). As discussed earlier in this chapter, there are several factors explaining why the divorce rate among Latinos is not as high as it is in other groups. Familismo and the Catholic religion both strongly discourage divorce. Latino couples traditionally considered marriage as a family or extended family matter, and its dissolution provoked strong negative sanctions by extended family members. However, there is concern about the increasing divorce rate among the younger, more acculturated Latinos who believe in the American ideal of romantic love and personal happiness in marriage (Benokraitis, 1993). Harmony within the family and the welfare of the children continue to be primary motivators in traditional Latino marriages. The process of immigration and acculturation has threatened many of these traditional values. Acculturated wives may find that they no longer wish to be "unequal" to their husbands. More acculturated husbands may also find traditional married lifestyles unromantic and boring. A spouse's dissatisfaction with a "business"-type spousal relationship may lead to infidelity and thus cause marital discord and divorce.

It is likely that the more highly acculturated and financially solvent client will seek divorce therapy. The majority of the divorce therapy clients come to the attention of the therapist during moments of crisis, such as when the husband abruptly decides to get a legal divorce, or the wife decides to divorce her husband because of physical abuse. In either instance, divorce therapy is conducted under extremely stressful circumstances. This requires quick decisions on the part of clients as well as therapists. The following recommendations are offered to ensure that these clients receive services responsive to their needs.

Exploring Divorce Experiences and Consequences

Traditional Latinos will consider divorce as the last resort to resolve their conflicts. The therapist should be attentive and nonjudgmental in assisting the individual or couple to determine if divorce is the final alternative. If the client is heavily indoctrinated in the Catholic religion, divorce can be a traumatic and guilt-ridden experience. This, coupled with feelings of family obligations, can temporarily immobilize or distort the individual's cognitive abilities. As therapists empathize with their client's anxiety or uncertainty about divorce, they also need to inform clients about the realities the client will face as the result of a divorce. Under no circumstances should a therapist offer moral judgment. Doing so would compound the client's feeling of guilt.

The final decision for divorce entails the husband and wife shifting from a collectivist orientation to an individualistic orientation. This may cause great pain and uncertainty and it also can temporarily immobilize a person's normal functioning. For individuals who have experienced a great deal of rejection and criticism in the past, the divorce experience can reactivate repressed negative self-images, causing the individual to feel unlovable, unworthy, and repulsive (Kohut, 1972). If the individual is a spiritualist, he or she may experience *despojo* or other emotional or physical symptoms requiring medical or folk healing attention. Hence the therapist's ability to assess the client's situation in an interpersonal, intrapersonal, and cultural content is extremely important during the early phase of divorce therapy.

Extended Family and Social Support

Once the divorce has been decided on, the therapist needs to assess the client's coping skills and capacities, along with the currently available social support system. The client's extended family is typically a good support source for economic, child care, and emotional needs. These resources will not be readily available to some clients, especially those who are newly arrived in the United States. Then the therapist's role is to link the client's needs with existing resources, taking advantage of agency resources provided by the mainstream society.

Because divorce may be seen as unacceptable in traditional Latino families, some divorced clients may find their extended families unsympathetic, hostile, and unsupportive. The therapist then becomes the client's only source of emotional support. The therapist should not interpret the client's behavior as overdependency. This reliance should be regarded as an expected normal transitory behavior characteristic of an individual experiencing emotional stress and cultural transition. If a client is unable to endure excessive emotional cutoff and strongly desires contact with the extended family, the therapist can serve as a mediator between the client and his or her extended family.

The client may be entrenched in the crisis of divorce and emotional alienation from the former spouse and possibly from the extended family. A divorced mother may require assistance in conducting her daily chores or such responsibilities as parenting. Again, the therapist can assume an active role, including transporting the children to school or clinics, to assist the client during this trying period.

Postdivorce Adjustment and New Relationships

Traditionally, the mother-child relationship among Latinos is strong. The absence of a father from the family because of divorce can easily intensify the mother-child transaction and foster enmeshment (Minuchin, 1974). To avoid this, therapy with the mother may include (a) sensitizing her to the dangers of enmeshment; (b) encouraging children to have more interaction with the extended family, peers, and other adults; (c) and encouraging the mother to capitalize on the divorce experience and to enjoy single life and friends.

The traditional hierarchical role structure of the Latino culture may not prepare the mother to assume a disciplinary role with her children or to assume the "executive" role essential to daily family living. The therapist may need to teach the mother single-parenting skills and assertiveness skills essential in dealing with matters outside of the home and on behalf of the family. A divorced mother may have strong feelings of family obligation and guilt. Some divorcees experience great difficulty in letting go of the ex-spouse. Her children's conscious or unconscious fantasy about or maneuvers to get their father back into the family certainly will not help the mother cope with divorce or the feeling of loss. The client's "unfinished business" (coping with the feeling of loss) may foster enmeshment with her children and may retard her effort and opportunity to establish a new emotional relationship. Referring the client to a divorce support group is beneficial to a divorcee who perceives her personal loss or unhappiness as unique and herself as helpless.

Single-Parent Therapy

Even with a low divorce rate, the number of Latino single-parent households is high (U.S. Census Bureau, 2000; Zinn & Wells, 2003). Generally speaking, there are great stresses and demands generated in two-parent households. When the parental or adult figures are reduced to one, the demands and stresses related to running a household become enormous; especially when the multiple stresses within the life space of ethnic minorities are thrown into the mix. The following suggestions aim to assist these families in resolving problems characteristic of single-parent households.

Mobilizing the Support System

One of the strengths of a Latino family is its strong familismo and extended family ties. When the father is absent from the family, a reduction in family income typically results. In addition, the mother has to assume double roles as both nurturer and disciplinarian to the children. Meanwhile, the mother can be deprived of a constant companion with whom to share problems and exchange emotional and physical needs. The therapist's intervention is to ascertain the level of need for all family members and to link the family members' needs to existing family system resources. During moments of crisis, it is not unusual for different siblings to be cared for by different relatives (Fitzpatrick, 1981). This practice is consistent with the Latino orientation of familismo.

Some Latinos, due to their new arrival status, geographic location away from major cities, or conflict with the extended family, need services provided by mainstream societal agencies. The therapist's role is that of a mediator or advocate whose primary responsibility is to assist the client in obtaining what she needs and is entitled to for her family.

Latina single parents needing to work outside of the home to provide for the family may lack employable skills. Some may also have great difficulty reading and writing English. The therapist's role is to refer them to local Latino social services or a cultural center or appropriate language- or job-training facilities where they can learn English and employable skills. It is important to attend to the basic needs of the single parent and her family prior to attending to the psychological and emotional transactional needs.

Restructuring the Family

The absence of the father from the spousal system and from the family as a whole requires family renegotiation and a restructuring of the family system boundary (Minuchin, 1974). The Latino hierarchical role structure by age and sex can easily place the oldest male child in the family in the absent father's role. Thus the intergenerational boundary between parent and child may be ruptured and an enmeshment may be created between mother and the oldest son. The traditional closeness of the mother-child relationship should not be misconstrued automatically as enmeshment. However, if the mother-child relationship excludes other siblings or extended family members, concern is justified as to whether the present relationship is conducive to the normal development and optimum functioning of the mother and the child.

In discerning the appropriateness or inappropriateness of a mother-child relationship, the therapist needs to consider the following factors: (a) the normal developmental needs of the child and the mother, (b) the degree to which the present mother-child relationship is meeting or not meeting the mother's needs or the child's needs, and (c) the relationship between the presenting family problems and the mother-child relationship. Generally, if the presenting problem is unrelated to the mother-child relationship, the therapist should not focus on the mother-child relationship.

To assist a single parent to function effectively, the therapist is advised to assess whether daily household tasks such as cooking, cleaning, children attending schools, and so on are properly taken care of. In addition, the therapist needs to assess whether the mother is effective in providing emotional nurturance for her children. In some instances, the mother also is expected to deal effectively with institutions and agencies such as schools, churches, or healthcare clinics. It is important that the single parent is aware of different roles she plays on behalf of the children and the family. It is also important that the therapist be supportive of the mother and not be unrealistically demanding of her.

The therapist may need to perform some of the essential duties for the single parent during this crisis-filled transitional period. As the crisis period subsides, the therapist needs to assist the mother in rearranging the family structure so that the essential tasks can be accomplished more efficiently without disturbing the intergenerational boundary. For example, older siblings can be assigned new tasks, including bringing home income like the father previously had done. Similarly, younger siblings can be expected to assume more household chores previously done by older siblings. The single parent can avoid quick burnout this way and can continue with the task of becoming self-sufficient enough to raise the children by herself.

Differentiation of Self

Latinas' traditional devotion to motherhood makes the adjustment to single parenthood a bit easier. Yet, the period of single parenthood created by divorce can reactivate repressed, unresolved emotions and conflicts. For some single parents, this period can reinforce feelings of low self-concept and unworthiness. It is important that the therapist assess developmentally where the client is and be attentive to her unresolved needs.

Bowen's (1978) concept of differentiation of self can be applicable at this stage of therapy. The client at this time needs to assess where she has been and where she wants to go. A Latina's sense of familismo and strong ties to the extended family are sources of strength. A single parent also needs to be aware of the fact that she is a separate individual and has some control over how others treat her and how she acts and reacts to others. This period of single parenthood can be capitalized on. The therapist can encourage the single mother to reflect upon her strengths and future direction. She needs to evaluate her previous marital relationship and to derive some self-understanding about the kind of person she is, as well as the kind of persons she wishes to meet. Clients from the lower socioeconomic status are overly burdened with the demands of survival. However, they also need self-understanding and normal growth development in addition to knowledge about surviving physically and materially. All of these skills are needed to help them manage their lives to achieve more satisfaction in life.

Reconstituted Family Therapy

Latinos have a strong sense of familismo and obligation to their family of origin. Problems can abound when there is a marriage of an ex-spouse with children from a previous marriage. If members of a reconstituted family carry with them unresolved conflicts from the previous spouse, or father or mother, their transactions with current reconstituted family members may become entangled. The following suggestions are offered for therapists providing family therapy for step- and blended Latino families.

Focus on Parental Coalition

Bowen (1978) emphasizes the importance of self-differentiation from family of origin. Minuchin (1974) stresses the necessity for establishing a strong spousal subsystem in family living. This is particularly important in the case of a blended family with children from previous marriages. Many individuals enter a blended or stepfamily without ever having successfully worked through or terminated previous relationships with ex-spouses. Such unresolved feelings are stumbling blocks to building a strong coalition with the present spouse. If the present marital relationship is not firmly grounded, child-rearing practices involving children from both previous and present spouses can cause confusion and difficulty. Too many step- and blended families are built upon the premise or fantasy that remarriage is good or essential to the normal development of their children from a previous marriage, because every child needs an adult male or female on whom to model. Children from the previous marriage are likely to experience ambivalence and difficulty within the present family context. The unspoken contract promised by the new marriage is, therefore, broken, and the new marriage may fail.

Therapy with a step- or blended family requires impressing upon the parents the necessity for a close reliance on each other. This may be more difficult in cases where Latina mothers are more devoted to maternal or motherly love for their children than to maintaining romantic relationships with husbands they traditionally respect and defer to. A Latina mother may feel that she owes loyalty to her children and nothing to her present husband, who before marriage was just a friend. Therefore, it is important that the therapist emphasize to the spouses that a strong marital coalition is a prerequisite to ensure the healthy and normal development of all children in a step- or blended family.

Building a strong parental coalition often is a brand-new concept to spouses in blended and stepfamilies. These spouses may come from familial backgrounds filled with marital conflicts. This, coupled with their most recent negative experiences with an ex-spouse, makes parental coalition an illusion. A strong parental coalition may require each spouse to modify traditional husband and wife roles. It may require a more egalitarian mode of interaction. The therapist, in being consistent with Latino culture, needs to emphasize the welfare of the children and the overall well-being of the entire family. Within this context, the couple can work to strengthen the marital relationship.

Define Roles and Expectations

The characteristics of a well-functioning family are its clear role definition and expectations. This has great implications as it applies to step- and blended families. Because of old habits and long-time familial obligations, each family member may have been taught and conditioned how he or she should behave in a family context. The reluctance on the part of some family members to cooperate in a step- or blended family may result from a lack of clear direction and expectations, as well as from loyalty to the member's own father, mother, or other family members. It is important that the therapist allow and encourage all family members to express their discomfort and ambivalence about the new familial composition. There should then be a consensus on the roles and functions of each family member. Latino culture prescribes that children respect all adults. It is a common practice among Latinos for adults to raise children who are not their own (Falicov, 1999; Garcia-Preto, 1982; Zinn & Well, 2003).

As a strategy to rectify problems with stepchildren in reconstituted families, some authors (Carter & McGoldrick, 1980; Haley, 1976; Minuchin, 1974) suggest that the stepmother take a passive role, leaving the father or stepfather to take charge of the children. This directive is in direct opposition to Latino culture, which prescribes that a woman's responsibility is to care for her children on a day-to-day basis. The Latina stepmother may feel totally displaced and resentful if she is advised to take a hands-off position in dealing with the children. If the therapeutic objective is to weaken the coalition between mother and child, the therapist may advise strengthening the parental subsystem boundary, and if the father-child subsystem is strengthened, then the coalition of the mother-child subsystem diminishes.

Extended Family Members

When a couple desires to establish a step- or blended family, members of the extended family may not be as eager. Some extended family members may have strong ties with the divorced spouses and the children. Reluctance and unreadiness on the part of the extended family can sabotage the development and functioning of a step- or blended family. This is particularly true with Latino families, who value familismo and extended family ties. Therefore, it is important in therapy with a step- or blended family that the therapist assess the level of enmeshment or differentiation that the divorced spouse and the children experience with relatives of the previous marriage. In addition to paying attention to the daily or weekly contact that the children maintain with relatives of the previous marriage, the therapist needs to ask each individual in the family about his or her present feelings and contact with relatives of the former marriage.

If there is excessive contact between the child and the relatives of a former marriage, the therapist needs to inform the parents of the potential setbacks such contacts will have on the reconstituted family. If necessary, the therapist can visit relatives or extended family members who are overly involved with the child. The therapist can solicit cooperation from the extended family members involved in the enmeshment. Once the extended family members are convinced that their overinvolvement may interfere with the normal development of the child in the reconstituted family, they will be likely to cooperate. If a child in the step- or blended family is unable to adjust, the extended family may care for the child temporarily. This is a common practice among Latino families (Falicov, 1999; Garcia-Preto, 1998; Zinn & Well, 2003).

PART 5: CONCLUSION

Latinos have become the largest racial minority group in America. Their socio-economic status, experience of political discrimination, and physical and mental health problems must not be overlooked. Latinos tend to relate their physical and mental health problems to improper interpersonal relationship and dysfunctional family transactions. They are receptive to family therapy provided the therapist is knowledgeable and respectful of their culture, which values familismo, personal-ismo, hierarchy, fatalism, and spiritualism.

Many Latinos are gradually acculturated to middle class mainstream society, but a vast majority are still struggling with basic survival needs. They experience racial discrimination, poverty, poor physical and mental health, and substandard housing and education. These are the families with whom therapists can expect to have frequent contact. These families need more than to feel good about them-selves and other family members; they need the basic necessities to survive. Hence the role of a therapist in working with Latinos extends beyond the psy-chologically oriented healer role to include other essential and functional roles. These may consist of roles as cultural broker, mediator, educator, and advocate. The therapist needs to involve and work cooperatively with priests and other spir-itual and indigenous leaders who are influential in the clients' lives. Finally, the strength of the Latino family lies within its familismo and extended family ties. These strengths should be employed as guideposts for assessment and therapy considerations.

This chapter has focused on a holistic view (an integration of historical, eco-nomic, social, political, psychological, physical, and cultural phenomena) and a Latincentric (emic-insider and culture-specific) approach in work with Latino families during different phases of (ecosystemically based) family therapy using a critical constructionist perspective.

5

Family Therapy With African Americans

PART 1: PRETHERAPY PHASE CONSIDERATIONS: A CRITICAL PERSPECTIVE

T he African American family is far more complex than has been recognized. The complexities of the African American family are reflected in Billingsley's (1992) definition of the African American family as an

intimate association of persons of African descent who are related to one another by a variety of means, including blood, marriage, formal adoption, informal adoption or by appropriation; sustained by a history of common residence in America; and deeply embedded in a network of social structures both internal to and external to itself. Numerous interlocking elements came together, forming an extraordinarily resilient institution. (p. 28)

Billingsley's definition suggests that the African American family, as a social system interacting with a number of other systems, must be understood within a historical perspective to comprehend its structure and function (Goldenberg & Goldenberg, 2002). His definition further suggests that the African American family structure should be perceived as an adaptation to a set of sociopolitical conditions existing in the family's wider social and ecological environment.

Within the framework of Billingsley's definition, Taylor (2003) takes the stance that to understand the African American family one must take a holistic perspective that emphasizes the influence of history, cultural, social, economic, and political forces in shaping contemporary African American family life. The confluence of these multiple forces not only contributes to the complexity of the African American family but also to its diversity, as there is no such entity as the singular "African American family." The African American family is in fact a social reality determined by a complicated interplay of factors, making African American families less than homogenous (Devore, 2001). The African American family, although "forming an extraordinary resilient institution" (Billingsley, 1992, p. 28), represents a collection of individual families with different religious and spiritual backgrounds, socioeconomic status, educational levels, skin colors, family structures, levels of acculturation, and diverse values and lifestyles (Boyd-Franklin, 1995).

Theoretical Perspectives on the African American Family

Unfortunately, attempts to understand the complexities and diversity of African American families have been marred by rather superficial analysis and scholarship. Hill (1993) identifies the following deficiencies in what he labels the "conventional perspective" in examining African American families. This perspective

- Reflects a superficial treatment of African American families. African American families are not considered to be an important unit of focus and thus are omitted entirely from or treated peripherally in family research. The conventional perspective assumes that African American families are automatically treated in all analyses that focus on African Americans as individuals.
- Accepts uncritically the assumptions of the "deficit model," which attributes most of the problems of African American families to internal deficiencies or pathologies.
- Fails to incorporate numerous new research findings and programmatic insights produced over the past two decades concerning African American families—many of which contradict the basic tenets of the deficit model.
- Fails to focus on positive policies, programs, and self-help and coping strategies that are successful in strengthening the functioning of African American families. (pp. 2-3)

In light of the obvious deficiencies of this perspective, scholars challenge this "deficit" orientation with what are known as "revisionist" theories about African American families. Contemporary theorists have now moved beyond these revisionist theories to more holistic perspectives. These holistic perspectives address the strengths and resiliencies of African American families. These perspectives further acknowledge the impact of structural factors such as poverty and racism, as well as cultural factors such as those residual African-based values that shape the distinctive experiences, modes of behavioral expression, and sociocultural adaptation of African Americans and their families. It is often the conflict between the structural and cultural factors that creates "bicultural tensions." The following section will briefly examine the conventional, revisionist, and holistic perspectives, with final attention given to an African-centered or *Africentric* framework for understanding the African American family.

The Conventional Perspective on African American Families

The "conventional perspective" on African American family life is reflected in the literature from 1870 to 1975. This body of literature defined almost all aspects of African American family life in pathological terms by focusing on lower income families. This "deficit"-oriented perspective failed not only to acknowledge middle class families but failed to distinguish between *poor blacks*—working people with stable family structures and the potential for gaining an education and achieving greater mobility—and the *black underclass*—unstable families with weak or no job skills, possibly third-generation welfare recipients with no hope of climbing out of poverty (Axelson, 1999). As Taylor (2003) points out, much of this literature on the African American family gave a distorted portrayal of the African American family by focusing overwhelmingly on those impoverished families in the Northeast and Midwest to the exclusion of the South, where more than 50% of African American families live.

The deficit orientation in studies of the African American family is reflected in the infamous 1965 Moynihan Report, which reiterated the thesis of E. Franklin Frazier's (1939) seminal work *The Negro Family in the United States*. In his study of the African American family, Frazer concluded that the dysfunctional patterns in the African American family are a result of the devastating impact of slavery and racism. The Moynihan Report expanded this theme and sought to apply it to the public welfare policy arena. The Moynihan Report supported the thesis that the dynamics of the African American family, influenced by the history of slavery and racial oppression, reflected a "tangle of pathology" that resulted in family instability, welfare dependence, and a matriarchal structure.

A Revisionist View of African American Families

In reaction to Moynihan's "tangle of pathology" thesis, a group of studies emerged that challenged the notion that slavery had an irreparably destructive impact on the family life of enslaved Africans. These studies document that a sense of "family" and a nuclear family structure was present among enslaved Africans (Gutman, 1976). Thus slavery did not destroy the African American family nor irreparably impair African American family structure. Other studies report that although this sense of family did exist among enslaved Africans, the various slave family configurations were determined by a variety of factors, including the cultural differences among the slaves themselves, the state or territory in which they lived, and the size of the plantation on which they resided (Taylor, 2003). As Stevenson (1995) states:

> The slave family was not a static, imitative institution that necessarily favored one form of family organization over another. Rather, it was a diverse phenomenon, sometimes assuming several forms even among the slaves of one community. . . . Far from having a negative impact, the diversity of slave marriage and family norms, as a measure of the slave family's enormous adaptive potential, allowed the slave and the slave family to survive. (p. 29)

The contribution that the revisionist studies made to the scholarship on African American families is an acknowledgment of the presence of an extended kinship network that prevailed under slavery. These studies further point to a sense of family intactness among enslaved Africans, albeit in various forms. Finally, these revisionist studies identify the strength, resilience, and endurance of African American families even while under the oppressive heel of slavery.

Holistic Perspectives

In recent years, scholars have challenged the deficit view of African American families and have adopted a more balanced perspective that includes articulating the strengths inherent in these families (Billingsley, 1968, 1992; Boyd-Franklin, 1989; Hines, Garcia-Preto, McGoldrick, Almeida, & Weltman, 1999). Current studies of the African American family focus on strengths and resilience, and there is also attention given to the adaptation of African American families to the oppressive conditions of racism and discrimination.

In one of the earlier works on the strengths of African American families, Hill (1972) identified several cultural themes or values that he believed formed the bases of survival for African American families. Although the expression of these values is often shaped by the sociocultural and socioeconomic influences of racism and oppression (Solomon, 1976), there are also themes that underlie the diversity of African American families and communities that give them coherence. These themes include (a) strong kinship bonds among a variety of households; (b) strong work, education, and achievement orientations; (c) a high level of flexibility in family roles; (d) a strong commitment to religious values and church participation; (e) humanistic orientation; and (f) endurance and resilience in the context of oppression. Understanding these themes and how they influence and shape African American family life can form a broader base for understanding and appreciating the patterns and functioning of African American families.

Pinderhughes (1982) contributes to this discussion of strengths and resilience by identifying the influences that affect how those themes identified by Hill

(1972) are expressed in a social context. According to Pinderhughes (1982), the cultural values of African American families are influenced by three major sources: (a) residual values from African cultural value systems; (b) identification with mainstream American values; and (c) adaptations and responses to a "victim-based" social system that is structured by the dynamics of racism, poverty, and oppression. Jones (1989) presents a similar schema in which he describes four domains that African Americans must negotiate throughout their lives. These domains include (a) developing a means of coping with racial oppression, (b) maintaining desired influences with respect to the majority culture, (c) establishing a connection with traditional African American culture, and (d) being aware of the influence of personal experiences and endowment.

"Double Consciousness" and Bicultural Challenges

What both Pinderhughes (1982) and Jones (1989) point out is that the psychological functioning of African Americans is affected by their ability to manage the tension created by coping with the influences of these multiple domains: (a) African and African American cultural values and worldviews; (b) the values of mainstream society; and (c) encounters with "systemic racism," or an institutionalized set of beliefs, attitudes, and concepts supporting and defending "white on black oppression" (Feagin, 2000, p. 102). Each of these domains represents an implicit worldview with a set of assumptions and beliefs about the social order and the individual's social location within that order. African Americans find themselves existing within these domains simultaneously, and for many African Americans, it is the sense of being of African descent and American at the same time. This sense of "two-ness" is reflected in the early thought of W.E.B. DuBois (1903) and his concept of "double consciousness" when he wrote

> It is a peculiar sensation, this double-consciousness, this sense of always looking at one's self through the eyes of others, of measuring one's soul by the tape of a world that looks on in amused contempt and pity. One ever feels his two-ness—an American, a Negro; two souls, two thoughts, two unreconciled strivings; two warring ideals in one dark body, whose dogged strength alone keeps it from being torn asunder. (p. 3)

The concept of "double consciousness" speaks to the bicultural tension that African Americans encounter in their efforts to manage their individual and family lives. Uncritical assimilation into dominant cultural values can cause a great deal of stress and strain on family relationships. Such assimilation can effectively create an "emotional cut-off" from one's family of origin and possibly the rich resources of African American culture and community life. Cultural immersion to the extent of rejecting the values of the dominant culture may effectively create a state of disconnection from the opportunity structures within mainstream society.

A different pace or level of acculturation between family members will tend to create tension and cultural value differences. College-educated young people may be influenced by changing ideas about family and incorporate a more individualistic concept, which may counter the collective notions of higher education. These differences in acculturation can led to *acculturative tensions* and *acculturative conflicts,* which can led to even more emotional distance within families (Rasheed & Rasheed, 1999) and, if left unresolved, can be primary contributing factors to emotional cutoff or disengagement between family members.

Disparate levels of acculturation and assimilation can be problematic for African American couples and can have a significant impact on the power dynamics within the relationship. These acculturative differences can also account for many conflicts over issues of child rearing, recreation, place of residence, friendship network, and so on. The sense of being "torn asunder" due to bicultural or acculturative tensions and bicultural or acculturative conflicts is often manifested in various racism-related psychosocial stressors that will be described later in this chapter. It is this bicultural tension and associated racism-related stressors that have a negative impact on the expression of the strengths and resilience of African American families.

The Africentric Perspective in
Understanding African American Families

As the holistic-oriented family theorists have focused on the strengths of African American families, there are those theorists who are giving increased attention to an African-centered or *Africentric* perspective for understanding African American families. The Africentric perspective seeks to identify the "residual values from Africa" as a source of strength and resilience for the African American family in the face of racism and oppression. As a conceptual framework for understanding African American families, this perspective not only provides a descriptive framework for analysis of African American families but can also be viewed as an intervention paradigm that promotes transformation of African Americans from a state of dependence to independence and self-reliance (Asante, 1980, 1987; Karenga, 1996).

The Africentric perspective directs us to the worldview and the cultural values and ethos of people of African descent. This perspective represents a set of beliefs, philosophical orientation, and assumptions that reflect basic African values as expressed within an American sociocultural and political context. As an "emerging paradigm in social work practice" (Schiele, 1996), the Africentric perspective provides a culturally sensitive framework for understanding the experiences of African American families. In addition, an Africentric perspective can guide us in developing intervention approaches that reflect the unique lived experiences, values, and worldview of African American families.

Africentrism is a perspective that reflects a distinct worldview from an African-based, yet American, frame of reference. An Africentric orientation combines the elements, science, mythology, and philosophy of the African Cultural System; juxtaposes African and American ways; and, finally, integrates values derived from the historic experiences of African Americans to give the clearest perspective on the unique group of people called African Americans (Asante, 1987). In essence, Africentrism reflects a philosophical and spiritual acceptance, the intellectual acknowledgment and celebration of the unique hybrid and historical development of the African American ethnocultural heritage.

Within an Africentric cosmology are basic assumptions about the human domain (Schiele, 1994, 1996; Swigonski, 1996). These assumptions are as follows:

- Human identity is a collective identity rather than an individual identity (i.e., "I am because we are")
- The spiritual or nonmaterial component of human beings is just as important and valid as the material components
- The affective approach to knowledge is epistemologically valid
- All things are interconnected; there is a oneness of mind, body, and spirit
- There is an appreciation of analogue thinking rather than dualistic thinking
- There is a phenomenological time (i.e., present oriented) tied to events
- There is a pervasive, experiential, and participatory spirituality

These assumptions undergird a worldview and value system that are believed to reflect, in an archetypal manner, the African American's existential mode of "being in the world."

The challenge for many Africentric-oriented social and behavioral scientists is the task of correcting the (mis)application of theories of human behavior that are based on a positivistic or Eurocentric worldview and are inappropriate to explain the behaviors of African Americans (Akbar, 1984; Bell, Bouie, & Baldwin, 1990; Kambon, 1992). This perspective is the basis for challenging deficit-oriented theories about African American families. Schiele (1996) views the Africentric perspective as making the following contributions: (a) It promotes an alternative social science paradigm that is reflective of the cultural and political reality of African Americans; (b) it dispels the negative distortions about people and families of African ancestry by legitimizing and disseminating a worldview that goes back thousands of years and resides in the collective memories of people of

African descent; and (c) it seeks to promote a worldview that facilitates human and societal transformation toward spiritual, moral, and humanistic ends.

The implications of the Africentric perspective are enormous. Africentrism counters the deficit model that focuses on the dysfunction of African American families by acknowledging the resilience that resides within those African cultural remnants that continue to remain in African American culture. This perspective is further seen as an intervention paradigm. Variations of the Africentric perspective have been used in the design and implementation of prevention programs for African American children and their families (Crawley, 1996). Finally, this perspective has provided a framework for theory, program development, and research within African American communities (Nobles & Goddard, 1992; Randolph & Banks, 1993).

Cultural, Social, and Economic Concerns of African Americans

What Is in a Name?

Ethnic identities are embedded in those collective narratives that ethnic groups recount as their distinctive "connectedness." In that sense, ethnic identities are socially constructed. How an ethnic minority group "labels" itself or the term used to identify the collective ethnic identity serves many purposes. The self-designated term or identity label may

- Represent the fact that the designated identity serves as a buffer against racism and oppression
- Serve as an experience of bonding that helps individuals form attachments with others who share similar cultural practices and worldviews
- Allow the group to adapt to a particular environment that may be more or less supportive of its cultural identity
- Serve as basis for pride and achievement (Parham & Brown, 2003).

The social and cultural history of African Americans speaks to their struggle for self-designation and self-definition. As with First Nations peoples and Latinos, the issue of an ethnic name has been the issue of achieving a state of self-determination and a sense of personal and collective empowerment. Terms such as Negro, colored, and even black, all of which have been used at one time or another in a pejorative sense, are labels that have been imposed upon a group of people of African descent in the Americas. These labels signify the operation of the "victim system," which places those of African descent in a marginalized, disempowered, and "invisible" position within the existing social order. The issue of "what is in a name" is also significant for many who come from other ethnic and cultural backgrounds and who are uncertain of the appropriate term with which to label those of African descent. In this chapter, the term *African American* refers to descendants of enslaved Africans brought to the United States. *Black* refers to all people of color and African descent in the "diaspora," including those from the West Indies, Africa, and the Americas (Grace, 1992; McRoy, 2003).

The other significance of "what is in a name" is reflected in the history of those of African descent who have within their genealogy the presence of other ethnic, racial, or cultural groups. This group has historically been designated by the existing term used for those of African descent, but there is an emerging group of individuals of bicultural and biracial descent who do not want to be referred to by any ethnic label (McRoy, 2003). The social and cultural ramifications of this emerging group on African American family life are only now beginning to be documented (Moran, 2001). The increasing number of interracial marriages and children resulting from such unions is only part of the story. We will discuss interracial marriages later in this chapter.

The presence of this multiracial group was reflected in part in the 2000 census.

In the 2000 census, between 34.7 million and 36.4 million United States citizens reported being black or African American. The reason for the range is that in the 2000 census individuals were able to check off more than one race, and 34.7 million identified themselves as black or African American only, but the remaining number indicated being both African American and another race. It is those from this latter group who are raising concern about where they fit in the existing social schema of racial classification. For many in this multiracial group, there are conflicted and divided loyalties. Others have achieved a sense of personal identity that is either inclusive of their multiple ethnic identities or transcends their multiple identities through the use of the term *multicultural*.

The Social and Economic Condition of African American Families

Socioeconomic data regarding African American families do reflect a grim picture of the current status of African American families (Kantrowitz & Wingert, 2001; McRoy, 2003). For example, the U.S. Census Bureau reported in 1999 that

- 36% of African American children are living in two-parent families, compared to 64% of Latino children and 74% white children
- 47% of African American families are married and living as couples, compared to 82% of white families
- 45% of African American families are maintained by women, with no spouse present, compared to 13% of white families

- 8% of African American families are maintained by African American men, with no spouse present, compared to 5% of white families
- 20% of African American married couples and 14% of African American families maintained by women have five or more members, compared to only 5% of white married couples
- 22% of African American families are at or below the poverty level of $17,000 per year
- 25% of African Americans in the middle class have incomes of $50,000 or more, yet these are median income levels, only 87% of what white counterparts earn
- Four million African American children (36%) resided with both parents in 1998. In 1997, 36% (1.4 million) of all children living in a grandparent's home were African American
- Unemployment rates for African Americans are twice the rate for whites (Karger & Stoesz, 2002)
- Black males (28.5%) are about six times more likely than white males (4.4%) to be incarcerated during their lifetime, and it is estimated that 7.9% of African American males (compared to 0.7% of white males) will enter state or federal prisons before they reach the age of 20 years and that 21.4% of African American males (versus 1.4% of white males) will be incarcerated before they are 30 years old
- About 62% of first-time offenders admitted to federal prisons and 31.1% of those admitted to state prisons are there for drug offenses. About 12% of drug users are African American, but African American males are involved in nearly 50% of drug possession arrests in the United States
- The African American mortality rate in the United States in 1997 was 13.7 per 1000 live births, more than twice that for whites (6.0/1000)
- African Americans had coronary deaths rates in 1997 of 136.2/100,000, compared to 97.7 for whites
- The African American HIV/AIDS infection rate in 1998 per 100,000 population was almost 10 times that for whites (42.5 versus 24.0)
- The pediatric AIDS rate for African American children under 14 years old in 1998 was 3.2 per 100,000, compared to 0.2 for white children
- In 1996, African American males had a life expectancy of 66.1 years, compared to 73.9 years for white males. For African American women, the life expectancy was 74.2 years, compared to 79. 7 for white women

Given these alarming data, a legitimate question can be raised as to how to reconcile the strength and resilience of African American families with statistics that speak to a crisis within African American families. The next section will answer this question, in part, by examining the structure of the African American family in terms of how African Americans and their families maintain, in the words of Billingsley (1992), an "intimate association [as well as being] deeply embedded in a network of social structures both internal and external to itself. . . . forming an extraordinarily resilient institution" (p. 29).

The African American Family Structure

Cultural Values in Relation to Family Structure

As we begin to examine the African American family from the perspective of resilience and strength, we see specific Africentric cultural themes that speak to the uniqueness of African American families. These themes are (a) strong kinship bonds, (b) strong education and work achievement orientations, (c) flexibility in family roles, (d) commitment to religious values and church participation, (e) a humanistic orientation, and (f) endurance in a hostile environment.

Strong kinship bonds. Strong kinship bonds and the extended family are heavily influenced by a traditional African cultural orientation that values collectivity above individualism. It is generally acknowledged that the African American kinship network is more cohesive and extensive than kinship relationships among the white population. For example, in 1992, approximately one in five African American families included extended family, compared to one in ten white families (Glick, 1997). Taylor (2003), Herskovits (1958), and Sudarkasa (1997) report that in comparative research on West African, Caribbean, and African American family patterns, they found evidence of cultural continuities in the significance attached to coresidence, formal kinship relations, and nuclear families among black populations in these areas. In contrast to European extended families, in which primacy is given to the conjugal unit, the African and African American extended family is centered primarily around extended blood ties (Taylor, 2003).

Strong kinship bonds can provide valuable functions and needed services to African American families. In an earlier work on African American extended families, Stack (1974) describes how problems occurring within an individual's life may reverberate within the extended kinship network. Other studies have revealed that the kinship network may assist extended family members with financial aid, child care, household chores, and other forms of mutual support (Martin & Martin, 1978; Shimkin, Shimkin, & Frate, 1978).

Many extended family members became a part of an individual African American family through informal adoption or informal foster parenting (Hatchett, Cochran, & Jackson, 1991). This form of child care, which has been practiced since the time of slavery, involves an adult relative in an extended family taking care of children whose parents are unable to care for them. Extended African American families may also include nonblood significant others who are considered relatives or "fictive kin" (Hill, 1993). These individuals may be given such designations as "play brother and sister" and are granted the same rights and responsibilities within the extended family as blood relatives. In summary, strong kinship bonds enhance the emotional relationships within the extended family network and beyond. They help the family to deal with environmental threats in such a way as to ensure the survival, security, and self-esteem of its members (Chestang, 1976).

Strong education and work achievement orientations. Parents in African American families have abundant experience with the harsh social realities of racism and oppression. Yet many African American parents still believe that the essential path to success in life is through higher education, work security, and social mobility (Billingsley, 1992; Boyd-Franklin, 1989; Staples & Johnson, 1993). Many parents who are without a college education strongly desire a college education for their children, as these parents expect their children to surpass them. As a result of their efforts, an overwhelming majority of African American college students are first-generation college students.

In the context of the extended family network, relatives, along with parents or older siblings, may make sacrifices to enable the younger members of the family to secure a good education. The extended family network may be involved in collective support to an individual family member to help him or her achieve a higher education, make a transition into a specific kind of work, or establish independent residence (Hines & Boyd-Franklin, 1996). This "reciprocal obligation" (McAdoo, 1978) process explains why some older children drop out of school. They enter the labor force as a means to support their younger siblings' education. Additionally, following the adage that "to whom much is given much is expected," many successful African American family members often feel that they have the responsibility to "give back" to needy family members and support their education.

Flexibility in family roles. The African American family has been described as egalitarian and characterized by complementary and flexible family roles (Billingsley, 1992; Hill, 1972; Taylor, 2003). The widely accepted standard (of the dominant society) that the husband-father performs the instrumental (i.e., economic) functions and the wife-mother carries out the expressive (i.e., domestic and emotional) functions does not necessarily apply to a large number of African American families. According to Billingsley (1968), such a framework for examining the functioning of African American families is too simplistic, for it fails to take into consideration the historical and political perspectives of African Americans.

Many African American husband-fathers perform expressive functions, and many wife-mothers perform instrumental functions. Using data gleaned from the National Survey of Black Americans (NSBA) on household composition and family structure, Hatchett, Cochran, and Jackson (1991) conclude that there is strong support among African American men for an egalitarian division of labor, regardless of their educational or socioeconomic status. This finding is not true among college-educated African American women. This latter group was more likely than women with less education to support the flexibility and interchange-ability of family roles and tasks. This gender difference in attitude toward the flexibility of family roles may be related to the fact that historically, the African American female had greater access to economic opportunity in the dominant structure of society than the African American male.

The fluid interchange of roles within the African American nuclear family is assumed to have emerged out of the economic imperatives of African American life. Yet this greater acceptance of role flexibility and power sharing in African American families may figure prominently in marital instability (Taylor, 2003). Gender role flexibility may present contradictory messages to young African American men in terms of encouraging them to embrace an androgynous gender role within the African American family although they are still expected to per-form according to the white male gender role paradigm in nonfamily contexts. The African American woman, on the other hand, may be socialized into a mes-sage of "be independent because it is hard to find an African American man to care for you," although she also hears the contradictory message of "find a man so he will care for you" (Franklin, 1986).

African American husbands in the early stages of marriage are found to have greater anxiety over their ability to function in the role of provider when they feel their wives have equal power in the family and when their wives feel there is not enough sharing of family tasks and responsibilities (Hatchett et al., 1991). This tension, although possibly reflecting changing attitudes and definitions of family roles among young African Americans, may more significantly reflect the African American male's anxiety over his economic viability and potential. It is impor-tant to note that the wife-mother's assumption of instrumental functions is not a reason for therapists to assume that African American families are matriarchal. The fact of African American woman assuming instrumental functions within the family may be more reflective of a socioeconomic structure that creates employ-ment barriers for African American men.

Commitment to religious values and church participation. African American churches have historically served a nurturing function for African Americans. A committed religious orientation was a major aspect of the lives of black people in Africa and during the era of slavery. Churches played a vital role in the escape of

African Americans from the oppression of slavery and continue to serve as advocates for social and political action against racism and discrimination. Today, in times of crisis, Christian churches and other African American faith communities, such as Islam, have been the supportive element in revitalizing hope for African Americans in the midst of the hopelessness and despair of racism and oppression. For some African Americans, church attendance and participation may not solely reflect a profound religious or spiritual orientation. Rather, the church may serve primarily as a social institution for social and communal affiliation. In this sense, churches provide a venue for the expression of the Africentric value of collectivity and communalism.

Churches are a source of psychosocial support and can have an impact on every aspect of life (McAdoo & Crawford, 1990). In addition to providing African American families with social services such as senior citizen activities, child care, educational groups, parenting groups, and housing development, churches also provide latent functions such as helping to maintain family solidarity, conferring social status, leadership development, release of emotional tensions, social and political activity, and recreation (Staples, 1976). Because the African American church has been ever present in the provision of human services, it has become an alternative social service delivery system for many African American families.

Humanistic orientation. In the midst of their daily struggle for survival in a racist society, African American families have not lost sight of the value and the importance of concern for each other. Solomon (1976) has referred to this value dimension of the African American family as "more humanistic and [of] greater validity than the hollow values of middle-class American society" (p. 169). This humanistic attitude is connected to the Africentric value of viewing the spiritual or nonmaterial component of the human being as coequal with the material aspect. This is in contrast to the materialistic and capitalist-driven characteristics of white American values, which are predominately task oriented and motivated by economic achievement to the exclusion of other values. The Africentric humanistic orientation stresses person-to-person relationships and their cultivation. African American cultural expressions in music, dance, and literature are suggestive of this humanistic aspect of African American culture. The humanistic orientation of African American culture can have strong implications during various therapeutic phases. It is the working alliance or relationship that is most significant or preferred over the accomplishment of a specific task according to a specific time frame.

Endurance in a hostile environment. In view of the adversity African Americans face, they have developed a great capacity for coping with conflict, stress, ambiguity, and ambivalence. Further, they have developed a "healthy cultural paranoia" (Grier & Cobbs, 1968) that makes them hypervigilant against acts of racism and oppression. Religion and spirituality have further provided a refuge from racism, as well as providing the spiritual power to support political and economic battles against racism and oppression. Yet in spite of their capacity for coping with racism and oppression, many African Americans have had acute psychological and physiological reactions to racism. Many of these reactions are the consequences of failed attempts to successfully manage bicultural or acculturative tensions and bicultural or acculturative stress. Utsey, Bolden, and Brown (2001) have identified key psychological and physiological process associated with the experience of racism. The racism-related reactions are as follows:

- *Race-related trauma* is the spiritual, psychological, and physiological devastation that African Americans experience following direct, personal experiences with racism, such as being victimized in regard to housing and employment, being humiliated and degraded in public places, witnessing and experiencing mob violence, or being arrested and/or beaten by police. Symptoms associated with race-related trauma include recurring thoughts, nightmares, anxiety, fear, sleeplessness, and depression.
- *Racism-related fatigue* is the psychological and physiological exhaustion that African Americans experience as a result of and in response to chronic exposure to racism and oppression on a daily basis.
- *Anticipatory racism reaction* is a defense mechanism that African Americans develop after being a victim, recipient, or combatant of racial discrimination and racially motivated hostility. This reaction is marked by a state of anxiety-ridden hypervigilance that may even exist in relatively nonthreatening environments.
- *Race-related stress disorders* are reactions such as tension headaches, intrusive thoughts regarding a specific race-related encounter, and a general sense of anxiety and tension resulting from chronic exposure to racism and oppression.
- *Race-related frustration* occurs when African Americans believe that they are powerless over the treatment that they receive because of their race. This frustration is marked by feelings of anger, irritability, aggravation, disappointment, dissatisfaction, and lack of fulfillment and satisfaction.
- *Race-related confusion* occurs when an African American begins to question the meaning and significance of his or her racial identity within the context of an oppressive environment: There is a sense of uncertainty as to "Who am I?" or "What have I done to cause this?"

These reactions affect the individual's psychological state and ability to cope with racism and oppression and can reverberate through a family system and create disruptions in the family's ability to cope with internal and external family stressors. Yet in spite of these reactions, the African American family has continued to survive. The African American family's efforts at coping with racism-related conflict, stress, ambiguity, ambivalence, and the psychological and physiological toll such coping exacts may partly explain their underuse of social services and high dropout rate in therapy. African American families may exhibit a cultural paranoia in light of their prior experiences with racism and oppression (Grier & Cobbs, 1968; Rasheed & Rasheed, 1999). This unwillingness to engage in a helping relationship may also reflect a reaction to the existing power differential between therapist and client. The therapy relationship becomes a reproduction of the power differential in society. This power differential, for many African Americans, can produce a sense of mistrust and distrust.

The African American cultural values of strong kinship bonds; education and work achievement orientations; flexibility in family roles; religiosity and church participation; humanistic orientation; and endurance in hostile, oppressive, and racist environments significantly influence African American family organization and structure. A discussion of how these values affect subunits and overall family interactions follows.

Mate Selection and Husband-Wife Relationships

Due to the excess number of African American women vis-à-vis African American men, African American women are experiencing great difficulty in finding a compatible mate. Factors contributing to the shortage of African American men include a high rate of mortality, incarceration, and intermarriage (Franklin, 2000). African American women outnumber men in each of the age categories from 20 to 29 years, resulting in a "marriage squeeze" that puts African American women at a disadvantage in the marriage market (Taylor, 2003). This fact may also contribute to the large number of female-headed households in the African American community, as remarriage may not be viewed as an option due to the low number of available or marriageable partners.

When it comes to finding a mate, the middle class woman has no advantage over her lower class counterpart, as many African American college women, especially those at African American college institutions, remain single. Many African American women who are college graduates marry men with less education. Such marriages have a greater statistical probability of ending in divorce (Franklin, 2000).

In times of high unemployment, African American women have historically worked outside the home and have often been the sole wage earners. Hence the husband-wife relationship of an African American couple has been more egalitarian than that of the white American couple. Regardless of socioeconomic status, most African American males expect recognition as the head of the household even though roles may be shared within the home. However, an individual African American male's inability to provide for his family due to discriminating practices in the workplace will more than likely greatly affect his role identity and involvement with his family. A family therapist should not misconstrue an African American father's inability to provide for his family financially as rendering him peripheral within his family system. Instead, creative approaches should be used to involve the father during family therapy (Boyd-Franklin, 1989).

Parent-Child Relationship

For many African American parents, their primary task as parents is to prepare their children to cope with the stress that will face them as African Americans. Thus African American children are socialized to successfully manage the world of the dominant culture, understand and negotiate their difference as it relates to the dominant culture, overcome the consequences of being different, immerse themselves in the world of the African American community, and combat the world of racial oppression (Jansen & Harris, 1997). These tasks are particularly crucial for raising African American males. As Boyd-Franklin and Franklin (2000) point out, parenting African American boys is particularly challenging. The challenge for parents of African American males is

- Keeping them alive past the age of 25 years, given the rate of homicide and violence among and against African American males
- Preparing them adequately for encounters with racism, prejudice, and discrimination that will affect their ability to take advantage of opportunities in life and achieve success
- Ensuring that they have a good education and helping them to see its importance and advantages as they chart their life path
- Helping them become responsible adults and persons who understand the importance of commitments, collective unity, and partnerships
- Helping them to develop a positive racial identity

These challenges are also important for parenting African American girls. One of the messages that a girl gets within an African American family is to be self-sufficient and independent and to not necessarily look to a male or husband for emotional or financial support. Yet this message may be contradictory to the message of finding a good husband or man to care for them (Taylor, 2003). Accordingly, the parents' expectations of the adolescent girl may carry with them an explicit objective of developing toughness and self-sufficiency in their daughter but covertly acknowledging that such traits may be a liability in attracting a mate in adulthood. It should be noted that these parental expectations are not perceived by the adolescent girl as rejection but as nurturing, caring, and preparing her for the future in a world in which racism may have an impact on life choices and mate selection.

Parenting African American children is an awesome task for African American parents. The parents' success in managing this task will be reflective of their childhood experiences as African American children and adults. One of the key areas of parenting that all parents struggle with, especially African American parents, is the issue of discipline. Discipline for African American parents is a part of the socialization process that prepares children to live and thrive as members of a racial and ethnic minority. Thus discipline serves at least two purposes for African American parents: (a) it is a means for children to learn to be sensitive and respectful to others within their family and extended family network, and (b) it can prepare and "toughen up" a child for encounters with the harsh race-based system existing outside the home and the "rules of engagement" in managing confrontations with systemic racism (Boyd-Franklin & Bry, 2000).

African American fathers' involvement with their children generally may be hindered by economic restrictions or obligations (working long hours or multiple jobs to care for his family), but African American mothers are generally recognized for their devotion and care of their children. Many African American women consider motherhood a more important role than that of wife (Bell, 1971). The role of the African American mother can be "doubly challenging for the [mother] must teach [her children not only] how to be human, but also how to be Black in White society" (Billingsley, 1968, p. 28).

It is generally recognized that an African American child's self-esteem and self-image is interwoven with group identity and group esteem. Studies have concluded that regardless of the region in which African American children live or their socioeconomic background, they are aware, between the ages of 5 and 7 years, of the social devaluation placed on their racial group by the dominant society (Wright, 1998). This information, however, should not lead to the conclusion that all African American children internalize these devalued images from the dominant society. Rosenberg (1979) has found that the level of self-esteem of African American school children does not differ a great deal from that of white school children and that African American children in racially homogeneous school situations who do not experience conflicting attitudes from the larger society have even higher images of self-worth than white school children. This factor may further indicate that many African American parents, especially middle class parents, have been able to nurture their child's sense of self-worth by finding ways to separate their personal sense of worth from the negative ascriptions placed on them by white society (Jenkins, 1988).

The frequent absence of the father or male figure within African American families has long been considered a negative factor in the psychological and emotional development of an African American child (Rainwater, 1966). This absence may be the case in specific families, but many theorists and practitioners have concluded that African American families by and large are "fatherless" families. As Boyd-Franklin (1989) points out, it is a serious error for a therapist to assume that because an African American father is not living in the home that he is not involved with his family. Rasheed and Rasheed (1999) further describe ways in which noncustodial low-income African American fathers continue to be involved with their families even though it is thought by public and human service professionals that they are not.

Earlier studies (Hare, 1975; Rubin, 1974) have concluded that the fatherless child does not significantly suffer from the absence of a father. Fatherlessness may, in part, be corrected by male role models among the male kinsmen in the African American child's extended family network. Staples (1976) offers another explanation for the relatively undamaged self-esteem of an African American child with an absent father. There are often other countervailing influences such as religion, reference groups, group identification, and positive experiences in the extended family that provide the ingredients for a secure sense of self.

Sibling Relationships

There are three important factors that characterize the sibling relationship within the African American family. First, there is generally equal treatment of both sexes, especially in middle class African American families. From infancy and early childhood, children of both sexes are treated equally, fostering a sense of personal uniqueness and intensity in interpersonal relations (Taylor, 1991). However, sex-based differences in socialization patterns do emerge in early adolescence. Both sexes are encouraged to complete their education, to find work, and to accept family responsibilities. Despite differences in parental expectation for adolescent boys and girls, there are few differences attached to preferred male and female personality types or traits. African American adolescents are taught that such traits as nurturing and assertiveness are desirable for any individual, regardless of sex (Boykin & Toms, 1986). Such nonbiased sex roles and traits are directly related to young African Americans' ability to relate to their future spouse in an egalitarian fashion and to prepare them for flexibility in performing various family roles.

Second, there are clear responsibilities assigned to siblings on the basis of age. After the age of 3 years, young children are frequently placed in the care of an older sibling, male or female, who may care for a group of children. The oldest child's authority as the "parental child" over the child group is strong, and so are his or her nurturing responsibilities for the younger siblings (Boyd-Franklin, 1989). The expectation that an older sibling or parental child will care for younger siblings represents a functional adaptation of families in which both parents or a single parent must work.

Third, the firstborn, regardless of sex, receives special preparation for a leadership role in the sibling group. It has been an established fact that, almost universally among African American families, the firstborn child receives more mothering and stimulation in infancy than do the children who follow (Lewis, 1975).

Intermarriage

Because laws against interracial marriage were declared unconstitutional by a United States Supreme Court decision in June 1967, intermarriage between African Americans and whites has increased rapidly. In 1980, there were 122,000 African American husband–white wife marriages and 45,000 white husband–African American wife marriages. Eighteen years later in 1998, the African American husband–white wife marriages had increased to 210,000, and the white husband–African American wife marriages had increased to 120,000 (Cose, 2003). The increase in numbers may be indicative of changing attitudes toward interracial marriages between African Americans and whites (interracial marriages also occur between African Americans and other ethnic groups).

Historically there has been a divergence of opinion in the African American community regarding African American–white marriages. Some view them as one channel through which equality can be achieved; others feel that such a marital union is inconsistent with the development of a sense of ethnic pride and a sense of "peoplehood." Others have speculated that those involved in African American–white marriages have certain "abnormal" social and psychological characteristics.

Furthermore, there is considerable concern among African Americans over the disproportionate number of African American men in intermarriages who are members of the middle class and have thus "robbed" the African American community of successful role models, as it is assumed that these individuals have given up their identification with the African American community. Traditional older African Americans and some African American females have been in opposition to interracial marriages. The African American woman's protest is mainly related to the disproportionate number of African American males to African American females. What is significant is that the number of African American female–white male marriages is increasing, which may indicate that African American women are altering their position on African American female–white male relationships, a change that may be attributed to the continued African American male shortage.

Although a great deal has been written about the "abnormal" social and psychological characteristics of those involved in African American–white marriages, Porterfield's (1978) research study indicates just the opposite. A majority of the respondents involved in the study indicated no sign of pathological abnormality or any personal crusade against prejudice. With few exceptions, the respondents' motives for intermarriage do not appear to be any different from those individuals marrying in the conventional style, that is, within their own race. As society continues to become more sensitive to individual freedom and personal rights, future African American–white marriages can be expected to have a more acceptable climate for success. Social scientists and family therapists can play a vital role in African American–white marriages by objectively analyzing this phenomenon so that many of the fears, myths, and misconceptions can be corrected.

Divorce and Remarriage

There has been a sharper increase in marital disruption and relatively low remarriage rates among African Americans (U.S. Census Bureau, 1996). Additionally, fewer than half (43%) of African American adults 18 years old and older were currently married as of 1996, down from 64% in 1970 (U.S. Census Bureau, 1996). This increase in marital disruption is in part explained by the following:

- Since 1960, there has been a sharp decline in the number of years African American women spent with their first husband and a corresponding rise in the interval of separation and divorce between the first and second marriage (Espenshade, 1985; Jaynes & Williams, 1989)
- Although African American women have a greater likelihood of separating from their husbands than do non-Latina white women, they are slower to obtain legal divorces, which may be due to their lower expectations of remarriage (Cherlin, 1996)
- The proportion of divorced African American women who remarry is lower than the proportion of non-Latina white women who remarry (Glick, 1997)
- The remarriage rate among African Americans is about one fourth the rate for whites (Staples & Johnson, 1993)
- Among African American women, twice as many college graduates were divorced or separated as white graduates (21% versus 11%). Among male college graduates, the rate of divorces was lower (15% for African American men and 9% for white men; Franklin, 2000)
- White (high-income) women married men who made more money, and African American high-income women married men who made less money (Franklin, 2000).

Despite African Americans' intense ties to family and their flexibility in family roles, marriage has proven to be an unstable institution for them regardless of socioeconomic class. Some social theorists have speculated that the institution of marriage has been weakened during the past few decades by the increasing economic independence of women and cultural drift within the younger African American community toward a more "individualized ethos" (Cherlin, 1992, p. 112). One factor that is clearly attributable to the high divorce rate among African Americans is American racist society, especially with regard to African American males. The high unemployment rate among African American males contributes neither to their self-concept nor to their performance as equal partners in marriage.

Middle class marriages among African Americans are negatively affected less by poverty than by the shortage of African American males, especially in the higher educational brackets. Many African American college women remain single. Those African American women who marry African American men with less education risk a high probability of having the marriage end in divorce. The shortage of African American males available for marriage is forcing African American women to reconsider the traditional idea of a long-lasting monogamous marriage with an African American male. Some African American women have now considered interracial marriages. Others have considered single parenthood through adoption, and those divorced have given up the idea of remarriage and have considered single parenthood as a possibly permanent lifestyle.

The continued shortage of African American males and African American females' coping with this phenomenon has significant implications in marriage and family therapy. Therapists may be able to understand the pressure African American males are under, being constantly sought for marriage, but therapists should also be empathetic toward African American females' barriers to a permanent marital relationship. Furthermore, the experience of becoming a female-headed household or a single-parent family should not automatically spell gloom for family members, because a household and an independent nuclear family are not synonymous. A close examination of the network of family relations that binds households together provokes an appreciation of the strength and richness of African American family life in its multiple forms.

The Impact of Discrimination, Migration, and Cultural Adjustments

Like every other ethnic minority group, African Americans are pressured to adapt to American mainstream society and cope with the reality of systemic racism. Although some families exhibit unusual strength and flexibility, tolerance for ambiguity, and creativity in their relationship with the larger sociopolitical, socioeconomic, and sociocultural system, other families consistently experience difficulty due to value conflicts and identity confusion. For example, American values of individualism, independence, autonomy, ownership of material goods, achievement, mastery, efficiency, and future planning are in direct opposition to Africentric cultural values that stress collectivity, sharing, affiliation, deference to authority, spirituality, and respect for the elderly.

In an attempt to survive the oppressive victim system, some African Americans adopt a value orientation that emphasizes (a) cooperation so that they will not experience feelings of powerlessness; (b) strict obedience to authority in response to experienced oppression; (c) toughness of character; and (d) creative activities in the form of art, music, and sports. Other African Americans challenge systemic racism through a form of critical consciousness and "liberating action" (Rasheed & Rasheed, 1999) in which they seek to reject the pernicious influence of the victim system on their sense of personhood. They act to create life options for themselves and others in spite of systemic racism. They seek empowerment and liberation.

There are other African Americans who, from their position of felt powerlessness and alienation, may engage in oppositional and transgressive behaviors that are marked by immediate gratification; manipulative relationships; and passive-aggressive, rebellious, or aggressive characteristics. While these latter values and behaviors may appear to be an adaptive response to powerlessness, they can also be maladaptive to a person's mental health and interpersonal relationships (Pinderhughes, 1989). Franz Fanon (1963), the Martinique psychiatrist who spoke to the impact of oppression on the black psyche, describes five aspects of alienation as a reaction to conditions of oppression:

1. Alienation from the self—to be alienated from one's personal identity

2. Alienation from the significant other—estrangement from one's family or group

3. Alienation from the general other—characterized by violence between blacks and whites

4. Alienation from one's culture and history—estrangement from one's language and history

5. Alienation from creative social praxis—denial or abdication of self-determination and of socialized and organized activity, which is at the core of human potential.

There are several strategies an African American family can use to adapt to racism and discrimination, such as (a) attempting to meet race-related crises as they arise, (b) physically removing themselves from any stresses caused by a racist society, (c) willfully maintaining externally imposed or self-imposed segregation, or (d) removing major barriers to assimilation into the opportunity structure. None of the above strategies alone can provide for successful family living. Recent suggestions involve developing an acculturation style that is a "dynamic, dialectical and/or circular process" (Landrine & Klonoff, 1996) that allows for movement within the cultural and economic space of the dominant culture but retains the important aspects of an Africentric cultural value base and maintains solidarity with the extended family and the African American community through its various institutional forms.

Family Help-Seeking Patterns and Behaviors

African American families often hesitate to seek mental health services. In addition to their general mistrust of mainstream institutions, African Americans rely heavily upon extended family ties and church organizations during times of crisis. Such patterns of help seeking are present in all African American families regardless of socioeconomic class (McAdoo, 1977). Reliance on natural support systems produces fewer feelings of defeat, humiliation, and powerlessness. Martin and Martin (1978) label such practice the "mutual aid system." It operates on the twin premises that families should seek security and independence, and when family integrity is threatened, sharing resources and exchanging services across households becomes even more crucial.

Many African Americans still view therapy as "strange" and think of it as a process for "strange or crazy people" only. Their contact with family therapy is usually precipitated by crises and happens when other sources of help have been depleted. The African American underuse of psychological help and family therapy is also related to their general mistrust of therapists, especially white therapists. African Americans' negative attitudes toward therapists may explain to some extent why African Americans have been found to drop out of therapy earlier and more frequently than whites (Sue & Sue, 1999).

Although African Americans do prefer African American therapists over white therapists, they also prefer competent therapists of whatever color over less-competent African American therapists. Competency in work with African Americans requires that the therapist take into consideration, from an African American perspective, the complexities of African American life, particularly family and community life.

There are several factors that characterize the use of individual and family psychotherapy among American Americans:

- African American women are more likely than men to seek both informal and professional help
- Persons with physical health problems are more likely than people with other types of problems to seek both professional and informal help

- Respondents with emotional problems are less likely than those with other types of problems to seek both informal and professional help
- People with physical problems are less likely than those with other types of problems to seek only informal help
- Respondents with emotional problems are more likely than persons with other types of problems to seek no help at all
- Gender, age, and problem type influence help-seeking behavior

McRoy (2003) and Dana (1993) indicate that African Americans do become involved in the helping process, but they initially may be guarded and reserved. They may later try to equalize the power differential between them and the therapist by challenging the therapist and questioning the background and experience of the therapist in understanding their situation as African Americans. The next stage may involve partial identification with the practitioner, and clients may begin to engage in the helping relationship. The work stage is then marked by a greater sense of comfort on the part of the African American client and by less defensiveness toward the therapist.

Applying Culturally Sensitive Family Theories, Models, and Approaches

Cultural and Political Factors Relevant in Family Therapy With African American Families

The first part of this chapter presented important ecological factors (historical, social, economic, political, psychological, and cultural) that operate to profoundly influence family life, structure, functioning, and processes. Below is a summary of key factors to consider in working with African American families. These factors include

- The African American poverty rate, which is much higher than that for non-Latino whites
- The psychological and physiological impact of racism and oppression
- Continued experiences with racism and discrimination practices in the labor market and related high rates of unemployment
- The drug epidemic (especially the use of crack cocaine and heroin) in the African American community
- The significant number of African American males who are incarcerated, many due to drug-related offenses
- The high rate of teen pregnancy

- The "marriage squeeze" for African American women due to the relative unavailability of African American men as marriage partners
- The significant number of single female–headed households (45%)
- The array of health concerns among African Americans (including high blood pressure, heart disease, diabetes, and other stress-induced illnesses)
- The high rate of HIV/AIDS in the African American community
- The lower life expectancy of African Americans compared to white Americans
- The high infant mortality rate
- Bicultural and acculturative tension and stress
- African-centered cultural values and worldview orientation
- The role of Christian churches and other faith communities in the African American experience

These factors affect the application of clinical approaches to family therapy with African Americans. Behavioral principles of family communication theory and family structure theory are discussed in this section. Practice principles derived from these theories will be reviewed in the context of critical sociocultural and economic factors affecting the African American family.

Family Communication Theory

Cultural and ethnic factors play an integral role in the communication process. Language is the vehicle through which individuals and families communicate their worldviews (Barranti, 2003). Given the significance of communication, family communication theory and practice offer enormous potential for family therapy with African American families. The following discussion focuses on family communication theories and therapy approaches and is organized into two parts. The first section describes principles of family communication behavior from the perspective of family communication theory. The second section describes practice principles derived from family communication therapy models.

Theories about communication have been an essential part of understanding families since the early days of some of the very first pioneers of family therapy (Duhl, 1989). Much of the following discussion about family communication theory and practice relies primarily on the work of Virginia Satir (1988; Satir et al., 1991). Satir is acknowledged by family therapy historians as the very first woman pioneer in family therapy (Duhl, 1989). Known to many as the "grandmother" of family therapy, Satir originally constructed her family therapy model with a focus on communication and problem solving (Duhl, 1989). During the course of her career, she experienced a shift of emphasis in her philosophy and began to incorporate existentialist philosophical notions into her already well-established and well-received family communication approach. Her revised family therapy model came to be known as the human validation process approach (Satir, 1988; Satir et al., 1991). Satir's revised approach retained important basic tenets of family communication behavior, such as the value of open and honest communication among family members and clarity of roles. However, her revised model also began to incorporate, in a very significant way, a humanistic focus with a spiritual, though nonreligious, sensitivity and awareness of human interconnectedness. The end result is a family communication model of therapy that is an excellent philosophical fit with the Africentric cultural values of African American families. Some of the most salient African-centered values are a sense of collectivity, the interrelationship of the spiritual and material worlds, and a humanistic orientation.

Specifically, Satir's (1988; Satir et al., 1991) revised human validation model emphasizes the growth potential of all individuals. Satir (1988) believes that one of the family's central and most critical functions is the enhancement of the self-esteem of its family members. To this end, Satir (1988) focuses on facilitating communication in the family that will enhance the self-esteem of individuals in the family. This approach has great significance for African Americans, as aspects of African American self-esteem (especially in adults) have been directly affected by racism.

Satir (1988, Satir et al., 1991) places a great deal of value on the therapist's roles of *observer, role model, advocate, culture broker,* and *educator.* The therapist's role as the Elder, so to speak, within these family sessions is also consistent with African American families' expectations that family members will derive a great deal of their learning through listening, observation, and emulation of Elders and family members who are seen as role models and teachers. A balance must be maintained between humility and openness ("not knowing," to prevent stereotyping) and showing expertise. Being direct but humble is interpreted as demonstrating awareness of the limitations of the therapist's knowledge and genuine respect for the family. For example, in therapy with an African American family, a therapist should not assume familiarity with adult family members via addressing these members by their first names without asking their permission. However, it is highly advisable that therapists refrain from seeking permission to address adult family members by their first names; rather, the therapist should wait and see if and when family members volunteer their permission.

The underlying values and theoretical assumptions in Satir's (1988; Satir et al., 1991) communication family therapy make it not only an excellent philosophical and existential fit with the critical constructionist practice perspective, but extremely compatible with social construction theory. (See chapter 1 for a discussion of social construction theory and the critical constructionist practice perspective.) Satir (1967, 1988) sees the therapist as having many important tasks. These tasks take on a decidedly social constructionist flavor in that she views them as observation and description of what is going on inside the family system from a position outside of the system (a concept central to the postmodernists), facilitation of a better understanding of the meanings behind communication, and empowerment of the family that makes it possible for family members to discover new ways of coping by *opening up space for alternative stories or actions.* Satir (1967, 1988; Satir et al., 1991) has always believed in the growth potential of individuals, their ability to make their own choices, and has clearly displayed within her practice model how much she values clients' knowledge of their own lives.

Satir (1988) believes that as a person experiences successes in good communication and problem solving, self-esteem is enhanced. She believes that family problems are a result of poor coping; and poor coping is a result of low self-esteem. She states, "The person is not the problem, the coping is the problem" (American Association of Marriage and Family Therapists, 1986). Satir (1988) believes that good communication and problem-solving skills are essential elements for a satisfying family life.

African American individuals and families coping with racism-related stressors and the experiences of alienation due to oppression may, over time, adapt dysfunctional (family) roles that do not serve them well. The *blamer, super-reasonable,* and *irrelevant* roles may be especially dysfunctional for African American families and their members, in view of prevailing collectivist cultural values that emphasize family cohesiveness. For example, a family member adoption the blamer stance dominates, finds fault, and accuses; one taking the super-reasonable stance remains detached, not emotionally involved in family processes; and a family member taking the irrelevant stance serves to distract other family members from the task at hand and seems to be unrelated and disinterested in anything that is going on in the family. Clearly, any of these stances would be diametrically opposed to African American and African-centered cultural values. These core cultural values are violated by these dysfunctional family stances, which should be viewed by the family therapist as serious threats to facilitating harmonious family life within African American families.

Other role conflicts may present themselves as challenges to African American families. *Role strain* and *role conflict* may result as a consequence of the experience of "double consciousness," resulting in bicultural tension and conflicts. This tension or sense of "two-ness" can occur both between and within African American family members, especially as this tension relates to different levels of connection with the values of the dominant, core culture and the ongoing connection with the communally oriented values of the African American community. For example, an African American male attempting to conform to the male gender role expectations of the dominant society may encounter images of black masculinity that represent stereotypes that exclude him from a viable position within mainstream society (Rasheed & Rasheed, 1999). Traditional roles that formerly helped to establish and define important developmental milestones for age, gender, community, or family roles may no longer be available to those who have suffered chronic racism-related stress and are alienated and disconnected from the community life and "creative social praxis" (Fanon, 1963). African American families will need assistance in communicating about these painful issues and will need even greater assistance to move toward problem resolution in the face of these experiences.

For African Americans, there is a wide range of communication styles, including a great reliance on nonverbal cues to convey a message rather than an open communication of feelings and intentions (McCollum, 1997). Hence traditional African American families are considered to be more of a *high-context communication culture* (Hall, 1976). A high-context culture relies heavily on the nonverbal aspect of a message (how it is said) to relay some of the most important and powerful aspects of a message. Conversely, in a *low-context communication culture,* the most important and powerful aspect of a message is contained within the verbal component of a given communication—as in the case in Eurocentric cultures. For African Americans, communication, regardless of socioeconomic status, may tend to be in generalities that may make conflict resolution difficult. Problem solving is generally thought to require communication skills that include specific communications and an open exchange of feelings and intentions. Engaging African American families in problem-solving activities necessitates the incorporation of nonverbal strategies. The therapist who has the knowledge and skill to understand and respond to the multiple levels and styles (the nonverbal component of a message, or how it is being said) of communication among African Americans will be better able to engage the African American family in the problem-solving aspects of therapy.

Linguistic obstacles may affect the family communication processes; that is, some African American family members may not be comfortable conducting an entire family therapy session in Standard English and may use a nonstandard English form of communication style known as "Black English" or "ebonics." The use of "Black English" is viewed by many as reflecting poor language skills, a lower level of intelligence, or a socioeconomic location in the lower class. Differences in communication and linguistic styles may render family sessions much more difficult to conduct for therapists who feel uncomfortable with this language style. As many African Americans are "bi-dialectical" (they have facility with both communication styles), the predominant use of one communication style over the other in therapy may reflect the family member's sociocultural position with respect to the victim system and class location.

Correspondingly, the use of one language style over the other in therapy may reflect issues of engagement by blocking effective communication between therapist and client. Additionally, different sociocultural positions and class locations within the same family can create bicultural or acculturative tensions within African American families. Differences in bicultural behaviors (especially within the realm of communicative behaviors) may complicate the communication process for African American families. Specifically, incongruous communication could occur, and other family members may perceive it as inappropriate or as behavior that is (however unintentionally) invalidating (Satir, 1986). For example, the use of Standard English by one family member in a communication context in which nonstandard or Black English is prevalent may create a perception that the Standard English speaker is attempting to disassociate from other family members or "putting down" those family members.

The effects of managing the bicultural tensions resulting from experiencing double consciousness has forced many African American couples to renegotiate their relationship. Their need for economic survival in a hostile environment (wherein all family members who are employable, including elder children, have to take on employment when available) may force their relationship to shift—upsetting the traditional hierarchy in the family system and subsystems, especially in the conjugal dyad, which may shift from a complementary or egalitarian relationship to a submissive-dominant conjugal relationship. This shift often complicates the couple's relationship and family life, as it occurs at a time when the family's emotional support system has been weakened and the demands for meeting basic family needs such as food, housing, and healthcare are greater than usual. African American couples (especially those couples that are experiencing bicultural tension and racism-related stress) need to be helped to "find their own way" so to speak, to determine for themselves what blend (if any) of conjugal behaviors will work for them. The family therapist is advised to facilitate the couple's effort to reauthor their *(ethnocultural) conjugal narrative,* which will help them to resolve the power issues and move past these dilemmas.

The problem of internalized racism, that is, viewing oneself in the same negative light as one's oppressor, is of concern and relevance in practice with African American families. This internalized oppression (accepting the negative messages and stereotypical images of others) is of general concern to people of color. Family members need to be empowered to *challenge these globalized interpretations* of their culture and *deconstruct these debilitating and nonpotentiating ethnocultural metanarratives,* which will enable them to *reconstruct* new, more *potentiating narratives* for themselves.

The painful racial experiences of those who grew up in communities where racism and oppression is overt (especially in the American South) may need help in dealing with these traumatic experiences, which can be emotionally intense and painful subjects. These emotionally laden issues may have become the source of *family secrets, myths,* and *rules* governing family and individual behavior.

There are many potential areas of unresolved grief that may have become forbidden subjects for family discussion. African American families and family members may be suffering from post-traumatic stress syndrome, and the family therapist can be helpful by engaging the family in *externalizing conversations* wherein the family provides accounts of trauma in their lives (emotional state, familial, peer) to externalize the problem so that it is not nested in the individual or within the family (Laird, 1993; White & Epston, 1990). Families can also be encouraged to *restory* some of these traumatic experiences, allowing the family and its members an opportunity to locate the (specific) origins of the immobilizing aspects of these experiences and losses (Laird, 1993). African American families and family members should then be encouraged to construct a *narration of oppression and resilience* that challenges disempowering sociopolitical and sociocultural meta-narratives. Reflective dialogue could provide a quiet, *culturally syntonic* forum in which the African American family and its members can critically reflect on their experiences, restory painful and debilitating experiences, and find or create new ways of coping with experiences of racism-based trauma (Rasheed & Rasheed, 1999). The family therapist will need to take great care and caution in approaching these subjects, especially as an outsider.

The principles of behavior derived from family communication theory can contribute significantly to understanding the dynamics and interaction of an African American family. The following discussion aims to further explicate the manner in which these family communication principles can be applied to actual work with African American families.

Communication Practice Principles

African American families may be very reluctant to seek help from white institutions, and this, in part, may be why African American families seek help from mainstream social agencies only as a last resort. The challenge on the part of the therapist working with African American families is to "join" the family and to be accepted by them. Specifically, *cultural joining* (Rasheed & Rasheed, 1999) is the technique of exploring ways to make changes that are the most culturally syntonic to the family, by including important cultural, religious, or civic leaders in the Black community. These persons can also serve as expert cultural consultants to the therapist and thus lend credibility to the therapy process, as well as serving as additional systems of social support to these families.

In the attempt to engage the entire family in the family's problem-solving efforts, the therapist should be cognizant of the African American family's inter-action communication rules. For example, many African American families believe that "children are to be seen but not heard," and "children should stay out of grown folks' business." If this rule is evident in a particular African American family, it should not be challenged in the initial stages of intervention with attempts to influence the family communication system according to the mainstream cultural ideals of democratic family decision making. It is advisable that beginning family therapy sessions be divided between the spouse subsystem and the sibling subsystem. Further, to respect the authoritarian parental position, parents should be interviewed first and children second.

Virginia Satir's (1967) communication theory can be used to help African American family members recognize the dysfunctional roles they sometimes assume as a maladaptation to bicultural stresses. She also challenges family members to be compassionate toward each other and to help each other to feel good and "respected." Honoring the extended kinship network is very important, and African Americans are expected to sacrifice self-interest to better other family members and the family as a whole. Satir's theory, which focuses on the "feeling good" (1967, 1986) component of each individual and the entire family, should greatly appeal to African American families and family members, and it is consistent with the African-centered cultural values of harmony, collaterality, collectivity, and cooperation. Her use of family history, which she calls the "family life chronology" (Satir, 1967), can be an invaluable *narrative* tool in helping the family reminisce and value its past, as well as work through aspects of racism-related trauma experienced by many African American individuals and their families. This discussion can also lead to the exploration of areas of strength and resilience that are an integral part of the family's chronology. Such exploration can give meaning to the African American spiritual "How I Got Over" (n.d.). Such explorations may be critical to helping family members better understand possibilities for new family system dynamics.

The reliance on the use of *storytelling techniques* is culturally syntonic and a natural fit with critical constructionist perspectives and techniques. African American families and family members can be encouraged to relive important aspects of their original traditions and ethnic and cultural heritage by storytelling and the use of metaphors and narratives, which may serve two purposes: (a) reinforcing positive self-images (or building potentiating ethnic narratives) to combat what family members may feel is forever lost to them and their families and (b) passing on important cultural images and memories to assist in nurturing positive ethnic identities (narratives) in children.

In light of the high-context nature of African American communication, with an emphasis on the nonverbal aspect of the communication or message in culturally immersed African American families, *family sculpting* and *family choreography* can be extremely useful techniques. Further, the family therapist will be able to encourage parents to "sculpt" their perception of family problems without fear of shame or embarrassment. Family sculpting and family choreography techniques can be especially helpful in their potential to bridge communication difficulties that arise when members of the same family do not have the same command of Standard English.

Satir (1988; Satir et al., 1991) employs a rich array of experiential techniques (e.g., sculpting, *drama, communication stances, family stress ballet, ropes, parts party*). These techniques are invaluable in their own right in that many do not heavily rely on verbal interchanges, making them particularly useful when, as discussed earlier, there are linguistic barriers, either between family members or between the family and the therapist. They can be considered to be nonverbal narratives in that the techniques encourage family members to tell their story *their* way, freeing family members to recreate their vision or perception of family relationships and family problems, as well as solutions to these problems.

Still, family therapists need to proceed with caution in implementing some of Satir's (1988; Satir et al., 1991) experiential techniques, such as family sculpting, family choreography, drama, communication stances, family stress ballet, ropes, and parts party. Although these techniques may be potentially very helpful in family therapy with African American families, family therapists must take great care not to intrude and otherwise impose their own sculpting suggestions (asking family members to take certain positions, etc.), which may violate (sex role and family) cultural norms and ideals of polite, respectful, and appropriate behavior.

To communicate effectively with an African American family, family therapists need to consider modifying their behaviors: limiting their verbosity and slowing their speech, for example. Therapists can communicate by paying attention to family members' needs and by respecting them as worthy and good individuals. Therapists can communicate effectively by not being overly dependent on the verbal mode of interaction; instead, the family and family members' use of metaphors in storytelling and within other oral African traditions, poetry, and journals, as well as artistic abilities, musical talents, and other natural assets can be used to facilitate communication. A more varied use of untapped clinical data and sources is very much a postmodernist notion (Rasheed, 1998, 1999). These families should be encouraged not to strive for consensus but to explore the *multiple (emotional) meanings* of important historical and cultural events and experiences. Family members then become empowered to take from these experiences what is most meaningful and helpful to them (Laird, 1993).

Interacting harmoniously during times of transition and crisis requires communicative skills, including effective styles. Traditionally, African Americans are taught to be cooperative, and "other-centered" in interpersonal relationships. An exchange of real feelings and intentions among all individuals at the early stage of therapy, therefore, may not be conducive to problem solving.

In summary, communication family therapy, especially as developed by Virginia Satir (1986) and discussed in this section, is a family practice approach that shares the cultural value assumptions and philosophical and existential position of traditional African American family life. Communication family therapy is also philosophically and existentially compatible with social construction theory. Furthermore, the varied roles that are prescribed for the therapist within this family therapy model (namely, educator and teacher, facilitator, mediator, advocate, and role model) are important and viable roles for those persons who seek to enhance the communication process of African American families.

Family Structure Theory

This discussion of family structure theory focuses on work developed and advanced by Bowen (1978) and Minuchin (1974). Reviewed here are behavioral principles and practice principles of structural family theory as they relate to assessment and therapy with African American families.

Bowenian family therapy incorporates important intergenerational processes, allowing family therapists to explore critical historical events and intergenerational patterns affecting current family functioning. Bowen's theory conceptualizes family change in a nonpathological framework as the family adapts to a stage in the life cycle such as marriage, the birth of a child, the departure of each child, retirement, aging, or death (Wimberly, 1997a). The *societal projection process,* identified by Bowen (1978), is relevant as it applies to the position of the relative powerlessness of African American families. This process creates "societal scapegoats" with which the African American individual, especially the male, clearly has been identified. In the societal projection process, one group (white society) maintains the illusion of competence at the expense of "unfortunates" by "helpfulness and benevolence." This group of "benefactors" assumes the blamer role, accusing the unfortunate of being inferior and undeserving. Such a societal projection process, like the *family projection process,* creates and maintains homeostasis for a social system.

We have introduced the concept of *invisible cultural triangles* (Rasheed & Rasheed, 1999) as an expansion of Bowen's *triangle* concept. A re-conceptualization of the concept of triangles, invisible cultural triangles refers to the existence of a third person, object, or event in a cultural system that exerts a powerful but not always apparent force on the systemic or dyadic relationship system. Historically, trauma and racism-related events and experiences can become *triangled* into the emotional system of African American families and create immobilizing and debilitating ethnocultural narratives. These sociopolitical narratives can take on a life of their own; thus a person or family can become a victim of a *collective narrativized past* or a narrative stance that does not work for the individual or the family.

A related term, also coined by us, is that of *invisible cultural loyalties* (Rasheed & Rasheed, 1999). This concept is an expansion of the family therapy (intergenerational) concept of *invisible loyalties,* also referred to as "relational indebtedness" or "family ledgers," as originally conceptualized by Ivan Boszormenyi-Nagy (1987). Invisible loyalties or family indebtedness can date back several generations and can also be a result of multigenerational and cross-generational unresolved conflicts or unrealized goals within the family (or tribal group) (Boszormenyi-Nagy, 1987). It is not hard to imagine it becoming difficult to preserve family legacies and continue family cultural traditions within cross-cultural, bicultural, and biracial families. It is easy to imagine the emotional conflict that family members may feel if these issues are not adequately addressed. Hence, family secrets, myths, and (powerful but unspoken) family rules may serve to further complicate and exacerbate emotional turmoil if they operate in tangent with invisible cultural loyalties or with invisible cultural triangles.

Structural family therapy is highly recommended with African American families because it incorporates a generational view, focuses on balancing the structure of the family, and uses a direct, concrete, here-and-now approach to problem solving (Wilson et al., 2000). The model's hierarchical parent-child relational position parallels African Americans' vertical communication style and reinforces the expected boundaries and rules within the family such as that children are not to be included in "grown folks' business." Similarly, the broad family framework, with a direct, no-nonsense, problem-solving approach, agrees with the preferred style of intervention among African Americans.

Minuchin (1974) views the structure of the African American family as characterized by strong family ties, egalitarian relationships, and flexible family roles. Under normal conditions, such a structure can produce cohesion conducive to the developmental growth of all family members. Minuchin points out, however, that "the stressful contact of the whole family with extrafamilial forces" (p. 63) can produce role confusion and power conflict within a family. By focusing on the extrafamilial forces, Minuchin shows sensitivity to the political, economic, social, and cross-cultural processes of poverty, racism, and discrimination faced by many African American families.

The African American family is typically large, and it is not unusual, therefore, for the older sibling to have the responsibility while both parents work outside of the home of caring for younger children and assisting with other household duties normally performed by adults. A therapist should avoid interpreting this as *boundary diffusion* and should not label an older child as "parentified child" (Minuchin, 1974, p. 53). This complementary accommodation between spouses and between parents and children characterizes the strength of the African American family structure. The family's ability to maintain traditional parent-child roles is often handicapped by the fact that both parents, and sometimes older siblings, have to work outside the home. Long working hours and different working schedules can create interactional problems and difficulty within a subsystem and between subsystems. For example, if the father (or even both parents) works a night shift, both parents will have little time to interact with each other and to maintain and solidify their spousal subsystem. The parents may also have too little time with their children, and older siblings may have to assume parenting responsibilities in the family. In this situation, the parental subsystem is disengaged from the children, thus creating a rupture in the caretaking relationship. As Minuchin (1974) cautions, such a family structure can be vulnerable if the parental delegation of authority is not explicit and the child lacks the power to carry out the responsibilities he or she attempts to assume. Moreover, if the parents abdicate their responsibilities, the child may be forced to become the main source of guidance, control, and decision making at a time when, developmentally, he or she is unprepared to handle these roles.

Family structure theory focusing on the family system's structural (contextual) dynamics, especially the creation, maintenance, and modification of boundaries, which are rules defining who participates and how (Minuchin, 1974), is useful in work with African American families. In an extended family system with multiple households, the subsystem boundaries between spouses, grandparents, parent and child, and siblings seldom are closed or rigid. These subsystems are functional historically because of cultural value reinforcements. As times change and as African American families continue to migrate to the suburbs and other integrated residential areas, the original extended family ties may have to be renegotiated. These factors, coupled with racial and cultural oppression and discrimination, make it difficult for African American individuals to retain culturally adaptive, functional family roles and traditional boundaries.

A different pace or level of biculturalism between family members will tend to create tension and cultural value differences. College-educated young people may be influenced by changing ideas about family and may absorb more individualistic notions that may run counter to the sense of collectivity that is a part of the social consciousness of many African American families. These bicultural tensions can lead to even more emotional distance within families (Rasheed & Rasheed, 1999) and, if left unresolved, can be primary contributing factors to emotional cutoff or disengagement between family members.

In response to the internal threats created by a racist society, African American families may protect themselves by maintaining rigid boundaries. The father's inconsistent involvement with the family due to job overload or unemployment can make the conjugal dyad highly susceptible to the process of triangulation, a three-person system that Bowen (1978) considers the building block of all emotional systems in and outside the family. Given the reality that many African American families are embedded in a complex kinship network of blood and unrelated persons, the process of triangulation may not have the same meaning and intensity as for a traditional white American nuclear family.

Because of their experiences with systemic racism, some African American parents are determined to create a more favorable environment or future for their children. They expect their children to earn greater rewards from the opportunity structure than they themselves were able to achieve. Many African American middle class parents actually warn their children of the consequences of associating with people who might interfere with their social and economic achievement (Scanzoni, 1971). Such intensity of purpose is relevant to Bowen's (1978) concepts of the "family projection process" and the "multigenerational transmission process." These processes are responsible for many couple difficulties and parent-child conflicts.

Family Structure Practice Principles

Bowen's (1978) societal projection process suggests that therapists be open to exploring the impact of the social, political, socioeconomic, and broader environmental conditions of the families with which they work. Those environmental conditions or systems most likely to impinge on African American families include welfare, the courts, schools, Medicaid, food stamps, public housing, and so on. These systems are the integral components of the daily functioning of many African American families. The therapist must be knowledgeable about social service systems and other help-providing agencies and be willing to work collaboratively with various service providers on behalf of the family.

"Differentiation of self" is a universal process, varying only in quantity and quality among different cultures. For example, white Americans may believe that sending an adolescent to work outside the home encourages the adolescent's differentiation of self. The same behavior should not be expected of an African American adolescent, whose parents may need him to assist with daily house chores. If the adolescent works, it is to reduce the financial burden on the family rather than for the adolescent to achieve a state of personal financial independence. Instead of self-differentiation, the general rule among African American families is not to separate but to maintain connectedness; the "we" takes precedence over the "I." The relational and interdependent nature of African American families corresponds with an individual understanding of the self-construct as a collective developmental process instead of as a differentiated, individualist self. Hence different cultures define and facilitate the process of "differentiation of self" differently. It is the responsibility of each therapist to learn about the specifics of the African American culture and to assist the client to differentiate accordingly.

Bowen's (1978) focus on obtaining, organizing, and understanding the family's history makes sense in terms of accurate assessment of individual and family needs. The process, however, may be antithetical to the African American "present" orientation. Those designated as "poor black" and "the black underclass" may be reluctant to invest energy, time, and financial resources to find out what is wrong with their parents, relatives, and ancestors. These family members may not feel comfortable and may remain unavailable for conjoint therapy. Bowen's (1978) technique of focusing on one individual, usually the more acculturated or respected member in the family (or whoever is willing to come), should be useful. In any case, this individual could be a grandparent, older sibling, other extended family (or "play relative": fictive kin). Although the therapist is working with an individual, the goal is to modify the structure of the emotional system of the family through that individual's change and effort. The Bowenian research process may be a more viable therapeutic tool with acculturated, middle class African American families.

Bowen's premise that parental relationship dictates the entire nuclear family's emotional system is logical. His preference for singling out the couple relationship as a therapeutic target (Bowen, 1978) may alienate the parents. The mother may feel more challenged to perform as a good mother than as a wife. Bowen's later emphasis on concentrating on the individual in family therapy can be applicable in dealing with a frustrated and emotionally depleted African American father and husband or mother and wife who may not tolerate challenges from their partner or children. In defending this one-to-one therapeutic technique, Bowen (1978) writes: "From my orientation, a theoretical system that 'thinks' in terms of family and works toward improving the family system is family psychotherapy" (p. 157). The one-to-one therapeutic modality may be the only workable resolution for many African American families. This is the preferred modality when the family as a whole is not amenable to family therapy because of mistrust, acculturative differences, or inadequate resources.

There are many advantages to the Bowenian family therapy approach in light of the traditional values of the African American family. Family work can still be conducted even when families are separated by long distances as a result of relocation to other states or cities for employment. Because all of the subsystems and dyads within the family are not required to be present at the same time for family therapy to proceed, potentially explosive and volatile cross-generational tensions and conflicts need not be exacerbated. Family members can sort through issues such as *generational splits* and acculturative tensions and conflicts. Family members can then repair emotional cutoffs (caused either by forced physical separation or via emotional detachment that acculturative conflicts may have exacerbated) and begin to repair other (emotional) damage that cultural transitioning may have had on family emotional relationships, in a much less emotionally charged atmosphere.

Bowen's (1978) concept of emotional cutoff has significant application in work with African American families. According to Bowen, everyone has some degree of unresolved emotional attachment to the previous generation. The "cutoff" consists of denial and isolation of the problem while living close to the parents or by physically running away, as in the case of (voluntary) immigration, or a combination of the two. As a rule, the more a nuclear family maintains emotional contact with previous generations, the calmer, more orderly, and less problematic the lives of family members will be (Bowen, 1978). Conversely, the greater the degree of cutoff, the more the nuclear family becomes a sort of emotional "pressure cooker." This concept indicates the importance of the extended family system of African Americans and the necessity for extended family members to be able to maintain consistent contact with each other.

Bowen's (1976, 1978) detached but interested, low-key approach to problem solving, during which he takes a careful family history (*multigenerational transmission records* or *ethnohistory*), reflects his sensitivity and respect for the cultural nurturance system, intergenerational perspective, and the need for individualizing each family.

Bowen (1976, 1978) believes that the therapist should take the roles of *coach, facilitator,* and *consultant.* This therapeutic style is very compatible with a social constructionist practice framework in that Bowen's primary goal in this therapy model is to coach the family and family members through a (self) discovery process by constructing a narrative of the family's history, primarily through the use of the *genogram* (a multigenerational diagram of family information). In this model of family therapy, the client is the expert in charge of the data collection process. The therapist is merely there to help the family and its members sort through their emotional reaction to the meanings that the family and family members ascribe to various family information gathered about family relationships, family patterns, and family (emotional) processes. For the most part, the family and family members set the goals and desired outcomes, as well as determining whether current family relationships will or will not change. Thus, Bowenian family therapy does not rely upon or employ the therapist's *privileged ways of knowing* about the family in this approach. The family and family members are free to *create or discover the collective narrative* of the family as the therapist creates a space for multiple meanings of the family's experiences.

In light of the emphasis on the rich historical, cultural, and familial traditions of African American culture, it is especially important for the family therapist to empower the African American family and its members to locate the origins of individual personal narratives—especially those narratives that are debilitating and nonpotentiating (Young, 1996). The genogram can provide a way for the family therapist to help the family and its members locate the origins of immobilizing, subjugating narratives and their context and significance (e.g., historical, political, economic, sociocultural, familial). This discovery process may uncover family myths and family secrets derived from generations of dysfunctional family emotional processes as the source of the emotional pain for the family or individual family member. The discovery process may uncover societal prejudice, discrimination, and racism at the root of troubling ethnic narratives (marginalized and negative stereotypical narratives), especially those of African American descent. Creating space for more *empowering liberating narratives,* making it possible for the family and its members to revise and reconstruct these stories (a reauthoring, restorying, or even *racial restorying process*), can offer possibilities for the acquisition of new information, new resources, and multiple opportunities (Freeman, 1992). These reauthored stories can reflect each family member's unique emotional experience and unique interpretation. Hence helping to maintain important close family ties as multiple (emotional) meanings is encouraged.

Minuchin's (1974) differential applications of joining techniques, which focus on the beginning phase of therapy, reflect his sensitivity to individual family differences and the wisdom that structural change in a family usually requires time and patience. His maintenance technique, in which the therapist follows the basic rules that regulate the transactional process in a specific family system, goes a long way toward helping to establish mutual respect and trust with the family.

While Minuchin's (1974) joining and maintenance techniques are compatible with African American family values and structure, his disequilibration techniques or family restructuring techniques generally do not share the same degree of congruence and effectiveness with this specific ethnic group. These techniques, including enactment and *boundary marking, escalating stress* (by emphasizing differences), *physical movement, utilizing the symptom* (by exaggerating it), and creating affective intensity by manipulating the mood (escalating the emotional intensity), are much too esoteric (not practical or immediately useful) and too manipulative. With modification, however, these techniques may work with bicultural, culturally immersed, or highly acculturated African American families and family members.

Minuchin's (1974) *tracking* technique aims to explore the content of family interaction and analyze family structure. When using this technique, the therapist should keep in mind the strong kinship bonds of the African American family. For example, the amorphous spousal subsystem boundary might be caused by the husband's need to do extra work to support the family. Interpreting less-intense spousal interaction as pathological is premature, insensitive, and irrelevant in this ethnic group. In addition, the African American family's flexibility in assuming different family roles should not be misconstrued as role confusion and family disorganization. It should be recognized and respected as a unique strength among African American families. To analyze an African American family structure without taking into consideration the strong extended family ties can do the client injustice and disservice. Thus Minuchin's (1974) system of boundary marking and restructuring techniques are helpful, provided they are adapted to the African American family's structured framework. In applying disequilibration (of boundary) techniques, Minuchin gives an example of how therapists can adapt this technique in work with an African American family whose structure includes a parental child. Minuchin (1974) suggests that "the therapeutic goal is to realign the family in such a way that the parental-child still helps the mother" (p. 98). The goal of the therapy is not to eliminate the child's parental role, which may be essential to the family's survival. Instead, the therapist needs to facilitate redistribution of the child's burdens and help the family make better use of the resources available to it.

Minuchin's (1974) "joining techniques" are generally sensitive to the African American family structure, but his family restructuring techniques, such as escalating stress (by emphasizing differences), utilizing the symptom (by exaggerating it), and manipulating mood (by escalating the emotional intensity), are highly emotional and confrontational. Some African American families may be confused by these techniques and interpret them as a means to undermine their authority, integrity, and respect. These techniques should not be attempted prior to developing a trusting relationship (if they are to be attempted at all).

An ethnohistorical approach to family therapy with African Americans can be useful. In this approach, a meticulous, detailed narrative account of each person's (unique) emotional experience of the many race-related stress and historical traumas has the ability to complement existing intergenerational approaches that focus primarily on intra- and interfamilial issues and events. Taking an ethnohistorical account of how African American families and family members have come to construct their own individual narrative, thus allowing for reflective dialogue, can lead, first, to the deconstruction of marginalizing, immobilizing ethnic narratives (as well as negative sociocultural metanarratives of the family group) and then empowerment of African American clients to reconstruct more liberating and potentiating narratives and begin the healing process.

The cultural values and structure of the African American family are explored in the preceding pages. Communication and structural family therapy theories are reviewed, along with their application in therapy with African American families and family members. Attention will now be directed to culturally relevant techniques and skills in three phases of therapy: beginning, problem solving, and termination-evaluation.

PART 2: CULTURALLY RELEVANT TECHNIQUES AND SKILLS IN DIFFERENT PHASES OF THERAPY

Beginning Phase

The engagement phase of therapy is a very critical period for African American clients. Many African American clients distrust the therapists who represent mainstream society; these clients use therapy for their problem only as a last resort. African Americans' strong endurance in the face of racism and oppression, religious beliefs, strong kinship bonds, and limited financial resources make family therapy less attractive and responsive to their needs. However, African Americans are beginning to use psychological services and family therapy more, including African Americans from the lower socioeconomic class. They are finding therapy that is short-term and with a focus on changing concrete behaviors to be extremely relevant and helpful.

The following discussion attempts to apply and integrate the cultural knowledge of African Americans and communication and structural family theories used during the beginning phase of family therapy. Specifically, five major skills and techniques are considered essential in therapy with an African American family in the beginning phase of therapy. These skills and techniques include (a) engaging the client or family, (b) cultural transitional mapping and data collection, (c) mutual goal setting, (d) selecting a focus or system for therapy, and (e) the use of an ecomap.

Engaging the Client or Family

Apprehension and distrust of (counseling) professionals attempting to "meddle" in family matters, emotional cutoff from family systems, and oppressive work schedules may render the engagement process of African Americans in family therapy a formidable process. Central to the task of engagement is one key dilemma.

The particular dilemma of the engagement of African Americans in family therapy is an ethical one and is rather straightforward in that the therapist is challenged to work a bit harder to engage all the subsystems of the family. This is to say, clinicians are confronted with the ethical dilemma of whether to take the easy way out and work with those family members who initially present at the door and those who are—with a little encouragement—willing to come in for therapy. However, family therapists can also elect to make a genuine effort to engage those family members who are initially resistant to the notion of coming in for family therapy, especially male members of the family.

One clinical strategy may enhance the engagement process with African American families: Avoid placing (textbook) "familial templates" on the family memberships of these complex and large systems. That is, allow the family members who do show up for therapy to inform the therapist as to who the important members of the family are. Therapists are reminded that the structure of the African American family is typically rendered even more complex when one considers the following factors: the fluidity of family membership (e.g., fictive kin change from time to time); the flexibility of roles, which dictates that given a certain issue some family members may be more central than others to specific matters; many of the more powerful and influential family members may not initially present for therapy but rather send in a proxy who may act as a sort of go-between or messenger between them and the therapist; and, finally, none of these factors or scenarios are necessarily dictated by household membership. If clinicians allow their initial outreach efforts to African American families to be informed by these unique factors, it is likely that engagement of African American family members (for those who initially come in, as well as for those who hesitate) will be enhanced. Clinicians who take a nonhierarchical position in the client-worker relationship and become more of a "cultural consult" to African American families, adopting the philosophy that the family is the real expert, may avoid initial resentment from family members. As African American families are especially attentive to and cognizant of outsiders deciding who makes up their family system and who is important to the resolution of family problems, showing this initial respect may operate to motivate others to come in for family therapy. Such an approach may allay some of their initial apprehensions about the paternalistic attitudes of professionals.

Transitional Mapping and Data Collection

Family communication theory focuses on analyzing the here-and-now trans-actions of the family. Family structural theory focuses on the family structure and functions in the present *and* in the past. Despite the African American family's responsiveness to problem-focused short-term therapy, some family problems cannot be successfully resolved without understanding the historical perspective of the family. The circumstances surrounding the development and maintenance of the African American family have resulted in a diversity of lifestyles among African American families.

In assessing the African American family, experiential information is more important than chronological and developmental data. Important experiential information includes the experiences of the parents as children growing up in their families of origin; the couple relationship; their perspective in child rearing; and the impact of social, economic, and political forces, with the important inclusion of their experiences with racism. Data collection has to be guided by the present-ing problem. For example, both parents' rigid child-rearing practices must be examined historically if the therapist and family are to resolve a child's current socialization difficulty. The data collection process will be incomplete if the extended family system is not also included. The genogram is a useful tool for gathering information about forces that affect the current structure and functioning of the family. Boyd-Franklin (1989) encourages the use of genograms to gather family information; however, she cautions therapists about attempting to formulate genograms too early on in the clinical process, before important joining activities occur. The authors suggest that practitioners consider engaging in cultural joining, that is, attempting to enter into the life space of the family— paying special attention to how gender, race, and social class issues may affect family members' life experiences both within and outside of the family. Practitioners also need to make special note of how the narratives of individual family members may differ from the narrative meanings assumed by others within the family: These differences have the potential to cause considerable pain and an increased sense of anomie, alienation, and isolation within the target family.

Again, clinicians are cautioned not to attempt to complete the genogram, or any other diagnostic activity for that matter, too early on in the clinical process, especially not in the initial interview with African American families (Boyd-Franklin, 1989). African American families are acutely aware of the negative and distorted perceptions a therapist might have about African American families. Family members initially may not feel like "going through the hassle" of convincing or educating a therapist about African American families.

The African American family is strongly present oriented, so the therapist should explain carefully to the family how such information may help them analyze and resolve present problems. The genogram should not be constructed during the early stage of therapy or before rapport has been developed. The therapist should look for an opportunity or opening to gather the desired information, rather than scheduling an agenda of data collection that the family might find insensitive and intrusive. One of the most important clinical dilemmas in conducting assessments in family therapy involving African American families is essentially the dilemma of challenging preconceived notions of African American families—notions that may have been informed by a conventional or "deficit" perspective. However, the clinical task in accomplishing this challenge involves conducting a skillful assessment of the various subsystems of these families and engaging the various dyads, subsystems, and invisible triangles in the important therapeutic tasks of joining and accommodating. Therapists are encouraged to use an *ethnographic (anthropological) approach* to studying families "and to view the family as tiny societies that over time, seem to develop their own systems of meanings and beliefs, their own mythologies and ritual practices, and their own subculture" (Laird, 1993).

Guided by one of the most important of the practice principles and guidelines emanating from the critical constructionist perspective is the need for clinicians to search their own "privileged ways of knowing" and examine their (practitioner) biases (Laird, 1993; White & Epston, 1990). That is, practitioners need to examine how they come to understand and "know" the African American family. Practitioners may find it necessary to deconstruct distorted, erroneous, and destructive perceptions and biases about the African American family. A more accurate, strengths-oriented perceptual and knowledge base about African American families will then need to be reconstructed by practitioners, with the assistance of their clients.

Next, therapists need to conduct a careful assessment of the various subsystems and dyads within the African American family, paying special attention to the presence of African American men, who may exist in important and powerful "invisible triangles." African American men are always present in African American families (physically, emotionally, spiritually, or via the collective communal associations). Sometimes, through their own filtered lenses, practitioners' internalization of (media-induced) overstatements regarding the absence of African American men in African American families renders their presence invisible in assessments and interventions. Critical constructionists offer a very helpful way of avoiding the use of outdated, distorted, or irrelevant information about African American families: They recommend that clinicians not derive their "clinical understandings or meanings" from "expert" knowledge or *global assessment schemes;* rather, "meaning" should be cocreated by the family and the practitioner within the clinical setting (Laird, 1993; White & Epston, 1990).

Mutual Goal Setting

Regardless of racial differences, all humans are goal directed. African American families share goals with their white counterparts (Berger & Simon, 1974; Scanzoni, 1971). However, African American families find their attainment of goals more difficult than whites due to the discrimination and prejudice inherent in many social, cultural, and economic institutions in the United States. Racism and oppression can also affect the internal dynamics of an African American family. Taylor (2003) and Franklin (2000) found that African American wives often become dissatisfied with their spouses' economic earning potential, and this becomes a major source of marital discord. The process of mutual goal setting with an African American family requires the therapist to assume an ecological and structural approach that considers a family's environment and community. The ecostructural reality or condition of poor or underclass African American families frequently includes welfare, the courts, schools, Medicaid, food stamps, and public housing. These families may face overwhelming socioeconomic problems, and survival needs should take precedence over family conflicts. Kilpatrick and Holland (2003) affirm that where patterns of change in the family are out of phase with the realities of extrafamilial systems, therapy will fail. Therapists should focus simultaneously on the problems and realities that are posed by external systems and on the way the family manages its relationship with them.

In formulating goals with the family, the therapist needs to pursue information in a problem-focused manner. Emphasis should be on the conditions maintaining the problem and how these conditions can be changed. Minuchin's (1974) tracking (data collection) technique is relevant in assisting the family to arrive at a goal that will ameliorate its immediate problem. This problem-focused approach should prevent the family's being overwhelmed with data-collecting attempts and can maximize the therapist's selection of a therapeutic goal congruent with the family's identified needs.

Selecting a Focus or System for Therapy

African American families face multiple problems, so it is important that the therapist assess rapidly and accurately how to reduce family stress, especially bicultural or acculturative tensions and racism-related stressors. For the therapist attempting to locate the proper system for therapy, the following guidelines are suggested.

Ecostructurally, a therapist needs to ascertain what systems are supportive or destructive to the present family problem. These systems may include external social systems such as school or social agencies and extended family, friends, and ministers. The discriminatory practice of the mainstream society toward African Americans is well documented. This system may well be the primary focus for the reduction of stress in the family. The strong kinship bonds among African Americans sometimes are a source of family conflicts. McAdoo (1977) has described how interference from extended family members may create marital difficulties when family members are unable to say no to unreasonable demands made by their relatives. If such is the case, the system for focus may include helping clients to differentiate between their extended and nuclear families and to develop healthy boundaries between them. To achieve these goals, Minuchin's (1974) structural approach, which requires seeing the family member and his or her relatives in separate sessions, is recommended. Once family boundaries are clarified, the therapist can focus on repairing or developing new boundaries within the nuclear family.

External systems and kinship bonds are integral to the survival of an African American family. Flexible boundaries between the family and external systems must exist to incorporate appropriate external supports. Also, there must be congruence in family members' perceptions of each other's roles. Such congruence may be interrupted by societal discriminatory practices, family life cycles, or idiosyncratic problems. Identifying stressors affecting the family, such as extrafamilial forces, family transitional points, idiosyncratic problems, and bicultural tensions, is a useful framework for assessing factors that are responsible for the confusion of roles among family members. Finally, there must be a stabilized power balance within the nuclear family system. An egalitarian relationship does not imply lack of leadership, which can cause the disorganization inherent in many problem-saturated families.

The Use of an Ecomap

Selecting a focus for therapy can be facilitated by the use of an ecomap. The ecomap, as developed by Hartman (1978), is a paper-and-pencil simulation that portrays in a dynamic way the ecological system whose boundaries include the client or family in the life space. It identifies and characterizes the significant nurturant or conflict-laden connection between the family and the environment. It makes available a more comprehensive picture of the major themes and patterns that give direction to the planning process and keeps both therapist and family from getting lost in detail. The actual use of an ecomap will be illustrated in the case illustration section of this chapter (Part 3). Specifically, an ecomap provides three major criteria from which the family and the therapist may select a plan or a unit of intervention. These criteria include

1. The family in relation to the ecological environment—the kinds of significant resources that are available in the family's world and information pertaining to the relationships (strong, stressed, and so on) between family and environment are important.

2. The family-environment boundary as measured by the number and quality of transactions—to protect against discriminatory practices, some African American families isolate themselves from the community environment. Such families may be closed off from new sources of energy and in danger of moving toward a state of entropy, that is, of randomization, disorganization, and, ultimately, dissolution.

3. Relationships within the family and its connection with the outside world—for example, unemployment outside of the home on the part of the African American father will affect his role as husband and father.

Similarly, for a mother, working two jobs and being overly active in church affairs will affect her relationship with her husband and children. An ecomap is particularly relevant in work with African American families who are more "visual" and responsive to activity-oriented intervention.

Problem-Solving Phase

The following discussion focuses on the problem-solving phase of therapy with African American families and considers the cultural norm, family structure, traditional help-seeking behavior, and capacities of this particular population. Additionally, the application of communication and structural family theories has been integrated into the therapeutic process. Specific skills and techniques that are of particular relevance in the problem-solving phase of therapy include mobilizing and restructuring the social and extended family network; self-observation as a tool for family restructuring; role-restructure for problem solving; religiosity as a therapeutic tool; employing the role model, educator, and advocate roles; and the team approach.

Mobilizing and Restructuring the Social and Extended Family Networks

In therapy with African American families, a therapist must recognize the survival issues that often take precedence over family conflicts. With such families, therapists should define themselves as system guides or brokers (Bowen, 1978) and help families learn skills to negotiate the complexities of the bureaucratic system and social service agencies.

Robert, an excellent student with unusual musical talent, was suspended from school when the music teacher claimed that he continued to violate the rule of not having his practice card signed daily by his parents. Robert's father was a truck driver who was away from home much of the time. Robert's mother was a relief nurse, and she worked an irregular schedule. Both parents worked hard at their jobs, and they had high expectations for Robert's academic achievement. They were disappointed about Robert's school suspension. Robert's appeal to the teacher to make an exception to the rule was not successful. Trapped in this dilemma, Robert lost interest in music and his performance in other school subjects suffered. Robert's parents, partly due to busy work schedules and partly due to lack of trust and experience in dealing with school personnel, blamed Robert for his problems. Robert developed severe headaches, and the physician's diagnosis was that they were caused by stress. The therapist arranged a meeting between Robert, his parents, and the music teacher in an effort to resolve Robert's school problem. His parents were most apprehensive about the meeting and feared that the teacher regarded them as unfit parents. The therapist reassured them about their concern and competence as parents, and he also rehearsed the questions the teacher might raise at the meeting with them. The meeting with the teacher went smoothly, and the teacher cooperated in resolving Robert's situation.

Hansell (1976) has outlined three major attachments to various resources that can be instrumental in helping the African American family cope with the type of distress that is usually experienced in bicultural adjustment and in the loss of social supports. These attachments include

1. Appropriate sources of information in which the therapist can connect the family with individuals or organizations, as illustrated in Robert's case.

2. Resources that will enable the family to realize its identity as a functioning unit. The therapist's task is to help the family establish connections with other families, or other persons, with whom members can share mutual interests and activities.

3. Groups of people who regard the family as members. These might include religious groups that have the capacity to assist the family with various tasks.

When support systems are disrupted, the task of the therapist is to effect connections where indicated. The main objective is to connect the African American family with others who "speak the same language" and with whom family members can feel comfortable, build trust, and gain a sense of self-esteem and a feeling of security.

Self-Observation as a Tool for Family Restructuring

African American clients may exhibit general distrust, unwillingness to express their feelings verbally, and differences in communication styles. A therapeutic process solely dependent on verbal exchange may fall short of helping the client understand and alter his or her way of interacting with others. The self-observation techniques of focusing on a client's here-and-now transaction with other family members can vividly illuminate behavioral patterns requiring change or restorying. The following case illustrates how self-observation can alter the wife's conjugal narrative and conjugal behavior.

In an attempt to persuade her husband to take a more active part in disciplining their teenage son, Mrs. Boren accused Mr. Boren of not wanting to do anything. When Mr. Boren finally explained how his effort was constantly undermined by his wife, Mrs. Boren would repeatedly interrupt her husband before he could finish what he had to say. The therapist's attempts to block Mrs. Boren's interruptions were unsuccessful. The therapist then said that he would sit next to Mr. Boren and dramatize how Mr. Boren might feel when he was interrupted. The couple agreed to this plan. As Mr. Boren continued to explain to his wife how much he resented her treating him like one of the kids, Mrs. Boren got angry and said, "As far as I'm concerned, the way you have been acting, you are worse than my kids." The therapist immediately dropped down on the floor and said nothing. As Mrs. Boren continued to berate Mr. Boren about his passivity and inability to hold a job outside the home, the therapist crawled toward the door and started pounding. This finally got Mrs. Boren's attention. She stopped and asked what the therapist's behavior was supposed to mean. The therapist redirected the question and asked if she could come up with an answer. After a short pause, Mrs. Boren reluctantly turned to her husband, "Did I really make you feel this bad?" Mr. Boren nodded, and said, "All the damn time!"

The therapist then empathized with Mrs. Boren's frustration at work and at home. A short-term goal was mutually arrived at whereby the therapist would teach the couple skills for effective communication. Other techniques to help clients gain self-observation and different perspectives include the use of a one-way mirror and audio- or videotape playbacks.

Role Restructure for Problem Solving

The membership, structure, roles, and functions of African American families have been widely documented as being complex, diverse, dense, dynamic, and (at times, by necessity) fluid (Billingsley, 1968; Hill, 1972; McAdoo, 1978; Stack, 1974; Staples, 1976). These characteristics are an inherent part of the strength, resilience, and adaptiveness of African American families. The role of the oldest siblings, regardless of sex, has long been both a strength and a potential liability for African American families. The following case illustrates how the role of the oldest daughter was restructured in consonance with the values and needs of an African American family.

Irene, at 16 years old, was the oldest of seven children in the Shaw family. Her father had been incapacitated and confined to a state mental hospital. Irene was an excellent student, and she also held a part-time job after school to supplement the family's income. Irene's mother, Mrs. Simpson, was irritated by her daughter's reluctance to take care of the younger siblings. The mother-daughter conflict finally came to blows when Irene was 2 hours late returning home from a date on the weekend. Mrs. Simpson was so upset with her daughter's "irresponsibility" that she notified the police and filed a missing person report. The police officer referred the family to the Transcultural Family Center for therapy.

At the first interview, Irene apologized for her irresponsible behavior and she volunteered that she sometimes hated to come home because of the "endless chores" awaiting her. Irene explained that she didn't mind taking care of her younger brothers and sisters, but she just couldn't do the house chores along with her homework and part-time job. Mrs. Simpson agreed that perhaps Irene was burdened with too much work, but she insisted that she had to do the same when she was Irene's age. The therapist empathized with Mrs. Simpson's demand for responsibility and her "bringing up Irene the right way." He suggested other arrangements (role restructure) be considered so that the responsibilities at home were divided and shared and that Irene and her mother make an effort to get along better.

Mrs. Simpson explained that the family needed the extra income from Irene's part-time job and that the 3-year-old child also needed proper care when the mother was away. Irene volunteered that she didn't mind taking care of the 3-year-old, but she just could not be responsible for keeping the house clean and clothes washed in addition to everything else. The therapist asked if other siblings could help out by performing some of these household chores. Mrs. Simpson paused and reflected, "Perhaps the other children need to chip in and help out." Considering Irene's age and her developmental needs, ideally she should not have been burdened by part-time employment outside the home while she was still a student. Unfortunately, the financial need of the family required that Irene work to supplement the family income. It is important that the therapist not impose his or her values in deciding "proper" or "improper" roles for each family member. The therapist's role as *culture researcher* or *coach* (Bowen, 1978) is to facilitate solutions that are compatible with the needs and structure of the African American family.

Religiosity as a Therapeutic Tool

Spiritual and religious worldviews and the integration of religious principles and values into the clinical or counseling process are implicitly discouraged in most professional (clinical) schools and training programs. This marginalization of religious values in the counseling process can serve to fragment the spiritual, psychological, and emotional realms of African Americans. Wimberly (1997a) encourages African American families to examine the spiritual context of their relationships; he holds that a religious worldview is a constant in the African American heritage.

Religion plays a vital role in the lives of many African American families, yet some family problems, unfortunately, emanate from a family's interpretation of and rigid adherence to certain religious beliefs. For example, the biblical principle "spare the rod, spoil the child," interpreted literally by some African American families, can be a potential source of physical abuse to children. A therapist may not share the family's religious beliefs, but he or she should respect and appreciate those beliefs. Therapists who convey no acceptance of the family's religious beliefs may find that they are not respected by the family. A religious African American family may refuse to associate with an outsider who deters them from "God's path and God's will."

If a therapist is unfamiliar with a family's religious beliefs and if these beliefs are contributing to the family problem, he should consult the minister with whom the family has close contact and whom the family respects. In some instances, the minister can be a cotherapist for family therapy. In cases where the therapist intervention is too threatening to a family, the minister can be used as a therapist helper (Landau, 1981). This approach allows the therapist to avoid direct confrontation with the family. The therapist helper approach also ensures that therapeutic changes on the part of the family are congruent with the family's cultural and religious background.

The Hopsons (1998) explain that African Americans have a "unique soul"— a deep sense of connectedness, strength, faith, focus, and passion to act upon their innermost feelings. Thus, therapists of African American families are urged to explore the spiritual, if not religious, realm of the family's internal and external relationships to help them express positive feelings, communicate more effectively, resolve conflicts, and, most important, "talk to God through prayer" (p. 1).

Employing the Role Model, Educator, and Advocate Roles

African American families exhibit a positive response to problem-focused, present-oriented, short-term therapy. Family therapists can effectively use themselves as role models to demonstrate how certain behaviors can produce positive changes in a familial relationship. Minuchin (1967) has observed that transactions among disadvantaged African Americans tend to have an all-or-nothing emotional expression. Therapists may alienate themselves from the family if they attempt to intellectualize a family's interactional style. Instead, the therapist should role-model by immediately identifying exchanges when they occur. For example, when one family related the death of a loved one with no apparent change of affect, the therapist pointed out to the family that their unusual calmness probably did not reflect their inner feelings of sadness. Therapists may use their own feelings to make a point as a means to role-model appropriate behavior. For example, if parents are calmly reflecting the injustice they receive from their children, the therapist can comment, "That angers me," or "I can't stand that." By modeling for the family, the therapist demonstrates that it is possible to be loving without being controlling and critical without being punitive.

In addition to role-modeling, Family therapists also need to assume the educator role. They should teach families about the role the social system plays in family problems. For example, a family can be commended for its efforts to protect the children from a hostile environment, yet it also needs to be shown that such overprotection can retard a child's normal development. It is important that the therapist's educative approach recognize the family's sincere effort to resolve its problem. Such recognition neutralizes any negative interpretations the family might give to what family members perceive as cultural insensitivity or disrespect from the therapist. African American families' responsiveness to a therapist's educator role is usually consistent with their achievement orientation.

The role of advocate is congruent with the family therapist's training as a system expert. At times, an African American's space can be invaded with well-intentioned but uncoordinated, inappropriate, and even destructive interventions. For example, a family with a schoolchild who receives service from a guidance clinic can be inundated by recommendations from the speech therapist, nurse, social worker, substance-abuse counselor, and psychologist. The speech therapist says the child's speech problem is caused by emotional stress. The nurse may advise the parents to be more permissive. Meanwhile, the social worker could be taking the parents for job interviews as a means to meet their basic needs, but the substance-abuse counselor may insist that the father's drinking problem be treated by attending Alcoholics Anonymous. The psychologist may recommend joint family therapy as the most effective tool to combat the child's school problems.

As an advocate of the family, the therapist needs to help the family prioritize and coordinate all these services so they will not fragment the family. At times, the therapist may need to assume a biased position to help the family negotiate and arrive at a workable solution to its problem. In view of the family's general feelings of powerlessness, it is important that the therapist's advocating efforts be realistic.

Team Approach

Many African American families face multiple problems. When intensive work is required to assist a family interacting with the environment, a team of therapists is recommended. The team approach offers several advantages. First, it simultaneously attends to the family's needs as well as to specific family members' needs. Second, a therapist team that contains members with different personalities, skills, and sensitivities maximizes the likelihood that each family member will be emotionally connected with at least one therapist. This is particularly important in the engagement stage of therapy, when the dropout rate is generally high. Third, a therapist team can provide the family with a role model for interaction and problem solving (Norlin & Ho, 1974). Such learning through observation is extremely relevant when working with African Americans, who are activity oriented. Fourth, team therapists generally can provide a more accurate assessment plan, and they can be more effective with the implementation of strategies (Mostwin, 1981). Fifth, team therapists ensure continuity of therapy, should one therapist become unavailable. Finally, team therapists avoid potential professional burnout, which is heightened when working with families who live under oppressive conditions. Note that if a team of therapists fails to work collaboratively or experience conflict, it can further fragment the family organization. Other drawbacks to team therapy are that it is time consuming and costly.

Evaluation and Termination Phase

In evaluating the outcome goals of family therapy with African American clients, it is important to distinguish between the goals of the family and the goals of the therapist. Family goals often focus on one member of the family who is the "identified patient." As therapy progresses, the family and the therapist often renegotiate and arrive at "compromised" goals. There may be a wide range of goals for which an African American family needs therapy. The goal for any family is the reduction or elimination of the presenting problems.

To determine if a specific goal has been accomplished through family therapy with an African American client, the ecological framework of assessment and therapy is particularly helpful. This framework consists of four major categories: family-environment interface, family structure, family processes (communication and interaction), and individual symptoms and character traits.

Family-environment interface. Goals to be evaluated during family-environment interface are the extent to which the family's basic needs (income, school, and shelter; safe neighborhoods; adequate health and medical resources; transportation; social connections with extended kin network or friends; shared ethnic cultured activities; employment; and so on) are met. Different individual members' adaptive balance with the environment is important, as is the overall adaptive relationship between the family and its environment.

Family structure. Two aspects of family structure are particularly important in family therapy with African Americans: family rules and programs and family roles and boundaries. Family rules are relationship agreements (conscious and unconscious) that prescribe and limit a family member's behavior over a wide variety of content areas. The egalitarian relationship orientation of African Americans under stress can confuse such family rules. Minuchin (1974) emphasizes the importance of intrafamilial role boundaries and sees most families who come for therapy as falling at one of two extremes on a continuum of boundary rigidity or flexibility. For African American families who need family therapy, the structure is a combination of *disengagement* and *enmeshment.* For example, a highly enmeshed subsystem of mother and children sometimes includes the father, who becomes disengaged in the extreme. According to Minuchin, a major goal of family therapy is improving family structure by recalibrating subsystem boundaries.

Family processes. Communication and conflict resolution are two key concepts in evaluating family processes with an African American family. As a result of successful family therapy, communication should become clear, congruent, non-contradictory, direct, and honest (Satir, 1967). More open and spontaneous expressions of feelings, wishes, ideals, and goals should occur. Conflict resolution as a result of therapy includes changes in the frequency, quality, and methods of handling intrafamilial conflicts (Aponte, 1979). However, Hines and Boyd-Franklin (1996) caution that family therapy goals with "conflict-avoidant" African American families should aim to increase the frequency of overt expression of conflict and, at the same time, decrease the frequency of covert conflict expression.

Symptoms and character traits of individual members. As a result of family therapy, the identified client should become more differentiated. Bowen (1978) defines differentiation as a process in which individuals come to assume responsibility for their own happiness and comfort and avoid the kind of thinking that tends to blame and hold others responsible for the person's own unhappiness or failures. To be differentiated does not imply total separation; rather, differentiated individuals possesses a sense of mature dependency in which they need to feel a sense of belonging and validate their self-worth.

Additionally, in assessing therapeutic goals relating to the family-environment interface, family structure and processes, and individual symptoms, therapists need to be cognizant of the unique cultural perspectives of African Americans. African American culture defines family structure and processes differently than white culture. Any evaluation of therapeutic goals should be considered in the appropriate cultural context.

African Americans may display strong feelings of interdependence and humanism (Foster & Perry, 1982). This, coupled with their priority for survival and possibly a lack of physical energy or a reluctance to burden the therapist, may cause a family to terminate therapy before the goal is realized. The therapist needs to reassure the family and point out to family members the potential negative consequences associated with premature termination. On the other hand, the African American client's value of humanism and kinship bonds may delay the termination process with a therapist who is accepted as trusted kin. It is important that therapists be comfortable with this element of cultural and human inclusiveness and make termination a natural and gradual process.

The preceding discussion should be helpful in understanding African American families and applying family structure and communication theories and culturally relevant (emic-based) principles. Part 3 of this chapter offers a case example to explicate and delineate how these family theoretical perspectives and emic-based practice principles can be integrated in actual therapy with an African American family.

PART 3: CASE ILLUSTRATION

Mr. Jackson, a 52-year-old African American man, was referred to Dr. Ho by an African American minister. A retired military man, Mr. Jackson works irregularly as a construction worker. When not working, Mr. Jackson has a tendency to drink heavily. He is married, with four children, but has a habit of not returning home when he drinks. Mr. Jackson has two "fairly close" female friends, whom he refers to as "drinking buddies," adding, "they don't mean much." Over the past 2 weeks, Mr. Jackson had two rather serious car accidents, and he was found asleep in his car on a cold night. The minister suggested that Mr. Jackson might be suicidal and in need of therapy. Mr. Jackson refused to go to the mental health clinic for therapy, claiming that he was not crazy and "those folks [counselors] know nothing." When I first

Recognizing strength.

met Mr. Jackson, he looked suspicious and extremely anxious. I introduced myself to him and he asked if I was Korean. I remarked that he was close, but I am Chinese. As I was thanking him for taking time to visit with me, he interrupted me by informing me that he was

Joining to help client feel at ease.

once stationed in Seoul, South Korea. I *encouraged him to relate* to me his overseas experience. Mr. Jackson volunteered that his experience in Korea was the best time of his life. I sensed some sadness in his voice, so I *empathized by saying,* "Life is full of happy

Tracking.

times as well as sad times." Mr. Jackson picked up my lead and said, "I have been living in hell the past few years, especially the past several months." I *encouraged Mr. Jackson* to *elaborate* on his present situation. He sighed and explained that since his retirement from the Army 2 years ago, things had been going downhill. Mr. Jackson

Taking narrative data.

volunteered that on the surface, he had a "good all-American family." He and his family were blessed with *no financial constraints,* and income from his wife, a licensed practical nurse; his retirement benefits; and his on-and-off construction

Basic needs not a problem source.

Problem identification.

Strenuous family relationship.

Joining.

Respect for client.

Identify strength in family.

Crisis intervention.

Problem identification.

Blamer role.

jobs helped "to pay the bills all right." His two oldest children, a son 31 years old and a daughter 28 years old, are married and live out of state. Two of his younger children, 17 (girl) and 15 (boy) years old, are still at home. Both are excellent athletes and students. They are very involved with their friends at school. The family's ecomap and genogram is shown in Figure 5.1.

Mr. Jackson continued, "My wife Gloria is an excellent mother and a busy body, working all the time and attending church activities at least four to five times a week." "You seem to have a happy family," I remarked. "Yes, for everybody except me." I asked if he would explain what he meant by that statement. "I feel out of place . . . in my own home. Nobody notices me . . . except when I am not there for a couple of days. Then all hell breaks loose. . . . Sometimes I have a feeling that they [family members] are ashamed of me and want to have nothing to do with me." Mr. Jackson broke into tears. I *empathized* by saying that nobody likes to be alone, especially in one's own home. After Mr. Jackson finished venting his frustration and disappointment toward his family, I *asked him if I could arrange* a joint meeting with him and his family. I briefly explained to him the joint meeting was to reunite everybody, for I sensed there was a *great deal* of love lost in this family. Mr. Jackson hesitated and asked if I would contact his wife for the meeting. I agreed.

The family meeting *took place 3 days later.* Although Mrs. Jackson and the children, Terri and Jason, appeared anxious and apprehensive, they were extremely polite and cooperative. After I thanked them for coming, I *asked if they understood the purpose behind the meeting.* Mrs. Jackson responded immediately that she was glad that *her husband finally sought help.* To

Shift from individual to family focus.	avoid focusing on (blaming) Mr. Jackson, I *asked how everybody got along at home.* Mrs. Jackson again responded by stating that everybody except her husband got along just fine. I then turned to Terri, who said that she wished her father was more a "part of the family." Jason nodded also. I
Attempts family restructure.	*asked what each of them was willing to do to involve* their father. They looked at each other and at their mother and said, "I don't know." I then directed my attention to Mr. Jackson by asking him how he felt when
Assist Mr. Jackson to reenter into family structure.	his children wished to involve him. Mr. Jackson hesitated and said, "Perhaps it was all my fault. . . . when I was in the service, I was not home often, and I really did not get to know my children." "You didn't get to know me either, for that matter," Mrs. Jackson interrupted angrily. Before he had
Reframing.	a chance to retaliate, I *reframed by asking* Mr. Jackson how he felt upon learning that his wife wanted to get to know him and be close to him. Mr. Jackson appeared to be
Changed family process.	surprised and he said that he *never realized that his family,* especially his wife, *wanted to be close to him.* Mrs. Jackson was very angry at this moment, and she began to enumerate the many occasions in which Mr. Jackson was indifferent and inconsiderate toward her, including countless embarrassments involving his drinking and being with other women. "You have pushed me and the children
Emotional cutoff.	away from you," cried Mrs. Jackson.
	In defense of his drinking and being with other women, Mr. Jackson complained about the disappointment and disrespect he experienced, and how he felt like a stranger in his own home. Before the session ended,
Summary evaluation.	I asked the family *what they had gotten* out of the session. Mrs. Jackson commented that she was tired of this kind of bickering, but *she did realize how lonely her husband might* have felt. I commented that she also might be feeling alone. Mrs. Jackson
New family process.	nodded and said, "Especially when the children are all grown."

Mr. Jackson commented that he felt bad for letting the family down, but he was comforted to see that the family still had love for him.

Terri said that she was saddened by what had happened to her father but was relieved that the family "is talking" again.

Family restructuring, father peripheral role shifts.

Jason asked his father *if he could attend his* basketball game Friday night. Realizing that family restructuring attempts to reenter the father into the nuclear family had just begun, and that the spousal subsystem boundary needed special attention, I suggested meeting only *with Mr. and Mrs. Jackson* for the next few sessions.

Focusing on a subsystem.

During the next meetings, the emphasis was to "restructure" the Jackson conjugal subsystem. A brief review of the couple's genogram revealed that Mrs. Jackson was a *firstborn* from a female-headed family. She was a parental child to her mother, who had "no respect for men." Mrs. Jackson had always excelled at whatever she did and ran the household "single handedly" when she was only a teenager. She had had no role model as to how a wife should interact with her husband, and even at this moment, she still recalls her *mother's injunction* that "men are not to be trusted." Mrs. Jackson maintains close contact with her mother. As her children grow older, she finds herself alone and occupies herself with church activities.

Negative (societal and familial) image of African American men.

Intergenerational transmission.

Family projection process.

Emotional cutoff from extended family.

Mr. Jackson, on the other hand, came from a two-parent family. Both of his parents died and he had no contact with his *other relatives due to geographic location*. After retiring from the military, he lost his role identity. He dislikes construction work and is in the process of looking for something more challenging. His *dissatisfaction* with his current role, retirement, present work,

Strenuous person-environment and person-family relationship.

and familial relationships caused him to drink excessively and to mingle with friends who would accept him.

The first marital therapy session was spent helping the Jacksons get reacquainted with each other. Their accusations and criticisms toward each other *were restoried* as wanting to be close to each other but without knowing how.

Restorying.

The second marital therapy session was devoted to assisting the couple in redefining their *roles as husband and wife* and their parental role in dealing with children. Mrs. Jackson, as expected, was reluctant to relinquish her central role and position with the family, especially in dealing with her children. In addition, she needed *to acquire* "mature dependency" in relation to becoming vulnerable in seeking love and affection from her husband. Mr. Jackson, on the other hand, needed directives in becoming more assertive in dealing with his wife. He also needed to forsake his passive-aggressive behavior by not drinking and not staying away from home to get attention.

Spousal restructuring.

Educative role.

The third and fourth marital sessions were spent in helping the couple creatively resolve conflicts. Effective problem-solving skills and styles were introduced.

The sixth and final session was spent in therapy with the whole family. Both *children reported* marked changes in the behavior of their father and mother and that the whole family had started doing things together more. Mr. Jackson volunteered that he "carried on" with his drinking *only one time* over the last 2 months and that he had never been absent from home since therapy started. "I even get him to go to *church with* me," quipped Mrs. Jackson. As the therapy ended, Mr. Jackson requested information about attending *vocational training* school.

Evaluation.

Improved family relationship.

Improved individual symptoms.

Improved environmental support.

Improved relationship with work world.

Figure 5.1   Jackson Family Ecomap and Genogram

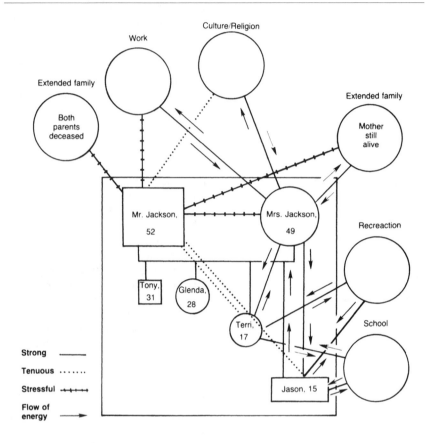

This case study demonstrates that even when there are no financial constraints, African American families still have problems like all families do. Such problems may manifest themselves in personal conflict and alcohol abuse, as in the case of Mr. Jackson. The therapist's sensitivity to the client's ethnic background and his transaction with his work environment and his family relationships helped to transform the presenting problem from one focused on the individual to one focused on the family. The therapist capitalized upon the family's strength in the kinship bond as well as in Mr. Jackson's motivation to be a part of the family. Through culturally relevant techniques such as joining, tracking, educating, and restructuring, the client is helped to reenter the family system successfully, and the system once again becomes intact.

The therapist's skill in conveying proper respect for Mr. Jackson reassures the latter that he is not "crazy." The therapist further emphasizes the family's humanistic orientation and flexibility in family roles, which later become the curative factors for Mr. Jackson's personal and family problems. By applying culturally relevant couple therapeutic techniques such as genograms, communication, problem-solving skills, and environmental support, the therapist assists the couple to improve the marital relationship and stabilize family relationships.

PART 4: CULTURALLY RELEVANT TECHNIQUES AND SKILLS FOR SPECIFIC THERAPEUTIC MODALITIES

Couple Therapy

The sociological and psychological research literature on African American marriages concludes that African American male-female relationships are no more problem ridden than male-female relationships within other ethnocultural groups (Aldridge, 1991). However, current research shows a significant decline in marriage, a significant increase in divorce, and increased separation between marriage and childbearing among African Americans (Dickson, 1993). Sociologists interpret these statistics as being more indicative of the destabilizing impact of the economy and the unavailability of African American men for marriage (in light of innumerable social problems), as opposed to being a statement about the quality of marriage relationships between African Americans (Dickson, 1993; Gibbs, 1988; Wilson, 1987).

Boyd-Franklin (1989) emphasizes that there is no such phenomenon as *the* African American couple or family; and that each couple or family should be evaluated for their own set of problems and concerns. Clinicians should also be prepared for an *elongated diagnostic phase* in couple and family therapy with African Americans, in light of the unique and complex societal factors facing African American families, which need to be understood with reference to their implications for couple therapy.

There are several factors that contribute to the prolonged assessment phase that is necessary in couple work with many African Americans. For instance, many clinicians observe that African American couples are more likely to enter the counseling process via a child-focused concern (Boyd-Franklin, 1989). Additionally, many African American couples may come to counseling when the presenting problem is initially financial, and they are not necessarily seeking couple counseling. The therapist's task in these situations is to carefully consider the couple's initial interpretation and even attempt an intervention to deal with the initial presenting problem (as deemed appropriate) as a gesture toward building trust and credibility with the couple. However, therapists are encouraged to get the couple to redirect these initial complaints, if indeed the clinician believes that the presenting problem is merely the surface of more complex dyadic difficulties.

Other ecological realities (e.g., racism and poverty) also serve to extend the assessment phase in couple and family work with African Americans by virtue of their complicating impact on the lives of these individuals. For instance, economic instability may have operated to undermine prior relationships, resulting in longer and more complex social histories that need to be taken and understood by the practitioner. In addition, larger, dense, more complex, and varied familial networks are likely to result in a longer assessment phase. Therefore, it is imperative that clinicians discard existing temporal templates for completing the assessment process and allow the couple's unique history to dictate the length of the diagnostic phase.

Boyd-Franklin (1989) further highlights the importance of giving special attention to helping African American couples negotiate boundaries between the conjugal dyad and the extended family. This therapeutic move can be an especially tricky one, in light of the need to preserve these important relational connections. Practitioners need to help African American couples find their own way in this regard, effecting boundaries that work for them as a couple. Therapists must pose this clinical question to themselves, as well as presenting it to clients: "Does the nature of these (extended family) boundaries work well for this couple?" It is indeed the central clinical question to be dealt with. Posing the question in this form can help therapists become more aware of their own (ethnocentric) biases and notions of "closeness" in the case of relationships with extended family.

Triangles are important in assessing the presenting problem of many African American couples because of the emphasis on and closeness within these extended families. The potential always exists for African American couples to draw others into their conjugal conflict (Wimberly, 1997a). Again, caution should be exercised by the clinician in detriangulating the couple from (familial) third parties, as it is important that there not be permanent damage done to these familial connections when sensitive issues are confronted.

The clinical issue of invisible loyalties has been previously mentioned in this chapter. However, the authors wish to expound upon the clinical issues in this regard. African American men, especially if they are spiritually or occupationally successful, as a result of strong support from their families of origin, can be particularly vulnerable to allowing invisible (family) loyalties to interfere with their conjugal relationship. This situation may be amplified within highly successful, strong African American families that strive to maintain their sense of (family and ethnic) history, family connectedness, family loyalty, and ethnic loyalty, especially if the extended family views these characteristics as part of the family's strength and survival strategies. Certainly, practitioners would not want to encourage a sense of ingratitude or aloofness in their clients toward these highly functional family values.

However, therapists may need to help the couple negotiate and resolve these invisible family and cultural loyalties in regard to the aforementioned "acculturative tensions" or "acculturative conflicts," to ease tension and facilitate a more harmonious conjugal relationship. Additionally, clinicians will need to help the couple negotiate how the partners can show their gratitude to their extended families and to their community as well as exploring and realizing new options that present in their own individual, conjugal, and familial experiences.

It must be further noted that the power dynamics within African American couples are vastly different from those within white couples, in some significant ways. What can be particularly confusing and misleading about the power dynamics and other gender issues within African American male-female relationships is that on the surface, or to the casual observer or untrained eye, these gender dynamics can appear to be no different than gender issues or power dynamics found within white couples. This is not to imply a homogeneity or lack of acculturative or assimilative differences existing within African American couples. Certainly, African American couples exhibit the full range of conjugal behaviors and dynamics seen in other ethnocultural groups. However, there are distinct and unique differences that also are, in part, due to African American women's unique sociopolitical "Africana Womanist" philosophy (Hudson-Weem, 1993).

Specifically, African American women may prioritize their feminism (or "Womanism") differently than do white women or women from other ethnocultural groups. That is, the "Africana Womanist" perceives (female) gender issues as having secondary importance and significance to her race position in American society (Hudson-Weem, 1993). Another key that is central to the difference in the "Womanist" prioritization of race and gender is the presence of racism and racial oppression within the sociocultural context of African American men. That is, given the hierarchy of economic, political, and social power in the United States (in which African American men are decidedly on the bottom rung), some African American women may view their conjugal issues and gender issues qualitatively and quantitatively differently than would a white woman. The "Africana Womanist" is cognizant of her mate's societal position—on the bottom rung of the socioeconomic ladder—and hence realizes that her mate is not the (societal) "oppressor" but that he is also a victim of white male institutional oppression. Thus these sociocultural differences can operate to create power dynamics within the conjugal dyad of African Americans that are vastly different from those of whites.

Family therapy may be indicated for the couple as well as for the extended family (as an adjunctive clinical process to the couple therapy) to help the wider familial system come to terms with family goals and unresolved conflicts that may hinder the growth of its individual members. To this end, concepts such as *family projection processes* and *multigenerational family transmission processes* can be used as a sort of umbrella within which to explore an entire rubric of family therapy processes, as defined and discussed in this chapter, such as invisible family loyalties, invisible cultural loyalties, acculturative tensions, acculturative conflicts, triangles (or rather interlocking triangles—in which there is an additional inter-generational or cross-generational component to the triangulation process.)

Improving Couple Relationships
Through Improved Parent-Child Relationships

With the exception of middle and upper class African American clients, many African Americans enter family therapy because of their child's problems. These couples are often more conscientious about their role as parents than their role as husband and wife. Partly because of the shortage of African American males, African American wives are not willing to risk a marriage failure. Therefore, couple therapy focusing exclusively on a couple's marital relationship is too threatening to the couple, especially the wife. Additionally, the couple may feel selfish or guilty should the partners perceive that their marital needs precede their child's needs. Therefore, it is important that the therapist not employ couple therapy prematurely as a means to resolve parent-child problems. Obviously, according to structural framework, the child's problems cannot be satisfactorily resolved without first repairing or realigning the parental or spousal subsystem. However, the spousal subsystem can be repaired directly or indirectly by focusing on the parents' newly learned alternative transactions with the child. For example, if the child's problem is related to the mother triangulating with the child against the father, who may be peripheral, the therapist can suggest that the parents join forces (restructuring the mother-son dyad to a father-mother dyad) to provide a more unified, firm, and consistent structure for their child, who may be seeking generational boundaries and directives.

Teaching Communication and Problem-Solving Skills

Communication among African American families tends to be in generalities more than in specifics. Regardless of whether the couple is from a disadvantaged or middle class background, communication skills required in conflict resolution and problem solving must go beyond generalities. Specific and open exchanges of affect and intentions are required. To make individual messages specific in communication, Satir et al. (1975) suggest that the couple learn when and how to use "I" statements. The partners need to further develop skills in communication feedback techniques and a transactional style that is congruent, direct, and open (Satir, 1967).

In view of the African American's cultural orientation of present (over past) and activity (over thought), couple therapy processes focusing on self-observation and immediate feedback through audio or videotapes are recommended. The use of cotherapists of both sexes can also provide a model for effective communication (Norlin & Ho, 1974).

Religiosity as a Source of Strength in Marriage

This chapter has discussed the importance that religion and church play in the lives of African American families. However, family therapists have yet to integrate this component of strength into couple therapy. For a religious African American client, no amount of knowledge and measure of communication skills can substitute for the level of marital commitment derived from religion. Without religious faith, an African American client is weakened in the internal strength, spirit, and commitment essential to becoming a happy individual and to achieving a successful marriage. A therapist needs to appreciate and respect the influence of religion on the well-being of the African American couple. When couples allow their religious faith to be a vital part of their marriage, they not only gain added strength and hope but also a model of love to guide their interactions. When religious faith is present in the couple's marriage, the partners become more fully aware of their responsibilities to themselves and to each other. Equality and problem solving in marriage can be pursued in open discussions, negotiations, and compromise.

During couple therapy, one partner may attempt to use certain biblical scriptures as a means to entice the therapist to side with him or her. The therapist should avoid being triangulated by such complicated intellectual or philosophical maneuvers. Instead, the therapist needs to help the couple focus on the issues to be solved.

Divorce Therapy

African American clients, particularly those from lower socioeconomic levels, seldom actively seek divorce therapy. The majority of divorce therapy clients seek help during moments of crisis, such as when the husband abruptly decides to end the marriage, when there are child custody or visitation or property issues to be settled, or when the wife contemplates ending the relationship because of repeated physical or mental abuse. Hence divorce therapy generally is crisis oriented, time limited, and extremely stressful for clients. The following recommendations are offered to therapists conducting divorce therapy with African American clients.

Exploring Divorce Experiences and Consequences

African American clients who grew up in a single-parent, female-headed family seldom seek divorce therapy as a means to end a marriage. A couple's relationship may be deteriorating, but the wife's strong desire to maintain a two-parent family generally is so strong that divorce is viewed as the last solution to the couple's problems. Although the therapist should consider and respect the client's decision about divorce, it is the therapist's responsibility to help the client point out the family problems or physical abuse problems causing unresolved marital stress. Under no circumstances should a therapist be judgmental about the client's decision.

Extended Family and Social Support

The strength of family ties among African Americans is a valuable resource to clients experiencing divorce. Extended families are the natural resources for emotional support and can often provide financial help, child care, household chores, and so on. The therapist at this stage should assist the client in taking advantage of the extended family system. The important objective is to help the client to make the necessary transitions and connections with the extended family without abdicating personal responsibility and allowing the extended family system to overstep the nuclear family system boundary. This may be difficult for a dependent client who, during stressful times, regresses to greater dependency on the family of origin. Bowen's (1978) theoretical concept of differentiation is applicable in helping the client to negotiate the family–extended family interface. Such negotiation may require conjoint sessions with extended family members. For clients who are experiencing divorce but because of geographical barriers or interpersonal conflicts are unable to use extended family help, the therapist's task is to link the family's needs with appropriate community resources. Such resources may include a human service department, health department, women's resource center, or child-care center. Because of the urgency of the client's need at the time of divorce, the therapist's roles can be those of resource mediator, child specialist, educator, and supporter to the client. The frequency and intensity of therapist-client contact at the time of divorce requires the therapist's flexibility in scheduling and conducting home visits and field activities.

Postdivorce Adjustment and New Relationships

Divorce can be a traumatic experience for both female and male clients. The divorcee generally has the support of the children and the extended family, and the male divorcee is often left totally without support. It is generally the female's responsibility to be with the children after divorce, so she generally receives more attention from various support sources, including the therapist. A divorcee is frequently confronted with the need for economic survival, which African American females seem better prepared to deal with than white females, even though they face economic and employment discrimination (Peters & deFord, 1978). After divorce, the mother must often do extra work outside the home and will have less time to spend with the children. The firstborn of the siblings can easily be coopted into assuming the parental child role (Minuchin, 1974). Although empathizing with the mother to assign more responsibilities to the firstborn, the therapist needs to point out to the mother the developmental needs of all children, including the eldest child.

Divorce usually is a devastating experience that can reactivate a person's feelings of unworthiness. A therapist needs to assess where the client is developmentally and the level of negative affect the divorce experience may have on the individual. Again, Bowen's (1978) differentiation concept is very helpful in ascertaining how emotionally divorced the client is and what areas of "unfinished business" the client may possess. Those undergoing divorce may perceive their experience as unique or unforgivable. A divorce support group can be very beneficial to such clients.

Single-Parent Therapy

Increased divorce and separation, as well as decisions to have children and not marry, have increased the number of female-headed families among African Americans. Single parents have the task of securing financial resources and support, maintaining a household, developing social and emotional relationships in the neighborhood and at work, and relating to children in a way that makes them productive members of society. For African American single-parent families, there are even fewer institutionalized sources of support informing them how to accomplish these tasks. Many African American single parents fit the description of the "at-risk" population that is socially isolated, is of a low socioeconomic status, and has a minimal social support network. The following suggestions aim to assist these high-risk single-parent African American families.

Mobilizing the Support System

The extended family can be a significant source of support and self-esteem for an African American single parent. It can be especially critical in providing emotional and instrumental assistance and can reduce feelings of loneliness and isolation. The family-of-origin network is important in providing the single-parent family with assistance in child care, finances, household chores, and emotional support. Geographical barriers or emotional strains may deny many African American single parents access to this valuable resource. In such cases, other extended network resources should be found. These can be new friendship ties, especially other single mothers, women's support groups, and social activity groups that can help the single-parent family adjust to this transitional period.

Mobilizing and Involving the Conjugal Network

When the father is absent from the family, a key male figure, or spouse equivalent, may be present in the single-parent household. This individual may or may not live with the mother in the single-parent household, yet he may have a great deal of influence in the daily transactions of the single parent and her children. Whether a single parent uses such a conjugal network depends on her personality, value orientation, and sex-role orientation. The therapist's task is to explore with the single parent the value of and need for such a network. If the therapist is aware of the conjugal partner, he or she can introduce the option of involving this individual in matters that concern the welfare of the single parent or child-rearing practices of the children. Rasheed and Rasheed (1999) reported that lower-class African American males contribute to the welfare of the family more than is commonly acknowledged and play an important role as a substitute father to the children of single mothers.

Restructuring the Family

The absence of the father from the family requires renegotiation and a restructuring of the family system boundary (Minuchin, 1974). Robert Weiss (1979) noted two major changes that can occur in the transformation from a two-parent to a single-parent family. First, the "echelon structure" collapses, with children being promoted to junior partner status and becoming more involved in decision making. Second, decompensation of the authority structure increases communication among family members. This situation may also be prompted by the African American egalitarian authority orientation. As a result of these structural changes, enmeshment between the single parent and the children can occur, resulting in parent-child conflict or idiosyncratic symptoms.

In view of the traditional closeness of the mother-child relationship within the African American family, the concept of enmeshment should be addressed only if it relates to the immediate problem to be solved. For example, in the case of parent-child conflict involving the single parent's unawareness or unwillingness to allow her teenage son to have peer relations, enmeshment should be explored. When enmeshment is present, new structural arrangements need to be developed to maintain the closeness of the parent-child relationship without emotionally suffocating the parent and child.

Reconstituted Family Therapy

The "remarriage family" is identified as a high-risk group for which society has not as yet established norms. Individuals with children who remarry are heirs to specific problems for which, on the whole, they are unprepared. The African

American's strong sense of kinship and humanistic individualism can produce split loyalties between members of a remarriage. The following suggestions are offered to therapists providing family therapy to a reconstituted (blended or step) African American family.

Focus on Parental Coalition

There is a consensus among all family therapy theorists that a strong spousal subsystem is essential to all family functioning. In view of the number of family members involved and their loyalties toward the spouse or in-laws from previous marriages, strong spousal subsystems are much more crucial in a reconstituted family. However, emphasizing the spousal subsystem to a reconstituted family experiencing parent-child conflict or child-related problems may be insensitive to the African American family's expectations for therapy. The task of the therapist is to assist the parents to work collaboratively for sake of their children and stepchildren. If the parents' differences remain unresolved, any treatment may at best result in a temporary resolution of the symptoms, which will have a high tendency to reappear in the future in the same manner or in a disguised form.

Interviewing the parents separately may help repair or establish the parental coalition. Both parents should be encouraged to express their feelings about their previous marriages and the legal settlement involving custody, visitation, and financial arrangements. They also need to be encouraged to discuss their child-rearing practices. To many parents, such a discussion can be highly informative and educational. To lessen the parents' sense of guilt and defensiveness, the therapist needs to adopt an educative approach during this stage of therapy. As therapy progresses, the therapist may need to shift to a more confrontational therapeutic role to modify rigid pattern acquired by the parents in the past.

The parental coalition emanates from the couple's commitment to function as a marital unit. It is important that the partners explore the motives or reasons behind their remarriages. Once their motives are identified, the couple should see more clearly the nature of the marital problem and how it affects the behavior of the children or stepchildren.

At the second interview, Mrs. Peters admitted that she decided to remarry simply because she wanted her two children to have an adult male figure at home. As she was growing up, she always regretted that there was not an adult male at home, and her grandfather and uncles lived out of state and had infrequent contact with the family. Mrs. Peters was afraid to confront Mr. Peters, her second husband, fearing that he might leave home as her first husband had done. Mrs. Peters was resentful and "unfeeling" toward Mr. Peters, whom the children from her previous marriage disliked. Mr. Peters was dissatisfied with his present marriage with Mrs. Peters and increasingly resented his stepchildren, whom Mrs. Peters claimed were her "number one priority and responsibility." At the fourth interview, Mrs. Peters began to see that she could enable Mr. Peters to be more loving toward her children by giving him more attention and affection.

Define Roles and Expectations

Many African American children of divorced persons retain relationships with the parent who is outside their current household. This may be attributed to strong kinship ties or perhaps to the need for a means to defend against a hostile external environment. This is the one permanent tie that links the present marriage with the previous marriage(s). Other areas of linkage include financial ties, previous in-laws, other relatives, and friends. Thus the reconstituted family is more vulnerable to role confusion and stress than is a first marriage (Kahn, 1974). Despite African Americans' general flexibility in assuming different family roles, role ambiguity and overload tend to create tensions and conflicts. Moreover, split loyalties can leave some instrumental and nurturing roles unfilled and the entire family disorganized.

In addition to helping the reconstituted family redefine essential roles, therapists need to help the family clarify the parental subsystem boundary so that the executive functions can be carried out with continuity and cohesion.

A strategy to decentralize the stepmother's role with her children in the reconstituted family may be antithetical to African American culture, which stipulates that a woman's responsibility is to care for her children on a day-to-day basis. To strengthen the spousal subsystem or father-stepchild subsystem will automatically dilute the mother-child enmeshment. To encourage husband-wife and father-child interaction is more consistent with African American culture's strong kinship bonds.

Involve Extended Family Members

The strong family ties of African Americans can also become a problem for the reconstituted family, whose loyalties are divided by more than one set of in-laws and relatives. On the other hand, in-laws and relatives can be added resources for the reconstituted family. If they are unsympathetic to and uncooperative with the reconstituted family, this can create unending demands and stress on the reconstituted family, especially on the stepparent. Interference by in-laws and relatives from a previous marriage may be unintentional, but reconstituted families often experience complexities centering on unspoken loyalties. Ecomaps and genograms are practical tools with which to portray to the reconstituted family the sources of strength and liability that emanate from their contacts with their extended families. It is important that the therapist constantly focus upon the problems to be solved within the reconstituted family. The nature of the kinship relationship should not necessarily be weakened, but it should be restructured to augment the functioning of the reconstituted family. If a child in the reconstituted family is unable to adjust, the extended family can be a viable temporary resource and shelter for the child.

PART 5: CONCLUSION

This chapter has focused on a holistic view (an integration of historical, economic, social, political, psychological, and cultural phenomena) and an Africentric (emic-insider and culture-specific) approach in work with African American families during different phases of (ecosystemically based) family therapy using a critical constructionist perspective. In view of the diversity of African American lifestyles and socioeconomic factors, any discussion pertaining to therapy with African American families risks overgeneralization and stereotyping. Yet there are specific factors that do set African American families apart from the dominant society and from other ethnic minority groups.

Family therapists must be willing to explore the impact of bicultural and acculturative tension and stress and social, political, socioeconomic, and broader environmental conditions on the families they serve. Inasmuch as the African American family is affected by systemic racism and social injustice, it has a rich cultural heritage and possesses enormous strength and potential. Family therapy with African Americans must take this into account and provide culturally relevant techniques and skills so that clients may be served effectively.

6

Family Therapy With Ethnic Minorities

Similarities and Differences

amily therapists will usually have the opportunity to work with many
different ethnic minorities. With the exception of ethnic culture centers or
agencies that limit their services to a specific client group, most agencies
and private practitioners provide family therapy to cross-cultural populations. It
is not uncommon for a family therapist to provide therapy to many different
ethnic minority families. The major objective of this chapter is to highlight and
analyze the similarities and differences of therapy with different ethnic minority
families at different therapeutic phases. Specifically, at the pretherapy phase, therapy similarities and differences pertaining to ethnic minority family structure are
analyzed along with the application of system, structural, and communication
theories. The similarities and differences in family therapy with various ethnic
minority families at the beginning, problem-solving, and evaluation phases are
examined and contrasted, together with the techniques and skills for specific therapy modalities, such as couple and divorce therapy, as well as extended, single-
parent, and reconstituted (step- and blended) family therapy.

PART 1: PRETHERAPY PHASE CONSIDERATIONS

The Ethnic Minority Family Structure

Cultural Values in Relation to Family Structure

Family therapy with ethnic minorities must be directed at the conflict, anxiety,
and defense systems within the individual and/or the family. The ecological
approach maintains that imbalance and conflict within a family may arise from
any point in the individual or family's transaction with the environment. The critical constructionist perspective further helps to contextualize the (individualized)
meaning of the lived experiences of ethnic minority families and family members
by locating their experiences within specific historical, economic, political, and

Table 6.1   Cultural Value Preferences of Middle Class White Americans and Ethnic Minorities: A Comparative Summary

Area of Relationships	Middle-Class White Americans	Asian and Pacific Islander Americans	First Nations Peoples	African Americans	Latino Americans
Man to nature and the environment	Mastery over	Harmony with	Harmony with	Harmony with	Harmony with
Time orientation	Future	Past-present	Present	Present	Past-present
Relations with people	Individual	Collateral	Collateral	Collateral	Collateral
Perferred mode of activity	Doing	Doing	Being-in-becoming	Doing	Being-in-becoming
Nature of humanity	Good and bad	Good	Good	Good and bad	Good

NOTE: For cultural value orientations, see Kluckhohn and Strodtbeck (1961).

sociocultural contexts. This is an important feature of our practice approach, considering that these families' experiences are largely and objectively negative, oppressive, nonaffirming, and depotentiating. For ethnic minority families undergoing acculturation and survival in a (mainstream) racist society, the strength and comfort that ethnic minority families derive from their cultural traditions and cultural values should be the focus from which to begin the therapeutic process.

According to Kluckhohn (Kluckhohn & Strodtbeck, 1961), individuals' value orientations influence their behavior, conception, and use of time; their relationship with their environment and with nature; and their interpersonal relationships. By focusing on the ethnic minority family's value orientation, a therapist gains understanding and insight into the family's view of the nature of the world and its problems, family members' feelings about their problems, and the direction the family adopts to resolve problems.

The major cultural values of selected ethnic minority families are summarized in Table 6.1 along with the middle class white American cultural orientation, which can serve as an informative guide for the family therapist.

Man to nature and the environment. Middle class, white American cultural values place man in control of nature and the environment. In contrast, ethnic minority groups emphasize man's harmony with his environment. According to the Asian Confucian system, man's quest for spiritual fulfillment is to achieve harmony in this world through observing five basic relationships in which loyalty and respect is expected on both sides, and especially toward the elderly in the family (Keyes, 1977). First Nations peoples hold nature as extremely important, for they realize that they are but one part of a greater whole. They believe the growing things of the earth and all animals have spirits or souls and that they should be treated as humanely as possible. An African American's cultural value of keeping harmony with the environment manifests itself in strong kinship bonds and collectivity above individualism (Clark, 1972). African Americans' strong religious or spiritual orientation is also a way to keep them in harmony with nature. They may view emotional difficulties as "the wages of sin" and interpersonal conflicts as not following the "Lord's teachings." In pursuit of spiritualism as a means to maintain harmony with nature, Latinos believe that the visible world is surrounded by an invisible world inhabited by good and evil spirits who influence human behavior (Delgado, 1978). To be protected by good spirits, an individual must perform good and charitable deeds in the secular world. Because the Latino cultural value is not to be preoccupied with mastering the world, Latinos may feel a keen sense of destiny and a sense of divine providence governing the world.

Ethnic minority cultural values of harmony with nature see no clash between humans and nature. Family problems develop when we have not attended properly to or kept our lives in balance with all sources of influence (heaven and earth). A therapist's "mastery over nature" orientation, which assumes that there are few (if any) problems that cannot be solved, may conflict with the values of ethnic minority clients. Recognizing this value difference, the therapist needs to respect and learn from the family how it views family problems and their solution.

Time orientation. Time in the mainstream society is oriented to the future, worshipping youth and material goods and making sacrifices for a "better" tomorrow. Other ethnic groups view the time orientation differently. Asian Americans honor their ancestors and emphasize the past, which represents respectability and wisdom. First Nations peoples, on the other hand, are very much grounded in what is happening in their lives at the moment and not always interested in making specific plans for future endeavors. They may view events as moving through time in a rhythmic, circular pattern and consider artificial impositions of schedules disruptive to the natural pattern. The strong spiritual foundation within the African American culture that has helped this race of people endure historical trauma may influence African Americans to focus on changing what is happening in the present. The strong hierarchical sense of Latino culture reminds Latinos of the importance of the past, and their value of *personalismo* makes their present encounters a spontaneous activity. In view of the overall present-time orientation of most ethnic minorities, concrete immediate problems and their solution will probably be considered more relevant than future-oriented, abstract, philosophical goals.

Relations with people. The middle-class white American subculture emphasizes individual autonomy and competition. Within ethnic minority cultures, there is an emphasis on cooperation and collectivity. The individual in traditional Asian and Pacific Islander cultures is protected securely in a wide network of kinship. He or she is clearly reminded that other social relationships or friendships should be secondary to the needs of family. In Asian and Pacific Islander societal structures, where interdependence is stressed, the actual or threatened withdrawal of support may shake a person's basic trust and cause him or her considerable anxiety over the thought of facing life alone. In the culture of First Nations peoples, the family and group take precedence over the individual, hence the importance of getting along with others—for the sake of the family. This concept of collaterality reflects an integrated view of the universe, wherein all people, animals, plants, and objects in nature have their place in creating a harmonious whole. African Americans' strong kinship bonds and extended family ties are heavily influenced by traditional African cultures, which value collectivity above individualism. Studies have revealed that kin help each other with financial aid, child care, house chores, and other forms of mutual support. In the Latino culture, the importance of family membership and belonging cuts across caste lines and socioeconomic conditions. Individuals' self-confidence, worth, security, and identity are determined by their relationships to other family members. During good times and during crisis, the family's name and family members' welfare always come first.

Ethnic minority Americans' adherence to collaterality is sure to conflict with the dominant culture's emphasis on individualism and competition. Children of ethnic minority groups can mistakenly be seen as "unmotivated" or "nonverbal" or "lazy" if they do not engage in the same competitive, individualistic behaviors as their (white) peers in the classroom or on the playground. The same may be true for ethnic minority adults in the workplace, in which being a "team player" is not rewarded to the same extent as distinguishing oneself from and competing with coworkers. However, the cooperative spirit of the minority family member can be revitalized and encouraged in the problem-solving process during a family crisis.

Preferred mode of activity. In the activity dimension, the "doing" orientation is basic to the middle class white American lifestyle. Thus competitiveness and upward mobility are the trademarks connected with *doing.* Asian and Pacific Islander Americans' "doing orientation" is manifested in the importance placed on having the ability to exercise self-discipline, which involves controlling one's feelings to properly fulfill one's responsibility and thus gain recognition, not for oneself, but for the family. *Gaman,* for a Japanese person, means to evince stoicism and patience, not to complain in the face of adversity, and to display tolerance for life's painful moments. African Americans share a similar doing orientation with Asian and Pacific Islander Americans. African Americans view endurance and suffering (of societal racism and individual prejudice) and education as essential paths to combat racism and discrimination and succeed in life, key elements of a survivor mentality.

First Nations peoples may prefer a "being-in-becoming" mode of activity. Their culture values what the human being *is* rather than what he or she *can achieve*. First Nations peoples do not emphasize the manipulation of nature or situations for their own comfort, convenience, or economic gain. The belief is that to attain maturity, which is learning to live with life (its evil as well as its good), one must face genuine suffering. Latinos may prefer a "being-in-becoming" mode of activity. Their culture defines individual self-worth in terms of those inner qualities that give an individual self-respect and earn the individual the respect of others. The emphasis is on an inner dignity (*dignidad*) and the expectation that others will show respect (*respeto*) for that dignidad.

Preferred mode of activity has important implications in family therapy with different ethnic minority groups. For example, a Latino or a First Nations person who believes in "being-in-becoming" will also believe that every individual has some sense of personal dignity, and these people will be sensitive about showing proper respect to others and demanding it for themselves. There may be some heightened sensitivity in regard to this expectation when a client first encounters a non-Latino or nonindigenous person. Thus a Latino or First Nations family may seek and perhaps benefit from family therapy not because of agency affiliation or the professional training of the therapist but simply because of the therapist's skill and ability to convey this sense of "being-in-becoming" when dealing with the family. "Being-in-becoming" translated into practice principles simply means to respect the client's right to self-determination and noninterference.

Nature of man. Both African American and Latino cultures share with middle class white American culture the view that the nature of humanity basically is that of neutrality: People are neither good nor bad, but more a product of their physical and nurturing environment. This explains the achievement orientation of these minorities, especially if they are members of the middle class. Because the belief is that the environment can influence the nature of man, there may be more receptivity to environmental sources for changes or improvement.

Asian American and First Nations cultures, on the other hand, share a belief that man basically is good. The Asian Buddhist canons state that qualities essential to harmonious living include compassion, a respect for life, moderation in behavior, and selflessness. In the indigenous culture, the belief is that human nature is always good. A person's misbehavior or problem is thought to result from lack of opportunity to be and to develop fully. There are always some people or things that are bad and deceitful. However, in the end, good people will

Table 6.2 Family Structure of Middle Class White Americans and Ethnic
Minorities: A Comparative Summary

Family Structural Relationships	Middle-Class White Americans	Asian and Pacific Islander Americans	First Nations Peoples	African Americans	Latino Americans
Kinship ties	Nuclear	Extended family	Extended family	Extended family	Extended family
Husband-wife	Egalitarian	Patriarchal	Patriarchal/ matriarchal	Egalitarian	Patriarchal
Parent-child	Hierarchical/ egalitarian	Hierarchical	Egalitarian	Hierarchical	Hierarchical
Siblings	Hierarchical	Hierarchical by age and sex	Egalitarian	Hierarchical	Hierarchical by age and sex

triumph just because they are good. The Asian American culture's belief of the
nature of man informs them that the best healing source for their problem is
within the family, not outside. Similarly, indigenous cultures believe that because
people basically are good, if a person is allowed to be left alone with people
within his or her own nurturing environment, goodness will outweigh evil.

These cultural value orientations significantly influence ethnic minority family
organization and structure. A discussion of how these values affect subsystems
and overall family interaction follows.

Traditional Family Structure and Extended Family Ties

To provide an informative guide for the family therapist, the traditional family
structures of selected ethnic minority families are summarized in Table 6.2, along
with the middle class white American family structure.

Studies indicate that ethnic minority extended family ties are more cohesive
and extensive than kinship relationships among the white population (Martin &
Martin, 1978; Padilla, Carlos, & Keefe, 1976; Shimkin et al., 1978; Stack, 1974).
Extended families in all ethnic groups include unrelated, lifelong friends. One
example is *compadrazgo*, a Filipino system, in which trusted friends and allies
can be recruited to serve as godparents to children (Ponce, 1977). Through
Catholic baptism, a Latino child can acquire a godmother (madrina) and godfather (padrino) who directly share responsibility for the child's welfare and thus
form coparent (compadre) bonds with the child's parents. Nonkin in an indigenous family can also become family members through naming ceremonies in
which a child becomes their namesake (Brave Heart, 2001). These individuals

then assume family obligations and responsibilities for child rearing and role modeling. Within the African American culture, a person can become lifelong friends with a family when he or she is "adopted" as a (fictive kin) *play mother* or *play brother* or *play uncle.* This individual can assume family responsibility, roles, and honor within this sacred (family) role.

Kinsmen of extended families provide essential functions for family members or members experiencing a crisis. For example, transferring children from one nuclear family to another within the extended family system is a common practice among all ethnic minorities. Unless the practice is regarded as a problem by the family, therapists should not criticize or attempt to alter such arrangements. The extended family network represents a relational field characterized by intense personal exchanges that have unending effects upon family members' perception, value systems, and behavior. It has immense practice implications in therapy with ethnic minority families. It sometimes represents the only natural source through which the family will seek help and benefit; it can also be the major source of blockage impeding the client's or family's progress in problem solving.

Mate selection and husband-wife relationships. In the area of mate selection and husband-wife relationships, there are a great many similarities among Asian and Pacific Islander Americans, First Nations peoples, and Latinos. Although the tradition of arranged marriage is gradually disappearing among these ethnic minority groups, the choice of mate is still heavily influenced by the families of both sides. Due to the influence of extended family ties, there is strong encouragement for young people to marry within their ethnic group. However, as previously cited and discussed in chapter 3, intertribal marriages are becoming more common, as entire tribes have been extinguished through systematic cultural and racial genocide.

Traditionally, a young Latino interested in a young Latina was expected to speak to the parents of the girl, particularly the father, to declare his intentions. A serious courtship could never even begin if the families disapproved. The patriarchal system of Asian and Pacific Islander Americans, some First Nations peoples, and Latinos places the wife in a submissive status in the family structure. Within a traditional Asian or Pacific Islander American family, the wife's position, in addition to being lower than that of her husband and her husband's parents, is also lower than that of her oldest son.

Traditionally, Inuit men took on a domineering role with their wives and were reluctant to establish close interpersonal contact (Hippler, 1974). Although traditional Latino husbands assume the instrumental dominant role of provider and protector of the family, Latina wives assume the expressive role of homemaker and caretaker. Because it is the wife's responsibility to care for the home and to keep the family together, the husband is not expected to assume household tasks or help care for the children in traditional Latino families. The Hopi say that "the man's place is on the outside of the house." This role arrangement sometimes results in wives assuming power behind the scenes although they overtly support their husband's authority (Brown & Shaughnessy, 1982; Hsu, 1972; Stevens, 1973).

Due to the high unemployment of African American males and the African American female's wage-earning ability, the husband-wife relationship of an African American couple has been more egalitarian than that of the other three ethnic minority groups and even far more so than for the white American couple. When the African American male or spouse is at home, he is more capable and willing to assume flexible roles and responsibilities than are white middle class American men. Women of all ethnic minority groups consider motherhood an important role equal to or exceeding the importance of the role of a wife (Bell, 1971; Brown & Shaughnessy, 1982; Hsu, 1972; Stevens, 1973). Given that it is the existence of children that validates and cements the marriage, motherly love is often viewed as a much greater force than wifely love.

During therapy with ethnic minority families, the marital subsystem may be the cause of the problem, but it should not receive the initial emphasis. The egalitarian relationship that is preferred by some middle class white Americans may not be the desired transactional relationship for minority couples. The romantic, egalitarian relationship should not be the criterion used to measure an ethnic minority couple's marriage and parental subsystem boundary. Partners in a couple should always be encouraged to communicate with each other clearly and effectively.

Parent-child relationship. The parental functions of both Asians and Latinos follow the cultural prescriptions for the husband-wife relationship. The father disciplines and controls and the mother provides nurturance and support. The child's responsibility at home is to obey and respect his or her parents. Love and affection are displayed openly when the child is an infant. The traditional Latino father generally is relaxed and playful with younger children and more stern and strict with older children, especially daughters (Fitzpatrick, 1981). Within African American and First Nations families, the basic parental disciplinary role may be shared among relatives of several generations. The biological parents are afforded the opportunity to engage in fun-oriented activities with their children. Despite the high number of single female–headed African American households, the effect on children of the absence of African American fathers is partly compensated for by male kinsmen in the extended family network. Recent literature also clarifies and rectifies the negative stereotypes of the neglectful, noncustodial African American father—especially poor, young fathers—with empirical information documenting the variety of creative ways in which these fathers have involved themselves in the lives of their children (Rasheed & Rasheed, 1999). African American mothers have been generally recognized for their devotion and care of their children; however, care must be taken by the family therapist not to assume that all African

American women want to or can assume the position of the family's "central switchboard operator" or take on the general "wonder woman" syndrome. With the declining resources available to African American families and the rising rates of teenage pregnancy, the African American grandmother is a sure candidate for burnout. However, one unique strength characteristic of all ethnic minorities is the involvement of the extended family in the rearing and guidance of children. Most ethnic minority children grow up in the midst of adults, not only their parents but members of the extended family. Ethnic minority children are seldom left at home with babysitters or other adults unknown to them.

Parents of Asian, Latino, and African American children usually engender the respect of their children through complementary transactions. They would not expect or want to be "friends" with their children. In disciplining children, some African American parents may use corporal punishment (although the authors' experiences with child welfare systems suggest this practice is slowly disappearing); however, physical punishment is done with love and care for the purposes of behavioral control, not out of anger or frustration with the child. Conversely, First Nations parents seldom physically punish their children (Lewis, 1970). The high status that the child is afforded in First Nations families is evidenced in some tribes where the mother and the daughter may be referred to by the same term (Brown & Shaughnessy, 1982). A daughter would properly address her mother as "mother-sister," and the mother would properly address the child as "child-sister." In terms of practice implications, a therapist must follow the authority stance of Asian, Latino, and African American families, which places the child in a subservient and obedient role. Attempts at the free and open expression characteristic of conjoint family therapy with white middle class families and family members should take into consideration that the communication patterns of ethnic minority families do not encourage children to challenge their parents with confrontive communication styles suggestive of an egalitarian (parent-child) relationship. These three ethnic groups believe in firm discipline of the children. Therapists should not automatically assume that children from female-headed families lack adult male influences or models, especially in the case of the "invisible triangle," in which the third member is an adult male whose presence is not apparent to the family therapist (e.g., an African American father or male companion of the mother who may or may not live with the African American family household but who still exerts a very powerful force on day-to-day family processes). Having been exposed to the companionship of many adults in an extended family, ethnic minority children are well aware of what socially approved patterns of behavior should be, as well as what other people think of them.

Sibling relationship. The sibling relationship within all ethnic minority families is influenced by the extended family network. Asians and Latinos further distinguish themselves in a vertical hierarchical structure and male sex-role dominance. Historically, through a son, Asian parents could be assured that the family's name and the memory of ancestors would continue. Due to the egalitarian orientation of the conjugal roles of African Americans and the different matrilineal and patrilineal patterns among some First Nations tribes, there is no distinct favoritism afforded to the First Nations or African American child. Parents of all ethnic minorities typically accord authority to older siblings and delegate supervisory and caretaking functions to them. The oldest son in a traditional Asian family is expected to be a role model and to provide continuous guidance to his younger siblings, not only when they are young but throughout their adult lives. Given the "superwoman" or "wonder-woman" stereotype of African American women, the oldest daughter of an African American family is often expected to be self-sufficient and independent early in life. Among Asians, Latinos, and First Nations peoples, cross-sex sibling companionship is curtailed at adolescence and is replaced by complementary functions such as girls doing household chores and boys working outside of the home and chaperoning the girls. African American adolescents are typically taught, however, that such traits as nurturing and assertiveness are desirable for any individual, regardless of sex. Because all ethnic minority children are taught respect, cooperation, and control of aggression (Hippler, 1974; Rothenberg, 1964; Sollenberger, 1962) at an early age (and the cooperative mentality that it takes to survive in such a racist society), there is typically little sibling rivalry. Emotional support, guidance, and practical help among siblings continue during adulthood. Family therapy with ethnic minorities should consider the significance of the sex, age, and sibling-order factors of children at the assessment phase. The intergenerational parent-child boundary within an ethnic minority family is often influenced by factors different than in the white middle-class American family. Therapists should take care not to use the latter as their frame of reference.

Intermarriages. The process of acculturation, social interaction, and increased tolerance of ethnic and racial differences are responsible for the gradual increase of intermarriage between members of ethnic minority groups and white Americans. Generally, upward mobility has been cited as positively associated with intermarriage (Grebler, Moore, & Guzman, 1970). Nevertheless, in view of the diverse cultural backgrounds and family patterns of the ethnic minorities and the dominant culture, intermarried couples may experience a high rate of conflict. The effects of intermarriage in family therapy also depend upon how relatives view the marriage. Some may see intermarriage as one channel through which equality can be achieved; others may feel that such a marital union may weaken nationality ties and the family of origin. Traditional older members of the respective ethnic minority families may thus oppose intermarriage. Their strong sentiment against intermarriage can make a couple's marriage vulnerable. Family therapists can play a role in counseling in intermarriage situations by becoming more knowledgeable about these unions so as to dispel the fears, myths, misconceptions, and prejudice historically associated with interracial and intercultural marriages.

Divorce and remarriage. Census data (U.S. Census Bureau, 2001a) have consistently supported the fact that the divorce rate for Asians and Latinos is lower than that for Anglo populations. Reasons include social ostracism, a female's realistic expectations of the wife's subservient role, and the predominant religion (Catholicism) among Latinos, which has a strong prohibition against divorce. Conversely, First Nations peoples and African Americans have a higher divorce rate than that of whites. In 2001, African Americans' divorce and separation rate more than doubled that of whites (U.S. Census Bureau, 2001a). Diversity of tribal cultures that conflict with the dominant culture, rising rates of unemployment, poverty, and a shortage of ("marriageable") males contribute to the high divorce rates for these two groups. Although an Asian or Latino divorcee may risk social ostracism, First Nations and African American divorcees typically have fewer problems with their families and extended families after divorce. Divorce and remarriage are more acceptable within these two cultures than among dominant culture families. The strong support of the extended family and multiple households offer the divorcee a place in the family. Family therapists who work with these ethnic groups should be cautious of the various implications and consequences that divorce has upon different ethnic minority members. They should be empathetic with Asians' and Latinos' reluctance to end their marriages. Should the marriage end in divorce, the strong support system among First Nations Peoples and among African Americans should be used to ensure a smooth post-divorce transition. Different ethnic minorities view divorce differently. Many therapeutic possibilities, including mobilizing the extended family and social support system, exist for the future adjustment of the divorcee in terms of single parenthood and remarriage.

Immigration, Migration, and Political and Cultural Adjustments

It is not uncommon for members of Asian and Pacific Islander and Latino families to migrate to the United States at different times. This migration pattern, along with age and gender factors, can contribute to marked differences in levels of acculturation. As a result, families may experience *acculturative tensions* and even more painful *acculturative conflict.* These conflicts may escalate even more as family members take on different (bicultural) ethnic identities that result from cultural transitioning. Bicultural conflicts, generational conflicts, and differences in acculturation may become serious threats to family cohesiveness. Additionally, the individual family member may experience role conflict, role loss, or role confusion when trying to integrate this new ethnic identity.

Both Asians and Latinos experience similar patterns of immigrational, political, and cultural adjustments. There are two interrelated levels of adaptive cultural transition that both Asian and Latino families in the process of immigration must face: (a) the physical and material, economic, educational, and language transitions and (b) the cognitive, affective, and psychological transition experienced by individual family members and the family as a unit. Immigration and migration produce a transitional crisis in the family, with predictable stages of resolution (Sluzki, 1979). Membership changes within the family during immigration may necessitate the restructuring by a family of its roles, functions, and transactions. The traditional hierarchical role structure of both Asian and Latino family members may conflict with a husband-father's unemployment. This, coupled with the wife's working outside of the home, can disrupt the traditional male-dominant role in the marriage. The faster acculturation rate of children can threaten authoritarian parents who may have to depend on their children to translate for them when they deal with community agencies, immigration authorities, and healthcare sources. Lack of support outside the family system and fear of crime, drug addiction, and more permissive sexual mores often cause parents to be overly strict with their children, who, in turn, may rebel against them. The children may also reject their parents' traditional customs, which they consider too "old-fashioned" compared to American mores.

First Nations peoples and African Americans are less affected by distant geographical separation, and they rarely experience language problems. However, First Nations families may have experienced forced relocation and hence separation from family members, as well as the physical distance that can create cutoffs between family members when some family members attempt to survive by going back and forth to the reservation as they seek employment opportunities. These groups have experienced what is now referred to in the literature as "historical trauma." The professional literature on First Nations peoples refers to this phenomenon as a "soul wound" that may take generations to heal (BraveHeart, 1999, 2000, 2001, in press a, in press b, in press c). Indigenous peoples, as well as African Americans, have experienced and endured cultural and racial genocide as a result of racist federal initiatives, programs, and policies. The results are bleak statistics for income, employment, education, health, mental health, and crime among both African Americans and First Nations peoples. Living against such ecological stresses as *race-related trauma* (stress, fatigue, frustration, and confusion), as well as daily threats to survival, the life of an indigenous or African American family is certain to be profoundly and adversely affected.

Thus family therapy with ethnic minorities must recognize the impact of immigration, political discrimination, and cultural adjustments. The therapist's role extends beyond a "talk therapy" therapeutic function; it also includes the roles of advocate, educator, cultural translator, mediator, and role model to help families form an open system with available community resources. The old natural support systems and the newly established network based on mutual aid developed by the therapist can provide needed economic, emotional, and educational assistance to families in cultural transition.

Ethnocultural Identity Formation

Ethnic minority families and family members' identities can range from that of a *traditional* ethnic identity (being very culturally immersed in one's original culture), to that of a *transitional* ethnic identity (being acculturated to Anglo values, perhaps even preferring the dominant middle class American cultural orientation), to a *bicultural* ethnic identity (being comfortable and accepting of both cultures), to a *marginal* ethnic identity (feeling alienated from both cultures) (Lin, Tazuma, & Matsuda, 1979; Sue & Sue, 1999).

One of the most critical clinical issues in working with ethnic minority individuals is for therapists to be able to assess and intervene in situations wherein the ethnic individual is experiencing *internalized racism*. That is, the individual has "identified with the aggressor," so to speak, and engages in self-deprecating attitudes and behaviors toward his or her own ethnocultural group. There is an idealization of Eurocentric cultural values and behaviors to the extent that the individual seeks to exclusively (or nearly exclusively) emulate Euro-American behavior and devalue his or her own cultural values and behaviors. The end result is a psychologically conflicted individual who has poor self-esteem, which may cause the individual to engage in dysfunctional defense mechanisms such as denial, avoidance, suppression, repression, reaction formation, and displacement of anger. However, for therapists to be helpful to families and family members suffering from this crippling mental health disorder, it is crucial that therapists already have engaged in candid (self) examination of their own "cultural countertransference" in reference to ethnic minority families' ethnic cultural values and behaviors. Therapists must be careful not to (consciously or unconsciously) *collude with debilitating and nonpotentiating ethnocultural narratives* that do not serve their clients well or collude with various members of the family system who may ascribe to negative societal ethnocultural stereotypes (as in the case of negative societal stereotypes heaped on the African American male). In these situations, it is incumbent upon therapists to empower the family and its members to *deconstruct these politicized (culturally dystonic) ethnocultural narratives* and to *reconstruct new (culturally syntonic) ethnocultural narratives* that are more appropriate for the individual's psyche.

Family Help-Seeking Patterns and Behaviors

Ethnic minority clients and families may not readily consider mental health services a solution to their emotional and family problems (Casas & Keefe, 1980; DeGeyndt, 1973; Kleinman & Lin, 1981; McAdoo, 1977). Reasons for their underutilization of health and mental services include (a) distrust of therapists, especially white therapists; (b) cultural and social class differences between therapists and clients; (c) an insufficient number of mental health facilities and professionals who are bicultural; (d) overuse or misuse of physicians for psychological problems; (e) language and linguistic barriers; (f) reluctance to recognize the urgency for help; and (g) lack of awareness of the existence of mental health clinics. Ethnic minorities typically consider the family and extended family their primary source of support. Reliance on natural support systems produces fewer feelings of defeat, humiliation of self and family, and powerlessness. When natural support systems are unavailable, ethnic minority clients or families may consult their folk healers, priests, or religious leaders. When all these fail, the family may seek help from the mainstream family and healthcare system. The ethnic minority client's fear and mistrust of therapists are caused by past oppression and discrimination and negative experiences with helping professionals from mainstream institutions. When minorities do seek mental health or family-related services, they may see the therapist as a physician who prescribes medication or gives directives.

Help-seeking patterns of ethnic minorities closely correspond to their specific needs and family types. Both Asian and Latino families can be categorized into three types: (a) recently arrived immigrant families, (b) immigrant-American families, and (c) immigrant-descendent families. Newly arrived immigrant families need information, referral, advocacy, and English-language instruction. Due to cultural and language barriers, they may not seek personal counseling and family therapy. Immigrant-American families, who are characterized by cultural conflict, may need help in resolving generational conflicts, communication problems, role clarification, and renegotiation. Immigrant-descendent families usually are acculturated, speak both languages at home, and can seek help from mainstream social and mental health agencies, including private practice family therapists. Red Horse's (1980b) classification of First Nations families also indicates that bicultural families are the ones most receptive to family therapy.

Neither traditional nor pantraditional families may be receptive to the idea of family therapy. Knowing the similarities and differences of help-seeking patterns among various ethnic minority groups makes a therapist better informed in terms of what to expect, especially during the initial contact phase with the client. Variations within each ethnic minority group also inform and remind the therapist of the need for individualization in therapy with ethnic minority families.

Applying Culturally Sensitive
Family Theories, Models, and Approaches

Family Communication Theory

Family communication theory pertaining to the daily interactions among family members has a great deal of relevance and applicability in therapy with ethnic minority families. The following discussion focuses on the contribution of family communication theory and is organized into two sections. The first section describes the principles of family behavior from the perspective of family communication theory. The second section describes practice principles derived from communication theory.

Communication Principles of Family Behavior as
They Relate to Understanding Ethnic Minority Families

In analyzing the communication patterns and interactions of ethnic minority families, the behavioral principle that all behavior is communicative is applicable to all groups. When First Nations peoples are confronted or under stress, they may communicate their anxiety through silence (Lewis & Ho, 1975). Latinos, governed by a hierarchical structure, may display no overt sign of displeasure when confronted, but they may not return for the next scheduled session (Falicov, 1998). Some Asians may communicate their stress and displeasure through a physical symptom, which is more acceptable in their culture than emotional symptoms. African Americans may respond to anxiety by either saying nothing or becoming aggressive, as well as through physical symptoms.

The process of *metacommunication,* defined as "the message within the message," (Haley, 1963), is further complicated by the process of immigration and acculturation among Asian and Latinos. Traditionally, these groups interact according to a prescribed vertical and hierarchical role structure, which is determined by age, sex, generation, and birth order of family members. First Nations peoples' use of indirect communication also is a form of metacommunication that requires sensitivity and reciprocity from others. When indirect communication is not properly received and reciprocated, there is a threat to the relationship. When an African American family's basic security and safety needs are threatened, metacommunication among family members in the manner of more confrontive behaviors may occur but should not automatically be interpreted by the family therapist as a precursor to physical violence—merely, a more expressive communication style.

The principle of the "punctuation" of communication sequences (Bateson, 1972) is experienced in an intergenerational parent-child conflict among various ethnic minority families. This principle of punctuation usually is triggered or related to "internal" stressors affecting the family (Minuchin, 1974), such as a family member's illness or parents coping with a child's or an adolescent's problems. For an ethnic minority family, punctuation of communication sequences may be caused by cultural value conflict, the acculturation process, or racist and discriminatory practices by mainstream society.

The communication concept of verbal and nonverbal communication has important implications in therapy with all ethnic minority families. Although many ethnic minority clients may be bilingual, some traditional Asian, Hispanic, and indigenous people are more comfortable with their native language when dealing with crises or problem-solving issues. Correspondingly, some African American families and family members who are not accustomed to "code switching" from Standard English to ebonics or slang may not feel comfortable discussing intense emotional situations entirely in Standard English. Clients who speak English or Standard English with difficulty may have the added demands of decoding and encoding the therapist's communications (Pitta, Marcos, & Alpert, 1978), which may cause clients' emotional reactions to appear "flat" or inappropriate. It is critical for family therapists in working with ethnic minority families and family members to be introspective regarding their cultural countertransference and general cultural attitudes about different languages and diverse dialectical styles.

Traditional ethnic minority families are considered to be *high-context communication cultures* (Hall, 1976) in that there is more reliance on nonverbal cues to relate a message. This concept describes a culture that relies heavily on the nonverbal aspect of a message (how it is said) to relay some of the most important and powerful aspects of the message. Conversely, in a *low-context communication culture,* the most important and powerful aspect of a message is contained within the verbal component of a given communication—as is the case in Eurocentric cultures.

The cultural transitional process and the strong influences of the egalitarian couple relationship of the dominant culture have greatly affected the traditional complementary (dominant-submissive) relationship of Asian and Latino couples. The husband may struggle to maintain a complementary (dominant-submissive) relationship and the wife may try to negotiate a symmetrical (equal) relationship. Conversely, First Nations and African American husbands try hard to maintain a symmetrical relationship with their wives, although the latter may have difficulty due to the wife's increased financial earning power and central role within the family.

Satir's (Satir et al., 1975) classification of family behavior for a family member under stress can explain an Asian, Latino, or African American husband-father's behavior during acculturation and other stressful periods. When a family transaction is out of (hierarchical) "structure," the husband-father easily falls into the *blamer* role, finding fault in others as a means of saving face, reaffirming his machismo, or defying or denying the negative (societal) images and stereotypes of African American men as fathers. The in-between position (between husband and children) occupied by the wife often places her in the *placatory role* of agreeing, pleasing, and apologizing. The consistent unemployment status of many African American males and the occupationally displaced status of many First Nations males may force them to assume placatory roles in their families. As they become demoralized by assuming the placatory role, they may shift into an *irrelevant* role, which, in turn, places them in a peripheral position in transactions with the children and other family members.

Linguistic obstacles may undermine family communication processes; that is, some family members may be bilingual, whereas others may speak only (or primarily) English, and still others may only (or primarily) speak their native language. This may in part be due to the fact that some family members may be at different levels of acculturation or assimilation, rendering family sessions much more difficult to conduct. Additionally, varying *levels of acculturation* within the same family can create acculturative tensions within Latino families. Differences in acculturative behaviors (especially within the realm of communicative behavior) may complicate the communication process for ethnic minority families. Specifically, incongruous communication could occur that other family members may perceive as inappropriate or (however unintentionally) invalidating (Satir, 1986). The family therapist is encouraged to pay special attention to the nonverbal content of family messages, given the high-context culture of more traditional ethnic minority families.

The effects of acculturation and assimilation, as well as the effects of immigration on the family life cycle, may have forced ethnic minority couples to renegotiate their relationship. Their need for economic survival in a hostile environment (wherein all family members who are employable—including elder children—have to take on employment when available) may force their relationships to shift, upsetting the traditional hierarchy in the family system and subsystems, especially in the conjugal dyad, which may shift from a complementary (dominant-submissive) relationship to a symmetrical (similar) conjugal relationship or vice versa. This shift often complicates the couple's relationship and family life, as it occurs at a time when the family's emotional support system has been weakened and the demands for meeting basic family needs such as food, housing, and healthcare are even greater than usual. Ethnic minority couples (especially those couples that have varying acculturative behaviors) need to be helped to "find their own way," so to speak, to determine for themselves what blend (if any) of traditional versus acculturated conjugal behaviors will work for them. The family therapist is advised to facilitate the couple to *reauthor the (ethnocultural) conjugal narrative,* which will help the partners to resolve power issues and move past these dilemmas.

The problem of internalized racism, that is, viewing oneself in the same negative light as one's oppressor, is of concern and relevance in practice with ethnic minority families. This internalized oppression (accepting the negative messages and stereotypical images of others) is of general concern to people of color, and family members need to be empowered to challenge these *globalized interpretations* of their culture and *deconstruct debilitating and nonpotentiating ethnocultural metanarratives* to enable the family to *reconstruct new, more potentiating narratives* for itself.

Clients who have been through painful migratory experiences and those from war-torn countries may need help in dealing with these traumatic experiences (coerced relocation, forced immigration, loss of national affiliation, relatives who were left behind and still remain in this politically volatile countries), which can be emotionally intense and painful subjects. These emotionally laden issues may have become the source of *family secrets, myths,* and *rules* governing family and individual behavior. There are many potential areas of unresolved grief that may have become forbidden subjects for family discussion. Ethnic minority families and family members may be suffering from post-traumatic stress syndrome, and the family therapist can be helpful by engaging the family in *externalizing conversations* wherein the family provides accounts of trauma in members' lives (emotional state, familial, peer), externalizing the problem so that it is not nested in the individual or within the family (Laird, 1993; White & Epston, 1990). Families can also be encouraged to *restory* some of these traumatic experiences to allow the family and its members an opportunity to locate the (specific) *origins of immobilizing aspects* of these experiences and losses (Laird, 1993). Ethnic minority families and family members should then be encouraged to *reconstruct a narration of oppression and resilience* that *challenges disempowering sociopolitical and sociocultural metanarratives. Reflective dialogue* could provide for a quiet, *culturally syntonic* forum in which family members can *critically reflect* on their experiences and *restory painful or debilitating experiences* to find or create new ways of coping with experiences of migratory trauma (Rasheed & Rasheed, 1999). The family therapist will need to take great care and caution in approaching these subjects, especially as an outsider.

The principles of behavior derived from communication theory have contributed significantly to understanding the dynamics and interaction of ethnic minority families. The following discussion aims to explicate the matter in which these principles can be applied in actual therapy with various ethnic clients.

Communication Practice Principles as They Relate to Work With Ethnic Minority Families

To communicate in a more culturally sensitive manner with Asian and Latino families, a therapist needs to consider the prescribed vertical and hierarchical role structure, as determined by the age, sex, generation, and birth order of family members. The hierarchical role structure places the father in a spokesman role that cannot be openly challenged, especially by his own children. Thus it is advisable that beginning family therapy sessions with Asian and Latino families be divided between the spouse subsystem and the sibling subsystem. Further, to respect the authoritarian parental position, when parents are interviewed with their children, their native language can be used to communicate with the parents and English can be used with the children (assuming the therapist is bilingual). An interchange of language is useful in delineating blurred generational boundaries (Falicov, 1982, 1998).

Conversely, because of the egalitarian power orientation within First Nations and African American families, the father should not be expected to lead the discussion during therapy. Fathers in these families may be acting in the role of protecting the family from hostile and unwelcome intrusion; hence less powerful family members may be more apt to speak first while the "general" assesses the situation further to determine if it is safe for his family to emotionally connect with this stranger and reveal real family business.

The role of the therapist, as defined by Haley (1976), is that of a "metagovernor of the family system," a role that requires intense active participation and, at times, manipulation. The therapist's active leadership role may easily be interpreted by the ethnic minority family as an unwelcome intrusion. Thus the therapist's activity should be guided by the cultural values of each group. This is particularly important at the engagement phase of the therapy. For example, in therapy with Latinos, the therapist should use the formal form of the pronoun "you" (*usted*) with adults to indicate respect. Children can be addressed with the family form (*tu*). Similarly, in therapy with an African American family, a therapist should not assume familiarity with adult family members via addressing these members by their first names without asking their permission. (It is highly advisable that therapists refrain from seeking permission to address adult family members by their first names; rather, wait and see if and when family members volunteer their permission.)

The technique of relabeling or reframing (by emphasizing the positive or behavior that can be changed) is consistent with ethnic minority families' emphasis on "spiritual optimism," interdependence, compassion, and harmonious living. The technique for *prescribing the symptom* (encouraging the usually dysfunctional behavior) may be perplexing at best and disrespectful at worst to most ethnic minority families.

Satir's (1967) emphasis on "good feelings" within the family and among family members is consistent with Asian Buddhists' teachings of harmonious living and compassion, Latinos' emphasis on *familismo* and respect, First Nations peoples' teaching of collaterality and the essential goodness of man, and African

Americans' humanistic orientation. Her cognitive approach of teaching family members to recognize and restructure rules appeals to ethnic minorities' expectations that the therapist will possess a certain degree of expertise that is to be shared with the family in a direct and straightforward fashion.

The reliance on the use of *storytelling techniques* using native culture stories and characters to deal with adjustment issues of children, also called *cuento* therapy (Constantino et al., 1986; Ramos-McKay et al., 1988); the use of *metaphors and images in narratives,* incorporating cultural values orientation, short stories, and religious icons to address gender issues, oppression and abuse (Bracero, 1998); and the use of *dichos*—Spanish proverbs, sayings, and words interjected to convey clients' behavior, thoughts, conflicts, and so on in storytelling or self-disclosure style (Zuniga, 1992) is *culturally syntonic* and a natural fit with critical constructionist perspectives and techniques. Ethnic minority families and family members can be encouraged to relive important aspects of their original traditions and ethnic or cultural heritage by *storytelling* and the use of *dichos, metaphors,* and *narratives,* which may serve two purposes: (a) reinforcing positive self-images (or *build potentiating ethnic narratives*) to combat what clients may feel is forever lost to them and their families and (b) serving to pass on these important cultural images and memories to nurture positive ethnic identities (*narratives*) in children. These families should also be encouraged to *construct or reenact missed (family or cultural) rituals and celebrations,* especially where there may have been cutoffs from various family members over time. Satir's (1967) use of family history, which she calls the "family life chronology," can help ethnic minority family members to recall and enjoy past cultural traditions that help to alleviate some of the stress experienced in these families' challenging environments.

In light of the high-context nature of communication in traditional ethnic minority families, with an emphasis on the nonverbal aspect of the communication or message, *family sculpting* and *family choreography* can be extremely useful techniques. Further, the family therapist will be able to encourage parents to "sculpt" their perception of family problems without fear of shame or embarrassment when there are language barriers or communication difficulties between the therapist and the parents and children (who may be acculturated at different levels).

Family sculpting and family choreography techniques can be especially helpful in their potential to bridge communication difficulties that arise when members of the same family do not have the same command of English or, worse, when all family members do not speak English or even the same language due to long periods of separation in the immigration or migratory process. Profound linguistic difficulties often are consequences of the result of different periods of immigration by family members to the United States and different rates of acculturation of these family members. It is not uncommon to find older members speaking only their native language and younger American-born members speaking only English. Because these family members may lack a common language in which they can communicate or share emotional exchanges, inappropriate, invalid, and confusing communicative exchanges are bound to occur.

Satir (1967, 1986, 1988; Satir et al., 1975, 1991) employs a rich array of experiential techniques (e.g., *sculpting, drama, communication stances, family stress ballet, ropes, parts party*). These techniques are invaluable in their own right in that many do not heavily rely on verbal interchanges, making them particularly useful when there are linguistic barriers, either between family members or between the family and the therapist, as discussed earlier. These strategies can be considered *nonverbal narratives* in that they encourage family members to tell their story, their way. Family members are free to recreate their visions and perceptions of family relationships and family problems, as well as solutions to these problems.

Family therapists need to proceed with caution in implementing some of Satir's (19674, 1986, 1988) experiential techniques, such as *family sculpting, family choreography, drama, communication stances, family stress ballet, ropes,* and *parts party.* These techniques may be potentially very helpful in family therapy with ethnic minority families, which emphasize learning by observation and participation, as well as a reliance on the rich oral traditions of storytelling and the use of metaphors to impart important messages and teaching. However, family therapists must take great care not to intrude and otherwise impose their own sculpting suggestions (asking family members to take certain positions, etc.) that may violate (sex role and family) cultural norms and ideals of polite, respectful, and appropriate behavior. Ethnic families should be encouraged not to strive for consensus but to *explore the multiple (emotional) meanings* of important historical and cultural events and experiences. Family members then become empowered to take from these experiences what is most meaningful and helpful to them (Laird, 1993).

In summary, communication family therapy, especially as developed by Virginia Satir (1986), is a family practice approach that shares many of the cultural value assumptions and philosophical and existential positions of traditional ethnic minority families. Communication family therapy is also philosophically and existentially compatible with social construction theory. Furthermore, the varied roles that are prescribed for the therapist within this family therapy model (namely, *educator and teacher, facilitator, mediator, advocate,* and *role model*) are important and viable roles for those persons who seek to enhance the communication process of ethnic minority families, including those who are indigenous, foreign born, refugee, and U.S. born. Satir's emphasis on those communication skills essential for congruent communication and effective feedback should also be taught to all ethnic minority families who may need constant renegotiation of role expectations within the family, in light of their constantly changing social and economic landscape.

Family Structure Theory

A theoretical discussion of family structure theory and its comparison with family communication theory was presented in chapter 1. The discussion of family structure theory here centers on behavioral principles and family practice principles. The first section examines behavioral principles of family structure theory. The second section presents family practice principles of structural family theory as they relate to assessment and therapy with ethnic minority families.

Behavioral Principles of Structural Family Theory as They Relate to Understanding Ethnic Minority Families

Structural family theory strongly adheres to the systems perspective and was primarily developed and advanced by Bowen (1976) and Minuchin (1974). The *societal projection process* (Bowen, 1976) creates societal scapegoats, with which all ethnic minorities have been identified. Through the societal projection process, one group (white society) maintains the illusion of competence at the expense of "unfortunates" by "helpfulness and benevolence." These "benefactors" (white society) assume the blamer role, and ethnic minorities are forced to assume the victim role. Thus *homeostasis* is maintained in the social system. Such a social system resembles the *family projection process*.

Given the reality that most ethnic minority families are embedded in a complex kinship network of blood kin and unrelated persons, the process of triangulation, which involves intense interaction among three people within a relatively long period, may not have the same meaning or intensity for an ethnic minority family. However, the process of immigration affecting Asian and Latino families and the process of migration affecting African American and First Nations families' responses to the external threats by a racist society may cause an ethnic minority family to protect itself by maintaining a rigid, closed system. In a multiple household that includes extended family members, where a child's interaction with parents is often shared by other extended family members, the *triangulation* process may occur and involve extended family members others than the typical parent-child dyad. To survive race-related trauma, parents in ethnic minority families are determined to create a better future for their children. They will sacrifice for their children, whom they expect to earn greater rewards from the opportunity structure than they themselves were able to achieve. Parents' intense wish for their children to achieve and to behave accordingly corresponds closely to Boszormenyi-Nagy's (1987) concept of "invisible (family) loyalties," also referred to as *family ledgers* or *relational indebtedness,* and Bowen's (1976) concepts of "family projection process" and the "multigenerational transmission process." Again, the traditional extended family structure of ethnic minorities needs to be considered in relation to the impact of these processes. For example, at times the close relationship between a child and grandparents within a First Nations family may have more to do with the family projection process than the relationship between the child and his or her biological parents.

Ethnic minority families must cope with the impact of acculturation and economic survival. Both of these processes may cause individual family members to move away from their extended families and close friends. These processes can also combine to create emotional cutoff, a reality for many ethnic minority families. Yet, the strong kinship bonds within these groups can be a source of strength to be relied upon in therapy with ethnic families.

The *level of differentiation* in an individual may not be determined strictly by the differentiated level of the individual's parents, sex, or *sibling position,* as advocated by Bowen (1976). The reason behind such uncertainty is that the typical ethnic minority child experiences a broader sphere of interaction with extended family members, compared to an Anglo child's limited interaction with only nuclear family members. Hence the importance that parental role, sex, and sibling position play in an individual's level of differentiation varies from one ethnic family to another. Thus in the assessment of an ethnic minority family relationship and an individual family member's level of differentiation, greater attention should be focused on extended family relationships and the extended family framework.

Family structural theory, which involves focusing on the family system's structural (contextual) dynamics, especially the creation, maintenance, and modification of boundaries (Minuchin, 1974), is useful in work with ethnic minority families. Under normal conditions, traditional ethnic minority families' structure, characterized by familismo, collaterality, and extended family ties, can produce cohesion conducive to the developmental growth of all family members. As Minuchin (1974) points out, however, "the stressful contact of the whole family with extra familial forces" can produce role confusion and power conflict within the family (p. 63). Additionally, the ethnic family's boundaries and environment may become closed or rigid as a defense against racism, discrimination, and oppression.

In defining family structure and system boundaries, Minuchin (1974) points out that the dominant culture's family structure places husband and wife in an equal relationship, with different levels of authority over their children. However, a therapist working with Asian and Latino families should not assume that the spouse boundary is diffuse just because the spousal system of these family groups is structured differently (hierarchical instead of egalitarian). The same also applies to a First Nations couple in which the partners consider "too much authority" detrimental to the development of a child's future decision-making ability and social maturity. Ethnic minority families are typically large, and parents are challenged with meeting the economic survival needs of a large family. Thus older siblings may be assigned the responsibility of caring for the young children and assisting with other household duties. A therapist should avoid interpreting this as boundary diffusion and should not automatically label an older child as a parentified child (Minuchin, 1974). This unique complementary accommodation between spouses and between parents and children characterizes the unique adaptive strength of the ethnic minority family structure.

Family Structural Theory Practice Principles in Therapy With Ethnic Minority Families

Bowen's (1978) societal process recommends, because the ethnic minority family and its members constantly face race-related challenges, that the therapist be a *culture broker* who is open to exploring the impact of the social, political, socioeconomic, and broader environmental conditions of ethnic minority families. Family group interaction characteristic of all ethnic minority cultures normally should be conducive to conjoint family therapy with every family member present. But the unnaturalness of the formal family therapy format, with the therapist in charge, may be too threatening and unfamiliar for many ethnic minority families. These families may prefer that family problems be resolved within the family itself. Bowen's technique of focusing upon one individual, usually the most acculturated member in the family, should be useful. Bowen's detached but interested, rational, calm, low-key approach to problem solving corresponds closely to the Asian, Latino, and First Nations cultural emphasis on moderation, patience, and self-discipline. Other techniques employed by Bowen to help a spouse define and clarify his or her relationship by speaking directly to the therapist, instead of directly confronting the other spouse, may also be helpful in therapy with these ethnic groups.

Bowen's (1978) preference for singling out the couple relationship as a therapeutic target may alienate the parents of these ethnic minority groups. The ethnic minority mother may feel more challenged to perform as a good mother than as a wife. Bowen's efforts in taking careful family history reflect sensitivity and respect of intergenerational perspectives and the cultural nurturing system, the migration process, and the need for individualizing each family. However, his heavy reliance on the client to be active and to do the research and the assessment may not be congruent with the ethnic minority client's need and perception of the therapist as an "expert."

An *ethnohistorical* approach to family therapy with ethnic minority families and family members involves a meticulous, detailed, narrative account of each person's unique emotional experience of his or her many losses and painful experiences. This approach has the ability to complement existing intergenerational approaches that focus primarily on intra- and interfamilial issues and events. An ethnohistorical account should be taken of how each family member has come to construct his or her own *individual narrative,* thus allowing for a *reflective dialogue* that can lead to, first, *deconstructing marginalizing, immobilizing ethnic narratives* (as well as *deconstructing negative sociocultural metanarratives* of the family group); next, empowerment of each individual family member to *reconstruct more liberating and potentiating narratives;* and, finally, the beginning of healing. The historical trauma experienced by ethnic minority families is a subject that is highly emotional and painful. Comas-Diaz (1994) suggests that ethnic minority families be given the opportunity to "release ethnocultural rage." However, therapists should not expect ethnic minority families to emote in the early stages of therapy, and persons of color may not ever be comfortable releasing this ethnocultural rage with a white therapist.

Minuchin's (1974) differential applications of "joining techniques" are especially helpful during the beginning phase of therapy with ethnic minority families. Application of these techniques reflects Minuchin's sensitivity to individual family differences and the wisdom that structural change in a family usually requires time and patience. In the joining process, Minuchin is also mindful of the ethnic minority family's need to accept the therapist as taking a leadership role aspired to and expected by all ethnic minority families. The purposeful use of the "maintenance" technique enables the therapist to adhere to the transactional process of a particular ethnic minority family system. For example, in therapy with a three-generation Asian or Latino family adhering to a rigid hierarchical structure, the therapist may find it advisable to address the grandfather first. For some First Nations tribes who follow matriarchal practices, the grandmother is the person to whom the therapist should speak. The technique of "tracking" also is helpful as a tool with which the therapist may explore the content of family interaction and analyze family structure. Here the therapist should keep in mind how ethnic minority family structures differ from the dominant culture. In view of their inclusive involvement with extended family ties, the degree of intensity within each subsystem usually varies from the dominant culture. For example, although the ethnic minority spouse subsystem may not be as emotionally intense as that of the dominant culture, the ethnic minority sibling subsystem and the extended family subsystem are much stronger and more emotionally intense. Likewise, to attempt to totally eliminate the parental child's parental role may be totally insensitive to the family's basic survival need, in cases where both parents have to work or in single-parent homes.

In applying Minuchin's (1974) disequilibrium technique, which aims to reestablish clear family subsystems and cross-generational boundaries, the therapist needs to use different modalities, including interviewing the parental subsystem separately and using native language (assuming the therapist is bilingual) to communicate with the parents or grandparents and using English when speaking to the children. Minuchin's (1974) joining, maintenance, and tracking techniques are compatible with ethnic minority family values and structure, but his "disequilibration techniques," or family restructuring techniques, need to be applied with caution. These techniques, including *escalating stress* (by emphasizing differences), *utilizing the symptom* (by exaggerating it), and *creating affective intensity* (by manipulating the mood and escalating the emotional intensity) may be antithetical to ethnic minority cultures that emphasize interdependence, harmonious living, and moderation of behavior.

The preceding discussions aim to analyze, compare, and integrate the cultural values and family structure of ethnic minority families. The communication and structural family therapy theories have been reviewed, along with their applications in therapy with different ethnic client groups. Attention will now be directed to comparison and integration of culturally relevant techniques and skills with different ethnic minority families in three phases of therapy: beginning, problem solving, and evaluation-termination.

PART 2: CULTURALLY RELEVANT TECHNIQUES AND SKILLS IN DIFFERENT PHASES OF THERAPY

A Critical Constructionist Perspective in Family Therapy With Ethnic Minorities

The critical constructionist perspective is informed by the assumption and ongoing analysis of the impact of sociocultural and sociopolitical factors on the presenting problems of ethnic minority families as an integral component of the clinical process. This approach is especially well suited to assist family therapists in bringing cultural and political realities into their work with these families. This perspective provides clear recognition of the social realities of racism and oppression and how they can operate to affect families and family members. Additionally, the emphasis on identifying and building on the strengths (individual, familial, cultural, and environmental) of ethnic minority families makes this approach a particularly vital one.

The critical practice perspective is an optimal framework for understanding the social and psychological distresses of oppressed, socially devalued, and marginalized ethnic minority families and family members. This proposed critical constructionist perspective has the potential to inform and guide family therapists to assist these families to challenge negative (societal) representations with an increased sense of mastery and dignity. One of the key goals of the critical constructionist perspective is to liberate these families to become the subjects of their own biographies rather than becoming the victims. This perspective shares many of the elements of the social work empowerment practice model (Gutierrez, Parsons, & Cox, 1998; Lee, 1994), as well as Lillian Comas-Diaz's (1994) integrative model for psychotherapeutic work with women of color. Like these models, the critical constructionist perspective as conceptually advanced and articulated in this text is not wedded to any particular theoretical school or practice model and is based on the following practice principles:

- Intervention is called for simultaneously at multiple levels (e.g., micro and macro) that target affective, cognitive, behavioral, and systemic changes.
- There must be recognition of the systemic and societal context of racism and oppression and social ideologies that are infused with the virulent disease of racism. Such recognition allows both practitioner and client to become aware of how their lived experience or personal narrative has been affected by these forces.
- There must be a deliberate effort by both the therapist and the client to be aware of how their location or position within the social political order shapes their identities and the context and content of the helping relationship.
- There must be identification of personal narratives, cognitive distortions, and language that reinforces a sense of disempowerment, pejorative classifications of difference, or a truncated sense of self-esteem (e.g., identifying dichotomous or binary thinking, such as "superior-inferior").
- There must be support for self-assertion and reaffirmation of both racial and gender identity, as well as development in the client of a more integrated identity as a person of color.
- There must be a search for increased self-mastery and achievement of autonomous dignity.
- There must be support for the ethnic minority family in their work toward social change by challenging racism and bias encountered within their ecological niche.

The critical constructionist perspective offers family therapists the opportunity to recognize the multiple voices and multiple realities of the heterogeneous population of ethnic minority families. Each "voice" is liberated to speak its own reality and is not confined to the *ethnocultural metanarrative* of the entire ethnic group.

The methodology for developing a "critical consciousness"—a key element of this approach—involves a *dialogical approach* to relationship building and engagement, which requires *critical reflection* as a part of the assessment process and promotes *readiness toward action* as part of the interventive planning (Freire, 1973). The phases of engagement as "reflective dialogue," assessment as "critical reflection," and intervention as "liberating action" are described in the remainder of this chapter.

Beginning Phase

The beginning phase of therapy is a critical period for all ethnic minority clients and families. The reason this phase of therapy is so important is due to several factors. Ethnic minority families tend to use family therapy only if all other traditional help-seeking attempts have failed. They may have very little knowledge of what family therapy is about. To rely on a family therapist who is considered an outsider (and very likely to be a member of the dominant [oppressive] society that has inflicted race-related trauma on the ethnic group) to resolve private family problems could be considered as antithetical to *filial piety* and a "betrayal" of ancestors. It also may be viewed as an unwelcome intrusion of self-determination. Family therapists also need to be cognizant of instances in which ethnic minority clients are uncomfortable with "talk" therapy because they are self-conscious about their limited ability in speaking English or Standard English. They may lack the financial resources to seek continuous (talk) therapy help. Many ethnic minority clients may have contacted a family therapist only because they are referred by mainstream societal agencies such as schools, mental and healthcare agencies, the courts, or social service agencies. If the beginning phase of therapy is not properly conducted, the first interviews will most likely be the last time the therapist will have contact with the client or family. Five major skills and techniques are essential in therapy with ethnic minority clients and families in the beginning therapeutic phase. These skills and techniques include (a) engaging the client and family, (b) cultural transitional mapping and data collection, (c) mutual goal setting, (d) selecting a focus or system for treatment, and (e) the use of an ecomap. Although these skills and techniques are considered generic and applicable to all ethnic minority groups, the following discussion attempts to draw some comparisons and conclusions of their strategic application in the beginning phase of therapy with different ethnic minorities.

Engagement as Reflective Dialogue

A common pitfall in family therapy with ethnic minorities is moving through the engagement process too quickly (Rasheed & Rasheed, 1999). Family therapists need to take more time in building these therapeutic relationships. Trust, respect, genuineness, and integrity are key aspects of building a clinical relationship (Franklin, 1994). Therapists are cautioned not to attempt to rush through this critical stage of the clinical process, for it may undermine the therapeutic bond. From a critical constructionist perspective, the first step in the clinical relationship is to engage the family and its members through the medium of trust, in a *reflective dialogical relationship* (Rasheed & Rasheed, 1999). Here the practitioner listens to their stories and explores the unique life experiences of each family member as they relate to (inter- and intra-) personal problems, historical trauma, and race-related stress. The family therapist also inquires about broader ethnocultural factors, such as race, social class or caste systems, culture, and gender, and their (potential) impact on each family member's (self or family) *narrative,* as well as their impact on the presenting problem.

The dialogical relationship involves the therapist taking a *nonhierarchical position* in the client-worker relationship and becoming more of a "cultural consultant" to the ethnic minority family. The family and its members become partners with the practitioner in exploring different and more empowering "ways of being." This is not to say that the therapist pretends not to have any areas of expertise or expert knowledge to derive professional credibility with families. However, the family and its member are viewed as the experts where their own lives are concerned, and therapists should develop this dialogue to complete their cultural knowledge of the family's ethnocultural background, using the relationship as a sort of royal road to cultural knowledge and understanding. This technique has the potential to become a more culturally sensitive and oppression-sensitive approach to family therapy with ethnic minority families.

As practitioners assume this position in the dialogical relationship, they must be aware of their own social position (in relation to race, culture, gender, and class) within the sociocultural and economic milieu. The practitioner's social location shapes the social context of the helping relationship and significantly affects the power dynamic. The dynamics of power and control are significant, however, regardless of the race, ethnicity, or gender of the practitioner in therapy with the family.

Engaging the Client and Family

Because some Asians and Latinos do not have the proper documents to reside in this country, it is important that therapists defines their role with the client early on. Additionally, some ethnic minority clients (Asians and African Americans) may perceive the role of a family therapist as that of a physician, or a medicine man (First Nations peoples), or a folk healer (Latinos). If there is a need to orient ethnic minority families as to how to make use of family therapy, such orientation should include exploring with the families their expectations of the therapy goals, the role of the therapist, and their involvement during the therapeutic process.

To foster an element of trust, therapists can help the client feel comfortable by displaying in their office objects, pictures, or symbols of different ethnic minority cultures. Race is a major factor undermining the ethnic minority client's sense of powerlessness. During this early stage of therapy, the therapist, therefore, may need to explore with the family the racial and cultural differences between the therapist and the family (Ho & McDowell, 1973).

A therapist needs to be sensitive to English language difficulties, especially by older, traditional clients who are Asian, Latino, and First Nations people. Using children as translators may reverse the authority structure of these families and threaten the parents, especially the father. When there are no native-speaking therapists available, an adult interpreter is recommended (Falicov, 1998; Kline et al., 1980).

Because therapists are perceived as authority figures, they need to assume an active role in the beginning phase of the therapy process. To minimize the unnaturalness of the initial therapist-family contact, Minuchin's (1974) maintenance technique, which "requires the therapist to be organized by the basic rules that regulate the transactional process in a specific family system" (p. 175), is helpful. For instance, given that the social interaction of the Latino is governed by a hierarchical role structure, the therapist should address the father first. The therapist's willingness to answer personal questions and receive a small token or gift is consistent with the Asian's "interpersonal grace" and Latino's "personalismo." Additionally, therapist should allow themselves and a First Nations family or family member ample time to gather their thoughts and emotions before pressing on to a new topic. Low-income ethnic minority families are often so overwhelmed by multiple problems and the anxiety associated with seeking help that informing them at the engagement phase that therapy will be long term and difficult may be self-defeating for the therapist.

Clinical Assessment as Critical Reflection

Family therapists should be prepared for an *elongated assessment phase* (Rasheed & Rasheed, 1999) because of the unique and complex societal factors affecting the lives of Latino families. Family therapists are also encouraged to use an *ethnographic* (anthropological) *approach* to assessing families (Rasheed & Rasheed, 1999) and to "view the family as tiny societies that over time, seem to develop their own systems of meaning and beliefs, their own mythologies, and ritual practices, and their own cultures" (Laird, 1993, p. 80).

Understanding and assessing the presenting problems of ethnic minority families requires a broad conceptual lens that includes multiple levels of assessment.

There is a unique constellation of data that needs to be collected in practice with ethnic minority families so that the family and the therapist may "coinvestigate" personal, social, and ethnocultural realities in the family's life space to identify meaningful themes related to sociopolitical and relational constraints (Rasheed & Rasheed, 1999). This stage of clinical assessment is followed by the process in which problems and contradictions in experiences are identified, with an emphasis on the contextual issues. As problems are identified, some are redefined, and an unfolding "restorying process" is initiated. A new liberating perspective is identified (Laird, 1989), and this liberating perspective is not just intra- or interpersonal; it takes on the quality of understanding how the ethnic minority family or family member's social, cultural, political, and economic context affects the family's or individual's sense of personal and social power. This process encourages a reconnection with self and culture. It also allows the individual to be aware of the ability to reconstruct his or her own reality.

Ivey (1995) provides the following assessment questions, which can be helpful at this stage of critical reflection:

- What do our family and our educational work history say about the development and operation of oppression?
- What is common to our stories? What are the patterns (themes)?
- How does each family member think (differently) about these stories, and how could each think about them differently?
- Which of your behaviors and thoughts are yours? Which of them come from your cultural surrounding and life history?
- How do family stories and family history relate to your conception of self? Of your cultural background? How do the two relate?
- What parts of you are driven by internal forces and what parts are driven by external forces? How can you tell the difference?
- Standing back, what inconsistencies can you identify in yourself?
- What rules (social, familial, cultural, etc.) have you (or anyone in the family) been operating under? Where did the rule come from? How might someone else describe that situation (another family member, a member of the dominant group, or another person of color)? How do these rules relate to us now?
- What shall we do now? How shall we do it together? What is our objective and how can we work together effectively? Or, how can the client-colleague manage his or her own affairs and take action as a leader in his or her own right? (pp. 68-69)

These questions have experiential and existential import—that is, they connect the presenting problem with the larger sociopolitical themes of ethnic minority families. The questions allow for critical inquiry about the specific social contexts or social locations in which these families' multiple experiences are embedded. This inquiry allows both the family therapist and the family member to identify the unique impact of the ethnic family's experiences with oppression and the inherent contradictions emerging from family members' positions with respect to multiple sociopolitical locations. Equally important, this critical reflection allows for an understanding of whether the ethnic minority family has internalized narratives that are supportive, liberating, and potentiating or narratives that are constricting or destructive.

Cultural Transitional Mapping and Data Collection

The techniques of *culture mapping* and *genograms* (Pendagast & Sherman, 1977) can provide insight into family members' intergenerational perspectives and differing levels of acculturation. Relevant personal, familial, and community information and cultural mapping can be extremely helpful in the assessment of ethnic minority families, which undergo rapid social change and cultural transition. Data that include the process (and stage) of cultural adaptation, as well as the acculturation level, are critical toward developing culturally relevant and culturally sensitive interventive goals for families and family members. Listed here is a summary of the social and cultural data that should be included.

- Assessment of migration stress: the stage of migration that the family is currently in and how it has dealt with previous migrational phases (and the age of each family member at the time of immigration); general migration history (e.g., reason for leaving; who left first and who was left behind; who was the sponsor; experiences of trauma before, during, and after migration; types of losses incurred by the family and its members); level of support from family, country, and friends; social and economic status of the family; and major political changes and events (during the preparatory stage and the migration)
- Language or dialect spoken (including the degree of comfort ability in "code switching" within the clinical interview)
- Foreign and/or Western medicines used, use of herbal remedies
- Help-seeking behavior patterns, including the use of indigenous folk healers
- Years in the United States, country of origin, and immigration status (the therapist must be very careful not to alarm family members who may have undocumented status)
- Work and school history in the country of origin and in the United States
- Position and life cycle stages of each individual and the family as a whole

- Family form and acculturation levels of extended family members
- Religion, religious participation
- Gender and age issues affecting level of acculturation and cultural adaptation
- Ethnic density of current neighborhood
- Ethnic and cultural pride
- Past and present exposure to Western culture

Techniques in data collection with ethnic minorities require more than the usual question and answer mode of communication. The use of home visits, family photographs, published poetry (as well as poetry written by family members), paintings, and native music can facilitate interaction and generate meaningful information (Ho & Settles, 1984).

Many ethnic minority families, especially Latinos, First Nations peoples, and African Americans, practice informal adoption or "child keeping." Consequently, their genograms seldom conform completely to bloodlines (Hines & Boyd-Franklin, 1996). Therefore, to obtain accurate information, the therapist needs to inquire about who the client considers to be in the family, the presence of fictive kin (e.g., "play relatives," compadrazcos, madrinas, padrinos), and who lives in the home.

Ethnic minority families have endured race-related trauma and "historical trauma," and therapists must thus be sensitive when asking questions. The therapist should look for an opportunity or a natural opening to gather the desired information, rather than adhering to an inflexible schedule. Patience and sensitivity in collecting the above data is likely to yield far better results than hurried, mechanistic data collecting.

Mutual Goal Setting

Therapeutic goals with ethnic minority families can be divided into three categories (Falicov, 1982, 1998): (a) goals related to situational stress (e.g., social isolation, poverty) caused by interface between the family and the new environment, (b) goals related to dysfunctional patterns of cultural transition (e.g., parent-child role reversal, conflictual child-rearing practices), and (c) goals related to transcultural dysfunctional patterns (e.g., universal family problems such as developmental impasses and limited range of repetitive interactional behaviors). Minorities are forced to adjust to mainstream society. Goal setting with an ethnic minority family requires an *ecostructural approach* (Aponte, 1979) that considers the "incompleteness" (basic survival needs) that many ethnic minority families experience.

The process of mutual goal formulation requires that the therapist adhere to the value orientation of a specific ethnic minority family. Individual psychologically oriented goals that are not accompanied by other ecosystemic interventions will not fit well with ethnic minorities' emphasis on familismo and interdependence. Therapy goals that do not reflect a person's determinants or self-centeredness but emphasize rehabilitation after physical or organic illness may be more acceptable to ethnic minorities, especially Asian Americans. An ethnic minority client may be reluctant to formulate goals that benefit only him- or herself. Ethnic family structure places strong emphasis on the parent-child relationship. Early therapeutic goals emphasizing only the improvement of the couple relationship are likely to meet with resistance. Because of the family's involvement with the extended family, the process of goal formulation should involve all family members, including extended family members. The hierarchical or egalitarian structure of the family should be recognized in the mutual goal formulation process.

Intergenerational perspectives can be influential; however, therapy goals should not dwell on the parents' families of origin or multigenerational transmission, because these subjects may be too threatening, too time-consuming, and antithetical to ethnic minorities' "present" and "doing" orientation. This orientation, in addition to linguistic complexities and language barriers, requires that therapeutic goals be problem focused, structured, realistic, concrete, practical, and readily achievable (Acosta et al., 1982; Edwards & Edwards, 1984; Murase & Johnson, 1974). Minuchin (1967) reaffirms that when patterns of change in the family are out of phase with the realities of extrafamilial systems, therapy will fail. He refers to the technique used to elicit information about this situation as "probing for flexibility in the system." Aponte (1979) also emphasizes the need to formulate therapeutic goals that can produce immediate success (power) in clients' lives.

Selecting a Focus or System for Therapy

Once the problem is identified and the therapeutic goal is formulated, the system selected for therapy can determine the outcome. Understanding and respecting the ethnic minority family's cultural norms and present social context are perhaps the most important skills when selecting a subsystem unit for therapy. Considering the intense involvement that ethnic minority families have with their extended family, some family problems can be resolved simply by involving the extended family members, especially the spokesperson, who typically may be the grandfather (with Asian and Latino families) or grandmother (African American and First Nations families). McAdoo (1977), however, points out that sometimes extended family kinship bonds can be a source of family conflict. Regardless, resolution of family problems within the immediate nuclear family will probably require the involvement of some extended family members.

The family's need for privacy and the hierarchical and vertical structure of Asian and Latino families may discourage family members from showing their true thoughts and negative feelings. A separate session with children may be in order so that issues they may not normally discuss in their parents' presence may be negotiated. The strengthening and restructuring of the sibling subsystem can extricate an overprotected child from the parental subsystem. A separate session with the parents need not focus exclusively on the conjugal relationship. Instead, emphasis can be on how the parents can relate to their child in a "united" manner that fosters a harmonious living environment desired by all family members. Considering the importance that machismo (Latino) and face (Asian) play in the father's role as head of the family, conjoint family sessions with every family member or with the wife present may be too threatening to the Asian or Latino father. Hence Bowen's (1978) therapeutic, flexible strategy of focusing only on one person (preferably, the father) may be most appropriate. This approach is also relevant to working with African American or First Nations fathers who feel peripheral in their family.

The Use of an Ecomap

In view of immigration, the acculturation process, cultural and language barriers, and poverty factors, therapy with ethnic minority clients must employ an ecostructural approach. The ecomap developed and advanced by Hartman (1979) is a useful and practical technique that visually depicts the family's relationship with its environment. It identifies and characterizes the important supportive or conflict-laden connection between the family and the environment. It also identifies emotional and interactive relationships within the family and its connection with the outside world. The comprehensive picture of the family's major themes and patterns identified by an ecomap, in turn, gives direction to the planning process and keeps both the therapist and the family from getting lost in details. The ecomap is a paper-and-pencil simulation of the family's life space, and it is visual, concrete, and easy to complete. It is highly relevant for all ethnic minority families who may be responsive to activity-oriented processes—especially those targeted at creating a more enabling niche in their life space.

Clinical Intervention as Liberating Action

Liberating action gives birth to a state of critical consciousness. Liberating action, then, is the basis and goal of intervention with ethnic minority families as critical reflection and action are the basis for personal, interpersonal, and social change. Franz Fanon (1967) gives direction to the need for liberating action:

When the Negro makes contact with the White world, a certain sensitizing action takes place. If his psychic structure is weak, one observes a collapse of the ego. The Black Man stops behaving as an actional person. The goal of his behavior will be The Other (in guise of a White man). For the Other alone can give his worth . . . self esteem. (p. 154)

Freire (1973) echoes these sentiments:

One of the basic elements of the relationship between the oppressors and the oppressed is prescription. Every prescription represents the imposition of one man's choice upon another, transforming the consciousness of the man transcribed into one that conforms with the prescriber's consciousness. Thus, the behavior of the oppressed is prescribed behavior, following as it does the guidelines of the oppressor. The oppressed having internalized the image of the oppressor and adopted his guidelines are fearful of freedom. Freedom would require them to reject this image and replace it with autonomy and responsibility. Freedom is acquired by conquest, not by gift. It must be pursued constantly and responsibly. Freedom is not an ideal located outside of man. (p. 31)

Hence, Fanon (1967) and Freire (1973) assert that one of the main impacts of racism and oppression is that it fragments the self and robs a person of a sense of "agency" or purpose. Thus, by implication, the goals of clinical intervention with ethnic minority families are to restore and strengthen the autonomous functioning of the ego, achieve a sense of autonomy from the "The Other" (i.e., the oppressor), and encourage ethnic minority family members to be "actional persons."

Liberation is achieved through the capacity to understand the internalization of oppression through narratives that prescribe behaviors gleaned from the perspective of the oppressor and to say "no" to those prescriptions. This rejection is achieved through the creation of alternate narratives, as Freire (1973) points out. This sense of autonomy may not be easily achieved; it requires inner struggle that leads to outside action.

The nature of this struggle is articulated by Wimberly (1997b) in his description of the process of reauthoring one's narrative. According to Wimberly, the reauthoring process, although possible and necessary, is not easy. Even though life narratives (worldviews) emerge from the lived experiences of the narrator and are given meaning through the process of social interaction, they often seem fixed, immutable, and have a sense of ontological authenticity. These narratives, however, can be challenged by significant life transitions and crisis (e.g., immigration, cultural transition, acculturation, ethnic identity crisis, and bicultural conflicts). Such a crisis can shatter the existing narrative and thus precipitate a restorying process

Table 6.3   Goal-Related Techniques and Skills for the Problem-Solving Phase of
Therapy With Ethnic Minority Families

	Therapeutic Goals	
Situational Stress	Cultural Transitional Conflicts	Conflicts Within the Family
Mobilizing and restructuring the extended family network	Indirectness	Self-observation as a tool for family restructuring
Collaborative work with a medicine person, folk healer, or paraprofessional	Social-moral and organic reframing	Paradoxical intervention
Home visits	Promoting interdependence, family obligation	Employing a therapist helper
Employing role models and the educator and advocate roles	Restructuring cultural taboos	Team approach

that enables one to meet new challenges or to explain a current situation that has
great emotional significance. Reauthoring, restorying, or reediting one's ethnic
(identity) narrative can open up new possibilities that might otherwise be hidden or
not allowed to come forth. White and Epston (1990) describe this process as dis-
covering hidden possibilities or "historically unique outcomes" (p. 56).

The Problem-Solving Phase

There are 12 generic techniques and skills that are particularly relevant in the
problem-solving phase of therapy with ethnic minority families. These techniques
and skills can be categorized according to the specific therapeutic goal to be
accomplished. As stated earlier, there are three therapeutic goals characteristic of
therapy with ethnic minorities (Falicov, 1998). These goals involve resolution of
(a) situational stress, (b) cultural transitional conflicts, and (c) conflicts within the
family. Table 6.3 presents goal-related techniques and skills in the problem-solving
phase of therapy with ethnic minority families.

Techniques and Skills in Resolving Situational Stress

There are myriad environmental issues (economic, political, and social) that
typically face ethnic minority families regardless of immigration, refugee, migration, or acculturation status. These very real ecological concerns can have a very

debilitating impact on families and family members' psyches and psychological functioning. It is not hard to imagine an individual who becomes defined by these numerous ecological obstacles. We recall a sermon given in 2002 by a guest minister in our church (who at the time had terminal cancer, but no one knew this). She spoke eloquently of "not allowing your problems to define who you are." She further admonished parishioners "not to carry their problems around like an albatross, allowing the problem to announce their entrance into a room." We couldn't help but reflect that her problem (terminal cancer) had the potential to totally define who she was and what she would become. None of us knew then that she would die within 6 months of that powerful sermon. In fact, no one would have faulted her if she had succumbed to the dying cancer patient identity, for that was the harsh reality of her existence.

Relating the above scenario to family therapy situations, one can also understand how the oppressed, victimized, powerless, and possibly traumatized ethnic minority individual or family can arrive at what the postmodernists refer to as a "problem-saturated narrative." The environmental problems are very real and quite sobering. To attempt to render these real problems as *annoying cognitive dilemmas* that can be *reframed away* is ludicrous. The family therapist, however, is in a position to engage the family in a process of *deconstructing the mechanisms of subjugation* by encouraging the *reauthoring of the ethnic narrative* by retrieving alternative knowledge of family endurance, perseverance, survival, and celebration. We support a movement away from the historically concept of the victim system, which we think can contribute to a victim mentality. All this is not to eschew other important functions and responsibilities of family therapists, specifically, to assist ethnic minority families to resolve situational stressors caused by the family's transactions with a hostile, racist, and oppressive environment.

Four techniques and skills are relevant in assisting the ethnic minority family to resolve situational stress caused by the family's interaction with a debilitating ecological niche. These techniques and skills include: mobilizing and restructuring the extended family network; collaborative work with a medicine person, folk healer, or paraprofessional; home visits; and employing role models, the educator role, and the advocate role.

Mobilizing and restructuring the extended family network. One of the factors plaguing many ethnic minority families is the lack of extended family support due to the fact that the family has immigrated (Asian and Latino) or migrated (First Nations peoples and African Americans) from its native environment where mutual inter- and intrafamily support was strong. Studies have indicated that ethnic minority families make use of the extended family network much more extensively than white American families (Hsu, 1972; McAdoo, 1978; Mindel, 1980; Red Horse, 1980b). A social support network is essential for ethnic minority

Americans who need a place and a way to bridge the ecological deficit, to ventilate frustration, to learn acculturated social skills, to form friendships, and to reconnect with their culture of origin. In an effort to mobilize social networks, the therapist's role may become that of a "social intermediary" (Minuchin, 1974, p. 63), a system guide, or a broker (Bowen, 1978).

Collaborative work with a medicine person, folk healer, or paraprofessional. Ethnic minority families may still resist certain aspects of the dominant culture, particularly the use of a healthcare provider or family therapist. A medicine person, shaman, or other religious or spiritual leader can play a vital role in resolving situational stress in the lives of many ethnic minority families. Even among bicultural families, the need for a medicine person or religious or spiritual leader is still prevalent. Latino folk practitioners ave demonstrated the acculturational function of "espiritismo" (Douglas, 1974), problem-solving skills of "santeria" (De La Cancela, 1978), and the reassurance of "curanderismo" (Kiev, 1968). Hence a family therapist should not hesitate to consult with a bonafide (culturally sanctioned) folk healer or religious or spiritual leader when the need arises. The folk healer or religious or spiritual leader should always be treated with professional integrity and respect.

Home visits. Ethnic minority families may lack specific knowledge about mental health services and family therapy. They may have limited financial resources and transportation problems. Home visits are a logical and practical tool for reaching such clients. The advantages of home visits in therapy with ethnic minority families include seeing the family in their natural environment (Carter, 1976), personalizing and joining the family in an emotional sense (Spiegel, 1959), and helping the family feel at ease. Home visits should be prearranged and conducted in a culturally appropriate manner that is nonintrusive but spontaneous and flexible.

Employing role models and the educator and advocate roles. Migration and acculturation often create confusion and disorganization for individual members as well as for the whole ethnic minority family. Traditional role modeling might have been functional in the past, but it becomes dysfunctional as family members experience different cultural norms and life cycles. Many First Nations peoples grew up and were educated in boarding schools and out-of-home placements. As a direct result, they lacked appropriate and clear parental role models. The therapist's roles of cultural translator, mediator, and model (DeAnda, 1984; Minuchin, 1974) are vital in helping the family resolve situational stress and form an open system with available community resources. Guided by communication practice principles, a therapist can teach a family, through role modeling, the skills essential for open and congruent communication (Satir, 1967).

Because many ethnic minority families are the victims of race-related trauma and intentional and unintentional indifference by agencies and institutions essential to their survival and well-being, the therapist may need to serve as an advocate for the family. Ethnic minority families do not wish to elicit sympathy or draw public attention to themselves. It is important that the therapist's biased advocate role on their behalf not subject them to further agency humiliation or discrimination.

Techniques and Skills in Resolving Cultural Transitional Problems

To assist ethnic minority families in resolving problems that are caused mainly by cultural conflict with the dominant society, specific techniques and skills are necessary. They include the use of *indirectness* and *postmodern problem-solving techniques* (*taking a narrative stance, engaging in reflective dialogue,* and *critically reflecting on the multiple [emotional] meanings of messages*).

Indirectness. Ethnic minority families, especially Asians, Latinos, and First Nations, may be highly sensitive to authority figures (including the therapist). The communication patterns of these families should be respected and observed. Thus the open, direct, congruent communication essential for problem solving may need some tempering, particularly during the early stage of therapy. Examples of direct communication such as, "Tell your wife what you really think of her," may need to be rephrased as, "Please comment on the things your wife does that contribute to the family." Such indirectness may be time consuming and nonspecific, but it conveys moderation and respect, which all ethnic minority families cherish. Indirectness can be altered when the family decides to deal with problems directly.

Postmodern problem-solving techniques. The meaning or interpretation that results when various family members take a *narrative stance* in attempts to sort out family problems may not be exact; hence the parties can be encouraged to engage in *reflective dialogue* and *critically reflect* on the *multiple emotional meanings* that each family member has attached to the presenting problem, as reflected in the individual narratives (Rasheed & Rasheed, 1999). For example, stressful experiences of migration can be reflected up to help family members become more attuned with how each family member uniquely experiences cultural transitions. Further exploration using this reflective dialogue can help the parties discover the positive feelings of concern, respect, and value that each has in their relationships with each other and the determination and desire for the family to survive stressful events such as the immigration, migration, acculturation, and assimilation processes.

Techniques and Skills for
Resolving Family Relationship Problems

To assist an ethnic minority family in resolving internal relationship conflicts, two generic techniques and skills are presented. They are employing a therapist-helper and the team approach.

Employing a therapist helper. The therapist helper approach is indicated when an ethnic minority family is highly resistant (especially in involuntary cases, e.g., court-mandated), when therapists suspect that the client is "misinterpreting" cultural practices in the service of resistance or is unfamiliar with the concept of family therapy, and when there is a definite language barrier between the therapist and the family. Additionally, this approach provides the family with a normal course of problem solving and an acculturation direction uninfluenced by the therapist. It is consistent with cultural norms and expectations to find a mature bicultural male compatible in therapy with a Latino or Asian American family. Grandparents of either sex may work well with African American or First Nations families. In some instances, the therapist helper does not need to be a member of the extended family but could be a highly trusted and respected individual. Extensive planning and consultative sessions with the therapist helper are needed to make the technique a success.

Team approach. The team approach is especially helpful in therapy with an ethnic minority family in which multiple members have numerous problems. Advantages of this approach include spontaneously meeting different family members' needs, provision of emotional and affective bondage with different family members, provision of a role model for problem solving, development of a more accurate assessment and interventive plan, assurance of continuity of therapy, and avoidance of professional burnout. Potential disadvantages of the team approach in work with ethnic minority families include disorganization and fragmentation, its time-consuming nature, therapists' conflicts, and excessive cost.

Evaluation and Termination Phase

To determine if a specific goal has been accomplished through family therapy with an ethnic minority family, the ecological framework of evaluation is particularly helpful. This framework consists of four major categories: the family-environment interface, family structure, family processes (communication and interaction), and individual symptoms and character traits. In assessing therapeutic goals relating to dysfunctional patterns of cultural transition or transcultural dysfunctional patterns, a therapist needs to be cognizant of the unique perspective of each ethnic minority culture. The intense interactive subsystem relationship characteristic of a nuclear family in a dominant society should not be used as a yardstick in evaluating the functional structure and transaction of an ethnic minority family. Instead, the inclusive, extended family framework should be kept in mind when evaluating a family's functioning.

Ethnic minority Americans may not verbally express the progress they make in therapy. Thus therapists may need to maximize their observational skills in evaluating the family's progress. A therapist may need to participate in and be a part of the family's activities, including home visits and participation in seasonal ceremonies and other cultural rituals.

The termination process should take into consideration the ethnic minority client's concept of time and space in a relationship. Some families may never want to end a good relationship, and they may learn to respect and love the therapist as a member of their family. It is important that a therapist be comfortable with this element of cultural and human inclusiveness and make termination a natural and gradual process.

PART 3: CULTURALLY RELEVANT TECHNIQUES AND SKILLS FOR SPECIFIC THERAPY MODALITIES

Couple Therapy

The divorce rate among Asians and Latinos is relatively low compared to the rate for First Nations peoples and African Americans (U.S. Census Bureau, 2001a). Nevertheless, the process of acculturation and the changed roles and status of both husband and wife make conjugal adjustment extremely vulnerable to difficulties. Factors contributing to the high divorce rate among African Americans and First Nations peoples include high rates of unemployment (for husbands), incarceration, mortality, homicide, and suicide.

Couple therapy with ethnic minorities must consider the extended family system framework. Therapists must be careful not to misinterpret close relationships with family-of-origin members as enmeshment. Bowen's (1978) intergenerational perspective can be used to assist the partners to work out inter- and multigenerational relational difficulties, especially those that arise out of acculturative conflicts and tensions. When they work collaboratively with respected extended family members (e.g., the padrino of the Latino family), couples' conflicts can be resolved in a culturally relevant manner. Couple therapy for family problem solving may be a very new concept to ethnic minority couples. Only the upper or middle class and more acculturated couples may seek couple therapy for their relationship problems (Falicov, 1998). Because of the hierarchical role structure of Asian and Latino couples' relationship, the wife may be reluctant to challenge her husband's traditional conjugal role as authoritarian, especially openly in the therapist's presence (particularly if the therapist is a female). Individual interviews can be used to bridge the gap. Advantages of using the individual interview at the beginning phase of couple therapy include development of rapport and trust (the technique is face saving for Asians and demonstrates personalismo with Latinos) and the possible disclosure of intimate information such as extramarital affairs or incest. Bowen's (1978) calm, unemotional, but interested approach can be most effective in assisting the individual spouse to gain a cognitive understanding of the problem.

Ethnic minority parents (especially the wife-mother) may feel a strong responsibility to their children. The therapist should not employ couple therapy prematurely as a means to resolve parent-child problems. The spousal subsystem can be repaired directly or indirectly by focusing on the parents' newly learned alternative transactions with the child.

Divorce Therapy

In addition to factors such as the breakdown of extended family ties, high rates of unemployment, unmet physical and economic needs, poor physical and mental health, high rates of alcoholism and attempted suicides, and intermarriages, First Nations' and African Americans' traditional respect for a person's right to make his or her own decisions and their strong belief in noninterference make divorce a socially acceptable behavior with very little negative stigma attached. Conversely, traditional Asian Americans consider divorce a family disgrace. The strong Catholic influence upon Latinos probably contributes to their relatively low divorce rate and, consequently, the stigma attached to divorce. The attitude of different ethnic groups toward divorce greatly affects the decision for divorce and the adjustment of the divorced partners. For instance, among First Nations peoples and African Americans, the extended family's relative acceptance of divorce greatly facilitates adjustment to a divorce. Contrarily, an Asian or Latino divorcee may risk ostracism from the extended family or the Catholic Church, making the adjustment more traumatic and difficult.

Typically only the more acculturated and financially secure ethnic minority couples will seek divorce therapy. The majority of divorce therapy clients seek help during moments of crisis, such as when the husband abruptly decides to get a legal divorce, the wife decides to divorce her husband because of excessive physical abuse, or in cases of child custody struggles. In either instance, divorce therapy with ethnic minority clients is often conducted under extremely stressful circumstances. It requires quick decisions on the part of the client and the therapist (especially in light of limited economic resources that will become even more scarce after the family separates).

The strength of family ties among ethnic minorities is a valuable asset for clients experiencing divorce. Extended families are the natural resource for emotional support and can often provide financial help, child care, household help, and so on. The therapist at this stage should assist the client in reconnecting with the extended family system. Some families, especially Asian and Latino, may withdraw support and sympathy from the client. The therapist's role is often that of a systems broker who helps the client secure new support systems, preferably with other divorced people who have shared similar experiences. In situations where there is a relatively nonromantic involvement, as is the case in some traditional ethnic minority marriages, especially among Asians, Latinos, and First Nations peoples, emotional termination and adjustment to life without the spouse may be less traumatic than in romantic marriages.

Single-Parent Therapy

The process of immigration and acculturation, increased divorce and separation, a dramatic increase in teen pregnancy (among Latinas and African American girls), as well as decisions to have children without the benefit of marriage has increased the number of female-headed families among ethnic minority Americans (National Urban League, 2002). Many such females fit the description of members of the "at-risk population," who are characterized by receiving Aid to Dependent Children, emotional depression, social isolation, and crisis emergencies. Although ethnic minority American women are known for their hard-working attitude and resourcefulness, the demands of single parenthood may far exceed the single parent's ability to cope.

The extended family can be a significant source of support and self-esteem for an ethnic minority single parent (Fitzpatrick, 1981; Hsu, 1972; Red Horse, 1980a; Stack, 1974). However, for recently arrived immigrants (Asians and Latinos), family support systems may not be readily available. Unemployment, pride, geographical location, differences in acculturative behaviors, reluctance to become a burden to aging parents, and strained relationships with parents can cause single parents not to return to their relatives after divorce. In such cases, other support network resources should be found. These can be new friendship ties, especially other single mothers, women's support groups, and social activity groups that can help the single-parent family adjust during this transitional period.

Among ethnic minority families, it is not unusual for a key male figure, such as an uncle, grandfather, or other spouse equivalent, to be present in the single-parent household (McLanahan, Wedemeyer, & Adelberg, 1981; Stack, 1974). Therapists who are aware of this individual or conjugal partner can introduce the option of involving this person in matters that concern the welfare of the single parent or in child-rearing practices.

The absence of the father from the household requires family renegotiation and a restructuring of the family system boundary (Minuchin, 1974). However, therapists are strongly cautioned not to relegate fathers to the margins of their practice efforts with single parent female-headed families, which serves only to reify societal stereotypes about the absentee (minority) father. Due to the acculturation process and single parents' possible lack of parenting skills, therapists need to adopt an educative role in assisting any single parent who is experiencing this transitional period. The collateral orientations of many ethnic minority clients who are single parents necessitate the therapist's focusing the attention first on the child (or children) and second on the care of the mother.

Reconstituted Family Therapy

Ethnic minority families have strong ties, obligations, and loyalties to their families of origin. Problems may abound when an exspouse with children remarries. Some ethnic minority Americans remarry because of love and affection for their children and a strong desire to do what is best for their children. Problems arise when children encounter conflicts with their stepparent or stepbrothers or stepsisters. If children are no longer happy, as originally anticipated by the parents, the second marriage may dissolve.

Many ethnic minority families (especially First Nations peoples and African Americans) have experienced living in extended families and households. The reconstituted family phenomenon (step- and blended families) should present fewer problems for them than it does for dominant culture families whose past experiences are limited to the single-household nuclear family. It has also been a common practice among African Americans and Latinos for adults to raise children who are not their own (Garcia-Preto, 1996b).

In therapy with a reconstituted ethnic minority family, the focus should be on repairing or strengthening the parental subsystem (Duberman, 1975; Satir, 1967). The therapist may encounter resistance, for many ethnic minority mothers are more devoted to motherly love for their children than to maintaining a close relationship with their husbands. It is important that the therapist emphasize to parents, especially the mother, that a strong conjugal coalition is a prerequisite to ensure the healthy and normal development of all children in a reconstituted family. Interviewing the parents separately has been found helpful in repairing or establishing the parental bond. Feelings about previous marriage(s) and the legal settlement involving custody, visitation, financial support, and current child-rearing practices need to be expressed and discussed by the couple. Some ethnic minority couples, especially Asians and Latinos, may need help in problem-solving skills characteristic of an egalitarian relationship. As a strategy to decentralize the stepmother's role in her children's lives in the reconstituted family, some authors (Carter & McGoldrick, 1980; Haley, 1976; Minuchin, 1974) suggest that she take a passive role, thus allowing the stepfather to take charge of the stepchildren. This directive may be in conflict with the beliefs of ethnic minority cultures that prescribe a woman's responsibility as the care of her children. A more culturally relevant directive that aims to dilute the mother-child emotional intensity is strengthening the spousal subsystem or father-stepchild subsystem. The reconstituted couple's extended family ties can be a source of interference, prohibiting the couple from forming a strong coalition or effectively rearing the children. The therapist may need to mediate between the reconstituted family and extended family members from previous marriages.

PART 5: SUMMARY

A close examination and analysis of different ethnic minority families' cultural values and family structure clearly indicate that although the traditional family therapy model, based on middle class white American culture, generally is helpful and applicable, it can sometimes be impractical, ineffective, and at times harmful. Certain commonalities are shared by middle class white American families and by different ethnic minority families, but vast differences also exist. These differences include the extent to which each ethnic minority family has to struggle daily with political discrimination, unemployment, poverty, poor physical and mental health, immigration and acculturation problems, and language and linguistic barriers. Between ethnic minority groups, there are both differences and similarities, including how each family group is structured and how it copes with a hostile external environment, negotiates differences, adjusts to changes, resolves problems, and responds to family therapy. This chapter represents an attempt to synthesize and systematize the degree of interethnic minority group variance regarding cultural orientation and the effect of this variance on the family therapy process and outcome for four ethnic groups: African Americans, Asian and Pacific Islander Americans, Latinos, and First Nations peoples.

The interventive principles of system communication and family structure theories have been demonstrated to be quite relevant in explaining how an ethnic minority family may respond to society and how family members may interact with each other within the family. The practice principles of these two family system theories need further exploration, elaboration, and specification to make them culturally relevant and ethnically specific. In addition, the ecological, systemic, and emic (culture-specific) approaches and the critical constructionist perspective must be the guiding framework by which to intervene effectively and prevent problems generally plaguing ethnic minority families.

The effectiveness of a family therapist also depends on the therapist's self-awareness of his or her own ethnic background and how this affects therapy with different ethnic minority groups. The need for bicultural and bilingual therapists is obvious. Effective family therapy with ethnic minority families requires that the therapist be sensitive and flexible in responding to the clients' cultural orientations regarding time and space. The routine 50-minute session within the 8:00 a.m. to 5:00 p.m. time frame conducted in an office is not a viable and responsive approach to all minority clients' needs. Instead, a block of time of 2 or 3 or more hours for a session in the client's own home environment may become more the rule than the exception in therapy with ethnic minority families. The extra time and effort demanded of a therapist can easily cause professional burnout. Hence ethnic-sensitive agency administrators or supervisors also need to provide therapists with reduced caseloads, greater flexibility of time, and more autonomy.

Family therapy with ethnic minority families still is in its infancy. A great effort is needed to continue to explore, explicate, and systematize family therapy knowledge and practice principles that are oppression-sensitive, culturally relevant, and ethnically specific.

Conclusion

Throughout this book, we have emphasized the importance of using a critical constructionist perspective within an ecological framework and incorporating culturally specific (emic) values in couple and family therapy with American ethnic minority families. This (theoretically and conceptually) integrative approach to family therapy is crucial to family-based interventions with ethnic minority families; it has the potential to move family practice beyond the narrow conceptualization of family-based problems and further integrate the roles of therapist and advocate. We hope that the result will be a more integrative approach that encourages family therapists to allow the family therapy process to be guided by a vision of social justice.

NOTES

1. There have been a number of different terms and definitions that have been applied to describe Asian and Pacific Islander Americans, First Nations peoples, Latinos, and African Americans in the United States. Examples of such terms include *people of color, Third World people, racial minorities, linguistic minorities, culturally different, oppressed minorities,* and *ethnic minorities.* In this book (and in keeping with the original term employed by Dr. Ho), the term *ethnic minority* is used because it encompasses elements that are important in providing effective service to this specific population. *Ethnicity* denotes cultural distinctiveness, which supplies meaning to the cross-cultural encounter between the therapist and the clients. *Minority* refers to a group of political and economic individuals who are relatively powerless, receive unequal treatment, and regard themselves as objects of discrimination.

2. We acknowledge and apologize for the use of any negative or pejorative meanings that may be inferred from the use of any terms used in this book to describe and classify certain ethnic groups. It is not our intent to determine or establish "correct" or even politically correct ethnic terms and definitions. At all times, we availed ourselves of the special knowledge and wisdom of culturally specific experts. We have no doubt that we may have inadvertently used an unfortunate term here or there despite our best efforts to avoid such. We invite the readers to write us at our respective universities to help us continue our own cultural sensitivity training.

3. The *therapeutic encounter* requires that the therapist learn from the clients about their cultural values, signs, and behavioral styles. Hence the term "ethnic minority" is more than a categorical description of race, culture, or color. It is the boundaries of separation and, in particular, how these boundaries are managed, protected, ritualized through stereotyping, and sometimes violated that is of primary interest and concern for family therapy.

4. The incorporation of the critical constructionist framework or perspective (carefully outlined in detail in chapter 1 of this book) is seen as an important conceptual development in the family practice field that occurred since the writing of the first edition of this book. Hence, this framework is incorporated into the second edition of this volume. The critical constructionist perspective is viewed as a critical, conceptual leap in our field, with the potential to appropriately acknowledge the deleterious (but quite varied) impact of racism and discrimination on the family life and process of ethnic minority families.

5. The apprehension that we felt in writing about ethnocultural groups outside of our own tripled as we approached the writing of this particular chapter. Instead of naming this chapter "Family Therapy with First Nations Peoples," we really wanted the title to read, "This Chapter Should Have Been Written by a First Nations Person." Undoubtedly, this chapter as well as the others would have been greatly enhanced if written from an insider perspective. However, had we not felt that it was possible to write or work with families outside of one's own ethnocultural group, there really would not be a need for this book at

all. We certainly hope that we did not do an injustice to this or any of the other ethnocultural groups previously or subsequently discussed in this volume. We also hope that our
willingness to study, read, and write about ethnocultural groups outside of our own
(African American) culture will be received positively and viewed as encouragement for
those family therapists faced with the challenge of working with families outside of their
own ethnocultural group.

6. In an excursion we took to the Southwest Pueblos, we had been told to be certain to
visit a particular roadside vendor who was widely known for his exquisite breads and
honey. We finally found this vendor, late in the day, only to find out that the vendor (a
member of the Taos Pueblos) had sold all of the food items that day. We were caught off
guard with the manner in which the vendor informed us that he had sold out; he cheerfully
(and unapologetically) told us to come back tomorrow. Instead of being apologetic and
viewing our request for his wares as some sort of unfortunate business mishap, his running
out of food items and his tone and mannerisms clearly expressed a sense of pride, joy, satisfaction, and accomplishment that he had, indeed, been able to sell all of his items that
day. He was clearly in a celebratory mood and seemed to expect that we would be happy
for him. We looked at each other, being both amused and ashamed of our (own) myopic
assumptions of how we had expected this vendor would respond to our requests. When we
piled back into the car, we affirmed how we both had interpreted the vendor's communication (and *metacommunication*). We left the site knowing that we had received an important education and had been exposed to a philosophy of life, a way of being that felt so
much more humanistic (and pragmatic) than our own.

7. For an in-depth understanding about how Latino families encounter life transitions
based on Latino value orientations, see Falicov (1998, 1999), Garcia-Preto (1996a, 1996b,
1998), Lyle and Faure (2000), and Santiago-Rivera et al. (2002).

REFERENCES

Abad, V., & Boyce, E. (1979). Issues in psychiatric evaluations of Puerto Ricans: A social-cultural perspective. *Journal of Operational Psychiatry, 10,* 28-30.

Abad, V., Ramos, G., & Boyce, E. (1974). A model for delivery of mental health services to Spanish speaking minorities. *American Journal of Orthopsychiatry, 44,* 585-495.

Acosta, F. X., Yamamoto, J., & Evans, L. A. (1982). *Effective psychotherapy with low-income and minority patients.* New York: Plenum.

Akbar, N. (1984). Africentric social sciences for human liberation. *Journal of Black Studies, 14,* 395-414.

Aldridge, D. P. (1991). *Focusing: Black male and female relationships.* Chicago: Third World.

American Association of Marriage and Family Therapists. (Producer). (1986). *Master series: Virginia Satir* [Motion picture]. (Available from the American Association of Marriage and Family Therapists, 112 S. Alfred St., Alexandria, VA 22314-3061)

Aponte, H. J. (1979). Family therapy and the community. In M. Gibbs & J. Lachenmeyer (Eds.), *Community psychology: Theoretical and empirical approaches.* New York: Gardner.

Aponte, H. J. (1994). *Bread and spirit: Therapy with the new poor.* New York: Norton.

Aponte, H. J., & DiCesare, E. J. (2000). Structural theory. In F. M. Dattilio & L. Bevilacqua (Eds.), *Comparative treatment of couples problems* (pp. 45-57). New York: Springer.

Aponte, J. E., & Wohl, J. (2000). *Psychological intervention and cultural diversity.* Des Moines, IA: Allyn & Bacon.

Ariel, S. (1999). *Culturally competent family therapy.* Westport, CT: Greenwood.

Arredondo, P., & Perez, P. (2003). Counseling paradigms and Latino/a Americans: contemporary perspectives. In F. D. Harper & J. McFadden (Eds.), *Culture and counseling* (pp. 115-132). Boston, MA: Allyn & Bacon.

Asante, M. K. (1980). *Afrocentricity: Theory of social change.* Buffalo, NY: Amulefi.

Asante, M. K. (1987). *The Afrocentric idea.* Philadelphia, PA: Temple University Press.

Attneave, C. (1982). American Indians and Alaska Native families. In M. McGoldrick, J. Giordano, & J. K. Pearce (Eds.), *Ethnicity and family therapy* (pp. 55-83). New York: Guilford.

Axelson, J. A. (1999). *Counseling and development in a multiracial society.* Pacific Grove, CA: Brooks/Cole.

Axinn, J., & Levin, H. (1997). *Social welfare: A history of American response to need.* New York: Longman.

Badillo-Ghali, S. (1974). Culture sensitivity and the Puerto Rican client. *Social Casework, 55,* 100-110.

Bamford, K. W. (1991). Bilingual issues in mental health assessment and treatment. *Hispanic Journal of Behavioral Sciences, 13*(4), 337-390.

Barlett, A. (1958). Toward clarification and improvement of social work practice. *Social Work, 3,* 3-9.

Barnett, L. D. (1963). Interracial marriage in Los Angeles, 1948-1959. *Social Force, 25,* 424-427.

Barranti, C. C. R. (2003). Communication framework. In J. Anderson & R. W. Carter (Eds.), *Diversity perspectives for social work practice.* Boston, MA: Allyn & Bacon.

Barrera, M. (1978). Mexican-American mental health service utilization: A critical examination of some proposed variables. *Community Mental Health Journal, 14,* 35-45.

Bateson, G. (1972). *Steps to an ecology of mind.* New York: Ballantine.

Bell, R. (1971). The relative importance of mother and wife roles for lower class women. In R. Staples (Ed.), *The black family: Essays and studies.* Belmont, CA: Wadsworth.

Bell, Y. R., Bouie, C. L., & Baldwin, J. (1990). Afrocentric cultural consciousness and African American male-female relationships. *Journal of Black Studies, 21,* 162-189.

Bennett, J. (1975). *The new ethnicity: Perspectives from ethnology.* St. Paul, MN: West.

Benokraitis, N. V. (1993). *Marriage and families.* Englewood Cliffs, NJ: Prentice Hall.

Berger, A., & Simon, W. (1974). Black families and the Moynihan Report: A research evaluation. *Social Problems, 22,* 145-161.

Bernal, G., & Flores-Ortiz, Y. (1982). Latino families in therapy. *Journal of Marital and Family Therapy, 8,* 357-365.

Bernal, G., & Shapiro, E. (1996). Cuban families. In M. McGoldrick, J.Giordano, & J. K. Pearce (Eds.), *Ethnicity and family therapy* (pp. 155-168). New York: Guilford.

Billingsley, A. (1968). *Black families in white America.* Englewood Cliffs, NJ: Prentice-Hall.

Billingsley, A. (1992). *Climbing Jacob's ladder: The enduring legacy of African American families.* New York: Simon & Schuster.

Blanchard, E. (1983). The growth and development of American and Alaskan Native children. In G. Powell, J. Yamamoto, A. Romero, & A. Morales (Eds.), *The psychosocial development of minority group children.* New York: Brunner/Mazel.

Boszorminyi-Nagy, I. (1987). *Foundations of contextual therapy.* New York: Brunner/Mazel.

Boszormenyi-Nagy, I., & Krasner, B. (1980). Trust based therapy: A contextual approach. *American Journal of Psychiatry, 137,* 767-775.

Bowen, M. (1976). Theory and practice of psychotherapy. In P. Guerin (Ed.), *Family therapy.* New York: Garden.

Bowen, M. (1978). *Family therapy in clinical practice.* New York: Jason Aronson.

Boyd-Franklin, N. (1989). *Black families in therapy.* New York: Guilford.

Boyd-Franklin, N. (1995). Therapy with African American inner city families. In R. H. Mikesell, D. Lusterman, & S. H. McDaniel (Eds.), *Integrating family therapy: Handbook of family psychology and systems theory.* Washington, DC: American Psychological Association.

Boyd-Franklin, N., & Bry, B. H. (2000). *Reaching out in family therapy.* New York: Guilford.

Boyd-Franklin, N., & Franklin, A. J. (2000). *Boys into men: Raising our African American teenage sons.* New York: Dutton.

Boykin, A., & Toms, F. D. (1986). Black child socialization: A conceptual framework. In H. P. McAdoo & J. L. McAdoo (Eds.), *Black children* (pp. 33-54). Beverly Hills, CA: Sage.

Bracero, W. (1998). Intimidades: Confianza, gender, and hierarchy in the construction of Latino-Latina therapeutic relationships. *Cultural Diversity and Mental Health, 4,* 264-277.

Bradford, D. T., & Munoz, A. (1993). Translation in bilingual psychotherapy. *Professional Psychology Research and Practice, 24,* 52-61.

Bradshaw, C. K. (1994). Asian and Asian American women: Historical and political considerations in psychotherapy. In L. Comas-Diaz & B. Greene (Eds.), *Women of color: Integrating ethnic and gender identities in psychotherapy* (pp. 27-113). New York: Guilford.

Brave Heart, M. Y. H. (1999). *Oyate ptayela*: Rebuilding the Lakota Nation through addressing historical trauma among Lakota parents. *Journal of Human Behavior in the Social Environment, 2*(1/2), 109-126.

Brave Heart, M. Y. H. (2000). *Wakiksuyapi*: Carrying the historical trauma of the Lakota. *Tulane Studies in Social Welfare, 21-22*, 245-266.

Brave Heart, M. Y. H. (2001). Culturally and historically congruent clinical social work assessment with Native clients. In R. Fong & S. Furuto (Eds.), *Culturally competent practice: Skills, interventions, and evaluations* (pp. 163-177). Needham Heights, MA: Allyn & Bacon.

Brave Heart, M. Y. H. (in press). Gender differences in the historical trauma response among the Lakota. *Journal of Health and Social Policy*.

Brave Heart-Jordan, M. Y. H. (1995). *The return to the sacred path: Healing from historical trauma and historical unresolved grief among the Lakota.* Unpublished doctoral dissertation, Smith College School for Social Work, Northampton, Massachusetts.

Brave Heart-Jordan, M., & DeBruyn, L. (1995). So she may walk in balance: Integrating the impact of historical trauma in the treatment of Native American Indian women. In J. Alderman & G. Enquidanos (Eds.), *Racism in the lives of women: Testimony, theory, and guide to anti-racist practice* (pp. 345-368). New York: Haworth.

Brave Heart-Jordan, M. Y. H., & DeBruyn, L. (1998). The American Indian holocaust: Healing historical unresolved grief. *American Indian and Alaska Native Mental Health Research, 8*(2), 56-78.

Brown, E., & Shaughnessy, T. (1982). *Education for social work practice with American Indian families.* Washington, DC: U.S. Department of Health and Human Services.

Brown, P. M., & Shallett, J. S. (Eds.). (1997). *Cross-cultural practice with couples and families.* New York: Haworth.

Bryde, G. (1971). *Modern Indian psychology.* Vermillion: University of South Dakota.

Bureau of Indian Affairs. (1971). *Information office statistics.* Washington, DC: Author.

Burkhardt, V. (1960). *Chinese creeds and customs* (Vol. 3). Hong Kong: South China Morning Post.

Bustamante, J., & Santa Cruz, A. (1975). *Psiquiatra transcultural.* Havana, Cuba: Editorial Cientifico-Technica.

Carter, E. (1976). Family therapy in the family therapist's own home. In P. Guerin (Ed.), *Family therapy: Theory and practice.* New York: Gardner.

Carter, E., & McGoldrick, M. (Eds.). (1980). *The family life cycle: A framework for family therapy.* New York: Gardner.

Casas, S., & Keefe, S. (1980). *Family and mental health in Mexican American Community.* Los Angeles: Spanish Speaking Mental Health Research Center.

Chavez, L. R. (1990). Coresidence and resistance: Strategies for survival among undocumented Mexicans and Central Americans in the United States. *Urban Anthropology, 19*, 31-61.

Chavez, L. R. (1992). *Shadowed lives: Undocumented immigrants in American society.* Fort Worth, TX: Holt, Rinehart & Winston.

Cherlin, A. (1992). *Marriage, divorce, remarriage.* Cambridge, MA: Harvard University Press.

Cherlin, A. (1996). *Public and private families.* New York: McGraw-Hill.

Chestang, L. (1976). The Black family and Black culture: A study of coping. In M. Satomayer (Ed.), *Cross cultural perspectives in social work practice and education*. Houston, TX: University of Houston, Graduate School of Social Work.

Cheung, F. K., & Snowden, L. R. (1990). Community mental health and ethnic minority populations. *Community Mental Health Journal, 26*, 277-291.

Cheung, M. (1997). Social construction theory and the Satir model: Toward a synthesis. *American Journal of Family Therapy, 25*(4), 331-342.

Chin, R. (1982). Conceptual paradigm for a racial-ethnic community: The case of the Chinese American community. In S. Sue & T. Moore (Eds.), *The pluralistic society: A community mental health perspective*. New York: Human Sciences Press.

Churchill, W. (1999). The crucible of American Indian identity: Native tradition versus colonial imposition in post conquest North America. *American Indian Culture and Research Journal, 23*(1), 39-67.

Clark, C. (1972). Black studies or the study of black people. In R. Jones (Ed.), *Black psychology*. New York: Harper & Row.

Coalition for Humane Immigrant Rights of Los Angeles (CHIRLA). (1995). *Hate unleashed: Los Angeles in the aftermath of 187* (pp. 4-19). Los Angeles: Author.

Cohen, F. S. (1982). *Felix S. Cohen handbook of federal Indian law*. Charlottesville, VA: Michie.

Comas-Diaz, L. (1994). An integrative approach. In L. Comas-Diaz & B. Greene (Eds.), *Women of color* (pp. 287-318). New York: Guilford.

Combs, D. (1978). *Crossing culture in therapy*. Monterey, CA: Brooks/Cole.

Constantino, G., Malgady, R. G., & Rogler, L. A. (1986). Cuento therapy: A culturally sensitive modality for Puerto Rican Children. *Journal of Consulting and Clinical Psychology, 54*, 639-645.

Cooper, R. L. (1995). *We stand together*. Chicago: Moody.

Cornell, S. (2000). That's the story of our lives. In P. Spickard & W. J. Burroughs (Eds.), *Narrative and multiplicity in constructing ethnic identity* (pp. 41-51). Philadelphia: Temple University Press.

Cose, E. (2003, March 3). The black gender gap. *Newsweek, 141*(9), 46-51.

Costa, R., & Henry, J. (1977). *Indian treaties: Two centuries of dishonor*. San Francisco: Indian Heritage.

Cowan, G., Martinez, L., & Mendiola, S. (1997, November). Predictors of attitudes toward illegal Latino immigrants. *Hispanic Journal of Behavioral Sciences, 19*(4), 430-415.

Crawley, B. H. (1996). Effective programs and services for African American families: An African-centered perspective. In S. Logan (Ed.), *The black family* (pp. 112-130). Boulder, CO: Westview.

Dana, R. H. (1993). *Multicultural assessment perspective for professional psychology*. Boston, MA: Allyn & Bacon.

DeAnda, D. (1984). Bicultural socialization: Factors affecting the minority experience. *Social Work, 29*, 101-107.

DeGeyndt, W. (1973). Health behavior and health needs in urban Indians in Minneapolis. *Health Service Reports, 88*, 360-366.

De La Cancela, V. (1978). Culture specific psychotherapy. In *Proceedings of the Fourth Annual Spring Conference of the New York Association of Black Psychologists* (pp. 128-152). New York: NYABP.

Delgado, G. (1978). *Steps to an ecology of mind*. New York: Ballantine.

Deloria, V., Jr. (1969). *Custer died for your sins: An Indian manifesto.* New York: Macmillan.

Demo, D. H., Allen, K. R., & Fine, M. A. (Eds). (2000). *Handbook of family diversity.* New York: Oxford University Press.

de Shazer, S. (1998). *Clues: Investigating solutions in brief therapy.* New York: Norton.

Devore, W. (2001). Whence came these people? An exploration of the values and ethics of African American individuals, families, and communities. In R. Fong & S. Furuto (Eds.), *Culturally competent practice: Skills, intervention and evaluations* (pp. 33-36). Needham Heights, MA: Allyn & Bacon.

DeVos, G. (1978). *Selective permeability and reference group sanctioning: Psychological continuities in role degradation.* Paper presented at: Seminar on Comparative Studies in Ethnicity and Nationality, University of Washington, Seattle.

Dickson, L. (1993). The future of marriage and family in black America. *Journal of Black Studies, 23*(4), 472-491.

DiNicola, V. (1997). *A stranger in the family.* New York: Norton.

Dorrington, C. (1995). Central American refugees in Los Angeles: Adjustment of children and families. In R. Zambrana (Ed.), *Understanding Latino families: Scholarship, policy, and practice* (pp. 107-129). Thousand Oaks, CA: Sage.

Douglas, F. (1974). Prescientific psychiatry in the urban setting. *American Journal of Psychiatry, 131,* 280-281.

Dreyfuss, B., & Lawrence, D. (1979). *Handbook for anti-racism.* Norman: University of Oklahoma Press.

Duberman, L. (1975). *The reconstituted family: A study of remarried couples and their children.* Chicago: Nelson-Hall.

DuBois, W. E. B. (1903). *The souls of black folks.* Chicago: McClurg.

DuBray, W. (1993). *American Indian values: Mental health intervention with people of color.* St. Paul, MN: West.

Duhl, B. (1989). Virginia Satir: In memoriam. *Journal of Marital and Family Therapy, 15*(2), 1001-1010.

Duran, E., & Duran, B. (1995). *Native American post-colonial psychology.* Albany: State University of New York Press.

Duran, E., Duran, B., Brave Heart, M.Y.H., & Yellow Horse-Davis. (1998). Healing the American Indian soul wound. In Y. Danieli (Ed.), *International handbook of multi-generational legacies of trauma* (pp. 341-354). New York: Plenum.

Edwards, D., & Edwards, M. (1984). Minorities: American Indians. In *Encyclopedia of social work.* Washington, DC: National Association of Social Workers.

Eggan, F. (1966). *The American Indian: Perspectives for the study of social change.* Chicago: Aldine.

Espenshade, T. (1985). Marriage trends in America: Estimates, implications, and underlying causes. *Population and Development Review, 11,* 193-245.

Espin, O. M. (1999). *Woman crossing boundaries: A psychology of immigration and transformation of sexuality.* New York: Routledge.

Estrada, L. F. (2000). *Children: A demographic profile.* Unpublished manuscript, University of California, Los Angeles, School of Public Policy and Social Research.

Falicov, C. J. (1982). Mexican families. In M. McGoldrick, J. Giordano, & J. K. Pearce (Eds.), *Ethnicity and family therapy.* New York: Guilford.

Falicov, C. J. (1983). Introduction. In C. J. Falicov (Ed), *Cultural perspectives in family therapy* (pp. xiv-xv). Rockville, MD: Aspen.

Falicov, C. J. (1996). Mexican families. In M. McGoldrick, J. Giordano, & J. K. Pearce (Eds), *Ethnicity and family therapy* (pp.155-182). New York: Guilford.

Falicov, C. J. (1998). *Latino families in therapy: A guide to multicultural practice*. New York: Guilford.

Falicov, C. J. (1999). Latino life cycle. In B. Carter & M. McGoldrick (Eds.), *The expanded life cycle: Individual, family, and social perspectives* (pp. 141-152). Boston, MA: Allyn & Bacon.

Fanon, F. (1963). *The wretched of the earth*. New York: Grove.

Fanon, F. (1967). *Black skin: White mask*. New York: Grove.

Farris, C. (1973). A White House conference on the American Indian. *Social Work, 18,* 80-86.

Fay, B. (1987). *Critical social science: Liberation and its limits*. Ithaca, NY: Cornell University Press.

Feagin, J. R. (2000). *Racist America*. New York: Routledge.

Fei, H. (1962). *Peasent life in China: A field study of country life in the Yangtze Valley*. London: Routledge & Kegan Paul.

Fine, M. (1992). Passions, power and politics. In M. Fine (Ed), *Disruptive voices: The possibility of feminist research* (pp. 205-231). Ann Arbor: University of Michigan Press.

Fish, V. (1993). Poststructualism in family therapy: Interrogating the narrative/conversational mode. *Journal of Marital and Family Therapy, 19*(3), 221-232.

Fitzpatrick, J. (1981). The Puerto Rican family. In C. Mindel & R. Habenstein (Eds.), *Ethnic families in America*. New York: Elsevier.

Flores, M. T. (2000). La familia Latina. In M. T. Flores & G. Carey (Eds.), *Family therapy with Hispanics: Toward appreciating diversity* (pp. 3-28). Boston, MA: Allyn & Bacon.

Flores, M. T., & Carey, G. (2000). *Family therapy with Hispanics: Toward appreciating diversity*. Boston, MA: Allyn & Bacon.

Foster, M., & Perry, L. (1982). Self-valuation among blacks. *Social Work, 27,* 60-66.

Franklin, C. (1986). Black male–black female conflict: Individually caused and culturally nurtured. In R. Staples (Ed.), *The black family: Essays and studies* (pp. 106-113). Belmont, CA: Wadsworth.

Franklin, C. (1994). Ain't I a man? The efficacy of black masculinities for men's studies in the 1990's. In R.G. Majors & J. U. Gordon (Eds), *The American black male* (pp. 285-299). Chicago: Nelson Hall.

Franklin, C., & Jordan, C. (1999). Family practice in today's practice context. In C. Franklin & C. Jordan (Eds.), *Family practice: Brief systems methods for social work* (pp. 3-21). Pacific Grove, CA: Brooks/Cole.

Franklin, D. (2000). *What's love got to do with it?* New York: Simon & Schuster.

Frazier, E. F. (1939). *The Negro family in the United States*. Chicago: University of Chicago Press.

Freeman, D. (1992). *Multigenerational family therapy*. New York: Haworth.

Freeman, J., & Combs, G. (1996). *Narrative therapy*. New York: W. W. Norton.

Freire, P. (1973). *Education for a critical consciousness*. New York: Beacon.

Fujii, S. (1976). Elderly Asian Americans and use of public service. *Social Casework, 57,* 202-207.

Garcia-Preto, N. (1996a). Latino families: An overview. In M. McGoldrick, J. Giordano, & J. K. Pearce (Eds.), *Ethnicity and family therapy* (pp. 141-154). New York: Guilford.

Garcia-Preto, N. (1996b). Puerto Rican families: An overview. In M. McGoldrick, J. Giordano, & J. K. Pearce (Eds.), *Ethnicity and family therapy* (pp. 183-199). New York: Guilford.

Garcia-Preto, N. (1998). Latinos in the United States: Building two bridges. In M. McGoldrick. (Ed), *Re-visioning family therapy: Race, culture, and gender in clinical practice* (pp. 330-346). New York: Guilford.

Garrison, V. (1977). Puerto Rican syndrome. In V. Garrison (Ed.), *Psychiatry and espiritism: Case studies in spirit possession.* New York: Wiley.

Gergen, K (1991). *The saturated self.* New York: Basic Books.

Germain, C. B., & Gitterman, A. (1996). *The life model of social work practice.* New York: Columbia University Press.

Gibbs, J. (1988). *Young, black and male in American: An endangered species.* Dover, MA: Auburn House.

Glick, P. (1997). Demographic pictures of African American families. In H. McAdoo (Ed.), *Black families* (pp. 118-138). Thousand Oaks, CA: Sage.

Goldenberg, H., & Goldenberg, I. (2002). *Counseling today's families.* Pacific Grove, CA: Brooks/Cole.

Gonzalez, J. (1978). Language factors affecting treatment of schizophrenics. *Psychiatric Annals, 8,* 68-70.

Gonzalez-Wippler, M. (1996). *Santeria: The religion.* St. Paul, MN: Llewellyn.

Gordon, W. E. (1969). Basic constructs for an integrative and generative conception of social work. In G. Hearn (Ed.), *The general systems approach: Contributions toward a holistic conception of social work.* New York: Council on Social Work.

Grace, C. A. (1992). Practical considerations for program professionals and evaluators working with African-American communities. In M. A. Orlandi (Ed.), *Cultural competence for evaluators: A guide for alcohol and other drug abuse prevention practitioners working with ethnic/racial communities* (pp. 55-74). Rockville, MD: U.S. Department of Health and Human Services, Office of Substance Abuse Prevention.

Grasmuck, S., & Pessar, P. R. (1996). Dominicans in the United States: First- and second-generation settlement, 1960-1990. In S. Pedrazo & R. G. Rumbaut (Eds.), *Origin and destinies: Immigration, race, and ethnicity in America* (pp. 280-292). Belmont, CA: Wadsworth.

Grebler, L., Moore, J., & Guzman, R. (1970). *The Mexican American people: The nation's second largest minority.* New York: Free Press.

Green, J. W. (1999). *Cultural awareness in the human services.* Boston, MA: Allyn & Bacon.

Green, R. J. (1998). Race and the field of family therapy. In M. McGoldrick (Ed), *Re-visioning family therapy: Race, culture, and gender in clinical practice* (pp. 93-110). New York: Guilford.

Greenbaum, S. (1991). What's in a label? Identity problem in southern tribes. *Journal of Ethnic Studies, 19,* 107-126.

Grier, W., & Cobbs, P. (1968). *Black rage.* New York: Basic Books.

Guerney, B. (1977). *Relationship enhancement.* San Francisco: Jossey-Bass.

Gutierrez, L. M., Parsons, R. J., & Cox, E. O. (1998). *Empowerment in social work practice.* Pacific Grove, CA: Brooks/Cole.

Gutman, H. (1976). *The Black family in slavery and freedom 1750-1925.* New York: Pantheon.

Haley, J. (1963). *Strategies of psychotherapy.* New York: Grune & Stratton.

Haley, J. (1976). *Problem-solving therapy: New strategies for effective family therapy.* San Francisco: Jossey-Bass.

Hall, E. T. (1976). *Beyond culture.* New York: Doubleday.

Hall, R. H. (1986). Alcohol treatment in American Indian population: An indigenous treatment modality compared with traditional approaches. *Annals of the New York Academy of Sciences, 472,* 168-178.

Hamilton, N., & Chinchilla, N. S. (1997). Central American migration: A framework for analysis. In M. Romero, P. Hondagnei-Sotelo, & V. Ortiz (Eds.), *Challenging fronteras: Structuring Latina and Latino lives in the U.S.* (pp. 81-100). New York: Routledge.

Hansell, B. (1976). *The person in distress.* New York: Human Science.

Hanson, W. (1980). The urban Indian woman and her family. *Social Casework, 61,* 476-484.

Hanson, W. (1981). Grief counseling with Native American Indians. In R. Dana (Ed.), *Human services for cultural minorities.* Baltimore, MD: University Park Press.

Hardy-Fanta, C., & MacMahon-Herrera, E. (1981). Adapting family therapy to the Hispanic family. *Social Casework, 62,* 138-148.

Hare, B. (1975). *Relationship at social background to the dimensions of self-concept.* Unpublished doctoral dissertation, University of Chicago.

Hartman, A. (1978). Diagrammatic assessment of family relationships. *Social Casework, 59,* 465-476.

Hartman, A. (1979). *Finding families: An ecological approach to family assessment in adoption.* Newbury Park, CA: Sage.

Hartman, A., & Laird, J. (1983). *Family centered social work practice.* New York: Free Press.

Hatchett, S., Cochran, D., & Jackson, J. (1991). Family life. In J. Jackson (Ed.), *Life in black America* (pp. 46-83). Newbury Park, CA: Sage.

Hawkes, G., & Taylor, M. (1975). Power structure in Mexican and Mexican American farm labor families. *Journal of Marriage and the Family, 31,* 807-811.

Healy, K. (2000). *Social work practices.* Thousand Oaks, CA: Sage.

Heiner, R. (2002). *Social problems: An introduction to critical constructionism.* New York: University Press.

Herskovits, M. J. (1958). *The myth of the Negro past.* Boston, MA: Beacon.

Hill, R. (1972). *The strength of black families.* New York: Emerson-Hall.

Hill, R. (1993). *Research on the African American family: a holistic perspective.* Westport, CT: Auburn House.

Hines, P. M., & Boyd-Franklin, N. (1996). African American families. In M. McGoldrick, J. Giordano, & J. K. Pearce (Eds), *Ethnicity and family therapy* (pp. 66-84). New York: Guilford.

Hines, P. M., Garcia-Preto, N., McGoldrick, M., Almeida, R., & Weltman, S. (1999). Culture and family life cycle. In B. Carter & M. McGoldrick (Eds.), *The expanded family life cycle* (pp. 69-87). Boston, MA: Allyn & Bacon.

Hippler, A. (1974). The North Alaska Eskimos: A culture and personality perspective. *American Ethnologist, 1,* 449-469.

Ho, M. (1976). Social work with Asian Americans. *Social Casework, 57,* 195-201.

Ho, M. (1980). Model to evaluate group work practice with ethnic minorities. Paper presented at: Social Work with Group Symposium, Arlington, Texas.

Ho, M. (1982). Building on the strength of minority groups. *Practice Digest, 5,* 6-7.

Ho, M., & McDowell, E. (1973). The black worker-white client relationship. *Clinical Social Work Journal, 1,* 161-167.

Ho, M., & Settles, A. (1984). The use of popular music in family therapy. *Social Work, 29,* 65-67.

Holmes, T., & Masuda, M. (1974). Life change and illness susceptibility. In B. Dohrenwend & P. Dohrenwend (Eds.), *Stressful life events: Their nature and effects.* New York: Wiley.

Homans, G. (1964). Contemporary theory in sociology. In R. Faris (Ed.), *Handbook of modern sociology.* Chicago: Rand McNally.

Hong, G. K. (1989). Application of cultural and environmental issues in family therapy with immigrant Chinese Americans. *Journal of Strategic and Systematic Therapies, 8*, 14-21.

Hong, G. K. (1993). Contexual factors in psychotherapy with Asian Americans. In J. L. Chin, J. L. Leim, & M. D. Hong (Eds.), *Transference and empathy in Asian American psychotherapy: Clinical values and treatment needs* (pp. 3-13). Westport, CT: Prager.

Hong, G. K. (1996). Culture and empowerment: Counseling services for Chinese American families. *Journal for the Professional Counselor, 11*(1), 69-80.

Hong, G. K., & Friedman, M. M. (1998). The Asian American family. In M. M. Friedman (Ed), *Family nursing: Theory and practice* (pp. 547-566). Norwalk, CT: Appleton & Lange.

Hong, G. K., & Ham, M. D. (1992). Impact of immigration on the family life cycle: Clinical implications for Chinese Americans. *Journal of Family Psychotherapy, 3*(3), 27-40.

Hong, G. K. & Ham, M. D. (2001). *Psychology and counseling with Asian American clients.* Thousand Oaks, CA: Sage.

Hopson, D. S., & Hopson, D. P. (1998). *The power of soul.* New York: William Morrow.

How I got over. (n.d.). Retrieved May 29, 2003, from http://www.negrospirituals.com/news-song/how_i_got_over.htm

Hsu, F. (1972). *American museum science book.* Garden City, NY: Doubleday.

Hudson-Weem, C. (1993). *Africana womanism: Reclaiming ourselves.* Troy, MI: Bedford.

Huffaker, C. (1967). *Nobody loves a drunken Indian.* New York: David McKay.

Ingrassia, M., King, P., Tizon, T., Scigliano, E., & Annin, P. (1994, April 4). America's new wave of runaways. *Newsweek, 123*(14), 64-65.

Ishii-Kuntz, M. (2000). Diversity with Asian American families. In D. Demo, K. R. Allen, & M. Fine (Eds.), *Handbook of family diversity* (pp. 274-293). New York: Oxford University Press.

Ivey, A. E. (1995). Psychotherapy as liberation. In J. G. Ponterotto, J. M. Casas, L. A. Suzuki, & C. M. Alexander (Eds.), *Handbook of multicultural counseling* (pp. 53-72). Thousand Oaks, CA: Sage.

Jackson, J. (1973). Family organization and ideology. In D. Miller (Ed.), *Comparative studies of Blacks and Whites in the United States.* New York: Seminar Press.

Jansen, C., & Harris, O. (1997). *Family treatment in social work practice.* Itasca, IL: Peacock.

Jansson, B. S. (2001). *The reluctant welfare state.* Belmont, CA: Brooks/Cole.

Jaynes, G., & Williams, R. (1989). *A common destiny: Blacks and American society.* Washington, DC: National Academy.

Jenkins, A. (1988). Black families: The nurturing of agency. In A. F. Comer-Edwards & J. Spurlock (Eds.), *Black families in crisis* (pp. 115-128). New York: Brunner/Mazel.

Johnson, C. A., & Johnson, D. L. (1998). Working with Native American families. *New Directions for Mental Health Services, 77*, 89-96.

Jones, A. C. (1989). Psychological functioning in African-American adults: Some elaborations on a model with clinical implications. In R. Jones (Ed.), *Black adult development and aging* (pp. 297-310). Berkeley, CA: Cobb & Henry.

Jones, D. (1977). The mystique of expertise in the social service. *Journal of Sociology and Social Welfare, 3*, 332-346.

Kagan, S., & Buriel, R. (1977). Field dependence-independence and Mexican-American culture and education. In J. Martinez (Ed.), *Chicano psychology.* New York: Academic Press.

Kahn, R. (1974). Conflict, ambiguity, and overload. In A. McLean (Ed.), *Occupational stress: Three elements in job stress*. Springfield, IL: Charles C Thomas.

Kambon, K. K. (1992). *The African personality in America: An African-centered framework*. Tallahassee, FL: Nubia Nations.

Kantrowitz, B., & Wingert, P. (2001, May 28). Unmarried with children. *Newsweek, 137*(3), 46-54.

Karenga, M. (1996). The nguzo saba (the seven principles): Their meaning and message. In M. K. Asante & A. S. Abarry (Eds.), *African intellectual heritage* (pp. 543-554). Philadelphia, PA: Temple University Press.

Karger, H. J., & Stoesz, D. (2002). *American welfare policy*. Boston, MA: Allyn & Bacon.

Katz, W. L. (1997). *Black Indians*. New York: Aladdin.

Kerr, M., & Bowen, M. (1988). *Family evaluation*. New York: Norton.

Keyes, C. (1977). *The golden peninsula*. New York: Macmillan.

Kiev, A. (1968). *Curanderismo: Mexican American folk psychiatry*. New York: Free Press.

Kikumura, A., & Kitano, H. (1973). Interracial marriage: A picture of the Japanese Americans. *Journal of Social Issues, 29*, 67-81.

Kilpatrick, A. C., & Holland, T. P. (2003). *Working with families*. Boston, MA: Allyn & Bacon.

Kim, B. (1978). *The Asian Americans: Changing patterns, changing needs*. Montclair, NJ: Association of Korean Christian Scholars in North America.

Kitano, H., & Yeung, W. (1982). Chinese interracial marriage. In C. Crester & J. Leon. (Eds.), *Intermarriage in the United States*. New York: Haworth.

Kleinman, A., & Lin, T. (Eds.). (1981). *Normal and deviant behavior in Chinese culture*. Hingham, MA: Reidel.

Kline, F., Austin, W., & Acosta, F. (1980). The misunderstood Spanish speaking patient. *American Journal of Psychiatry, 137*, 1530-1533.

Kluckhohn, F. (1951). Values and value orientation. In T. Parsons & E. Shils (Eds.), *Toward a general theory of actions*. Cambridge, MA: Harvard University Press.

Kluckhohn, F., & Strodtbeck, F. (1961). *Variations in value orientation*. New York: Harper & Row.

Kohut, H. (1972). Thoughts on narcissism and narcissistic rage. *Psychoanalytic Study of the Child, 27*, 360-400.

Kuerschner, S. (1997). Childrearing today: The traditional way. *Pathways, 12*(5/6), 1-2, 24-25.

LaFramboise, T., Trimble, J., & Mohatt, G. (1990). Counseling interventions and American Indian tradition: An interpretive approach. *The Counseling Psychologist, 18*(4), 628-654.

Laird, J. (1989). Women and stories: Restorying women's self construction. In M. McGoldrick, C. H. Anderson, & F. Walsh (Eds.), *Women in families* (pp. 427-450). New York: Norton.

Laird, J. (Ed.). (1993). *Revisioning social work education: A social constructionist approach*. New York: Haworth.

Laird, J. (1998). Theorizing culture: Narrative ideas and practice principles. In M. McGoldrick (Ed), *Re-visioning family therapy* (pp. 20-36). New York: Guilford.

Landau, J. (1981). Link therapy as a family therapy technique for transitional extended families. *Psychotherapy, 7*, 390.

Landrine, H., & Klonoff, E. A. (1996). *African American acculturation*. Thousand Oaks, CA: Sage.

Le, C. N. (2003). Interracial dating & marriage. *Asian-Nation: The Landscape of Asian America*. Retrieved June 10, 2003, from http://www.asian-nation.org/interracial.shtml

Lee, E. (1982). A social system approach to assessment and treatment for Chinese American families. In M. McGoldrick, J. Giordano, & J. K. Pearce (Eds.), *Ethnicity and family therapy*. New York: Guilford.

Lee, E. (Ed.). (1997). *Working with Asian Americans: A guide for clinicians*. New York: Guilford.

Lee, J. A. B. (1987). *The empowerment approach*. New York: Columbia University Press.

Leonard, P. (1994). Knowledge/power and postmodernism: Implications for the practice of critical social work education. *Canadian Social Service Review, 11*(1), 11-26.

Levine, E., & Padilla, A. (1980). *Crossing cultures in therapy: Pluralistic counseling for the Hispanic*. Monterey, CA: Brooks/Cole.

Lewis, C. (1970). *Indian families of the northwest coast: The impact of change*. Chicago: University of Chicago Press.

Lewis, D. (1975). The black family: Socialization and sex roles. *Phylon, 2*, 221-237.

Lewis, R. (1984). The strengths of Indian families. In *Proceedings of Indian Child Abuse Conference*. Tulsa, OK: National Indian Child Abuse Center.

Lewis, R., & Ho, M. (1975). Social work with Native Americans. *Social Work, 20*, 379-382.

Lin, T. Y., Tazuma, L., & Matsuda, M. (1979). Adaptational problems of Vietnamese refugees. *Health and Mental Status Archives of General Psychiatry, 36*, 955-961.

Logan, S. M. L. (1990). Diversity among Black families: Assessing structure and function. In S. Logan, E. M. Freeman, & R. G. McRoy (Eds.), *Social work with Black families* (pp. 73-96). New York: Longman.

Logan, S. M. L., Freeman, E. M., & McRoy, R. G. (1987). Racial identity problems of biracial clients: Implication of social work practice. *Journal of Intergroup Relations, 25*(2), 11-14.

Longres, J. F. (2000). *Human behavior in the social environment*. Itasca, NY: Peacock.

Loo, C., & Yu, C. (1980). *Chinatown: Recording reality, destroying myths*. Paper presented at: American Psychological Association Convention, Montreal, Québec.

Lopez, D. E., Popkin, E., & Telles, E. (1996). Central Americans: At the bottom, struggling to get ahead. In R. Waldinger & M. Bosorgmeher (Eds.), *Ethnic Los Angeles* (pp. 279-304). New York: Russell Sage Foundation.

Lopez-Baez, S. (1999). Marianismo. In J. S. Mio, J. E. Trimble, P. Arredondo, H. E. Cheatham, & D. Sue (Eds.), *Key words in multicultural interventions: A dictionary* (p. 183). Westport, CT: Greenwood.

Lott, J. (1998). *Asian Americans: From racial category to multiple identities*. Walnut Creek, CA: Altamira.

Lum, D. (Ed.). (2002). *Culturally competent practice*. Pacific Grove, CA: Brooks/Cole.

Lyle, R. R., & Faure, F. (2000). Life-cycle development, divorce and the Hispanic family. In M. T. Flores & G. Carey (Eds.), *Family therapy with Hispanics: Toward appreciating diversity* (pp.185-203). Boston, MA: Allyn & Bacon.

Madsen, W. (1964). *The Mexican-American of South Texas*. New York: Holt, Rinehart, & Winston.

Marin, G., & Marin, B. V. (1991). *Research with Hispanic populations*. Newbury Park, CA: Sage.

Marin, G., & Triandis, H. C. (1985). Allocentrism as an important characteristic of the behavior of Latin Americans and Hispanics. In R. Diaz-Guerrero (Ed.), *Cross-cultural and national studies in social psychology* (pp. 85-104). Amsterdam, Holland: North Holland.

Martin, E., & Martin, J. (1978). *The black extended family*. Chicago: University of Chicago Press.

Mass, A. I. (1976). Asians as individuals: The Japanese community. *Social Casework, 57,* 160-164.

Massey, D. S., Zambrana, R. E., & Bell, S. A. (1995). Contemporary issues for Latino families: Future directions for research, policy, and practice. In R. E. Zambrana (Ed.), *Understanding Latino families* (pp. 190-204). Thousand Oaks, CA: Sage.

McAdoo, H. (1977). Family therapy in the black community. *Journal of the American Orthopsychiatric Association, 47,* 74-79.

McAdoo, H. (1978). The impact of upward mobility on kin-help pattern and the reciprocal obligations in Black families. *Journal of Marriage and the Family, 4,* 761-776.

McAdoo, H., & Crawford, V. (1990). The black church and family support programs. *Prevention and Human Services, 9,* 193-203.

McCollum, V. J. C. (1997). Evolution of the African American family personality: Considerations for family therapy. *Journal of Multicultural Counseling and Development, 25,* 219-229.

McGoldrick, M. (Ed). (1998). *Re-visioning family therapy: Race, culture and gender in clinical practice.* New York: Guilford.

McGoldrick, M., Giordano, J., & Pearce, J. K. (Eds.). (1996). *Ethnicity and family therapy.* New York: Guilford.

McLanahan, S., Wedemeyer, N. V., & Adelberg, T. (1981). Network support, social support, and psychological well-being in the single-parent family. *Journal of Marriage and the Family, 43,* 601-612.

McRoy, R. (2003). Cultural competence with African Americans. In D. Lum (Ed.), *Culturally competent practice* (pp. 217-237). Pacific Grove, CA: Brooks/Cole.

Mead, G. H. (1934). *Mind, self and society.* Chicago: University of Chicago Press.

Medicine, B. (1978). *The Native American woman: A perspective.* Austin, TX: National Education Lab.

Merian, L. (1977). The effects of boarding schools on Indian family life: 1928. In L. Merian (Ed.), *The destruction of American Indian families.* New York: Association on American Indian Affairs.

Merton, R. (1957). *Social theory and social structure.* New York: Free Press.

Miller, S., Nunnally, E., & Wackman, D. (1975). *Alive and aware.* Minneapolis, MN: Interpersonal Communication Program.

Miller, W. (1959). Implications of urban lower class culture of social work. *Social Service Review, 33,* 219-236.

Mindel, C. (1980). Extended familism among urban Mexican Americans, Anglos, and blacks. *Hispanic Journal of Behavioral Sciences, 2,* 21-34.

Minuchin, S. (1967). *Families of the slums.* New York: Basic Books.

Minuchin, S. (1974). *Families and family therapy.* Cambridge, MA: Harvard University Press.

Mizio, E. (1979). *Puerto Rican task report: Project on ethnicity.* New York: Family Service Association.

Mizio, E., & Delaney, A. (Eds.). (1981). *Training for service delivery to minority clients.* New York: Family Service Association of America.

Moll, L. C., Rueda, R. S., Reza, R., Herrera, J., & Vasquez, L. P. (1976). Mental health services in East Los Angeles. In M. Miranda (Ed.), *Psychotherapy with the Spanish speaking: Issues in research and service delivery* (Monograph No. 3, pp. 52-65). Los Angeles: University of California, Spanish Speaking Mental Health Research Center.

Momaday, N. (1974). I am alive. In N. Momaday (Ed.), *The world of the American Indian.* Washington, DC: National Geographic Society.

Montalvo, F. (1991). *Phenotyping, acculturation and biracial assimilation of Mexican Americans: Empowering Hispanic families, a critical issue for the 90's.* Milwaukee, OH: Family Services America.

Moore, J., & Pachon, H. (1985). *Hispanics in the United States.* Englewood Cliffs, NJ: Prentice Hall.

Morales, E. (1996). Gender roles among Latin gay and bisexual men: Implication for family and couple relationships. In J. Laird & R. Green (Eds.), *Lesbians and gays in couples and families: A handbook for therapists* (pp. 272-297). San Francisco: Jossey-Bass.

Morales-Dorta, S. (1976). *Puerto Rican espiritismo: Religion and psychotherapy.* New York: Vantage.

Moran, R. F. (2001). *Interracial intimacy.* Chicago: University of Chicago Press.

Morelli, P. (2001). Culturally competent assessment of Cambodian American survivors of killing fields: A tool for social justice. In R. Fong & S. Furuto (Eds.), *Culturally competent practice: Skills, intervention and evaluations.* (pp. 196-210). Needham Heights, MA: Allyn & Bacon.

Morey, S., & Gilliam, O. (Eds.). (1974). *Respect for life.* Garden City, NY: Waldorf.

Mostwin, D. (1981). Multidimensional model of working with the family. *Social Casework, 55,* 209-215.

Mouseau, J. (1975). The family, prison of love. *Psychology Today, 9,* 53-58.

Moynihan, D. P. (1965). *The Negro family: The case for national action.* Washington, DC: U.S. Government Printing Office.

Muguia, E. (1982). *Chicano intermarriage.* San Antonio, TX: Trinity University Press.

Murase, T., & Johnson, F. (1974). Naikan, morita and Western psychotherapy. *Archives of General Psychiatry, 31,* 121-128.

Murillo, N. (1971). The Mexican American family. In N. Wagner & M. Huag (Eds.), *Chicanos: Social and psychological perspectives.* St. Louis, MO: Mosby.

National Urban League. (2002). *National Urban League report: State of black America.* New York: Author.

Native American Research Group. (1979). *American Indian socialization to urban life.* San Francisco: Scientific Analysis Corp.

Ngo, D., Tran, T., Gibbons, J., & Oliver, J. (2001). Acculturation, pre-migration, traumatic experiences, and depression among Vietnamese Americans. In N. Choi (Ed), *Psychological aspects of the Asian American experience: Diversity within diversity* (pp. 225-242). New York: Haworth.

Nichols, M. P., & Schwartz, R. C. (2001). *Family therapy.* Boston, MA: Allyn & Bacon.

Nobles, W. W., & Goddard, L. L. (1992). *An African centered model of prevention for African American youth of high risk* (DHHS Publication No. ADM 92-1925). Washington, DC: Department of Public Health.

Norbeck, E., & DeVos, G. (1972). Culture and personality: The Japanese. In F. Hsu (Ed.), *Psychological anthropology in the behavioral sciences.* Cambridge, MA: Schenkman.

Norlin, J., & Ho, M. (1974). Co-worker approach to working with families. *Clinical Social Work, 2,* 127-134.

Norton, D. (1978). Black family life patterns, the development of self and cognitive development of Black children. In G. Powell, J. Yamamoto, A. Romero, & A. Morales (Eds.), *The psychosocial development of minority group children.* New York: Brunner/ Mazel.

Office of Special Concerns, Office of the Assistant Secretary for Planning and Evaluation, Department of Health, Education and Welfare. (1974). *A study of selected socio-economic* characteristics of ethnic minorities based on the 1970 census. Vol. 2. Asian Americans. Washington, DC: U.S. Government Printing Office.

Ortiz, C. (1972). The Chicano family: A review of research. Social Work, 18, 22-23.

Padilla, A., Carlos, M., & Keefe, S. (1976). Mental health service utilization by Mexican Americans. In M. R. Miranda (Ed.), Psychotherapy with the Spanish-speaking: Issues in research and service delivery. Los Angeles: Spanish Speaking Mental Health Research Center, University of California.

Papajohn, J., & Speigel, J. (1975). Transactions in families. San Francisco: Jossey-Bass.

Parham, T. A., & Brown, S. (2003). Therapeutic approaches with African American populations. In F. Harper & J. McFadden (Eds.), Culture and counseling (pp. 81-98). Boston, MA: Allyn & Bacon.

Parsons, T. (1951). The social system. New York: Free Press.

Penalosa, F. (1968). Mexican family roles. Journal of Marriage and the Family, 30, 680-689.

Pendagast, S., & Sherman, R. (1977). Diagrammatic assessment of family relationships. Social Casework, 59, 465-476.

Perez Foster, R. M. (2001, April). When immigration is trauma: Guidelines for the individual and family clinician: American Journal of Orthopsychiatry, 71(1), 153-170.

Perez-Stable, M., & Uriarte, M. (1993). Cubans and the declining economy of Miami. In R. Morales & F. Bonilla (Eds.), Latinos in a changing U.S. economy: Comparative perspectives in growing inequality (pp. 133-159). Newbury Park, CA: Sage.

Peters, M., & deFord, C. (1978). The solo mother. In R. Staples (Ed.), The black family: Essays and studies. Belmont, CA: Wadsworth.

Pinderhughes, E. (1982). Afro-American families and the victim system. In M. McGoldrick, J. Giordano, & J. K. Pearce (Eds.), Ethnicity and family therapy. New York: Guilford.

Pinderhughes, E. (1989). Understanding race, ethnicity, and power. New York: Free Press.

Pitta, P., Marcos, L., & Alpert, M. (1978). Language switching as a treatment strategy with bilingual patients. American Journal of Psychoanalysis, 38, 255-258.

Polkinghorne, D. E. (1988). Narrative knowing and the human sciences. Albany: State University of New York.

Polacca, M. (1995). Cross-cultural variation in mental health treatment of aging Native Americans. Unpublished manuscript, School of Social Work, Arizona State University.

Ponce, D. E. (1977). Intercultural perspectives on mate selection. In W. S. Tseng, J. F. McDermott, & T. W. Maretzki (Eds.), Adjustment in intercultural marriage. Honolulu: University Press of Hawaii.

Porterfield, E. (1978). Black and white mixed marriages: An ethnographic study of black-white families. Chicago: Nelson Hall.

Price, J. (1981). North American Indian families. In C. Mindel & R. Habenstein (Eds.), Ethnic families in America. New York: Elsevier.

Purdy, B., Pellman, R., Flores, S., & Bluestone, H. (1970). Mellaril or medium, stelazine or séance? A study of spiritism as it affects communication, diagnosis, and treatment of Puerto Rican people. American Journal of Orthopsychiatry, 40, 239-240.

Rainwater, L. (1966). The crucible of identity: The lower class Negro family. Daedalus, 95, 258-264.

Ramirez, R. (1979). Machismo: A bridge rather than a barrier to family counseling. In P. Martin (Ed.), La Frontera perspective: Providing mental health services to Mexican Americans. Tucson, AZ: La Frontera Center.

Ramos-McKay, J. M., Comas-Diaz, L., & Rivera, L. A. (1988). Puerto Ricans. In L. Comas-Diaz & E. E. H. Griffith (Eds.), Clinical guidelines in cross-cultural mental health (pp. 204-232). New York: Wiley.

Randolph, S. M., & Banks, D. (1993). Making a way out of no way: The promises of Africentric approaches to HIV prevention. *Journal of Black Psychology, 19*(2), 215-222.

Rasheed, J. M. (1998). The adult life cycle of poor African American fathers. *Journal of Human Behavior and the Social Environment, 1*(2/3), 265-280.

Rasheed, J. M. (1999). Obstacles to the parental role functions of inner-city, low-income, noncustodial African American fathers. *Journal of African American Men, 4*(1), 9-23.

Rasheed, J. M., & Rasheed, M. N. (1999). *Social work practice with African American men: The invisible presence.* Thousand Oaks, CA: Sage.

Red Horse, J. (1980a). American Indian elders: Unifiers of Indian families. *Social Casework, 61*, 490-493.

Red Horse, J. (1980b). Family structure and value orientation in American Indians. *Social Casework, 61*, 462-467.

Red Horse, J. G. (1982). Clinical strategies for American Indian families in crisis. *Urban and Social Change Review, 15*(2), 17-20.

Red Horse, J. G., Lewis, R., Feit, M., & Decker, J. (1978). Family behavior of urban American Indians. *Social Casework, 59*, 67-72.

Ridley, C. R. (1995). *Overcoming unintentional racism in counseling and therapy.* Thousand Oaks, CA: Sage.

Ritter, E., Ritter, R., & Spector, S. (1965). *Our Oriental Americans.* New York: McGraw-Hill.

Rogler, L., & Hollingshead, A. (1965). *Trapped: Families and schizophrenia.* New York: Wiley.

Romero, A. J. (2000). Assessing and treating Latinos: Overview of research. In I. Cuellar & F. Paniaqua (Eds.), *Handbook of multicultural mental health* (pp. 209-223). New York: Wiley.

Rosen, P., & Proctor, D. (1978). The study of the family. *Family Process, 4*, 1-20.

Rosenburg, M. (1979). *Convicting the self.* New York: Basic Books.

Rothenberg, A. (1964). Puerto Ricans and aggression. *American Journal of Psychiatry, 20*, 962-970.

Rubin, R. (1974). Adult male absence and the self-attitudes of black children. *Child Study Journal, 4*, 33-44.

Ruiz, R. (1977). *The delivery of mental health: Report of the Task Panel on Special Populations* (Vol. 4). Washington, DC: U.S. Government Printing Office.

Saleeby, D. (1997). *The strength perspective in social work practice.* White Plains, NY: Longman.

Santiago-Rivera, A. L., Arredondo, P., & Gallardo-Cooper, M. (2002). *Counseling Latinos and la familia.* Thousand Oaks, CA: Sage.

Satir, V. (1967). *Conjoint family therapy.* Palo Alto, CA: Science and Behavior Books.

Satir, V. (1986). A partial portrait of a family therapist in process. In H. C. Fishman & B. L. Rosman (Eds.), *Evolving models for family change: A volume in honor of Salavador Minuchin.* New York: Guilford.

Satir, V. (1988). *The new peoplemaking.* Palo Alto, CA: Science and Behavior.

Satir, V., Banmen, J., Gerber, J., & Gomori, M. (1991). *The Satir model: Family therapy and beyond.* Palo Alto, CA: Science and Behavior Books.

Satir, V., Stachowiak, J., & Taschman, H. (1975). *Helping families to change.* New York: Jason Aronson.

Scanzoni, J. (1971). *The black family in modern society: Patterns of stability and security.* Chicago: University of Chicago Press.

Schiele, J. (1994). Afrocentricity as an alternative world view for equality. *Journal of Progressive Human Services, 5*(1), 5-25.

Schiele, J. (1996). Afocentricity: An emerging paradigm in social work practice. *Social Work, 41*(3), 284-294.

Seijo, R., Gomez, H., & Freidenberg, J. (1991). Language as a communication barrier in medical care for Hispanic families. *Hispanic Journal of Behavioral Sciences, 13*, 363-376.

Shimkin, D., Shimkin, E., & Frate, D. (Eds.). (1978). *The extended family in black societies.* The Hague: Mouton.

Shon, S., & Ja, D. (1982). Asian families. In M. McGoldrick, J. Giordano, J. K. Pearce, & J. Giordano (Eds.), *Ethnicity and family therapy.* New York: Guilford.

Sluzki, C. (1979). Migration and family conflict. *Family Process, 18,* 379-439.

Sollenberger, R. (1962). Chinese-American child-rearing practices and juvenile delinquency. *Journal of Social Psychology, 74,* 13-23.

Solomon, B. (1976). *Black empowerment.* New York: Columbia University Press.

Speck, R., & Attneave, C. (1974). *Family networks.* New York: Vintage.

Speigel, J. (1959). Some cultural aspects of transference and counter-transference. In G. Masserman (Ed.), *Individual and family dynamics.* New York: Grune & Stratton.

Spencer, F., Szapocznik, J., Santisteban, D., & Rodrigues, A. (1981, March). *Cuban crisis 1980: Mental health care issues.* Paper presented at the Southeastern Psychological Association, Atlanta.

Spindler, G., & Spindler, L. (1971). Male and female adaptations to culture change. In G. Spindler & L. Spindler (Eds.), *Man in adaptation: The institutional framework.* Chicago: Aldine-Atherton.

Stack, C. (1974). *All our kin.* New York: Harper & Row.

Staples, R. (1976). *The black family: Essays and studies* (Vol. 2). Belmont, CA: Wadsworth.

Staples, R., & Johnson, L. B. (1993). *Black families at the crossroads.* San Francisco: Jossey-Bass.

Stevens, E. (1973). Marianismo: The other face of machismo. In A. Pescatello (Ed.), *Female and male in Latin America.* Pittsburgh, PA: University of Pittsburgh Press.

Stevens, P. E. (1989). A critical social reconceptualization of environment in nursing: Implications for methodology. *Advances in Nursing Science, 11*(4), 56-68.

Stevenson, B. (1995). Black family structure in colonial and antebellum Virginia: Amending the revisionist perspective. In M. B. Tucker & C. Mitchell-Kernan (Eds.), *The decline in marriage among African Americans* (pp. 27-56). New York: Russell Sage Foundation.

Stuart, P. (1977). United States Indian policy. *Social Service Review, 47,* 451-463.

Sudarkasa, N. (1997). African American families and family values. In H. P. McAdoo (Ed.), *Black families* (pp. 9-40). Thousand Oaks, CA: Sage.

Sue, S., & Morishima, J. (1982). *The mental health of Asian Americans.* San Francisco: Jossey-Bass.

Sue, D. W., & Sue, D. (1999). *Counseling the culturally different.* New York: Wiley.

Sung, B. (1967). *Mountain of gold.* New York: Macmillan.

Suro, R. (1999). Mixed doubles. *American Demographics, 21,* 56-62.

Sutton, C. T., & Broken Nose, M. A. (1996). American Indian families: An overview. In M. McGoldrick, J. Giordano, & J. K. Pearce (Eds.), *Ethnicity and family therapy.* (pp. 31-44). New York: Guilford.

Sweet, J. A., & Bumpass, L. L. (1987). *American families and households.* New York: Russell Sage Foundation.

Swigonski, M. E. (1996). Challenging privilege through Africentric social work practice. *Social Work, 41,* 153-161.

Szapocznik, J., Scopetta, M., & Tillman, W. (1978). What changes, what remains the same, and what affects acculturation change in Cuban immigrant families. In J. Szapocznik (Ed.), *Cuban Americans: Acculturation, adjustment, and the family.* Washington, DC: National Coalition of Hispanic and Human Service Organizations.

Taylor, J. B. (1997). Niche practices: Extending the ecological perspective. In D. Saleeby (Ed.), *The strength perspective in social work practice* (pp. 217-227). New York: Longman.

Taylor, R. L. (1991). Poverty and adolescent black males: The subculture of disengagement. In P. Edelman & J. Ladner (Eds.), *Adolescence and poverty: Challenge for the 1990's* (pp. 139-162). Washington, DC: Center for National Policy.

Taylor, R. L. (2003). Diversity within African American families. In A. S. Skolnick & J. Skolnick (Eds.), *Family in transition* (pp. 365-388). New York: Allyn & Bacon.

Thomas, E., & Carter, R. (1971). Instigative modification with a multi-problem family. *Social Casework, 52,* 444-455.

Thomas, N. D. (2000). Generalist practice with people of color. In J. Poulin (Ed.), *Collaborative social work* (pp. 265-325). Itasca, IL: F. E. Peacock.

Thomas, R. (1969). Lecture on nationalism. In G. Wikerson (Ed.), *The American Indian reader.* Albuquerque, NM: National Indian Youth Council.

Torres, A., & Bonilla, F. (1993). Decline within decline: The New York perspective. In R. Morales & F. Bonilla (Eds.), *Latinos in a changing U. S. economy: Comparative perspective and growing inequality* (pp. 85-108). Newbury Park, CA: Sage.

Tracks, J. (1973). Native American non-interference. *Social Work, 18,* 30-34.

Tseng, W., & McDermott, J. (1975). Psychotherapy: Historical roots, universal elements, and cultural variations. *American Journal of Psychiatry, 132,* 378-384.

Ulibarri, H. (1970). Social and attitudinal characteristics of Spanish speaking migrants and ex-migrant workers in the Southwest. In J. Burma (Ed.), *Mexican Americans in the United States.* Cambridge, MA: Schenkman.

United States Census Bureau. (1980). *Estimates of the population of the United States by age, race, and sex* (Series p-25, no. 870). Washington, DC: U.S. Government Printing Office.

United States Census Bureau. (1993). *1990 census of the population: Persons of Hispanic origin in the United States.* Washington, DC: U.S. Government Printing Office.

United States Census Bureau. (1996). *Statistical abstracts of the United States, 1996.* Washington, DC: U.S. Government Printing Office.

United States Census Bureau. (1998). *California leads states and Los Angeles County, Calif., tops counties in Asian and Pacific Islander population increase, Census Bureau reports* (CB98-161). Retrieved May 14, 2003, from http://www.census.gov/ Press-Release/cb 98-161.html

United States Census Bureau. (1999a). *The Asian or Pacific Islander population in the United States: March 1999 (update) (PPL-131).* Retrieved June 6, 2003 from http:// landview.census.gov/population/www/socdemo/race/api99.html

United States Census Bureau. (1999b). *Black population in the U.S. March 1999: List of tables (PPL-130).* Retrieved May 29, 2003, from www.census.gov/population/www/ socdemo/race/black99tabs.html.

United States Census Bureau. (2000a). *Current population survey.* Washington, DC: U.S. Government Printing Office.

United States Census Bureau. (2001a). *The Hispanic population: Census brief* (C2kbr/01-3). Washington, DC: U.S. Government Printing Office.

United States Census Bureau. (2001b). *The Hispanic population in the United States: 2000 March CPS.* Retrieved May 14, 2003, from http://www.census.gov/population/www/socdemo/hispanic/ho00.html

United States Commission on Civil Rights. (1992). *Civil rights facing Asian Americans in the 1990's.* Washington, DC: U.S. Government Printing Office.

Utsey, S. O., Bolden, M. A., & Brown, A. L. (2001). Visions of revolution from the spirit of Franz Fanon: A psychology of liberation for counseling African Americans confronting societal racism and oppression. In J. G. Panterotto, J. M. Casus, L. A. Suzuki, & C. M. Alexander (Eds.), *Handbook of multicultural counseling* (pp. 311-336). Thousand Oaks, CA: Sage.

Utter, J. (2001). *American Indians.* Norman: University of Oklahoma Press.

Vega, W. A. (1995). The study of Latino families: A point of departure. In R. E. Zambrana (Ed.). *Understanding Latino families* (pp. 3-17). Thousand Oaks, CA: Sage.

Vidal de Haymes, M., Barbour, L., Kwong, K., Lammers, M., Liss, W. P., van Stradten, J., et al. (2002). *The Indian child welfare act of 1978: A child welfare professional training curriculum.* Chicago: Loyola University of Chicago.

Wachtel, S. (1982). To think about the unthinkable. *Social Casework, 51,* 467-474.

Wahrhaftig, A. (1969). The folk society on type. In G. Wikerson (Ed.), *The American Indian reader.* Albuquerque: National Indian Youth Council.

Walter, J., & Peller, J. (1992). *Becoming solution-focused in brief therapy.* New York: Brunner/Mazel.

Weaver, H. N. (2001). Organizations and community assessment with First Nations people. In R. Fong & S. Furuto (Eds.), *Culturally competent practice: Skills, intervention and evaluations* (pp. 178-195). Needham Heights, MA: Allyn & Bacon.

Weaver, H. N. (2003). Cultural competence with First Nations peoples. In D. Lum (Ed.), *Culturally competent practice* (pp. 197-217). Pacific Grove, CA: Brooks/Cole.

Weiss, R. (1979). Growing up a little faster: The experience of growing up in a single-parent household. *Journal of Social Issues, 35,* 97-111.

White, M., & Epston, D. (1990). *Narrative means to therapeutic ends.* New York: Norton.

Williams, E. E., & Ellison, F. (1996). Culturally informed social work practice with American Indian clients: Guidelines for non-Indian social workers. *Social Work, 41*(2), 147-151.

Wilson, M. N., Kohn, L. P., & Lee, T. S. (2000). Cultural relativistic approach toward ethnic minorities in family therapy. In J. F. Aponte & J. Wohl (Eds.*)*, *Psychological intervention and cultural diversity* (pp. 92-109). Needham Heights, MA: Allyn & Bacon.

Wilson, W. J. (1987). *The truly disadvantaged: the inner city, the underclass, and public policy.* Chicago: University of Chicago Press.

Wimberly, E. (1997a). *Counseling African American marriages and families.* Louisville, KY: Westminster John Knox.

Wimberly, E. (1997b). The men's movement and pastoral care of African American men. In C. C. Neuger & J. N. Poling (Eds.), *The care of men* (pp. 104-121). Nashville, TN: Abingdon.

Wintemute, G., & Messer, B. (Eds.). (1982). *Social work practice with Native American families.* Mitchell, SD: Dakota Wesleyan University.

Witkins, S. L. (1995). Family social work: A critical constructionist perspective. *Journal of Family Social Work, 1,* 33-45.

Wright, H. (1998). Therapeutic intervention with troubled children. In A. F. Comer-Edwards & J. Spurlock (Eds.), *Black families in crisis.* New York: Brunner/Mazel.

Yang, C. (1959). *A Chinese family in the communist revolution.* Boston, MA: MIT Press.

Yellow Bird, M. J. (1999). What we want to be called: Indigenous people's perspective on racial and ethnic identity labels. *American Indian Quarterly, 23*(3), 1-21.

Yellow Bird, M. J. (2001). Critical values and First Nations peoples. In R. Fong & S. Furuto (Eds), *Culturally competent practice: Skills, interventions, and evaluations.* (pp. 61-74). Needham Heights, MA: Allyn & Bacon.

Young, T. (1996). Using narrative theory and self psychology with a multigenerational family systems perspective. In J. Brandell (Ed.), *Narrative and therapeutic action* (pp. 137-155). New York: Haworth.

Zinn, M. B., & Well, B. (2003). Diversity with Latino families: New lessons for family social science. In A. S. Skolnick & J. H. Skolnick (Eds.), *Family in transition* (pp. 389-415). Boston, MA: Allyn & Bacon.

Zintz, M. (1963). *Education across cultures.* Dubuque, IA: William C. Brown.

Zuniga, M. E. (1992). Families with Latino roots. In E. W. Lynch & M. J. Hanson (Eds), *Developing cross-cultural competence: A guide for work with young children and their families* (pp. 151-179). Baltimore, MD: Brooks/Cole.

Zuniga, M. E. (2003). Cultural competence with Latino Americans. In D. Lunn (Ed.), *Culturally competent practice* (pp. 238-260). Pacific Grove, CA: Brooks/Cole.

INDEX

First Nation peoples and, 87-89
See also Immigration
Minority populations.
 See Ethnic minorities
Minuchin, S., 18, 50, 54, 105, 111, 114,
 116, 132, 139, 173, 177, 180, 189,
 190, 201, 209, 245, 246, 251, 257,
 263, 265, 305, 306, 308, 313, 317
Morelli, P., 25
Moynihan Report, 214
Multi-racial population, 30

Narrative-based approaches, 3
 communicative competence and, 3-4
 family life chronology, 103
 reauthoring/restorying process,
  49-50, 103
 social constructionist framework
  and, 14
 storytelling, metaphor use and,
  103-104
Narrative identity formulation, 10-11, 12
National Survey of Black Americans
 (NSBA), 224
Native Americans. *See* First Nation
 peoples
Norton, D., 3

Obligation, 24, 57, 190-191
Oppression, 5-6, 12
 African American experience of,
  225-227, 233-235, 241-242
 historical trauma, 101, 108, 111-112,
  214, 215, 316
 Latino history, 146-149
 narrative of, 10-11
 power dynamics and, 12
 social class and, 9
 See also Critical constructionist
  framework

Pacific Islander Americans.
 See Asian/Pacific Islander
 Americans

Parent-child relationships:
 African Americans and, 228-230
 Asian/Pacific Islander Americans
  and, 27-28
 couple relationships and, 276
 ethnic minorities and, 291-292
 First Nations peoples and, 84-85
 immigration process and, 34-35
 Latinos and, 156-157
Parsons, T., 18
Pathology framework, 12
Perez, P., 145, 149
Personalismo, 152
Person-in-environment. *See* Ecosystem
 theoretical framework
Pinderhughes, E., 215, 216
Porterfield, E., 232
Postmodern constructivism, 3
Powerlessness, 11, 12, 234, 235
Power struggles, 15, 38, 50
Puerto Ricans, 147

Racism, 5-6, 7
 African American reactions
  to, 225-227
 immigration process and, 32-33
 internalized racism, 101, 168,
  241-242, 301
 Latino experience of, 146-149
 narratives of oppression/resiliency
  and, 10-11
 See also Historical trauma
Rasheed, J. M., 230, 280
Rasheed, M. N., 230, 280
Reconstituted-family therapy:
 African Americans and, 280-283
 Asian/Pacific Islander Americans
  and, 71-73
 ethnic minorities and, 328-329
 family narratives, restorying of, 72
 First Nation peoples and, 139-140
 kinship networks and, 73, 140,
  210-211, 282-283
 Latinos and, 208-211

About the Authors

Dr. Man Keung Ho (deceased) was Professor of Social Work at the University of Oklahoma. He was Approved Supervisor and Clinical Member in the American Association for Marriage and Family Therapy and served on the editorial board of *Practice Digest* and as External Examiner for the Chinese University of Hong Kong. Maintaining an active practice in individual, marital, and family therapy, he also found time to act as Director of the Moore Transcultural Family Study Institute. He was the author of *Building a Successful Intermarriage* (Abbey Press, 1984), as well as innumerable articles and chapters in prestigious professional journals and books.

Janice Matthews Rasheed is Associate Professor of Social Work at Loyola University Chicago's School of Social Work. She received her master's degree in social work from the University of Michigan, Ann Arbor, and her doctorate in social welfare from Columbia University. She was the coprincipal investigator for a multiyear research grant funded by the John D. and Catherine T. MacArthur Foundation for the study of poor, noncustodial African American fathers. She has published articles in the *Journal of Community Practice, Journal of Human Behavior and the Social Environment, Journal of African American Men,* and *Journal of Evaluation and Program Planning.* She is also the author of several chapters in books dealing with the subjects of African American men and families. She is a coauthor of *Social Work Practice with African American Men: The Invisible Presence* (Sage, 1999). She has taught clinical practice and research courses in the undergraduate, master's, and doctoral programs (e.g., couple therapy; family therapy; advanced family therapy; crosscultural practice; culture, race and ethnicity; and a course titled "Black Men in America: Race, Gender and Class") and conducts workshops and training programs. She is a licensed clinical social worker in Illinois and has maintained a private practice since 1978, specializing in people of color, couples, and families. She has served as Approved Supervisor (in training) at the Northwestern Family Institute.

Mikal N. Rasheed is Associate Professor and Chair of the Justice Studies and Social Work Department at Northeastern Illinois University. He formerly served on the faculty of the George Williams College of Social Work at Aurora University and was also Director of the Department of Social Work at Texas Southern University. He received his masters degree from the University of Chicago School of Social Service Administration and his doctorate in social work from Loyola University Chicago. He is a coauthor of *Social Work Practice with African American Men: The Invisible Presence* (Sage, 1999). He has taught courses on family therapy, couple therapy, cross-cultural practice, child welfare practice, generalist social work practice, clinical supervision, and clinical practice with men and conducts workshops and training in these areas. He is a licensed clinical social worker in the Illinois and has maintained a private practice for more than 20 years in which he specializes in men's issues, practice with people of color, and couple and family therapy.